Administrator's Guide to Sybase® ASE 12.5

Jeffrey Garbus
Alvin Chang
Gary Tyrrell
Penny Garbus

Contributing authors: Brian Davignon, Rick Kinnaird, Christine Lindsay, Jim Nimmo, Sheri Page, and Brian Taylor

Wordware Publishing, Inc.

Library of Congress Cataloging-in-Publication Data

Administrator's guide to Sybase ASE 12.5 / by Jeffrey Garbus ... [et al.]
p. cm.
Includes index.
ISBN 1-55622-307-2 (pb)
1. Client/server computing. 2. Sybase. I. Garbus, Jeffrey R.

QA76.9.C55 A36 2001
005.75'8--dc21 2001057364

2320 Los Rios Boulevard
Plano, Texas 75074

Printed in the United States of America

ISBN 1-55622-307-2

10 9 8 7 6 5 4 3 2 1
0111

Portions of Chapter 16 are from the Sybase *Troubleshooting Guide* and are used with the permission of Sybase, Inc. Appendix E is used with the permission of Imperial Technology, Inc. Appendix F and Appendix G are used with the permission of White Sands Technology, Inc.

All inquiries for volume purchases of this book should be addressed to Wordware Publishing, Inc., at the above address. Telephone inquiries may be made by calling:

(972) 423-0090

Dedication

For my love

Jeff Garbus

To Helen, for her time, patience, and indulgence.

Gary Tyrrell

For all my parents, George, Bea, Sharon, Stanley,
and my kids, Gillian, Max, Devon, Brandon.

Penny Garbus

About the Authors

Jeff Garbus' background includes a B.S. degree from Rensselaer Polytechnic Institute, and work experience from PCs to mainframes and back again. He has many years of Microsoft and Sybase SQL Server experience, with a special emphasis on assisting clients in migrating from existing systems to pilot and large-scale projects. He is well known in the industry, having spoken at user conferences and user groups for many years, written articles and columns for many magazines nationally and internationally, as well as having written several books. Recently his focus has been on Very Large Databases, data warehousing, training, and remote database administration.

Jeff has been in consulting for fourteen years, training for nine, and in the software business for eighteen. He has a demonstrated talent for staying at the leading edge of technology, as well as transferring his knowledge to others.

Jeff currently is CEO of Soaring Eagle Consulting, an RDBMS consulting and training firm based in Tampa, which specializes in solving business problems as well as performance problems. Soaring Eagle now offers remote database administration services.

Gary Tyrrell is a Principal Instructor with Sybase, where he teaches a wide variety of courses on ASE, ASA, Replication Server, SQL, and database design. He is not the same Gary Tyrrell from the famous 1982 Stanford–California game, so please stop asking him what happened to the trombone.

Alvin Chang is a technical trainer, author, and consultant working for Soaring Eagle Consulting, a Tampa-based consulting and training firm. He has taught Adaptive Server Enterprise throughout the United States. Currently specializing in Sybase and Microsoft System Administration, Alvin started as a technical trainer for products like Microsoft Office, Lotus Smartsuite, and Lotus Notes before moving into RDBMSs. This is his fifth book.

He can be reached at alvin@soaringeagleltd.com.

As a technical writer and project lead for Soaring Eagle Consulting, **Penny Garbus** has written literally thousands of pages of Sybase training over the last several years, from versions 10 through 12.5.

Contents

Foreword

Dear Reader,

I am responsible for strategic oversight of Sybase, Inc.'s core database and middleware business including that of Sybase's flagship product, Adaptive Server® Enterprise (ASE). For over 15 years, this RDBMS has been supporting mission-critical OLTP and DSS applications for thousands of customers in an array of industries.

The most recent version of Sybase's RDBMS, ASE 12.5, builds upon this solid foundation with innovations that help meet the emerging needs of businesses as they transition to e-Business, including efficient tools for handling new e-Business data types, dynamic performance management to address the unpredictable nature of Internet-based computing, and enhanced security to protect business data in a highly distributed Web-based environment.

Over the past few years, there have been a number of titles released on the Sybase enterprise data management software platform. This release of *Administrator's Guide to Sybase ASE 12.5*, introduces consultants and administrators to one of the most comprehensive, up-to-date, and authoritative titles on this widely used software.

Jeffrey Garbus is considered throughout the Sybase community as one of the most experienced database administrators, consultants, and authors for the ASE enterprise data management software. He's widely known as the author of *Sybase SQL Server 11 Unleashed*, lauded by many database administrators I've spoken to as one of the most respected Sybase titles published.

Garbus covers an expanse of new ground as the series editor for the *Jeffrey Garbus Official Sybase ASE 12.5 Library* from Wordware Publishing, Inc. I believe that this series will be an invaluable asset to Sybase database administrators and consultants.

Dr. Raj Nathan
Senior Vice President and General Manager
Enterprise Solutions Division
Sybase, Inc.

Preface

It was pretty much a toss-up.

When offered the opportunity by Wordware to write a book about Sybase databases again, I had to decide what was most topical. What did I want to write about first? My inclinations were systems administration and performance and tuning, as they encompass what has changed the most since the last Sybase books had been published.

I made the (somewhat arbitrary) decision that there are more people performing systems administrator duties daily than performance and tuning, so I chose to do the SA book (this book). Since starting this book, I've been asked to write/series-edit five more, so fortunately, I get to do both, which simply makes the SA book "first."

I hope you get as much benefit out of using this book as we had fun writing it.

Jeff Garbus

Acknowledgments

First, I'd like to thank Celeste Noren and Dale Engle, for having the vision to pursue a new ASE book. I'd like to thank all of the people whose time and support helped make this possible: Jim Hill and Wes Beckwith at Wordware; Omkar Bhongir and Jan Gipe, who coordinated things on the Sybase side; and my coauthors, many of whom suddenly realized the amount of work that goes into a book. Early versions of the book were reviewed by the Sybase ASE engineering team, which provided feedback. The final version was done by the auther based on the review received from engineering. Wordware and I are especially grateful for the extra effort the Sybase engineering staff made reviewing this book before publication.

Most of all, I'd like to thank my family, without whose support I might never have slept. Thank you, all.

Further Acknowledgments:

A very special thanks to these talented DBAs who helped with this book by writing or reviewing a chapter or two, but who didn't have time to help with the entire book:

Brian Davignon
Rick Kinnaird
Jim Nimmo
Brian Taylor
Penny Garbus
Christine Lindsay
Sheri Page

Jeff Garbus

Jeff and Alvin made this project a pleasure to work on. My colleagues over the years have generously shared their knowledge and made me smarter; special thanks to Ray Rankins, Mitch Fleischman, Tony Haber, Chris Amidei, Jay Cramblet, Brian Knauff, and Dean Rock (who went over to the Dark Side). Stacey Cooper and Brian Wesselink have supported me in my work on this book, and in all my efforts at Sybase. And I wouldn't be a technical instructor without the example of Doctors Frank Acker, Jovan Lebaric, Andy Mech, Peter Parshall, Thad Smith, and Art Western — I hope that someday I'm as good in the classroom as they are.

Gary Tyrrell

I would like to thank Jeff Garbus for providing me the opportunity to contribute to this book. Thanks to my brother, Basil, my sounding board and source of my phone bills. And thanks to my parents, Yuling and Yuching Chang, who got me started on computers in the first place.

Alvin Chang

I'd like to thank my coauthors, Jeff, Alvin, and Gary. It's always great working with you.

Penny Garbus

Introduction

What does systems administration mean to you? Installing a server? Making sure it stays up and running? Tuning it? Managing security? Tuning problem queries?

I think that if you ask 100 people, you will get 100 different answers. That might make it hard to limit the scope of this book. As it is, we will try to define a few roles ourselves.

Systems Administration

Systems administration is the function of installing, maintaining, operating, and controlling the Sybase ASE. A systems administrator (SA) is responsible, at the server level, for maintaining a secure, stable operating environment; for forecasting capacity requirements of the CPU; and for planning and executing future expansion. Further, an SA is responsible for overall performance at the server level.

Database Administration

Database administration is the act of migrating a logical model into a physical design, and performing all tasks essential to consistent, secure, prompt database access. A database administrator (DBA) is responsible for access, consistency, and performance within the scope of the database.

Overlap

Because the database is part of the server, taking responsibility for server-wide performance means that the SA often takes over the role of DBA when it is time to identify bottlenecks. Further, most shops combine these roles, further engendering confusion. And, to add to the confusion, those shops I've seen that divide the roles between separate people often end up with interpersonal conflicts caused by one or the other unable to complete a task without waiting on an associate.

Other shops have individuals who are production DBAs, which seems to mean that all preventive maintenance and disaster recovery work are performed by these individuals, as well as development DBAs, those who tune queries, perform schema changes, and work with developers to write good code.

Scope of This Book

We're not here to pass judgment over roles and responsibilities at different shops. Frankly, if it works, it's obvious, and if it doesn't work, it's also obvious. As long as it works, as the saying goes, don't fix it.

This book is about systems administration. We also talk about the tasks that a DBA needs to perform as they, in our judgment, overlap. After reading this book, you should be able to perform any task that encompasses the creation or maintenance of a server.

The only exception to this is tuning (other than server configuration parameters), which is a separate book in and of itself.

Chapter 1

Systems Administration Overview

Architecture Overview

The Sybase Adaptive Server Enterprise (ASE) is a relational database using client/server technology. The ASE is a process on the machine that controls all necessary memory usage, disk access, network functions, and OS processes or threads.

E.F. Codd created the concept of *relational databases*, and described the characteristics of the relational database management system. Such systems consist of rows of data within tables, with the tables having relationships to one another. For example, a table named Authors may contain instances of authors, each of which has a unique author ID that uniquely identifies different authors; a table named Titles may likewise contain instances of titles, each of which has a unique title ID that uniquely identifies different books. However, neither table by itself is sufficient to indicate which authors contributed to which books; this is resolved by associating author IDs with title IDs. This *relationship* (which may take different forms, according to basic design rules) shows the user which authors contributed to which books.

The term "relational" indicates how the data is represented, while the term "client/server" indicates what kind of technology is used to access the data. In such systems, there is a division of effort between the client application (which makes a request for data) and the server (which determines if the client has access to the data, and returns any results to the client). The client can exist on the same machine as the server. More typically, however, it is on a different machine to spread system load.

Responsibilities of the Sybase Systems Administrator

The systems administrator of a Sybase ASE (also referred to as SA, database administrator, or sometimes DBA) is responsible for all aspects of creating, maintaining, and monitoring the server and database environment, including:

- Installing the Sybase Adaptive Server
- Establishing connectivity between clients and servers
- Installing and maintaining user databases
- Establishing security for the ASE
- Maintaining and troubleshooting the ASE
- Establishing disaster recovery procedures
- Monitoring ASE
- Use of utilities

This list is not comprehensive; there are many duties implied by this list that may fall to the DBA/SA. For example, if a stored procedure that previously ran in 30 seconds has recently been running for over an hour, as SA, you will need to find out why it is taking longer now than before. If it is a configuration problem, then it falls into the troubleshooting category for the SA to resolve. But if the SQL inside the procedure was poorly written, then tuning the SQL falls into a gray zone. In some shops, the programmer is responsible for the P&T (performance and tuning) of the procedure; in others (and our recommendation!), it is up to the DBA to review all procedures going in the production system, and approve the procedure based on knowledge of the system and optimizer; either way, it usually falls to the DBA/SA to resolve optimizer problems. In the end the SA is responsible for the server. All aspects of the ASE are in the domain of the SA.

Installing the Sybase Adaptive Server

The process of installing a Sybase ASE is the first step towards a productive database management system. Always read the Sybase *Installation Guide* specific to your platform, as there are differing requirements and recommendations for different operating systems. In particular, walk through the checklist provided and make sure that you meet or exceed all operating system requirements. Analyze the user databases you intend to create on this new server, and size your disk space, memory, and other configurable resources to accommodate the current needs. Be sure to also estimate growth in the foreseeable future, and see to it that the resources you will need will be available. There are many calculations in the Sybase *System Administration Guide* to help you calculate resource needs, especially in the chapter titled "Configuring and Tuning the Server."

Establishing Connectivity Between Clients and Servers

For clients and servers to communicate, they must be able to locate each other; this is done by creating an address listing. On UNIX machines, this address listing is called the interfaces file, and on NT it is called the sql.ini file (the term "interfaces" is used to generically refer to any of these files, regardless of O/S). Within these files you will list all servers (ASE servers, backup servers, monitor servers, XP servers) with their network addresses; clients will use these files to find the server they wish to query, and servers will use them to listen for client requests.

Within these interfaces files, there may be multiple server entries, each of which may contain multiple services. A *service* is a specific address used for a specific purpose. The master service (featuring the keyword "master") is used for servers to track incoming requests; the query service (with the keyword "query") is used by clients to locate a server when sending data queries or commands. Each service will contain a specific network location and information about supported network protocols. These entries look different depending on the operating system.

Example:

```
SYBASE
     query tcp ether my_machine 4500
     master tcp ether my_machine 4500
```

The easiest way to maintain these files is with the dsedit utility.

New with 12.5, you may instead choose to use Lightweight Directory Access Protocol (LDAP) to replace the interfaces file. LDAP is an industry standard for accessing directory services. Directory services allow components to look up information by a distinguished name (DN) from an LDAP server that stores and manages server, user, and software information that is used throughout the enterprise or over a network.

The LDAP server can be located on a different platform/machine from the one on which Adaptive Server or the clients are running. LDAP defines the communication protocol and the contents of messages exchanged between clients and servers. Messages are operators, such as client requests for read, write, and query, and server responses, including data-format information.

The LDAP server stores and retrieves information about:

- Adaptive Server, such as IP address, port number, and network protocol
- Security mechanisms and filters
- High availability companion server name

The LDAP server can be configured with these access restrictions:

- Anonymous authentication — all data is visible to any user.
- User name and password authentication — Adaptive Server uses the default user name and password

Installing and Maintaining User Databases

Before a user database may be created, space must be made available to the server. This is performed using the disk init command.

Syntax:

```
disk init
name = "device_name" ,
physname = "physicalname" ,
size = number_of_blocks
[, vstart = virtual_address ,
cntrltype = controller_number ]
 [, dsync = {true|false}]
```

Detailed syntax and usage for disk init and other device-related commands are found in Chapter 3, "Defining Physical and Sybase-Mirrored Devices to the Server." Once the devices have been initialized, the create database command can be issued.

NOTE: Prior to 12.5, you needed to provide a virtual device number (vdevno), but with 12.5 that is automatically assigned.

Syntax:

```
create database database_name
[on {default | database_device} [= size]
    [, {default | database_device} [= size]]...]
[log on {default | database_device} [= size]
    [, {default | database_device} [= size]]...]
[with {override | default_location = "pathname"}]
[for {load | proxy_update}]
```

Once the database is created, tables, indexes, users, and permissions can be added. Creation of databases is covered in more detail in Chapter 4, "Databases."

Establishing Security for Adaptive Server Enterprise

Security is critical for the protection of Adaptive Server Enterprise and the data contained within. Sensitive data must be protected from improper access, whether by reading or modification.

There are several levels of security within Adaptive Server Enterprise. At the server level, a *login* allows a connection to be established; at the database level, a *user* has access to the storage structures of data; at the object level, *permissions* allow the use of data creation and manipulation syntax.

It takes a combination of these security measures to successfully create a secure Adaptive Server Enterprise environment.

Once you've put your chosen security scheme in place, the ASE auditing feature may be enabled at the SA's discretion. Auditing allows monitoring of users, commands, and administrative tasks (but adds overhead to the server). Auditing must be installed, and requires its own database (sybsecurity) in which it retains auditing information; reports can be generated from the auditing tables to track trends.

Kerberos/Distributed Computing Environment (DCE) (New in 12.0)

In a distributed client/server computing environment, intruders can view or tamper with confidential data. Adaptive Server works with third-party providers to give you security services that:

- Authenticate users, clients, and servers — Make sure they are who they say they are.
- Provide data confidentiality with encryption — Ensure that data cannot be read by an intruder.
- Provide data integrity — Prevent data tampering and detect when it has occurred.

SSL (New in 12.5)

Adaptive Server Enterprise security services now support Secure Sockets Layer (SSL) session-based security. SSL is the standard for securing the transmission of sensitive information, such as credit card numbers, stock trades, and banking transactions, over the Internet.

The implementation of Adaptive Server SSL features assume that there is a knowledgeable system security officer who is familiar with the security policies and needs of your site, and who has general understanding of SSL and public-key cryptography.

Security is covered completely in Chapter 6, "Security" and Chapter 7, "Auditing."

Maintaining and Troubleshooting the ASE

Putting the application database into place and setting up user access to Adaptive Server Enterprise is your first step, but you still need to do some work to keep the server running. Logs will fill, data will outgrow its allotted space, indexes will become inefficient, and data could become corrupt. Many of these things can be detected early or avoided by general maintenance being performed on a scheduled basis. There are several maintenance processes you should consider implementing, including:

- DBCC (database consistency checker), a series of commands that detect structural problems within your system. Some of these are highly resource intensive and should only be run during slow times.
- Periodic rebuilding of indexes to improve performance; this is more important on highly volatile data (lots of inserts, updates, or deletes) than on static data.
- Maintenance of statistics to improve query optimization.
- Adding thresholds to warn when space is becoming too full.

These topics are discussed in Chapter 14, "Periodic Maintenance," and Chapter 15, "Troubleshooting."

Establishing Disaster Recovery Procedures

Disasters happen. If you don't believe it, ask those folks at the Board of Trade building in Chicago about when the tunnels flooded and the CBOT lost all electricity. Whatever the nature of your disaster, you must be prepared to move the complete business (or part of the business) operation to a new location, and be up and ready in a short amount of time. A well thought-out and thoroughly practiced plan must be available to deal with any contingency. Some things to consider:

- Spare machines with sufficient resources to run the business will be required.
- Networking needs must be addressed.
- Connectivity issues must be addressed and tested.
- Good backups of the databases will need to be accessible from off-site.
- Installation disks for all components (clients, servers, applications,...) must be accessible from off-site.
- Timetables for acceptable recovery time must be established.
- A step-by-step disaster recovery plan must be created.
- Personnel must be designated for disaster recovery.
- A failover site with warm or hot backups should be evaluated (is it an option or mandatory for business survival?).

- The plan must be tested. No matter how impressive it is on paper, it still may fall apart. Test it repeatedly.

There are books on disaster recovery and how to prepare. Each site will have different requirements and possibly different approaches to this subject matter. Just remember that it can happen to you and be prepared. More information is found in Chapter 8, "Backing Up and Restoring."

Monitoring ASE

There are many ways to monitor the ASE. There are system stored procedures, which present information about the state of the server. There are the Monitor and Historical Servers, which obtain and track performance statistics. There are third-party applications that can be run with the ASE. Whatever the tool or technique, monitoring is essential to the health of the ASE; knowing which resources are overused (or available in excess) allows you to maximize the performance of the ASE. Most mature shops have their own set of monitoring tools, which have been developed over time.

Use of Utilities

Sybase utilities are used at the operating system level to perform special services against the ASE. These utilities are:

- srvbuild — a UNIX-based program to create the ASE once it is unloaded from the CD.
- srvconfig — an NT-based program to create the ASE once it is unloaded from the CD.
- dsedit — edits the server entries in the interfaces file and LDAP servers.
- bcp — the bulk copy program allows mass loading (or unloading) of data files into (or out of) tables.
- defncopy — creates script files containing data definition language for specific database objects.
- optdiag — used to display (and in some cases, modify) statistics pertaining to tables and the optimizer.

Databases

Within a server, a database provides the context for data. There are four types of databases stored in the ASE.

- System databases essential to the ASE operation:

  master contains information needed to start the server, as well as all the system tables needed to govern the ASE; anything that has to do with the ASE as a whole is stored in master (including permitted logins, existing databases, space allocation, and other broad-scope items). master is the first database to be brought online when you power up an ASE; therefore it should be kept small and without user tables for faster access and startup of your ASE.

  model is the database used as a template when new databases are created; the contents of model are copied to each newly created database. Therefore, all changes that are made to model are reflected in new databases.

  tempdb is the temporary working area. Temporary tables are automatically created to hold intermediate results in some queries (especially when sorting is involved), and users may create temporary tables for their own purposes. Remember that the contents of tempdb are not permanent: tempdb is cleared and re-created each time the ASE is started, and some temporary tables will delete themselves even without a server restart. tempdb is heavily used by the ASE, and will require careful monitoring to avoid performance bottlenecks.

  sybsystemprocs contains the stored procedures that are installed by the server (known as *system procedures*), which are used to query and change the contents of system tables.

  sybsystemdb is used for the data change processes known as *distributed transactions* (most transactions take place in a single database, but distributed transactions span multiple databases, and sometimes multiple servers).

- Special functionality:

  dbccdb is used to store output from the dbcc checkstorage command.

  sybsecurity is the auditing database; it must be installed prior to turning on the auditing options.

  sybdiag is installed by Sybase Technical Support to help debug problems.

- Sample databases:

  pubs2 and **pubs3** are optional databases; they are the source of syntax examples in the documentation set and are used in many Sybase classes for labs. The installation scripts are provided with ASE.

- User databases:

  These are databases created specifically for applications.

System Tables Overview

The system tables govern the ASE and/or the databases within the ASE. In addition to the master system tables that pertain to the ASE as a whole (see Table 1-1 for a list of these system tables), every database (including master) contains a set of system tables that refer only to that database (see Table 1-2). These tables are maintained and modified with the use of Transact-SQL statements (create, drop, disk init, etc.) and system procedures (sp_addlogin, sp_adduser, sp_configure, etc.).

Table 1-1 System tables

System Table	Contents
syscharsets	One row for each character set or sort order
sysconfigures	One row for each server configuration parameter
syscurconfigs	Information about configuration parameters currently being used by Adaptive Server
sysdatabases	One row for each database on Adaptive Server
sysdevices	One row for each data device and dump device
sysengines	One row for each Adaptive Server engine currently online
syslanguages	One row for each language (except U.S. English) known to the server
syslisteners	One row for each type of network connection used by current Adaptive Server
syslocks	Information about active locks
sysloginroles	One row for each server login that possesses a system role
syslogins	One row for each Adaptive Server login
syslogshold	Information about the oldest active transaction for each database
sysmessages	One row for each system error or warning
sysmonitors	One row for each monitor counter
sysprocesses	Information about server processes
sysremotelogins	One row for each remote user
sysresourcelimits	One row for each resource limit
syssecmechs	Information about the security services available for each security mechanism that is available to Adaptive Server
sysservers	One row for each remote Adaptive Server and for the server itself
syssessions	Only used when Adaptive Server is configured for Sybase's Companion Server in a high availability system
syssrvroles	One row for each server-wide role
systimeranges	One row for each named time range
systransactions	One row for each transaction
sysusages	One row for each disk piece allocated to a database

Table 1-2 All databases

System Table	Contents
sysalternates	One row for each aliased user
sysattributes	One row for each object attribute definition
syscolumns	One row for each column in a table or view, and for each parameter in a procedure
syscomments	One or more rows for each view, rule, default, trigger, and procedure, giving SQL definition statement
sysconstraints	One row for each referential and check constraint associated with a table or column
sysdepends	One row for each procedure, view, or table that is referenced by a procedure, view, or trigger
sysgams	Allocation bitmaps for an entire database
sysindexes	One or more rows for each table and its indexes
sysjars	One row for each Java archive (JAR) file that is retained in the database.
syskeys	One row for each primary, foreign, or common key; set by user (not maintained by Adaptive Server)
syslogs	Transaction log
sysobjects	One row for each table, view, procedure, rule, trigger default, log, and (in tempdb only) temporary object
syspartitions	One row for each page chain of a partitioned table
sysprocedures	One row for each view, rule, default, trigger, and procedure, giving internal definition
sysprotects	User permissions information
sysqueryplans	Abstract query plans and SQL text
sysreferences	One row for each referential integrity constraint declared on a table or column
sysroles	Maps server-wide roles to local database groups
syssegments	One row for each segment (named collection of disk pieces)
sysstatistics	One or more rows for user-designated columns; used in query optimization
systabstats	One row for each table, plus one row for each nonclustered index
systhresholds	One row for each threshold defined for the database
systypes	One row for each system-supplied and user-defined data type
sysusermessages	One row for each user-defined message
sysusers	One row for each user allowed in the database
sysxtypes	One row for each extended, Java-SQL data type

System Tables in Special Uses Databases

The sybsecurity and sybsystemdb databases contain some unique system tables that are particular to their activities. See Tables 1-3 and 1-4 for a list of these tables.

Table 1-3 sybsecurity system tables

System Table	Contents
sysauditoptions	One row for each global audit option
sysaudits_01 - sysaudits_08	The audit trail. Each audit table contains one row for each audit record

Table 1-4 sybsystemdb system tables

System Table	Contents
syscoordinations	One row for each remote participant of a distributed transaction

Sybase System Stored Procedures

Sybase provides a variety of stored procedures to help the DBA/SA maintain and monitor the ASE. These special stored procedures will be found in the sybsystemprocs database (there are a few stored procedures needed for startup that will be found in the master database). These procedures use the following naming schema: "sp_xxx" where xxx is a descriptive name. Procedures provided by Sybase have the special ability to modify system tables. Changes to system tables should only be made by means of stored procedures (except under the most extreme circumstances), as this will guarantee the integrity of the system table data.

Chapter 2

Adaptive Server Installation

When dealing with installation, one must remember that Adaptive Server has been written to run on many different platforms. Since each platform, whether NT, Linux, Solaris, or other flavors of UNIX, has its own way of getting things done, each platform has a slightly different installation routine. However, each server installation does have a few things that are common.

The first common point is planning. The installation of Adaptive Server requires a certain amount of planning in order to be successful. During the installation process, many questions will be asked that will affect the final outcome. The answers to these questions should be prepared in advance.

Among the questions that will need to be addressed:

- What is the destination drive and directory for the Adaptive Server software?
- Will raw partitions or file system devices be used?
- What is the destination and size for the master device?
- What is the destination and size for the sybsystemprocs device?
- If you are going to install auditing, what is the destination and size for the sysaudits device?
- What character set and sort order are you going to use?
- What network protocols and addresses are you going to support?

Some of these issues (particularly raw vs. file and device location) will recur as we use the server; others (like sort order and character set) are really only referenced during installation.

The sort order defines how Adaptive Server will order storage bytes in the server, how it will compare values in queries, and how it will order query results that request sorting (including order by and group by queries).

The ASE default is binary order, which stores the information in ASCII-numeric order, meaning capital letters are sorted before lowercase letters, because capital letters are numerically smaller in the ASCII character set. The remaining sort orders are variations on dictionary sort order, combining various forms of case- and accent-sensitivity.

Adaptive Server supports the following network types:

- TCP/IP
- Named pipes (NT only)

NOTE: Not all network protocols are supported with all operating systems. On some operating systems Adaptive Server will support multiple protocols simultaneously.

Step 1: Preparation

The first step to performing the installation is to prepare. Read through the installation manual for the platform you are installing to; since all platforms are slightly different, there will be differences between them. The specific steps required for installing to the platform will be laid out in the installation manual (including platform-specific OS configurations). It is important to document all of the choices (and keep the documentation for future reference).

Typical information needed includes:

- Logical page size
- Physical device information for system databases
  - Type
  - Size
  - Location
- Server name
- Networking information
  - IP address/host name
  - Port number/socket number
  - Named Pipe address
- Any Sybase Software Asset Manager (SySAM) feature activation codes
- Serial numbers (Get this off the tape or CD before inserting it into the drive; not asked for on NT)
- Character set, sort order, and default language
- Backup Server/XP Server/Monitor Server/Historical Server information
  - Name
  - Networking information
- Security configuration
  - SSL
  - Kerberos

The installation will be quicker and easier if you have made all of these decisions beforehand. Some of these parameters can be left at default values, and some will require inputs.

Logical Page Size

Adaptive Server 12.5 allows for configuration of a logical page size at installation. The default size is 2 K. The options are 4 K, 8 K, and 16 K.

Database	Minimum Size	Minimum Recommended Size
master	13 MB for 2 K pages	30 MB
	25 MB for 4 K pages	60 MB
	49 MB for 8 K pages	120 MB
	97 MB for 16 K pages	240 MB
sybsystemprocs	90 MB	90-120 MB
sybsystemdb	4 MB	5-20 MB
sybsecurity	0-5 MB	7 MB

Physical Devices

The installation program initializes a master device which provides the context for the master, model, sybsystemdb, and tempdb databases, and a device for sybsystemprocs. Optionally, a device can also be defined for the sybsecurity database.

Adaptive Server has always allowed administrators to have a choice of where and how they would create their physical devices. However, prior to ASE 12, Sybase normally recommended that database devices be created on raw partitions. The primary reason behind this was the fact that most file systems had some form of OS buffering; this meant that when ASE would write to the device there was the possibility that the write did not really happen. The write would actually occur in a buffer or in cache (memory), which would later be flushed to disk (this could result in significantly faster reads and writes). But this could be disastrous should the server lose power before writing to disk, since whatever data was stored in memory would be lost.

However, with the advent of changes in file systems to allow direct writes to disk, Sybase was able to change its recommendation. Beginning in ASE 12, devices may reliably be placed on raw partitions or on file system devices, provided that the file system supported direct writes to disk (see Chapter 3, "Defining Physical and Sybase-Mirrored Devices to the Server," for a full discussion). The key exception to this has been Windows NT, where it is recommended that you create file system devices on the NTFS file system.

When defining the master device the size may be requested in blocks (2 K pages), megabytes, kilobytes, or gigabytes. The master device should be at least 30 MB. The defined minimum is 13 MB, but this is usually just adequate to build the databases. The sybsystemprocs database can be placed on the master device, but it is recommended that it be placed on a separate device.

Avoid making the master device too large; keeping the master device reserved for system databases makes recovery easier and faster.

Server Names

If you do not want the default value of SYB_machinename on UNIX, you need to specify the server name. On NT the default is just machine_name.

For the Backup Server, if you do not want the default value of SYB_machinename_BACK on UNIX (for NT, default is machine_name_BS), you need to specify the server name. Similar defaults exist for the XP Server, Monitor Server, and Historical Server.

Using the default names will work, but in a multi-server environment, it is best to adopt a server naming standard early and stick with it. If you install multiple servers, the names must be unique.

Networking Information

The most common way for ASE to communicate with clients is over TCP/IP; the client does not need to establish a login on the host machine that ASE is running on. Instead, the client will send its requests to a particular host name and port number. ASE will listen directly to the network, and respond to any incoming network packets that use the same port number that ASE is using.

In this way, many TCP/IP-enabled processes (including multiple ASEs) can all run simultaneously on one machine, each paying attention only to their own network traffic, as long as each process has a unique port number. The host name portion of the network addressing will be set by your network administrators. You should either generate a port number that you know is not in use (and will not be used by any subsequent processes), or ask the network administrators to generate one for you. Port numbers default to 5000.

Sybase Software Asset Manager

Starting with version 12.0, the SySAM application enforces installation of premium server features. It is activated automatically at the beginning of installation and asks for license key values that go into the licensing file. At startup, ASE checks the license file to determine available features. Technically, you do not need to enter any keys into SySAM, but you will not be able use any of the premium features (such as Java in the Database and High Availability Companion Server) unless you provide their keys and the key for the basic ASE server.

Sybase will provide certificates with feature authorization codes to enable the premium features that you have purchased. It is very important that you do not lose these certificates, in case machine or disk failure ever requires you to re-enter the license keys.

The purpose of Step 1 is to plan out how the server will be built and to document it. This will be helpful in the event you have to reinstall and wish to refer to what you did the first time. The *Installation Guide* of the documentation set always has a form to fill out, which basically requires you to think about what you are putting on the server and where you are putting it. This worksheet should be saved for future reference and should be updated if any of the installation choices is later changed.

Step 2: File Transfer

The installation process will require that you use an operating system login to unload the CD (and later, perform the installation and start the server). This login is generically referred to as the *sybase login*, but may be named anything you wish. The sybase login should have ownership over the areas of disk where you will unload and install the server (and later, create devices); on NT, the sybase login must be a member of the Administrators group.

> **NOTE:** The implication here is that you already have an OS-level login called sybase. If you don't, then create one. Installing as root (or administrator on NT) can create ownership/startup problems later.

Once signed in as the sybase login, you will need to make available a large area (see platform-specific documentation, typically 60 to 500 MB) of drive space for the Adaptive Server software to reside on. Use operating-system specific commands to unload software from the CD; on some operating systems, the install program will perform the unload.

At the end of Step 2, you will have copied all the necessary files to create the server, as well as the software to install and configure the new server. On most systems, the install program will automatically move on to Step 3.

Step 3: Running Installation

The install program will begin to ask questions about the Adaptive Server to be created; the worksheets filled out in Step 1 should provide the answers. The install program will prompt the installer for information about the size and location of the master device, master database, and other system devices and databases. Once all the questions have been answered, the Adaptive Server will be built to the specs from your answers. The tasks performed by the install include:

- Initialization of the master device and sybsystemprocs device
- Creation of the master, model, sybsystemprocs, sybsystemdb, and tempdb databases
- Startup of the server (optionally the backup server, depending on platform)
- (Optional) Installation of auditing and creation of the sybsecurity database and device

At the end of Step 3, the new Adaptive Server should be up and running. The new server will contain at least one initialized device for master (optional — but recommended on a busy system — initialized devices for sybsystemprocs and sybsecurity), and there should be at least five databases: master, model, tempdb, sybsystemdb, and sybsystemprocs. On NT, the necessary registry entries will be created.

A good way to test the server is to run the isql command and attempt to connect to the server.

```
isql -U login_name -P password -S servername
```

Initially, you may use the login sa, which has a null password (leave the parameter empty). This initial login/password combination is very privileged and presently constitutes a security hole, and should be changed as soon as possible (see Chapter 6, "Security").

NOTE: Do not supply the password on the command line, as this will give your password to anybody OS savvy enough to use their OS equivalent of a ps command. Instead, leave the password off, and allow the server to prompt you.

You should also notice that several files have been created as a part of the installation:

- Interfaces file
- Runserver file
- Errorlog file
- syb_olympus.cfg (Note that this is *servername*.cfg)

Interfaces File

The interfaces file (named sql.ini on NT systems; otherwise named interfaces or interfac, depending on OS naming limitations) is actually part of the Open Client/Server (OCS) aspect of Adaptive Server. The interfaces file is located in the $SYBASE directory, and provides the connectivity information for the client/server architecture that ASE uses. Each client application and each server that exist in your architecture need to be able to access a copy of the interfaces file; clients use it to find the servers they will connect to, and servers use it to know which inbound network packets to pay attention to (and to communicate with other servers).

Sample UNIX Interfaces Entries

In this example, olympus is the name of the machine upon which Adaptive Server Enterprise is running, and syb_olympus is the name of the Adaptive Server Enterprise instance:

```
syb_olympus
     master tli tcp /dev/tcp \x000207ee390601e80000000000000000
     query tli tcp /dev/tcp \x000207ee390601e80000000000000000

syb_olympus_bak
     master tli tcp /dev/tcp \x000207ef390601e80000000000000000
     query tli tcp /dev/tcp \x000207ef390601e80000000000000000
```

Above, you can translate the hex entries. 07ee and 07ef are the port numbers. The IP address is 390601e8.

You can also choose to do this without all of the hex entries:

```
syb_olympus
     master tli tcp olympus 2030
     query  tli tcp olympus 2030
```

Sample NT sql.ini Entries

```
;; Sybase Interfaces file
;; <link_type>=<network_driver>,<connection_info>
;; Examples:
;; [JUPITER]
;; QUERY=NLMSNMP,\\JUPITER\pipe\sybase\query
;; WIN3_QUERY=WNLNMP,\\JUPITER\pipe\sybase\query

[TENCHI]
master=tcp,tenchi,2030
query=tcp,tenchi,2030

[TENCHI_XP]
master=tcp,tenchi,2032
query=tcp,tenchi,2032
```

Although the formats differ, in each case the file contains the names of servers (such as syb_olympus and tenchi) and details of how to connect to them. A detail consists of a service type (the master service used by the server, and the query service used by the client), a reference to the protocol used (on UNIX, the protocol name, like tcp; on NT, the protocols are represented by the names of DLLs), and address information (normally machine name and port number in plain text; Solaris uses a hexadecimal encoding; NT named pipes uses a directory location format).

Incorporating SSL into Your Interfaces File

Adaptive Server Enterprise security services now support Secure Sockets Layer (SSL) session-based security. SSL is the standard for securing the transmission of sensitive information, such as credit card numbers, stock trades, and banking transactions, over the Internet. The implementation of Adaptive Server SSL features assumes that there is a knowledgeable system security officer who is familiar with the security policies and needs of your site, and who has general understanding of SSL and public key cryptography.

You can enable a server to use SSL by adding an ssl parameter to the interfaces file entry:

```
syb_olympus
     master tli tcp olympus 2030 ssl
     query tli tcp olympus 2030 ssl
```

You can also configure a server to accept both SSL and non-SSL transactions:

```
syb_olympus
     master tli tcp olympus 2030 ssl
     query tli tcp olympus 2030 ssl
     master tli tcp olympus 2030
```

Sybase's books online has an excellent section on SSL if you choose to implement this. Check www.sybase.com/manuals.

LDAP as a 12.5 Alternative to the Interfaces File

Lightweight Directory Access Protocol is an industry standard for accessing directory services. Directory services allow components to look up information by a distinguished name (DN) from an LDAP server that stores and manages server, user, and software information that is used throughout the enterprise or over a network. The LDAP server can be located on a different platform from the one on which Adaptive Server or the clients are running. LDAP defines the communication protocol and the contents of messages exchanged between clients and servers. Messages are operators, such as client requests for read, write, and query, and server responses, including data-format information.

The LDAP server can be configured with these access restrictions:

- Anonymous authentication — all data is visible to any user
- User name and password authentication

LDAP Directory Services vs. the Sybase Interfaces File

The LDAP driver implements directory services for use with an LDAP server. LDAP directories are an infrastructure that provide:

- A network-based alternative to the traditional Sybase interfaces file.
- A single, hierarchical view of information, including users, software, resources, networks, files, and so on.

Performance when using an LDAP server may be slower than when using an interfaces file because the LDAP server requires time to make a network connection and retrieve data. Since this connection is made when Adaptive Server is started, changes in performance will be seen at login time, if at all. During normal system load, the delay should not be noticeable. During high system load with many connections, especially repeated connections with short duration, the overall performance difference of using an LDAP server versus the traditional interfaces file might be noticeable.

Runserver File

The runserver file is also created at server installation time; it contains the various settings used to start up the server. This file calls the dataserver program with various parameters, including the servername, location of the master device, the location of the errorlog file, the page size, and shared memory location. This file is, by default, named RUN_SERVERNAME, and is created in the $SYBASE/$SYBASE_ASE/install directory.

Note that while NT does contain a batch file that resembles the runserver file, the actual startup parameters are stored in the registry. The batch file is used in certain emergency restart situations, and changing its settings in the batch file will not affect normal startups. If you need to change startup parameters, edit this registry key: My Computer\ HKEY_LOCAL_MACHINE\ SOFTWARE\SYBASE\Server\servername\Parameters.

UNIX example:

```
#!/bin/sh
#
# Adaptive Server name: olympus
# ASE page size (KB):   2k
# Master device path:   /clwprod/sybase/data/master.dat
# Error log path:       /clwprod/sybase/ASE-12_5/install/errorlog
# Directory for shared memory files:  /clwprod/sybase
#
/clwprod/sybase/ASE-12_5/bin/dataserver \
-solympus \
-z2k \
-d/clwprod/sybase/data/master.dat \
-e/clwprod/sybase/ASE-12_5/install/errorlog \
-M/clwprod/sybase \
```

NT example:

```
rem
rem Adaptive Server Information:
rem  name:                          TENCHI
rem  master device:                 f:\sybase\data\master.dat
rem  server page size:              2048
rem  master device size:            30
rem  errorlog:                      f:\sybase\ASE-12_5\install\errorlog
rem  interfaces:                    f:\sybase\ini
rem
f:\sybase\ASE-12_5\bin\sqlsrvr.exe -df:\sybase\data\master.dat -sTENCHI
-z2048 -ef:\sybase\ASE-12_5\install\errorlog -if:\sybase\ini
-Mf:\sybase\ASE-12_5
```

NOTES: UNIX is case sensitive, as are the various switches in the command. The actual file is really a dataserver command (the sybase executable), followed by a series of parameters.

The page size is for documentation only.

-z2k is not needed for boot; in fact, it is ignored by Adaptive Server Enterprise. It is for documentation, and will not change page sizes at boot time.

Runserver Parameters

The following table describes the parameters used in the runserver file.

Parameter	Description
-c	Location and name of the .cfg file
-d	Location and name of the master device
-e	Location and name of the errorlog
-i	Location and name of the interfaces file
-M	Location of the shared memory directory
-r	Location of master mirror
-s	Name of the server
-z	Logical page size of the server

Parameter	Description
-m	Master recovery mode: server starts single-user to repair a failed master
-p	Password recovery mode: used to generate an SSO password at startup
-u	Unlock login mode: used to unlock a single locked login at startup

For use of the runserver file, see the "Starting the Server" section later in this chapter.

Errorlog File

The Sybase errorlog is an operating system file, which receives all operator/console messages. Its default location is:

$SYBASE/$SYBASE_ASE/install

It can be read directly on every operating system, though on NT many tools that check to see if the file is in use will not open the file.

On NT, Adaptive Server can be configured to send the messages to the machine's eventlog. Looking at the errorlog from time to time is part of a preventative maintenance regimen.

servername.cfg — Server Configuration File

The server has a wide variety of configuration options that determine how resources are allocated and used; the setting of these parameters is an ongoing process, fully described in Chapter 11, "Configuring and Tuning the Server." These settings are stored in the servername.cfg file, which is stored in $SYBASE by default. Each time a configurational change is made, the current version of the .cfg file is copied to an archive file named *servername.<three-digit integer>,* starting from *servername*.001 and going up. These files are useful for historical analysis, or if you misconfigure the server and need to revert to an earlier configuration; if no longer needed, these numbered files may be deleted. A copy of a .cfg file is shown in Chapter 11.

SSL in Adaptive Server

Adaptive Server's implementation of SSL provides several levels of security. It authenticates itself, and once the SSL session is established, the client requesting a connection can send his user name and password over the secure, encrypted connection.

A comparison of the digital signature on the server certificate can determine whether the data received by the client was modified before reaching the intended recipient. Adaptive Server uses the SSL Plus™ library API from Certicom Corp.

SSL Filter

Adaptive Server's directory service, such as the interfaces file, NT registry, or LDAP service, defines the server address and port numbers, and determines the security protocols that are enforced for client connections.

Adaptive Server implements the SSL protocol as a filter that is appended to the master and query lines of the directory services. The addresses and port numbers on which Adaptive Server accepts connections are configurable so that multiple network and security protocols can be enabled for a single server. Server connection attributes are specified with directory services, such as LDAP or DCE, or with the traditional Sybase interfaces file.

All connection attempts to a master or query entry in the interfaces file with an SSL filter must support the SSL protocol. A server can be configured to accept SSL connections and have other connections that accept clear text (unencrypted data), or use other security mechanisms.

Note that having a clear text port to accept connections along with an SSL port to accept connections is possible but not recommended, because allowing cleartext defeats the purpose of SSL connections. However, it may be useful during migration to SSL or along with other security measures.

The SSL filter is different from other security mechanisms, such as DCE and Kerberos, which are defined with SECMECH (security mechanism) lines in the interfaces file (sql.ini on Windows).

Authentication Via the Certificate

The SSL protocol requires server authentication via a server certificate to enable an encrypted session. Likewise, when Adaptive Server is functioning as a client during RPCs there must be a repository of trusted CAs that a client connection can access to validate the server certificate. Each Adaptive Server must have its own server certificate file that is loaded at startup. The default location for the certificates file is:

UNIX — *$SYBASE/$SYBASE_ASE/certificates/*servername.*crt*

NT — *%SYBASE%\%SYBASE_ASE%\certificates*\servername.*crt*

The server certificate file consists of encoded data, including the server's certificate and the encrypted private key for the server certificate. Alternatively, you can specify the location of the server certificate file when using sp_ssladmin.

NOTE: To make a successful client connection, the common name in the certificate must match the Adaptive Server name in the interfaces file.

The CA Trusted Roots Certificate

The list of trusted CAs is loaded by Adaptive Server at startup from the trusted roots file. The trusted roots file is similar in format to a certificate file, except that it contains certificates for CAs known to Adaptive Server. A trusted roots file is accessible by the local Adaptive Server in:

UNIX — $SYBASE/$SYBASE_ASE/certificates/*servername*.txt

NT — %SYBASE%\%SYBASE_ASE\certificates*servername*.txt

The trusted roots file is only used by Adaptive Server when it is functioning as a client, such as when performing (RPC) calls or Component Integration Services (CIS) connections.

The system security officer adds and deletes CAs that are to be accepted by Adaptive Server, using a standard ASCII text editor.

Environmental Variables

In order to locate the appropriate components of Adaptive Server (and Backup Server and Open Client), it is necessary to set some environmental variables for the operating system. The installation manual will provide a list of the required settings for your environment. Some of the common environment variables are:

Variable	Description
SYBASE	The base directory in which you installed the software
DSQUERY	The entry within the interfaces file to be used by clients as the default Adaptive Server to connect to
DSLISTEN	The default interfaces entry for the server to listen on, if none is specified in the runserver file
SYBASE_ASE	The subdirectory where the Adaptive Server Enterprise server files are located
SYBASE_EJB	The subdirectory where the Enterprise Java Beans server is located
SYBASE_OCS	The subdirectory where Open Client/Server files are located
SYBASE_SYSAM	The subdirectory where the Software Asset Manager is located

In UNIX systems, the variables may be preceded by a "$"; on NT, the variables are bracketed by a pair of "%".

Note that the directory structure used by ASE changed significantly in version 12.0, and administrators of prior versions may find directories in slightly unfamiliar locations. The top level of the installation is the $SYBASE directory, which contains items like the interfaces file and .cfg file.

Underneath the $SYBASE directory are a series of subdirectories, some of which are product- or executable-specific, and some of which are common. The common subdirectories (like charsets, collate, installed, and locales) contain files that may be used by multiple Sybase products (various versions of ASE, Adaptive Server Anywhere, Adaptive Server IQ, Replication Server, and others). The product- or executable-specific subdirectories are each named for a specific type and version of server (such as ASE-12_0, ASE-12_5, or REP-12_0), and contain the installation that is particular to a single product.

Some of the subdirectory names you should be familiar with include:

Subdirectory Name	Description
ASE-12_5	Top level of the ASE installation
EJB-12_5	Top level of the Enterprise Java Beans installation
jconnect-5_5	Top level of the Java connectivity installation
jutils-2_0	Top level of the Java-based utilities (jisql, ribo) installation
OCS-12_5	Top level of the Open Client/Server utilities installation
SYSAM-1_0	Top level of the Sybase Software Asset Manager installation

As a result of the directory shift, some of the directories you were familiar with have shifted to new locations:

Task	Old Location	New Location
start the server	$SYBASE/install	$SYBASE/ASE-12_5/install
run isql/bcp	$SYBASE/bin	$SYBASE/OCS-12_5/bin
read the errorlog	$SYBASE/install	$SYBASE/ASE-12_5/install

Step 4: Front-End Installation

With the installation of the front-end (or *client*) application, the database now has a user interface. This application will connect to the database, request tasks of the server, and display the results of its requests. These applications may be pre-written, third-party applications, or products specifically built for an organization. Regardless, the application will need to talk to the database over a network, and it will need to use Open Client.

Open Client is the portion of the Adaptive Server Architecture that provides network transparency. This connectivity layer allows for client applications (regardless of the platform) to talk to servers (also regardless of the platform), provided they both are communicating with the same network protocol. If a server is capable of communicating with multiple protocols, this means that the clients can communicate to the server using any protocol the server already uses. This also means that regardless of the protocol used, the application is coded the same way.

Figure 2-1

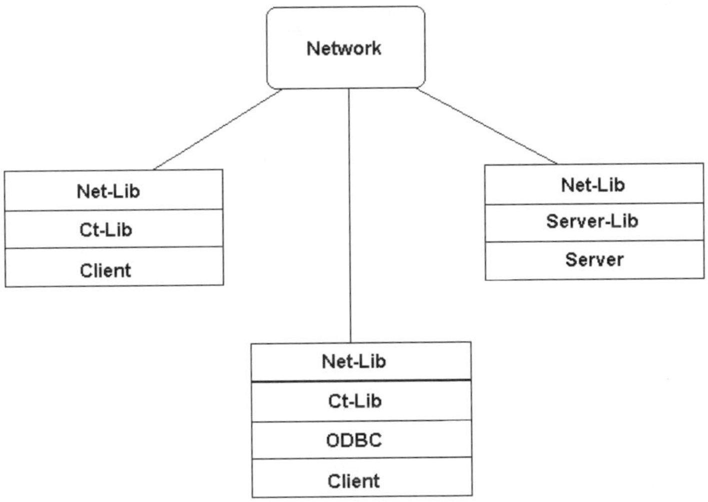

On the client side, the application is written to take advantage of the connectivity of Open Client. The particular Open Client libraries (CT-Lib) take any requests and convert them into a generic form known as the Tabular Data Stream (TDS), which the Net-Lib can understand and transmit over the specified network protocol. The Net-Lib is a driver written to accept TDS from the CT-Lib or from the network. On the server side, there is a server equivalent to the CT-Lib, called the Server-Lib, which is part of the ASE executable. It also communicates with the Net-Lib.

In brief, the CT-Lib translates the requests of the client application into a generic form, which is further translated by the Net-Lib according to the network protocol used. On the server side, the Net-Lib translates the incoming network stream into a form that the Server-Lib can understand, which then translates the request into particular server calls. When the Adaptive Server produces results, they are transmitted back to the client by traversing the same layers in reverse: Server-Lib translates results into a generic form; Net-Lib translates according to the protocol; Net-Lib translates from network protocol to generic; CT-Lib translates from generic to a specific form understood by the client application, which then displays the results. As a result, any portion of this translation process could be replaced (a new client application written or a new network protocol used, for example) without having to replace or re-create all of the other layers.

ODBC

Another popular method of getting connectivity to the Adaptive Server is through the use of Open Database Connectivity (ODBC). While ASE supports connectivity to its databases through the ODBC, it is usually an additional layer of connectivity and still requires a complete installation of the Open Client.

The ultimate goal behind the use of Open Client is that any client should be able to connect to any kind of server regardless of platform.

Starting the Server

As simple as it may sound, one of the most sought-after tasks for an ASE administrator is to start and shutdown (or restart) the server. Since the startup and shutdown can have a drastic effect on users, these tasks require special permission. Starting a server will require access to the runserver file and permission to use the dataserver executable (UNIX), or membership in the Administrators group (NT); shutting down the server will require the ASE sa_role (see Chapter 6, "Security"). Like many other aspects of computing, there may be slight differences between the startup processes for different platforms. And there usually is an alternative method or two for getting the server running.

The following examples will look at some generic UNIX startup options and some NT startup options.

Normal UNIX Startup

Use the startserver utility, which will put the running server process in the background automatically. Otherwise, unless you manually place the ASE process in the background (using "&"), the server will stop running when you log out of the connection used for startup. The startserver utility is provided in the $SYBASE/$SYBASE_ASE/install directory.

1. Sign in as the sybase user.
2. Change to the $SYBASE/$SYBASE_ASE/install directory.
3. Execute the RUNSERVER file using the startserver utility.

```
startserver -f RUN_olympus
```

The -f option is followed by the name of the runserver file with the necessary startup parameters; if you wish to start multiple servers (say, a dataserver and its associated Backup Server), you may use multiple instances of -f with runserver files:

```
startserver -f RUN_olympus -f RUN_olympus_back
```

Normal NT Startup

Windows NT may also start the Adaptive Server from the command line, but will do so via a slightly different method. As mentioned above, the batch file equivalent to the runserver file isn't meant for ordinary startups; instead, we will start the ASE service using the NT net start command.

1. Sign in as a member of the Administrators group.
2. Open a DOS prompt.
3. Run net start with the service name (which will be sybsql_*<name of server>*).

```
net start sybsql_olympus
```

Manual UNIX Startup

For a manual startup, instead of the startserver utility starting up the server, a manual execution of the dataserver command is used. The steps in the manual process differ at step 3. For manual startup, the environment variables are manually declared and the server is run by using the dataserver command. The runserver file will have all the necessary parameters for a manual startup.

Manual UNIX Startup

1-2. Same as previous.

3. Set the DSLISTEN environment variable (the server-side equivalent of the DSQUERY environment variable).
4. Make sure your path statement includes the $SYBASE/$SYBASE_ASE/bin directory.
5. Execute the dataserver command as a background process.

```
%setenv DSLISTEN SYBASE
%/home/sybase/bin/dataserver -d/dev/rsd01 &
%/home/sybase/bin/dataserver -d/dev/rsd01
-s SYBASE &
```

In order for the manual startup to work, Sybase Adaptive Server must have the network up and loaded before Sybase can load properly. An alternative for setting the DSLISTEN variable is to pass the server name with the -s parameter. In both cases the trailing "&" says, "start that as a background job." If the network fails to load, regardless of the operating system, Adaptive Server Enterprise will not start. Both the network and Adaptive Server Enterprise will send error messages to the OS errorlog if this occurs.

Automatic System Boot

This is the preferred method of starting an Adaptive Server, in part because it takes some of the work out of the process. The goal is to get the ASE server to start automatically when the system is started. This way the administrator does not have to worry about running the startup command, just whether the startup completed successfully.

UNIX Start

ASE startup at boot time is usually done by placing startserver commands in your operating system's automatic startup file. Some versions/platforms have these instructions in the installation manual. The major key to success at automatic startup is to ensure that the network is completely up before applying Adaptive Server startup; otherwise, startup will fail. Also, remember not to start the server as root; this can inadvertently change file permissions. Issue the UNIX swapuser command (usually su) prior to startup.

NT Start

Adaptive Server is configured to start automatically by using the SERVICES application in the Control Panel application. By setting the STARTUP of the Sybase Adaptive Server to automatic, Adaptive Server will load automatically.

Verifying the Server is Running

Once the server has been started, the next administrative task is to verify that the startup was successful and a server process exists on the machine.

Adaptive Server for UNIX

On a UNIX platform, this must be done by locating the dataserver process on the machine. Sybase provides showserver, an operating system level tool to verify that the server is up and is located in the $SYBASE/$SYBASE_ASE/install directory. The execute permission for showserver defaults to only the sybase user. Some operating systems show detailed statistics on the process, while others merely verify that the server is up. It is a common recommendation that the showserver utility be executable by any user.

Adaptive Server for NT

In an NT environment, server verification is done using the GUI tools provided by Windows, or from the command prompt.

Use NT Services Manager

You may verify if an NT-based Adaptive Server is running by checking the NT Services list. If the process has started successfully, the service status should be listed as "Started."

Figure 2-2

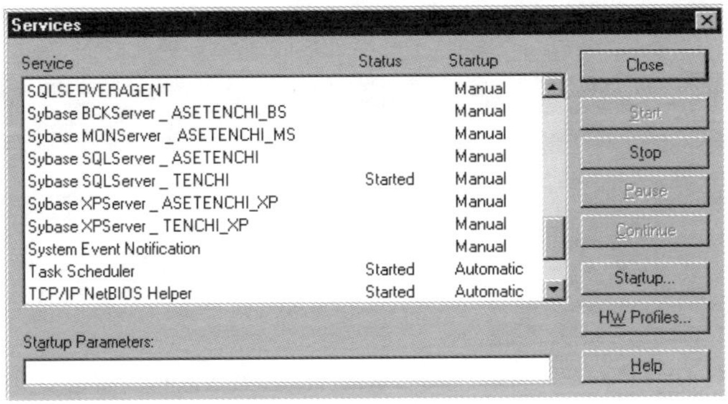

Use NT Task Manager

The NT Task Manager is also capable of indicating whether or not the Adaptive Server has successfully started. If the server has not failed, then a process should exist on the task list.

Figure 2-3

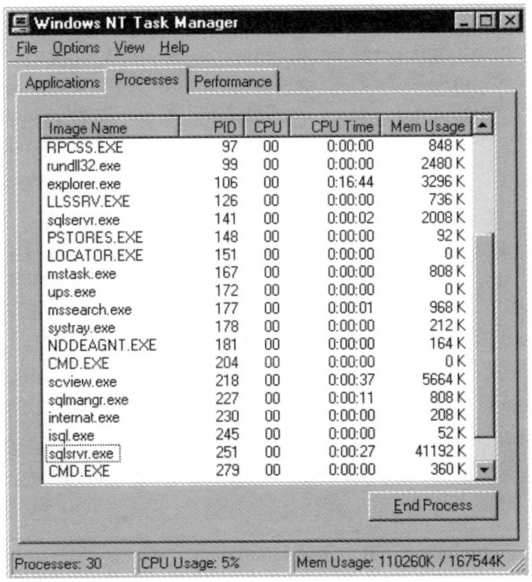

Use the Net Start Command

Finally, you may verify that the server is running by executing the net start command with no arguments; this will list all of the running services on the server (this is merely a command-line equivalent to using the Services Manager).

Shutting the Server Down

The other task that is strictly reserved for administrators is the act of shutting down the server or stopping it. ASE shutdowns come in two flavors: graceful and immediate.

Graceful Shutdowns

A *graceful* shutdown allows Adaptive Server to unload itself from memory, but to completely process existing statements on current user connections, as well as checkpoint all databases before finally shutting down.

To perform a graceful shutdown:

1. Log in as anyone with the sa_role using a query editor (like isql).
2. Type the shutdown command from client application.

In this instance "shutdown" represents an Adaptive Server keyword for Transact-SQL. The shutdown disables all logins (except those with SA privileges), waits for currently executing transactions and procedures to complete, checkpoints the databases, and shuts down the dataserver process (this is also called "cycling" or "bouncing" the server).

The "stop" option doesn't show up in Java SybCent, just "disconnect."

Shutdown with nowait

In certain circumstances, it may not be possible to gracefully shut down the server; in these cases, the with nowait option will force Adaptive Server to close immediately. This still allows the dataserver executable to remove itself from the operating system and close its own memory allocations, but it tells Adaptive Server to unload directly from the operating system, without waiting for user connections to complete their work. This usually means that any in-progress transactions will be lost, and also does not checkpoint the various databases. The nowait option shuts everything down immediately, terminating all processes without regard to status, just as if you had suddenly yanked out the power cord.

The two shutdown options are the primary method of turning off an Adaptive Server. If they fail to complete, the remaining, less desirable option is available. When all else fails, kill the Adaptive Server process from the O/S or reboot the machine. Note that this is a last-ditch solution.

Maintenance Shutdowns

While it is very popular to discuss 24x7 (24 hours/7 days per week) availability of a server, the practical availability of a single server is not always that continuous. Adaptive Server Enterprise will require a restart under certain conditions:

- When changing certain configuration options
- When aborted transaction(s) in the log keep the dump transaction from cleaning it out
- To set a variety of system trace flags

Certain configuration options require the reallocation of memory, which may only occur at server start time. Changing configuration options that are not dynamic will require shutdown and restart for that option to take effect.

Aborted transactions in the log may keep the dump tran from cleaning it out — this is a bad thing — and usually reflects neglectful DBAs or improperly coded (long-running) transactions.

Chapter 3

Defining Physical and Sybase-Mirrored Devices to the Server

The Need for Devices

Now that the server is installed, you will want to start creating your user databases so that you can begin building your tables and other database objects. Before you can do that, you must first define the storage areas that the databases will require. This chapter will describe that process. We will also look at methods of protecting the databases from device failure and optimizing the performance of those database devices.

Logical vs. Physical Devices

Unlike some other database servers, ASE uses logical rather than physical devices to store and manage database space. A logical device is simply a name that is mapped to a physical area on disk, which is identified by a filename. In the case of UNIX operating systems, the filename could be either a raw device or a regular file. (NT also allows for raw devices, but the NTFS file system is preferred.) The differences between those two types of devices will be discussed later in this chapter. Regardless of the type of physical device you choose, the syntax for creating and managing the logical device is the same.

Using logical devices provides you with more manageable and flexible control over your database and object placement, because your database is not tied directly to a file. A single database can span multiple devices, and multiple databases can share the same device. Each database is made up of one or more fragments (contiguous allocations of physical storage), with each fragment mapped to part or all of a logical device.

Performance Implications

Where you choose to place your databases and their individual fragments can play a major role in how they will perform. You will want to make the most out of your available disk drives so that you don't overwork one drive while another sits mostly idle. For that reason, you may want to create multiple logical devices across many physical drives so that when you create your database, it will not reside entirely on one physical disk. Additionally, the type of device you choose to create can impact performance. Keep these facts in mind as you begin defining your devices. We'll look at load balancing and device types in more detail later in this chapter.

Creating and Dropping Devices

Managing your devices is handled through a series of commands and stored procedures. The device information and database mapping is stored in a set of system tables in the master database, which can be queried directly or through predefined stored procedures. Creating and modifying your devices should never be done by direct modification of the system tables; ASE provides all the commands and procedures necessary to do this safely.

Don't wait until you need database space to create your devices. You should have a set of devices predefined so that if your database runs out of space, you can quickly allocate more space to the database without having to scramble to find available disk space and define new logical devices. Additionally, choosing a standard set of sizes for your devices simplifies administration, record-keeping, and emergency repairs.

The master device and the device used to house the sybsystemprocs database (typically sysprocsdev) are created through the server installation process. The devices used to house the sybsecurity database are created through the auditinit utility. All other database devices are created using the disk init command. Each device created will be stored as a single row in the sysdevices system table in the master database, regardless of how the device was created.

TIP: Remember to dump the master database after any allocation of system resources.

Creating Database Devices

You use the disk init command to create database devices. Its syntax is as follows:

```
disk init
name = "device_name" ,
physname = "physicalname" ,
size = size_of_device
[vdevno = virtual_device_number , ]
 [, vstart = virtual_address ,] [cntrltype = controller_number]
[, dsync = {true | false}]
```

The first parameter is name. This is the logical name of the device, and it will be the name referred to when allocating database space to this physical device. It is also the name you will reference when mirroring or assigning default devices. The name can be anything you like, but it must be unique to this server and cannot contain any spaces or punctuation. As is true with objects and databases, the name is case sensitive and must be 30 characters or less.

It's a good idea to name devices to identify their use. For instance, creating devices called dev1, dev2, and dev3 is far less informative than sales_data1, products_data1, and sales_index1. If you were to run out of index space in the sales database, you can quickly identify which logical device to use to expand the database and extend your index segment.

The second parameter is physname. This is the physical file that the logical name maps to and is the actual storage area that will house your database fragment. Depending on whether you are using a raw device or a regular file for the new device, the sybase account must have read-write permissions on either the raw device itself or the directory that will contain the regular file. Without proper permissions, the disk init command will fail.

> **NOTE:** You must fully qualify the physical filename with its path. Otherwise, the command may fail or a new file will be created in the wrong location. For instance, if you specify a device name of sales_data1.dat, that file will be created in the directory from which the server was started, when perhaps what you really wanted was to create the file under the /devices directory. The correct physname should have been /devices/sales_data1.dat. In the case of a raw device, if you were to specify dev/rdsk/c0t1d0s2, the command will likely fail since the server would be looking for a directory called $SYBASE/dev/rdsk to create the new file c0t1d0s2 in. If the directory does not exist, the command fails. The correct physname would have included a leading "/" to fully qualify the raw device location. Similar path rules apply for NT servers.
>
> Caveat: There is one reason for using relative device names: It may simplify moving the server to another physical location. It is unusual to see this in practice.

The third parameter is size. By default, this is specified in number of virtual pages (the page size for the server), not megabytes. Note that size allocations are not an area in which ASE provides consistency; if you don't remember the units when you're using a command, Look it up! A simple calculation to determine the number of 2 K pages is to multiply the number of megabytes by 512.

New for 12.5, you may instead choose to specify the units for disk init. "k" or "K" indicate kilobytes, "m" or "M" indicate megabytes, and "g" or "G" indicate gigabytes. Although it is optional, Sybase recommends that you always include the unit specifier in both the disk init and create database commands to avoid confusion in the actual number of pages allocated. You must enclose the unit specifier in single or double quotes. Don't use float; while you can specify a float, documentation differs as to whether any numbers after the decimal are truncated (for example, if you specify size as "4.5 G", it is initialized as "4"), or are converted to the lower multiple of 2 K pages. We recommend that you simply avoid the problem.

This chapter assumes 2 K pages, which is the default (and the only size available prior to 12.5). If you are using larger page sizes, make sure you alter your calculations accordingly. Devices have only one page size: 2 K. It is when we allocate the devices to databases that we begin to use the alternate sizes.

You must be certain that the raw device is not smaller than the specified size, or in the case of regular files, that the directory has enough free space to create the new file.

TIP: Unlike regular files, where you can define many files under one directory, when using raw devices to define your logical devices, use the entire raw device size. Only one logical device can map to any given raw device, so if you don't use it all, you are wasting space. You may have a 2 GB directory that contains many smaller regular files, but if you have a 2 GB raw device, use the entire 2 GB. Take this into account when working with your UNIX Admin to carve up your physical disks into multiple raw device slices. If you want to define your devices as 500 MB, then make sure your UNIX Admin defines your raw devices as 500 MB each.

The fourth parameter is vdevno. This is the virtual device number, which is a unique identifier assigned to each device. It must be a number that is not already used by another device, and must be less than the configured number of devices. If the number is 25, vdevno can be no higher than 24. If you have used up all available device numbers, you must reconfigure for more devices, using sp_configure. New with 12.5, you can skip this parameter and the server will automatically assign the next available virtual device number. This is recommended, as keeping track of available virtual device numbers can be tedious.

TIP: To determine the configured number of devices, run sp_configure 'number of devices', or look for "number of devices" in your configuration file (ServerName.cfg).

To determine which device numbers are currently in use, run sp_helpdevice or the following query:

```
select low/16777216
from sysdevices where cntrltype=0
order by low
```

On large servers where you have more than 127 devices, try this instead:

```
select low/power(2,24) + ((low/power(2,24)) & 128) * 2
from sysdevices where cntrltype=0
order by 1
```

The fifth line, which defines your virtual starting address and the controller number, is optional and generally not used. Both values default to 0. Do not specify them unless directed to by Sybase Technical Support.

The last parameter defines whether the dsync option is on or off for this device. This will be covered in detail later in this chapter.

Let's take a look at some examples of logical device creation.

```
disk init
name = sales_data1,
physname = '/dev/rdsk/c0t1d0s2',
size = 51200

disk init
name = tempdb_dev1,
physname = '/tmp/tempdb_devices/tempdb_dev1.dat',
size = "300M"

disk init
```

```
name = sales_index1,
physname = 'D:\Database_Devices\Sales\sales_index1.dat',
size = "150M"
```

The first example shows how to create a logical device called sales_data1 on a raw device in a UNIX environment. Remember that the physical device /dev/rdsk/c0t1d0s2 must have read-write access for the Sybase account, and the device size should be exactly the same as the size specified so that no space is wasted. In this case the size is 100 MB, or 51,200 2 K pages. Also note the logical name sales_data1 must be unique.

The second example shows how to create a logical device called tempdb_dev1 as a regular file with a size of 300 MB. In this example I've used the /tmp directory to improve performance. This is mapped to the swap area, which is essentially the same as mapping it to memory so I get better performance than I would from a slow disk drive. Since /tmp is cleared out when the UNIX server is recycled, I'll want to make sure that I modify my Sybase startup script to check for the existence of the tempdb_devices directory and the tempdb_dev1.dat file prior to starting the server. If they don't exist, the script should create them or the server will not start properly. If the tempdb database is not available after startup, the server is unusable.

The last example shows how to create a logical device called sales_index1 on a regular file in a PC-based environment. Note that all syntax is the same, with the only difference being how you reference the physical filename.

One last note on device creation. You may have noticed that I used the file extension .dat when defining my physical filenames. This is not a requirement, it's merely my preference. The only thing you should make sure of is that you are consistent with how you name your devices, and that the names are meaningful to you, so define your naming conventions ahead of time.

Creating Default Devices

To create a default device, use the following:

```
exec sp_defaultdisk logical_device_name, 'defaultoff | defaulton'
```

After server installation, the master device is the only default device. This should be changed immediately so that you do not accidentally allocate user database space to the master device. The master device should only contain system databases, not user databases. If the master database becomes full, and there is no space left on the master device, this can be a big problem since the master database can only be allocated to the master device. The example below illustrates how to take the master device out of the default device pool, and add other devices to the pool.

```
exec sp_defaultdisk 'master','defaultoff'
exec sp_defaultdisk 'data_dev1','defaulton'
exec sp_defaultdisk 'data_dev2','defaulton'
```

Execution of this stored procedure will update the status column of the sysdevices table to identify whether the device is part of the default device pool. If you were to create or extend a database without specifying which device to use, space would be allocated to one or more of the default devices, using them up in alphabetical order (by logical name). So if you were going to create a 500 MB database, but data_dev1 only had 300 MB free, it would use up that 300 MB, and then use 200 MB of the data_dev2 device, assuming space is available.

Dropping Database Devices

So why would you want to remove a device? You may have made a mistake when you created it, such as defining the wrong size or location or name. Or perhaps you want to reallocate your device space to achieve better load balancing. Maybe you've reached the limit of number of devices, so you need to combine smaller devices into larger ones. It could be that you had a disk drive fail, and after installing a new drive, you need to reallocate the device. Replacing a slower drive with a faster one is another good reason. Whatever your reason happens to be, ASE provides a means for dropping database devices.

As mentioned previously, the device information is stored in the sysdevices system table, which is located in the master database. It's OK to query this table, but just like you should never directly modify this table to add devices, the same holds true for removing devices. Instead, a stored procedure named sp_dropdevice should be used.

```
exec sp_dropdevice 'logical_device_name'
```

To remove the device, you specify the logical device name, not the physical name. When you execute this stored procedure, it removes the entry from the sysdevices table. It does not remove the physical file, so you will need to do that manually to free up the directory space or to reuse that physical filename. Of course, you should only remove the physical file if it's a regular file, not if it's a raw device.

NOTE: You cannot drop a database device if any part of a database is currently allocated to it. Don't worry, you can't make this mistake. If you try to do this, you will get a warning message stating that the device is currently in use. Of course, it doesn't tell you which databases are using it. You'll have to figure that out on your own! Here's how:

```
select distinct db_name(su.dbid)
from master..sysusages su, master..sysdevices sd
where su.vstart between sd.low and sd.high
and sd.name = 'logical device name'
```

Raw vs. Filesystem

I've mentioned raw devices and regular files, but only from an operational standpoint. So what about from a functional standpoint? The main difference between a raw device and a regular file is not in how you reference them or how you remove them, but in how they are actually written to and what this can mean to the safety of your database.

A regular file uses buffered writes. Without going into detail, what this essentially means is that as you are performing data modifications in your databases, ASE writes these changes to the database devices on disk. Or at least it thinks it's doing that. In reality, the operating system tells ASE that the writes have been completed, when, in fact, they have been buffered in cache and only truly written to disk when a certain amount of write operations have occurred. If the server were to suddenly shut down in a less than graceful manner, you could end up with corruption in your index or page linkage. What does this mean to you? Well, corruption can cause partial or full data loss in the affected table. Not a good thing, obviously.

Raw devices on the other hand, do not buffer their writes. Instead, when ASE sends a write, the information is actually written to disk before ASE receives confirmation of the write. As you can see, this is a much safer type of device to use, and it is highly recommended for your system databases.

Safety is not the only difference between raw devices and regular files. Performance is also a consideration. Since regular files will use buffered writes and raw devices must actually write to disk, regular files tend to outperform raw devices. Depending on how heavily you are writing to your database and how fast your disk drives are, this can turn out to be a significant difference in performance. However, this performance difference may vary widely (or even be negligible), depending on the hardware and operating system of your host machine.

Manageability is another key difference. Managing raw devices tends to take a lot more effort and planning than using regular files, and is more restrictive. When you use regular files, you simply define a new device by pointing to a particular directory and assigning a new filename. With raw devices, you are limited to how many slices you can have per disk drive, unless you are using some volume management software, and you must plan ahead to determine how big each raw device should be.

It's up to you to decide which is more important for each database and server. As with almost everything, there are tradeoffs. Some databases are less critical than others. If corruption occurs, maybe restoring from yesterday's backup is acceptable, while slow performance is not. In that case, you might consider using regular files. You might choose to go with raw devices for production servers, while choosing the manageability of regular files for your development environments.

Dsync Option

A nice feature that was added in Version 12.0 was the dsync option. With this feature, you can combine the ease of use of regular files with the safety of raw devices. Basically, it eliminates the buffered behavior of regular files by telling UNIX to open the database device with the dsync flag. In other words, all writes are guaranteed, so the safety of your database is maintained. This is not to say you still can't have corruption occur for other reasons, but the chances of it occurring due to missed writes is greatly reduced. On the other hand, it is slower than using files with OS-supported buffering. There is a real, very noticeable difference between OS files with dsync on or off.

Another benefit of using the dsync option is that although your writes will be slower, your reads will be faster than raw devices. This is because regular files typically use buffered reads in addition to buffered writes. So, in effect, you have a hybrid device — one that has the safety and slowness of raw device writes, but the read speed and flexibility of regular files.

Again, your performance may vary, and you should carefully test whether or not a dsync'ed file device is faster than a non-dsync'ed raw device in your shop. As a general rule, devices intended for tempdb should be heavily buffered file devices with dsync off. If not specified in the disk init command, dsync will default to true, even for raw devices (for these devices, dsync should be set to false). Lastly, the dsync flag is ignored by NT-hosted servers; for the best mix of safety and performance on NT, use file devices on the NTFS file system.

> **NOTE:** Because the master database is so crucial to your server, dsync is always set to true if you define your master device to a regular file. You cannot change this, and if you attempt to, you will receive a warning message.

Besides setting the dsync option at disk initialization, you can also change it after the device has already been created. This is done via the sp_deviceattr stored procedure. Before the change takes effect, you must restart Adaptive Server.

The stored procedure is defined as:

```
exec sp_deviceattr 'logical_name', 'option_name', 'option_value'
```

Here is an example:

```
exec sp_deviceattr 'sales_data1','dsync','true'
```

Device Limitations and Restrictions

Following are limitations and restrictions associated with database devices.

- Logical device names — must be unique, case sensitive, up to 30 characters (no spaces or punctuation)
- Device sizes — system dependent, but generally 32 GB without making changes to O/S.
- Number of devices — 256
- Vdevno — 1 through 255, with 0 reserved for the master device
- Dsync — ignored for raw partitions and PC file systems. Always on for master device.
- Location — physical file must be local to the machine where Adaptive Server resides (cannot be a network or remote mounted drive). You should fully qualify the path name, which must be 255 characters in length or less.

Master Device Creation

The master device is the first device created at installation time. It used to be a strong recommendation to put the master device on a raw partition rather than a regular file, but with dsync, this is no longer a concern, since writes are ensured.

Once installation is complete, you will have four databases occupying space on the master device. Obviously the master database is one of them, but the model database, the first 2 MB of tempdb, and sybsystemdb will also reside there. (If upgrading from a pre-12.0 server, sybsystemdb is probably on a non-master device; if installing 12.0 or 12.5, sybsystemdb resides on master.) You should keep it that way. Do not add user databases to the master device because you will want to keep the space free to allow for master database expansion. With that said, be sure to define the master device with enough space to allow for expansion of the master database. Typically, the master database gets larger with each new release of Adaptive Server.

Building the Master Device

The buildmaster utility (or bldmastr on Windows NT) is no longer used to build or rebuild the master device. In previous versions, it was used to re-create your master device and/or database in certain emergency situations where you had to resize the device or re-create the database due to corruption, disk failure, or other serious problems. That functionality still exists, but it is now handled through the dataserver executable, which also happens to be the Adaptive Server engine.

The dataserver executable is defined as follows:

```
dataserver -d master_device_name
   (-e, -c, -T, -I, etc.)
   [-b master_device_size [k|K|m|M|g|G]]
   [-z logical_page_size [k|K]]
```

The -d option specifies the physical location and name of the master device to create.

The -b option specifies the number of virtual pages to allocate for the device. Virtual pages are always 2 K in size, so this is similar to the disk init command where you multiply megabytes by 512 to determine the number of pages. Note that you can optionally specify the device size by specifying the size in kilobytes, megabytes, or gigabytes. You do not have to use whole numbers when using megabytes or gigabytes, for instance, 210.5 M and 1.5 G are both valid sizes.

> **TIP:** Adaptive Server Enterprise uses 8 KB at the beginning of the master device for housekeeping purposes. Also, space must be allocated to databases in groups of 256 logical pages (an allocation unit), with a minimum of 1 M per unit. When using an OS file for the master database, take this into account so that you don't potentially waste space in the file. For instance, on a 4 K page size, specifying "50 M" provides ample space for system databases with only a few hundred bytes that can't be allocated.

The -z option specifies the logical page size to use. This has nothing to do with physical storage, since all database devices are stored as 2 K pages grouped in 512 K allocation units. This is defining how the databases will logically use space, and it can be defined as 2 K, 4 K, 8 K, or 16 K logical pages. If you do not use the K in your syntax, then it represents the number of bytes per logical page. In other words, -z8192 is the same as -z8K, since four 2 K pages equals 8 K. The default is 2 K if you leave out this option.

I mentioned that dataserver also happens to be the Adaptive Server engine. This is an important point because you do not want to specify the -z or -b options during normal operations, also known as the boot phase. The runserver file contains the startup commands to identify the location of the master device (-d), the errorlog location (-e), the configuration file location (-c), and various other options to control how the server runs. The -b and -z options should only be used during the build phase; otherwise, every time you reboot your server, you'll be attempting to rebuild your master device, and you certainly don't want that! (The server checks, and won't overwrite OS files unless you use the -force option.)

Mirroring and Volume Management

Once disks are initialized, you need to decide what mechanisms are appropriate to minimize the risk of disk failure. Sybase mirroring enables you to keep a copy of a physical disk by using Sybase software. You can, if you like, utilize hardware to perform the same task.

Sybase Mirroring

What happens when one of your disk drives fails? Unless you've done something to protect yourself, you will end up having to replace the failed drive, reinitialize database devices that were mapped to the drive, re-create one or more databases, and then restore the databases from backups. Depending on how you're handling backups and how you've allocated your databases and transaction logs, you may end up losing data. Even if you've set things up so you don't lose any data, you're definitely going to have some downtime, which is not going to please your users or your management. It's a good way to find yourself quickly hunting for a new job!

Thankfully, Adaptive Server provides you with a method of protecting your database devices (and your job!). That method is called mirroring, and that's what we'll be exploring in the following sections. *Mirroring* basically means that each write to a primary device is subsequently written to a secondary device, so that you have a complete copy of your data. Of course, the secondary device should be defined on a completely separate physical disk drive or it doesn't do you much good. An even better approach is to place the secondary device on a drive that uses a different controller, to further protect you in the event of a controller failure.

You use the disk mirror command to mirror, as follows:

```
disk mirror
name = 'logical_device_name',
mirror = 'physical_mirror_name'
[, writes = {serial | noserial}]
```

The disk mirror syntax is similar to the disk init syntax because you must specify a logical and a physical device name. That's where the similarities end. Since it is a mirror of the database device, it does not require a size or vdevno value. It does not create a new entry in the sysdevices table, but instead modifies information about the logical device that you are mirroring.

The first parameter is name, which represents the logical name of the device you want to mirror. It must refer to a database device that already exists.

The second parameter is mirror, which is the physical location of the secondary, or mirror, device. This follows the same rules as the physname parameter of the disk init command. The sybase account must have read-write access to the location, it should be a fully qualified path (unless you are using relative paths), the file cannot already exist (unless it is a raw device), and there must be enough free space to create the file. The size of the mirror device will be exactly the same as the database device you are mirroring. If the device or directory is too small, the command will fail. As was the case with disk init, if your physical device is a raw partition, don't waste space by only using part of it, because no other device or mirror can point to it; make sure your sizes match, because the server won't.

The third parameter is writes, and it tells Adaptive Server whether to use synchronous or asynchronous writes for the mirror device. This is similar to the difference between using regular files and raw devices. If you choose noserial, then as soon as the write to the primary side completes, processing continues, even if the mirror side hasn't completed its write. If the server were to go down suddenly, there's no guarantee that the mirror side is in synch with the primary side, which is a big problem. If you choose serial writes, then both sides must complete their writes before processing continues. This guarantees that the mirror and primary side are always in synch. As is the case with raw devices, there is a performance penalty to pay, since you are now doubling your writes, so keep that in mind as you weigh your options.

Example:

```
disk mirror
name = 'data_dev1',
mirror = '/sybase/mirror_devices/data_dev1_mir.dat',
writes = noserial
```

When you run the disk mirror command, it may take a while to complete because it must copy all used pages from the primary database device to the mirror device. Be sure to run this during periods of little or no activity so you do not impact the users. Once the pages are copied, it will update the row in sysdevices for the corresponding database device. This update will identify the physical location of the mirror device, and update the status column to identify it as mirrored and whether writes are serial or not.

NOTE: As of System 10, reads are only done from the primary side. Prior to that, reads could be done from both the primary and mirror devices, but the performance benefits were found to be minimal.

What Should You Mirror?

Keep in mind that since you are mirroring devices and not databases, you should make sure that if your database spans multiple database devices, you mirror them all; otherwise you are only partially protecting your database. Depending on your goals and available space, you have several options as far as a mirroring strategy.

If you want to ensure full nonstop access to the database devices, mirror all database devices. This means you will be protecting your user databases and your system databases, and you will be protecting your data and your transaction logs. If any of your disk drives fail, your server and all databases will still be accessible, and the users will not even know anything has happened. This safety does have a cost associated with it, though. You will require twice as much disk space, but thankfully disk prices continue to drop. Perhaps the larger cost is the performance hit you will take because, again, you are doubling the number of writes.

If you want to reduce the costs but still protect your data, you might consider only mirroring your critical databases. This depends on whether you can afford any downtime, and how much effort will be involved in recovering your databases. You may have a database that is read-only. In this case, mirroring doesn't cost you anything as far as write speed is concerned, but it does cost you disk space. Since the database is read-only, and maybe you can afford for that database to be unavailable for a while, you can leave it unmirrored and then just restore from your nightly backup if the device takes a hit. This leaves disk space available to mirror only your more mission-critical databases.

Another option is to only mirror the transaction log devices. As you'll discover in later chapters, the transaction log is the only part of a database that is really needed to achieve up-to-the-minute recoverability. By using this mirroring strategy, you minimize your space requirements and performance hit by not having to mirror your data devices, while still ensuring no loss of data. The downside is that you will have some downtime while you replace your data devices and perform other recovery tasks.

Of course, probably the most important database device to mirror is your master device. Without it, the entire server goes down, not just some of your user databases. In addition to mirroring the master device with the disk mirror command, another step is required. Since Adaptive Server reads the sysdevices table during startup to determine where all its mirror devices are, if the master device becomes damaged while the server is down, it cannot come back up because it cannot read the sysdevices table. To get around this problem, you must update the command line in the RUN_SERVER file to identify the location of the mirror device, as shown below. If the primary side is damaged, Adaptive Server will attempt to start from the mirror device. In theory, the server will figure this out anyway, but in practice it's a good idea.

```
dataserver -d/sybase/devices/master.dat
-r/sybase/mirrors/master_mir.dat -e.....etc.
```

As you can see, there are a lot of decisions to be made, and every system has its own needs, so you'll need to work out a mirroring strategy that works best for you.

Disabling Mirroring

Mirroring can be disabled either automatically or manually.

Automatic Disabling

If Adaptive Server determines that there is an I/O error on one of the devices in a mirrored set, mirroring is disabled. At that point, all reads and writes are redirected to the device that is still functioning. This happens very quickly and the users should not even notice. A message is written to the errorlog, and the status column in the sysdevices table is modified to set the status to disabled. You should manually inspect the errorlog frequently so that you can spot this error and correct it before your remaining device fails. Optionally, you can automate this process by writing a script that will scan the errorlog and notify you via e-mail or page when mirroring is disabled.

Another option is to use a mirrorexit process. This is done via the waitfor command, shown below. Note that the sp_sendmail stored procedure is not a system procedure, it's just an example of a proc that you might write to handle sending of e-mails. You can have the process do anything you like, but generally you want it to perform some action that will cause you to be notified of the failed device. The only trick to this method is that it is not persistent. In other words, you must execute this command each time the Adaptive Server is restarted.

```
waitfor mirrorexit
begin
exec sp_sendmail 'dba_group','Mirroring error detected, please see errorlog
for details'
end
```

Manual Disabling

There are certain times when you might want to intentionally disable mirroring of a particular database device. This can be accomplished with the disk unmirror command, shown below. It has the same effect as automatic disabling. All reads and writes will now be against the remaining device in the mirror set, and sysdevices will be updated to reflect the change. It does run much faster than the disk mirror command, since all it is really doing is updating a single row in sysdevices.

Unmirroring

```
disk unmirror
name = 'logical_device_name'
[ ,side= {'primary' | 'secondary'}]
[ ,mode = {'retain' | 'remove'}]
```

The first parameter is name. It identifies the logical database device you want to unmirror and is the only required parameter.

The second parameter is side, which specifies whether you want to stop writing to the secondary (mirror) side or the primary side. The default value is secondary.

The last parameter is mode. The retain value causes a temporary disabling, meaning you can reenable mirroring with the disk remirror command, which we'll cover later in the next section. It resets the status bits in sysdevices indicating that mirroring is disabled, but retains the physical name of the secondary device. When you use remove, it will update the status bits to show no mirroring and it removes the physical name of the secondary device. In order to remirror, you would need to use disk mirror, not disk remirror since there is no record of any previous mirroring on that device.

TIP: You might find a need to relocate a logical device to a faster disk or to improve load balancing. One way to do this would be to drop all databases that reside on the affected devices, drop the devices, re-create the devices on different physical disks, and re-create and then reload the databases from backup. This would require a lot of work and a lot of downtime. Instead, you could simply use mirroring commands like the following:

```
disk mirror
name = 'data_dev1',
mirror = '/sybase/mirrors/data_dev1_mir.dat'

disk unmirror
name = 'data_dev1,'
side = 'primary',
mode = 'remove'
```

First, data_dev1 is copied to a mirror location. The primary side is then dropped, making /sybase/mirrors/data_dev1_mir.dat the new physical location of data_dev1, and then removing any record of mirroring. It's just copying and repointing, and it can be done while users are on the system (with some impact, of course).

Remirroring

As mentioned earlier, once you've unmirrored a device with the retain option, you can go back at a later point and remirror. This essentially synchs up the mirror side with the primary side, but it performs a complete copy of the primary device to the mirror side, not just changes that occurred since mirroring was disabled. The main advantage remirror has over mirror is not speed; it's that you don't have to specify a physical name or any other options.

```
disk remirror
Name = 'unmirrored_logical_device_name'
```

Software- and Hardware-Level Mirroring

While Sybase provides mirroring capabilities within Adaptive Server, there are other options that may work better for you. Using Sybase mirroring is effective, but it does involve a lot of planning and setup, and it can be slow. In this section we'll discuss hardware- and software-level mirroring, as well as RAID (Redundant Array of Inexpensive Drives).

Hardware-Level Mirroring

Because hardware mirroring is handled by the controller, it reduces the CPU cost that Adaptive Server and the operating system would otherwise incur. That means the CPUs can spend their time doing real work instead of managing the disk. That means it's typically faster than software mirroring. It also protects the areas of disk that Sybase mirroring can't, such as the Adaptive Server's software and other file systems. This type of mirroring tends to be very reliable and better performing, but is also more expensive.

Software-Level Mirroring

Adaptive Server's mirroring is software-level mirroring. Windows NT provides disk striping and mirroring capabilities, which is also software-level mirroring. There are many types, but they all have one thing in common: it is software that is managing the disk mirroring, which can be expensive in terms of CPU cycles. In its favor, software mirroring allows you to fragment your physical disks so that you can pick and choose which parts of the disk to mirror. This provides you with more control but also more administration by having to plan, set up, monitor, and adjust as needed.

RAID

RAID stands for Redundant Array of Inexpensive Drives (some say Independent drives, which is also true). RAID has many different configurations (levels), but the most common are 0, 1, and 5. In some cases, RAID incorporates mirroring, in some cases striping, and in others both mirroring and striping. RAID uses hash information stored on one or more disks to "mirror" the information stored as regular data. If one of the devices fails, the data is "re-created" from the hash information. This should be transparent to users. Without going into details on RAID, mirroring protects your data by keeping a "copy" of it in another location, and striping helps balance your I/O load across available disks to improve performance. With striping, blocks of data are written to successive devices instead of to just one. So if you are writing 64 KB of data to disk, it might write 16 KB to each of four disks if you were using a 16 KB stripe size. This can greatly improve read and write performance. You may want to use different RAID levels for your data devices than you do for your log devices, a common practice that can achieve protection where you want it and performance where you need it. The bottom line is, investigate the various RAID levels and then choose the one that works best for you.

Volume Management

Volume management refers to software that you can use to enhance the usability of your devices. It can help to improve load balancing, reduce maintenance, and provide you with much more usable devices. While not going into great detail, this section is intended to introduce you to the concept. Talk to your O/S admin to determine what is available on your system.

Maintenance and Ease of Use

In many UNIX environments, you are limited in how many raw device partitions you can have on a single disk drive, typically six. With limited disk drives, you can only have so many Sybase logical devices defined. It's much simpler with filesystem devices because you can create many logical devices under one directory.

Volume management allows you to define logical raw partitions, greatly increasing the number of raw partitions you can define, which means more flexibility in creating your Sybase logical devices. If you have four drives, you are no longer limited to having 24 partitions; you may have 50, 100, or more. Unused raw partitions can be recarved to better suit your needs as they evolve.

Load Balancing

Volume management software typically includes not only a way of "carving" your physical disks with more control than without, it also tends to include striping capabilities. With it, you can create a single logical raw partition that might span many physical raw partitions across many disks. The logical raw partition provides you with the same safety of the underlying physical raw partitions, that is, the writes are not buffered. Striping them across many physical disks is one way of offsetting the performance cost associated with choosing raw instead of file system devices, while maintaining peace of mind.

System Info

Once you've defined your disk management, you want to make sure the system sees the disks the way you've defined them. Alternatively, if you are taking over for another DBA, you may need to see how your predecessor has set things up.

System Procedures

```
sp_helpdevice ['logical_device_name']
```

Returns a listing of all database devices and their attributes or a single specified device.

```
sp_dropdevice 'logical_device_name'
```

Removes the device entry from sysdevices. The device cannot be occupied by any database or the procedure will fail.

```
sp_diskdefault 'logical_device_name', {'defaulton' | 'defaultoff'}
```

Adds or removes a logical device from the default device pool.

`sp_deviceattr 'logical_device_name', 'option', 'setting'`

Changes an attribute of a logical device.

`sp_configure 'number of devices'`

Displays or changes the configuration value for number of logical devices allowed.

`sp_helpdb 'database_name'`

Displays basic database info as well as which fragments reside on which logical devices and what each fragment's use is.

Examples:

```
sp_helpdevice 'test_dev1'
device_name   physical_name                   description
------------  ------------------------------  ----------------------------------------
test_dev1     /sybase/devices/test_dev1.dat   special, MIRROR DISABLED, mirror = '',
                                              nonserial writes, physical disk, 2048.00

status      cntrltype   device_number    low              high
--------    ----------  ---------------  ---------------  -------------
16386          0              8          134217728        135266303
```

```
sp_dropdevice 'test_dev1'
  Device dropped.
```

```
sp_diskdefault 'test_dev1', 'defaultoff'
  (return status = 0)
```

```
sp_deviceattr 'test_dev1', 'dsync', 'false'
```

```
sp_configure 'number of devices', 50
Parameter Name       Default   Memory Used  Config Value   Run Value
------------------ --------- ------------ ------------- -------------
number of devices     10          #14           50            50

Configuration option changed. The SQL Server need not be rebooted since the option is
dynamic.
```

```
sp_helpdb test_db
name      db_size    owner     dbid  created          status
--------  --------   --------  ----- ---------------  --------------------------------
test_db   75.0 MB     sa         7   Feb 11, 2001     select into/bulkcopy/pllsort

device_fragments      size          usage          free kbytes
--------------------- ------------- -------------- ----------------
test_dev1             40.0 MB       data only      31948
test_dev2             20.0 MB       data only      13107
test_log              15.0 MB       log only       not applicable

--------------------------------------------------------------
log only free kbytes = 15344
```

System Tables

sysdevices

Contains one row for each database or dump device, even if mirrored.

sysusages

Contains one row for each database fragment and is loosely related to sysdevices by joining vstart to the low and high columns of sysdevices. If vstart falls between low and high, the database fragment resides on that logical device.

sysdatabases

Contains one row for each database and is related to sysusages. Referenced by sp_helpdb to determine which devices the database resides on.

Querying System Tables

Adaptive Server does provide many stored procedures to help you administer your server, but it doesn't do everything for you. You should familiarize yourself with the tables, their contents, and their relationships so that you can write your own custom queries or procedures to further enhance your administrative capabilities (read: reduce work!). The following is a sample of one to get you started. You can enhance it further to show you the usage (data or log) of the device fragment, sort by lstart, etc., or run it as is. (Note: The 512 presumes a 2 K data page. This should be the number of pages in a megabyte.)

Display space used for a device:

```
select dev_name=d.name, db_name=db_name(u.dbid), size_in_mb=u.size/512
from master..sysusages u, master..sysdevices d
where u.vstart between d.low and d.high
and d.name = @logical_dev_name
```

Modifying System Tables

Unless absolutely necessary, you should never directly modify system tables. The results could be disastrous. If you want to add a new device, use disk init; don't insert a row manually into sysdevices. If you want to drop a device, run sp_dropdevice; don't manually delete the row. If you want to enable mirroring, don't update the row; run disk mirror or disk remirror. In other words, you have all the commands and procedures you need in order to manage your disk resources without having to directly modify the system tables.

There are occasions where you may need to update system tables. But as far as the sysdevices table is concerned, I can see no reason to modify it directly, unless directed to by Sybase Technical Support.

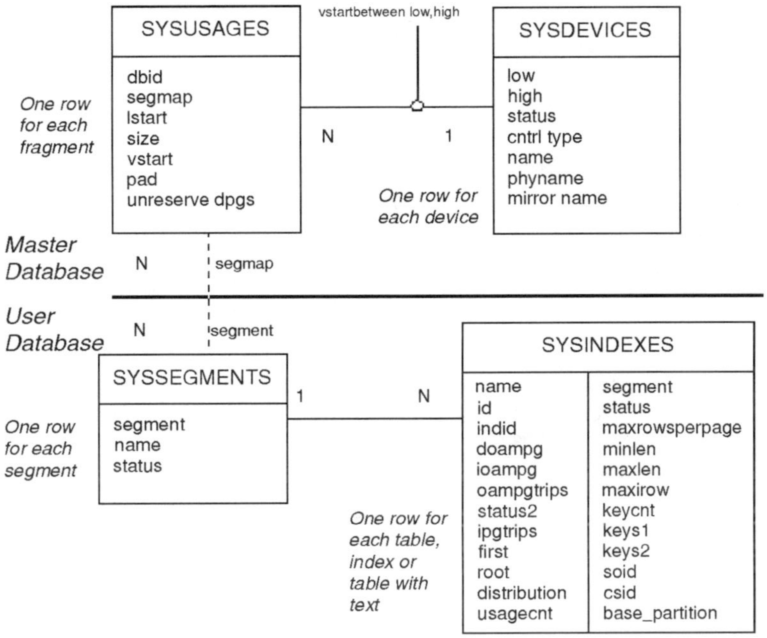

Figure 3-1
System tables diagram

Here's part of the system schema that identifies the relationships between devices and the objects upon them, in case you'd like to write your own queries.

Disaster Recovery

In the event of a disaster, where you lost your entire machine, you'll want to get the system back up and running as quickly as possible. Some important system info will be required to make it quicker and easier to accomplish. Although not required, you'll probably want to create your devices and databases with the same or similar layout on your physical disks. Once you've identified a suitable replacement for your machine, you'll want to quickly install Adaptive Server and begin creating your devices and databases so you can restore from backup. Therefore, it is very important that you keep a record of, or better yet an extraction of, your system table info.

An easy way to do this is to bcp out your sysdevices, sysusages, and sysdatabases tables, then copy the bcp files to tape. (See a discussion of bcp in Chapter 17, "Tools.") This should be done routinely, depending on how often the system info changes. In addition, running the sp_helpdb and sp_helpdevices procedures and saving off the reports can help speed and verify the recovery process. The reports can be run via isql and the output saved to disk, so they too can be copied off to tape. Finally, a diagram of your devices (and the databases built on them) can be an invaluable tool for determining what resources are available or needed. This picture may be worth a thousand lines of script.

Summary

How you choose to implement your device strategy is an important step in setting up and modifying your database environment. You need to choose which types of devices to use for each database, whether to use default disks, what to mirror, and how you want to implement mirroring. You can decide to implement load balancing with disk striping or with user-defined segments, and you can choose whether or not to use volume management software. Regardless of what you choose, if there's one thing I've learned, it's better to do the planning up front than to have to rework it all later.

For Geeks Like Us

The more you work with ASE, the better acquainted you'll become with system tables. System tables contain metadata (information about how the information is stored). You've seen a few queries that identify specific information from the system tables; here's a more in-depth study of what's happening inside.

Sysdevices

The definition of a device is stored in the system table sysdevices; the columns in this table record how a device was created and how it is configured. Several of the columns in *sysdevices* can be directly interpreted based on the disk init command that created the device; in this example, the name and phyname columns correspond to the name and physname arguments of the creation script. Note that unlike the disk init argument, the column is spelled p-h-y-n-a-m-e (no "s").

```
low       high      status  cntrltype  name         phyname              mirrorname
--------  --------  ------  ---------  -----------  ----------           ----------
       0     25599       2          0  master       <path>/master.dat      NULL
16777216  16828415   16386          0  sysprocsdev  /dev/rdsk/c0t1d1s0     NULL
     ...       ...     ...        ...  ...          ...                    ...
```

Other columns in sysdevices are derived from disk init, but do not record the exact values that you used; for example, both the vdevno and size arguments are used to calculate the values of the low and high columns, and later commands (such as disk mirror/unmirror) and procedures (like sp_diskdefault and sp_deviceattr) are used to calculate the values of the status and mirrorname columns. While these derivations are not difficult, they do take some explaining.

Low and High

In order to track each page in the server with no chance of confusion, ASE must address every page on the device in a wholly unique fashion. There are many ways to accomplish this, but the one that is used here is to allow for unique, non-overlapping ranges of page numbers for each device. A helpful analogy may be found in a typical American city street: Fifth Avenue in New York City.

Imagine you're at the extreme southern end of Fifth Avenue, standing in the middle of the street, facing north; the buildings on your right are even-numbered starting from 2, and on your left, odd-numbered starting from 1. Now start walking north and note the street numbers — on your right you pass by 2, 4, 6, and 8, and on your left, 1, 3, 5, and 7. Occasionally, a number is skipped where a series of buildings were torn down and replaced with a single structure, but the series continue upward pretty smoothly. This pattern continues for a while, but when you cross the first cross-street, you notice something funny has happened: all the street numbers have jumped. You were looking at 28 (on the right) and 27 (on the left), and all of a sudden, you find yourself between 100 (right) and 101 (left).

In order to avoid confusion when different builders added buildings to Fifth Avenue, each block was pre-assigned a range of street numbers to use: the first block gets to use 1-99 and 2-98; the second block is assigned 101-199 and 100-198, and so forth. We could put up as many buildings as we want on either side of the street, as long as the numbers increase as we go north, and we don't run outside of our range; if we don't use all of the assigned numbers (as in this case), the unused range is wasted. At the same time, we're limited to how many buildings we can put up on one side of the block by the number of available addresses (although it's unlikely that we could fit more than 50 buildings on one side of the block). But the alternative is trying to coordinate all of the builders up and down Fifth Avenue, hoping for perfect communication, and praying that no two of them decide to use the same street address. In this case, wasting some potentially usable street numbers seems better than the risk of putting up two buildings with the same number.

ASE does the same thing with devices, only the pre-allocated ranges aren't in ranges of 100; ASE uses a 3-byte address to locate pages on a device, which allows up to 2^24 = 16,777,216 pages per device. Each device is pre-assigned a unique range of 2^24 page numbers; any numbers not actually used (because most devices won't be large enough to require the full range of page numbers) are wasted.

This information is stored in the columns low and high, which represent (respectively) the first and last page numbers assigned to the device. The value of low is calculated by multiplying the vdevno used to create the device by 2^24; since each device is only allowed a maximum of 2^24 pages, this allows for non-overlapping ranges of page numbers for each device. For the first few integer values of vdevno, this gives us:

```
vdevno = 0
low = 0 * 2^24 = 0
max number of pages = 16, 777, 216
max range starting from low = 0 to 16,777,215 (inclusive)

vdevno = 1
low = 1 * 2^24 = 16,777,216
max number of pages = 16, 777, 216
max range starting from low = 16,777,216 to 33,554,431 (inclusive)

vdevno = 2
low = 2 * 2^24 = 33,554,432
max number of pages = 16, 777, 216
max range starting from low = 33,554,432 to 50,331,647
```

The value of high for any device is derived from low and the size argument of disk init; each device has size pages, starting from low, and ending on high. Note that because the page range is inclusive:

high = low + size – 1
size = high – low + 1

For the sample sysdevices given above, we can derive the following information:

master:	low	= 0	high	= 25599
	vdevno	= low/2^24	size	= high – low + 1
		= 0 / 2^24		= 25599 – 0 + 1
		= 0		= 25600 virtual pages
sysprocsdev:	low	= 16777216	high	= 16828415
	vdevno	= low / 2^24	size	= high – low + 1
		= 16777216/2^24		= 16828415 – 16777216 + 1
		= 1		= 51200 virtual pages

While most users will find these calculations sufficient, those with large numbers of devices will find one other behavior in the calculation of low. At large values of vdevno (128-255 inclusive), low and high suddenly jump to very large negative numbers. This happens because Adaptive Server Enterprise has no way to represent unsigned numbers. Below are some sample values from sysdevices:

```
low          high         status  cntrltype  name        ...
-----------  -----------  ------  ---------  ----------  ...
-2147483648  -2147483137  16386           0  testdev1    ...
-2130706432  -2130705921  16386           0  testdev2    ...
-2113929216  -2113928705  16386           0  testdev3    ...
```

Given these numbers and the formulas above, we can calculate the following:

testdev1	vdevno = –128	size = 512
testdev2	vdevno = –127	size = 512
testdev3	vdevno = –126	size = 512

The low and high columns use an integer data type to store their values, which has a maximum value of 2,147,483,647; this value is enough to store all of the possible pages for devices with vdevno values 0 to 127, but no higher. But the integer data type is signed, and also allows storage of negative numbers down to –2,147,483,648, which is enough space to store another 128 devices; since ASE will allow up to 256 devices per server to be configured, this requires that negative values be used in low and high.

For vdevno values in the range 128-255 (inclusive):

low = (vdevno – 256) * 2 ^ 24
vdevno = (low / 2^24) + 256

For our three devices:

testdev1:	low	= –2147483648	high	= –2147483137
	vdevno	= (low/2^24) + 256	size	= high – low + 1
		= 128		= 512 pages
testdev2:	low	= –2130706432	high	= –2130705921
	vdevno	= (low/2^24) + 256	size	= high – low + 1
		= 129		= 512 pages
testdev3:	low	= –2113929216	high	= –2113928705
	vdevno	= (low/2^24) + 256	size	= high – low + 1
		= 130		= 512 pages

The value of vdevno for any device can be calculated with:

```
select convert(int,(low/power(2,24))) & 255
from sysdevices
order by 1
```

status, cntrltype, and mirrorname

The status column is an integer number that describes the presence or absence of other attributes of a device. About 15 different characteristics, each true or false, could be used in combination to describe your device. For example:

```
This is a default device (1)
This device is mirrored (64)
This device has the dsync flag enabled (16384)
```

If the characteristic is true for a device, the binary value in parentheses is added to the status column; if false, a zero is added instead. If all of the possible characteristics for a device are false, the status value would be 0. If only the default device characteristic were true, the status value would be 1. If the device were dsync enabled, mirrored, and a default device, then the status value would be 16449 (1 + 64 + 16384). This bitmap value allows for a large number of combinations of characteristics to be stored in very little space. The status column can be translated into verbal descriptions with the sp_helpdevice procedure, and a full list of status values can be found in the documentation set.

The cntrltype column is used to distinguish between *database devices* (every device discussed in this chapter) and *dump devices*; dump devices are used solely for storing backups, and are discussed in Chapter 9. For reference, all dump devices will have cntrltype values greater than 0, and status values of 16. Dump devices will also have values of low and high that do not follow the rules given above and cannot be mirrored.

The mirrorname column is used to store the physical name of the device's mirror; if no mirror is defined for the device, mirrorname is Null.

Chapter 4

Databases

One of the most important aspects of understanding Sybase Adaptive Server Enterprise is the concept and application of the database. Simply put, a database is a container for all the data and objects needed for an application. Most of the physical space of the database will be taken up by user tables (those holding your data), but other items will be present as well: other objects that support the tables (indexes, views, procedures, triggers, etc.); the transaction log (see Chapter 5, "Database Logging and Recovery"); and system tables (special tables that keep track of what exists in the database; see more below).

In addition, the database is Sybase's basic unit of recovery. You will back up and restore your data at the database level. As a result, when creating databases, you will often allow your backup and recovery elapsed time (as driven by your business) to control maximum database size.

Before creating new databases, it is useful to understand the structures that define databases. Each database stores all the information that describes its existence and behavior in its system tables, or catalogs. These look and behave like regular tables, but have a few unique characteristics: they all have names that start with "sys"; they may be queried but not changed by standard SQL commands (even by the SA); and they contain information that is necessary to keep the database running. If a table is to exist, it must be listed in the sysobjects system table; granting a user permission to access data requires that the permission be listed in the sysprotects table; a user exists in a database only so long as a corresponding row exists in the sysusers table; and so on. Approximately two dozen of these tables exist in every database, and they refer only to the database they occupy.

A partial list of system tables is given in the following table.

System Table	Description
sysobjects	List of all items that exist in the database
sysindexes	List of indexes and tables in the database
syscolumns	List of all columns that exist in the tables of the database, as well as parameters for stored procedures
sysprocedures	List of stored procedures and other pre-compiled objects
syscomments	Creation scripts of procedures, triggers, and certain other objects
syssegments	List of segments that exist in the database
syslogs	Transaction log for this database
sysprotects	List of permissions for objects/users in this database
sysusers	List of users allowed to use this database

ASE also stores all information necessary for its own proper operation within special *system databases*. Just as the system tables in a given database record and define the existence of that database, there are special databases that define the structure of the ASE as a whole.

This chapter will discuss all aspects of databases and database creation. This includes the system databases, those which Adaptive Server Enterprise uses for internal purposes, as well as how to create "user" databases, for your own tables.

System Databases

System databases are mandatory, required for the running of the server, and are created when the Adaptive Server is installed. Each of these system databases is described in the following table.

System Database	Description
master	Records overall structure of the server, including the existence of all databases
model	Template used for the creation of new databases
tempdb	Holds temporary results and non-permanent objects
sybsystemprocs	Holds system stored procedures
sybsystemdb	Used for distributed transactions

The master database is the single most important structure in the server. At startup time, ASE knows exactly one thing: where to find master. Other databases that exist and their physical locations, logins permitted to connect, how to spend allocated resources, all other server-related information is known only after master is loaded. The single most important task for the SA is to ensure the continued existence and reliability of master; backups of this database must always be kept (in fact, failure to back up the master database may be the single most common big mistake made by administrators). User data should never be stored there.

As with all databases, master contains a series of system tables that define its own structure, but unlike other databases, it also contains additional system tables that define the server as a whole. In addition to the standard system tables, there are about two dozen additional system tables found only in master, some of which are described below.

Master System Tables	Description
sysdatabases	List of all databases that exist in the server
sysdevices	List of devices that are defined for the server
sysusages	Relates database space allocations to the devices used
syslogins	List of users permitted to connect to the server
sysconfigures	List of server configuration options and settings
sysmessages	List of server error messages
sysprocesses	List of current running tasks within the server
syslocks	List of locks presently isolating transaction data
sysservers	List of all servers this server is aware of (including itself)

The model database is a template for the creation of databases; when a new database is created, it receives a copy of all items found in model. As a result, all databases must be at least as large as model when they are created, or the creation statement will fail. Any modifications made to the model database will be reflected in all subsequent database creations. Although it sounds as if model is merely a convenience, model is also the mechanism with which system tables are added to new databases; without these, the new database could not exist, so model is just as important as any system database.

Probably the most-changed and heavily-used database, tempdb is used to hold non-permanent data. Every query that requires multi-stage processing (like sorting) will automatically create *work tables* in tempdb to hold the preliminary results before moving on to final processing. Additionally, users may create *temporary tables* in tempdb; these are like ordinary tables, but (depending on their creation syntax) may automatically drop themselves when the user's connection is ended. Even if the temp table (or another object created in tempdb) does not automatically drop, it will still have a limited existence, as tempdb will always be dropped and rebuilt from scratch every time the server is started.

As tempdb is needed for certain startup processes, creating it is one of the first things done during server boot. Since tempdb will be used almost continuously, it may be a bottleneck for performance problems in the server, and its size and location will be critical issues for the SA.

The default database size for tempdb is at least 3 MB, but may be larger based on the chosen server's page size. Each database holds at least 1,024 logical pages.

Stored procedures supplied with the ASE installation are known as system stored procedures, and are stored in the sybsystemprocs database. These procedures are generally used to query and modify the contents of system tables, and unlike regular procedures, may be called from any database. A few special-purpose system procedures may be stored in other databases (master, for example), but for the most part they'll be found in sybsystemprocs.

Lastly, the sybsystemdb database is used to track and coordinate distributed transactions. Where transactions usually are defined in one database (see Chapter 5, "Database Logging and Recovery"), sometimes they must span database boundaries; in cases like this, the transaction is actually broken into multiple single-database transactions, which are coordinated by an exterior process. In such cases, the coordination information is stored in sybsystemdb. Prior to ASE 12.0, sybsystemdb was an optional database only installed when needed, but is now mandatory.

Other Sybase-Provided Databases

There are databases used primarily by the system for optional server capabilities, but which are not absolutely necessary to the running of the server; if needed or desired, they may be installed from scripts provided by Sybase. Also, there are databases that are intended primarily as examples, and are not required for the use of any features; they may be installed at the discretion of the SA.

The sybsecurity database, when present, is used by the auditing feature of Adaptive Server. When auditing is installed and enabled, ASE will track actions, commands, and users as directed by the SSO (see Chapter 7, "Auditing"); the records of this tracking (or *audit trail*) are stored in sybsecurity.

As part of the maintenance of the server, the SA will use a series of utilities known as dbcc's (database consistency checkers); there are many variations on dbcc, some of which are diagnostic and some reparative. One particular utility, dbcc checkstorage, is commonly used because it is very fast, thorough, and accurate, but it requires a dedicated database in which to perform its calculations. This working database, if present, is called dbccdb.

Similar to the UNIX man command, ASE provides a stored procedure called sp_syntax that can be used to retrieve brief syntactical information about SQL commands and procedures. In order to use sp_syntax, the sybsyntax database must be installed.

> **NOTE:** sp_syntax was dropped in ASE 12, but it appears to be back (at least, the script is included in my 12.5 beta installation).

The ASE documentation set uses a pair of databases called pubs2 and pubs3 for examples; if you wish to follow along with the examples, one or both may be installed from scripts included in the Sybase\install directory (or for NT users, sybase\install).

Creating a Database

A database is created with the create database command.

The create database Command

Syntax:

```
create database database_name
[on {default | database_device} [= size]
[, database_device [= size]]...]
[log on database_device [= size]
[, database_device [= size]]...]
[with {override | default_location = "pathname"}]
[for {load | proxy_update}]
```

Parameters:

database_device: A logical database device name.

size: The amount of space to be allocated on the database device, expressed as a number or a string. If a number is used, the size is in megabytes. If a string is used, the string must be enclosed in quotes and may include a unit of measurement. Adaptive Server uses these units:

K or k — Kilobytes
M or m — Megabytes
G or g — Gigabytes

> **NOTE:** Previous versions did not allow for units to be declared, forcing all databases to be sized in megabytes.

override: By default ASE will disable dump transaction for databases with data and log on the same device. Although the override option will permit dump transaction for these databases, it is highly recommended that log be placed on separate devices, both for performance reasons and to allow a wider range of repair options in the event of a device failure (see the "Creating Database Logs on Separate Devices" section below).

default_location: Allows for a specific location to store new tables. This is required when using the "for proxy_update" option.

proxy_update: Allows Adaptive Server to retrieve metadata from a remote source and creates the proxy table; this gives the user the ability to access databases that are physically stored in other servers as if they were stored in the local server (if the SA has configured the Component Integration Services feature).

for load: Creates the database with a streamlined process (approximately 250 times faster) so the database can be loaded from database dump. Databases that are created with the for load option may not be used in any way; the only commands that will work on such a database are alter database … for load, load database, and drop database.

When the create database command is executed, several events take place:

- The Adaptive Server verifies that the new database has a unique name.
- The database is assigned a unique ID number, and a row is inserted into the master..sysdatabases table to represent the new database.
- The database is assigned space on the devices specified by the create database command. These space allocations are recorded in the master..sysusages table.
- The objects in the model database are copied into the new structure. This will create all the necessary database system tables, and any data objects or data (for example, user-defined data types) that have been placed in the model database.
- The remaining pages in the database are initialized and marked as available for allocation.

This final step, clearing of database pages, can take a while depending on the size of the database and the speed of the devices; this step is also performed when loading a database from a dump. So when creating a database specifically to be loaded from a backup, it is recommended that the database be created for load. This prevents the clearing of pages during the create process, since they will be cleared during the load.

Who Can Create a Database

Initially, the SA or a user with the sa_role has the exclusive right to create databases.

The ability to create a database may be granted to a user by the SA (see Chapter 6, "Security, User Administration, Roles"). However, since disk space is often a closely guarded resource on a database server, most administrators will not grant this permission freely.

Creating a Default Database

The bare minimum syntax for creating a database is similar to the following example.

Syntax:

```
create database defaultdb
```

There are problems with creating a database using this particular syntax: it will create a database using the default settings. While the database would be created successfully, the default settings are usually inconvenient for a production database.

The typical defaults are:

Database size = minimum configured database size = 2 MB
Data device = Default device (possibly master device)
Log Device = Default device (possibly master device)

> **NOTE:** The minimum database size is 4 allocation units, so a 4 K page would be 4 MB, etc.

These are generally inappropriate choices for creating most databases, for the following reasons:

- A minimum-size database is barely large enough to store its own system tables, much less any user objects and data. The database would need to be expanded very quickly.
- As discussed in Chapter 4, the use of default devices is not encouraged; it is vitally important for the SA to carefully track available system resources (including available device space), and default devices allow databases to be created without explicit references to devices. Under these circumstances, it is difficult to know which devices are being used. Additionally, if the SA has not changed the installation defaults, the master device may still have default status. User databases do not belong on the master device!

> **NOTE:** When asked why the master device is a default device, the engineers answer: "It's an historical accident." We recommend you turn off the default option on this device.

- As mentioned previously, log should be separated from data within the database; unless you specify log on device_name, log and data will both end up on the same device, complicating backups and recovery.

The following example code relieves most of the potential problems:

```
create database practicedb1
       on datadev1 = "20M"
```

The statement creates a new database called practicedb1 on a device called datadev1. In this case the database has been sized to 20 megabytes, however, the database log is still on the same device as the data.

Creating Database Logs on Separate Devices

The database log stores all the changes that have occurred in the database. It is used in the server's recovery process to ensure that all the recorded changes in the log are reflected in the database data. When a log is defined on the same devices as the data, several problems arise. The first is the competition for space (see Chapter 5, "Database Logging and Recovery," for the dangers of log running out of space). The second problem is that if the device containing both log and data were to fail, all of the database would be lost; if on separate devices and the log survives a failure, it may be possible to restore the lost data (see Chapter 8, "Backing Up and Restoring," and the topic of emergency log dumps). Third, even if there is sufficient space and no possibility of device failure, separation of the log is necessary to allow incremental backups of the database.

While it may be acceptable for practice or dummy databases to share space between data and log, it is not recommended for production. Thus, the preferred (or even "correct") form of the create database command will resemble:

```
create database practicedb2
       on datadev1 = "20M"
       log on logdev1 = "8M"
```

This code will create a 28 MB database called practicedb2; 20 MB of space will be allocated on datadev1 (for data) and 8 MB will be allocated on logdev1 for the database log.

It is also possible to create multiple allocations to either data or log in the create database statement:

```
create database practicedb3
       on datadev1 = "8M",
       datadev2 = "8M"
       log on logdev1 = "4M",
       logdev2 = "4M"
```

This will create a 24 MB database called practicedb3. There will be 8 MB of space will be allocated to the database on datadev1 and an additional 8 MB will be available on datadev2. The database log will be allocated 4 MB on logdev1, and 4 MB on logdev2.

You can customize the default database size by executing the following configuration command:

```
sp_configure 'default database size', 20
```

However, recall that using such a simple enough form of create database that the default size would be used is not recommended, so there is little practical need for this adjustment.

Sizing a Database

When creating a user database, the database should be large enough to hold all the data that will be entered into it; the estimated sizes of the user tables, indexes, and system tables must be considered. Something else to take under consideration is whether or not there will be any additional data entered into the database. If the database will grow, additional space should be estimated to allow for the anticipated growth (for example: consider leaving 25% of the space free).

TIP: Remember also that the database is ASE's restore unit, so you do not want to make the database bigger than what you can restore in your business-defined recovery window. This size can only be determined by experimentation on your own equipment.

Adaptive Server includes a system procedure called sp_estspace that can produce an estimate of the space required for a table based on the anticipated number of rows that the table will hold; sp_estspace will also calculate the sizes of indexes if they exist on the table when the procedure is executed. The following shows an example.

```
sp_estspace 'payroll', 100

name          type          idx_level   Pages   Kbytes
----------    ------------  ---------   -----   ------
payroll       data          0           318     637
payroll_x0    clustered     0           6       12
payroll_x0    clustered     1           1       2
payroll_x1    nonclustered  0           77      152
payroll_x1    nonclustered  1           1       2

Total_Mbytes
------------
1.10

name          type          total_pages    time_mins
----------    ------------  -----------    ---------
payroll_x0    clustered     326            1
payroll_x1    nonclustered  78             0
```

It is usually better to underestimate the size of a database than to overestimate. If the database size is too small, the database can easily be altered (see the next section) to increase its size. However, if the database is too large, there is no other remedy than to make a new database of the appropriate size and move all the data over to the new smaller database a table at a time (or wait for the data to grow and fill the database space). There is no practical means to shrink a database once it has been assigned space.

One notable exception to this rule is that you can shrink tempdb by directly modifying the system tables; check the troubleshooting guide for more details.

The Alter Database Command

The alter database command allows for expansions in database size or changes to certain options to be made.

Syntax:

```
alter database database_name
[on {default | database_device } [= size]
[, database_device [= size]]...]
[log on { default | database_device } [ = size ]
[ , database_device [= size]]...]
[with override]
[for load]
[for proxy_update]
```

The alter database syntax allows the database owner to increase the amount of database space, log space, or both by defining new allocations for the databases.

The command is similar to create database. Note that the size parameter will specify the amount of additional space allocated to the database.

The following example shows how to expand the database sampledb4 from its original size of 20 MB (16 MB data, 4 MB log) to a total of 40 MB (16 MB additional data, 4 MB additional log).

```
create database sampledb4
on datadev4 = "16M"
log on logdev4 = "4M"
```

```
<database used for some time>
```

```
alter database sampledb4
on datadev5 = "16M"
log on logdev4 = "4M"
```

Note that it is not possible to alter a database before it is created; if the two commands above were executed in the same command batch, the alter syntax would not have a database to work on and would fail with an error. Note also that the data and log can be altered independently.

Database Options

Adaptive Server supports the setting of specific database-wide options. These options only apply toward an individual database and can control how the database works with transactions, the performance of recovery and non-logged operations, and how the database maintains the log. The options supported in ASE 12.5 are:

- abort tran on log full — When enabled, will force a transaction to abort if it crosses the last-chance threshold in the log.
- allow nulls by default — When set to true, changes the default behavior of a database. The default behavior when creating a database table is that its columns will not accept null values; this option reverses that behavior.

- auto identity — Forces all tables to be built with a column called SYB_IDENTITY_COL. This column is a 10-digit identity column, and is not visible to select * queries.
- dbo use only — Only the database owner may use the database. This option is typically used when you are performing maintenance tasks and want to keep other users out of the database.
- ddl in tran — When enabled, this option allows for the use of Data Definition Language (DDL) statements (e.g., create procedure, create index) to be used in explicit transactions.
- identity in nonunique index — This option makes existing identity columns in a table part of any non-unique index. The additional unique column allows the index to be effectively unique.
- no chkpt on recovery — When true, the database will not perform a checkpoint following the recovery process when the server is restarted. This is useful when a copy of a database is left as a standby. The lack of the checkpoint after restart and recovery of a server prevents the transaction log from changing enough to prevent additional loads from the later transaction dumps.
- no free space acctg — Used to accelerate recovery time by suspending the calculation of free space for any non-log segments and preventing the execution of any free-space threshold procedures.
- read only — When true, the database can no longer be modified.
- select into/bulkcopy/pllsort – Activating this option will allow the execution of minimally logged operations:
  - "Select into" queries
  - Use of the writetext utility
  - Use of the fast version of bulkcopy (bcp)
  - Parallel sorting
- single user — The database will only allow only one user to access the database at a time (typically used when the SA is performing maintenance tasks and wants to keep other users out of the database). This option is not permitted for the tempdb database.
- trunc. log on chkpt. — Adaptive Server will attempt to truncate the transaction log approximately once a minute, when the background checkpoint task wakes up; dbo-issued checkpoints have no effect on this option. If the log is very small (less than 50 records), the truncation will be skipped. Note that this option is always enabled for tempdb. This option is typically used in a development environment where incremental backups are not required. For more information, refer to Chapter 8, "Backing Up and Restoring."
- unique auto_identity index — Includes an IDENTITY column with any unique, non-clustered index for new tables.
- disable alias access — Prevents cross-database access by users aliased to other users in a database, who are not otherwise owners of objects in that database.

Setting Database Options

Database options are set via the system procedure sp_dboption:

```
sp_dboption database_name, "option_name",{"true"|"false"}
```

All database options are enabled by setting the option to true or disabled by setting the option to false. Note that none of the database options will actually be enabled until the dbo issues a checkpoint in the named database, and that option changes for the master database will be ignored.

Example:

```
use master
go
sp_dboption pubs2, "select into/bulkcopy/pllsort", true
go
use pubs2
go
checkpoint
go
```

This will allow the pubs2 database to perform minimally logged operations like "select into" queries.

Accessing Database Information

A complete description of a database (size, device allocations, owner, options) can be obtained by querying the system tables, but this usually involves elaborate joins and interpretation of coded information. A simpler method is to use the system procedure sp_helpdb, which will present the database information in an easy-to-read format.

Syntax:

```
sp_helpdb [database_name]
```

By itself, sp_helpdb will list the different databases on the server along with information on when each was created, its size, enabled options, and current status.

Example:

```
sp_helpdb

name              db_size    owner  dbid    createdstatus
--------------    -------    -----  -----   ------------------------------
master            6.0 MB     sa     1       Apr 03, 2001 no options set
model             2.0 MB     sa     3       Apr 03, 2001 no options set
pubs2             3.0 MB     sa     4       Apr 04, 2001 trunc log on chkpt
sybsystemdb       2.0 MB     sa     31513   Apr 03, 2001 no options set
sybsystemprocs    90.0 MB    sa     31514   Apr 04, 2001 trunc log on chkpt
tempdb            2.0 MB     sa     2       Apr 04, 2001 select
                                                         into/bulkcopy/pllsort,
                                                         trunc log on chkpt
```

When the database name parameter is used, sp_helpdb will display information for only the database requested. It will also supply additional information about the fragments of the database devices used (including size of the fragments, their purpose, and the number of unallocated pages remaining on the fragment).

Example:

```
sp_helpdb pubs2
name     db_size    owner    dbid     created status
-----    -------    -----    ----     --------------------------------
pubs2    3.0 MB     sa       4        Apr 04, 2001 trunc log on chkpt

(1 row affected)

device_fragments    size      usage           free kbytes
----------------    ------    -----           -----------
master              3.0 MB    data and log    1068

(return status = 0)
```

If sp_helpdb is executed with a database name from within the context of the database, the output will also include information about the segments that have been defined for the database as well as free space information.

Example:

```
sp_helpdb pubs2

name     db_size    owner    dbid     createdstatus
-----    -------    -----    ----     --------------------------------
pubs2    3.0 MB     sa       4        Apr 04, 2001 trunc log on chkpt

(1 row affected)

device_fragments    size      usage           free kbytes
----------------    ----      -----           -----------
master              3.0 MB    data and log    1068

device      segment
------      ----------
master      default
master      logsegment
master      system

(return status = 0)
```

Dropping Databases

If a database is no longer required on an Adaptive Server, it can be dropped from the server using the drop database command. Databases can be dropped under the following conditions:

- No users are currently connected to the database.
- The databases are not referenced by other databases.
- The drop command is issued from the master database.
- The command is issued by the dbo or SA.

Syntax:

```
drop database database_name [,database_name]…
```

Example:

```
drop database testdb4
```

WARNING: There is no "undrop" command; data is lost forever.

Database Ownership

In Adaptive Server, database ownership is determined at creation: the user who creates the database owns the database. Database ownership can be easily transferred via the sp_changedbowner system procedure.

Syntax:

```
sp_changedbowner login_name [, true]
```

For successful execution of the procedure, the following conditions must be true:

- The procedure must be executed from the database being altered.
- The new owner must not already be a user in the database.

The second parameter, " true", is optional and used to transfer aliases and permissions to the new database owner.

Note that sp_changedbowner may not be used to transfer the ownership of system databases. Also, it can only be run by system administrators.

System Tables

Defining information about databases is stored in the master system tables sysdatabases, sysusages, and sysdevices. These tables describe all databases' physical layout, according to some key relationships:

sysdatabases ← dbid → sysusages
sysusages ← vstart – low/high → sysdevices

Figure 4-1

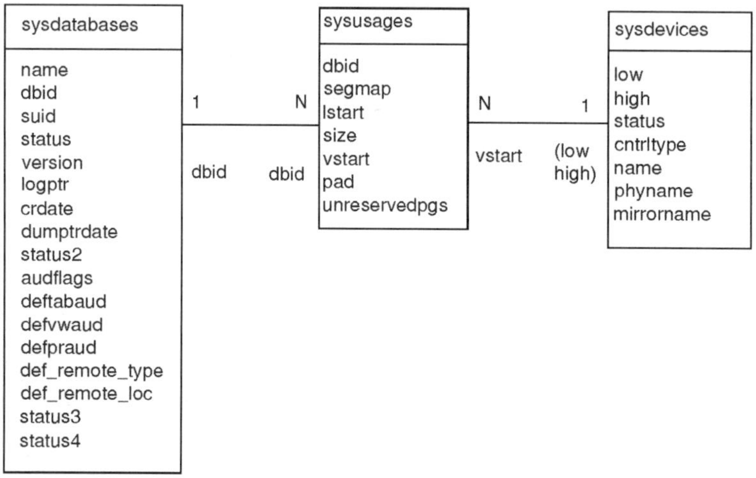

In the sysusages-sysdevices relationship, vstart is between low and high; note that between is inclusive. Note also that sysdevices names a database device, not a backup device.

sysdatabases

The sysdatabases table is the list of all databases in the Adaptive Server. Each time a database is created, a row is added to the sysdatabases table. Commonly queried columns include:

- name — The name of the database.
- dbid — The unique ID number for the database.
- suid — The unique ID number of the database owner.
- status — An integer storing the configured options and the status of the database; additional status information is stored in the columns status2, status3, and status4.
- crdate — The creation date of the database.
- dumptrdate — The date and time when an incremental database dump was last performed.

sysdevices

The sysdevices table holds the list of all database devices configured to work with the Adaptive Server. Each time a disk init command is executed a new row is added to this table. The structure and columns of sysdevices is described in Chapter 3, "Defining Physical and Sybase-Mirrored Devices to the Server."

sysusages

The sysusages table describes the distribution of pages from the devices and the allocations provided to the various databases; each allocation to a database (fragment) is entered as a row in the sysusages table. Columns related to sysdevices and sysdatabases are:

- dbid — The database assigned to the fragment.
- segmap — An integer storing the segment information for the fragment.
- lstart — The logical start page for the fragment (that is, sequence within the database).
- size — The size of the fragment.
- vstart — The virtual start page for the fragment (that is, sequence within the logical device).

Note that one logical page equals one or more virtual pages. Virtual pages are always 2 K in size, but logical pages are 2 K to 16 K.

The segmap value is related to the syssegments table (which is a database-specific system table, not a master system table) to indicate what sort of data are allowed to be added to the fragment. The value of segmap is an integer that is calculated by adding up other integers that indicate certain types of data. There may be up to 32 segments defined in a database, but only three are required and always present:

system	used by system tables	segmap value = 1
default	used by ordinary data	segmap value = 2
logsegment	used by transaction log	segmap value = 7

The lstart value indicates which range of pages will be used by the fragment; each database starts from page number zero and consists of a continuous range of increasing page numbers. Although page numbers are unique within the database, the same page numbers may be found in other databases and are not necessarily unique within the server.

The vstart value is unique within the server, since it is one of the device-level page numbers as described in Chapter 3. As we showed there, each pair of low and high values from sysdevices uniquely bound a single device, and so a value of vstart may be mapped to only one device. Note that the sysdevices and sysusages tables are joined using the "between" operator. A common query on these three system tables would display the name of the database that owns each fragment, along with the name of the device that holds the fragment:

```
select distinct "db name" = d.name, "device name" = v.name
from master..sysdatabases d, master..sysusages u, master..sysdevices v
where d.dbid = u.dbid
and u.vstart between v.low and v.high
```

```
create database payroll
      on data1 = 50
  log on log1  = 60

sysdatabases
name         dbid      crdate
-------      ----      ------------------
payroll      7         Apr 20 2001 6:42PM

sysusages
dbid  segmap   lstart   size         vstart          pad    unreservedpgs
----  ------   ------   ----------   -----------     ---    -------------
7 3   0        25600    1241513984   (null) 9368
7 4   25600    30720    1258291200   (null) 30712

sysdevices
low              high             name       phyname
-----------      -----------      -----      ---------------
1241513984       1241616383       data1      /dev/rdsk/data1
1258291200       1258342399       log1       /dev/rdsk/log1
```

Chapter 5

Database Logging and Recovery

In this chapter we're going to encounter a few more terms that require redefinition. Specifically, recovery is often misused to describe the process of restoring a database from a stored backup copy (a database dump). Adaptive Server Enterprise uses the term "recovery" to refer to the process of synchronizing the log with the physical database when the server is started. How does it become desynchronized? Well, that is what this chapter is about: the way the database log interacts with the data to ensure consistency.

In order to ensure that the database is always consistent and can reproduce all the changes made to the database, Adaptive Server databases must maintain a list of the changes that have been made to the database. This list of changes is the transaction log.

Transactions

What is a transaction? The most common response to this question is: a transaction is a "unit of work."

This is almost a cliché, but it is an excellent description of what a transaction is. A transaction is a task that, no matter how large or small, simple or complicated, cannot (for business or practical reasons) be broken down. In databases, a transaction is a set of work which can only be completed in full or not at all; there is no middle ground.

For example, database transactions are often compared to bank transactions. Simple banking transactions are easy to understand: money can be deposited into an account, or money can be withdrawn from an account. But more complicated tasks can also exist, like a transfer from one account to another; this can be interpreted as a withdrawal from one account and a deposit into another, or two distinct tasks. If the transfer is treated as two distinct tasks, then an error in the processing of either task can result in one of three possible outcomes.

1. The money was transferred successfully.
2. The money was withdrawn from the first account but did not get deposited into the second account.
3. The money was withdrawn from the first account but the money was returned when an error occurred.

Outcomes 1 and 3 are perfectly acceptable options; in these cases, no money is lost. But there is no satisfactory resolution to Outcome 2 — the money may be left with no place to go.

If the funds transfer were defined as a transaction, Outcome 2 would not only be unacceptable, it would be impossible. The transfer must be successful in all of its individual actions, or the transaction reverses all changes. No matter how many intermediate steps it takes to complete the task, the whole task must be completed in full or not at all.

So, when the squirrel chews through the transformer cable, are you still a happy customer, or are you going to have a little chat with the bank manager in the morning?

The Transaction Log

In Adaptive Server Enterprise, the transaction log is actually a system table called syslogs. This table contains a list of all modifications made to the database and information needed to ensure the integrity of the database. It cannot be directly modified by any user.

Adaptive Server Enterprise uses what is known as a *write-ahead log*. This means that all changes to the database will be recorded to the log before any attempt is made to reflect the data changes in the database. The syslogs table may be queried with an ordinary SELECT statement, but its output is not very useful or understandable to the naked eye (there are special utilities, such as dbcc log, that can translate a log's contents into a more useful form).

> **NOTE:** Past versions of Adaptive Server Enterprise have had 813 run-time errors linked to the dbcc log command if the "Dump log on checkpoint" option is turned on in the database; this is no longer the case. We haven't seen this problem since version 4.8, but have been careful ever since.

Another good reason to turn off the option is that we want to preserve the evidence of the problem to be diagnosed.

Transaction Modes

The behavior of transactions within SQL is defined by the ANSI standard, which identifies two distinct types of transactions: chained mode and unchained mode. A *chained mode* transaction may be thought of as "auto-starting"; when you log in and begin any SQL statement, ASE invisibly begins a transaction which will continue until you explicitly end it. In this way, you are always making all changes as part of a transaction, and may choose to end a transaction either by accepting your changes or by rejecting and removing them. As soon as your transaction is finished, a new one is started by the next SQL statement.

In *unchained mode*, the rules shift in an important manner: while any single data change statement is treated as a transaction, groups of statements are not transactions without an explicit command to begin a transaction. In unchained mode, you can be assured that any single INSERT, UPDATE, or DELETE (regardless of how many rows are changed) will complete in full or not at all. If, however, a series of data change commands need to complete or fail as a group, you will have to explicitly begin and end the transaction.

At first glance, it might seem that chained mode is "better" than unchained: transactions are always defined, and work (no matter how many statements are involved) is always protected against undesired outcomes. However, it's important to remember that a defining characteristic of transactions is that they isolate data. In order to ensure that different changes don't contradict one another, the data being altered by the transaction is locked. Depending on session settings and the particular commands involved, data may be partially or wholly unavailable to other users until the transaction finishes.

If your user began making changes to a table (say, giving a 3% increase to all the values in the price column of the Inventory table), thus making all of the rows in the table unavailable to all other users until the transaction finishes, and your user didn't know that a transaction was active, and decides to take a long lunch without logging out, then you may have a database that's all but useless.

This sort of situation is less likely in unchained mode — a user must specifically begin a transaction, which means that (hopefully!) she'll remember to finish the transaction at the end of the data change. However, it's still possible to forget and leave a long-running open transaction. Not only will this prevent other users from accessing data, it may prevent you from truncating the log to free up space; this may not only prevent access to a given table, but potentially can prevent all changes in the entire database (see "When the Transaction Log is Full," later in this chapter).

ASE will always default to unchained mode; the remainder of this chapter will assume that unchained mode is being used. Individual users may change their transaction mode while logged in (so long as a transaction is not active!), but should not necessarily do so. The choice of mode should be a standard that all users adhere to, in order to promote consistent application usage. Regardless of transaction mode, transactions should be kept as short as possible, and users should not be allowed interaction within the boundaries of a transaction (e.g., don't prompt a user to approve changes before finishing the transaction; prompt the user before beginning the transaction; and then begin and finish the transaction in a single batch).

Note that this is an application design decision. Very few shops seem to choose chained mode.

Transaction Control Statements

In order for Adaptive Server to control a transaction, the server must be aware of when a transaction starts and ends (whether successfully or not). This is accomplished by the use of transaction control statements. The transaction control statements permitted by Transact-SQL are:

- Begin transaction or begin tran — Marks the start of a transaction.
- Commit transaction or commit tran — Marks the end of a transaction and applies all data changes.
- Rollback transaction or rollback tran — Marks the end of a transaction and reverses all data changes.
- Save tran — A bookmark that allows you to roll back the transaction to a specific point in time, while leaving the transaction active.

Transaction control statements can be nested; however, this is not especially meaningful, as the transaction is never complete until the outermost transaction is complete. There must be at least one commit tran executed for each begin tran statement executed; the begin tran/commit tran pairs are not scanned syntactically the way begin/end code is scanned. But, regardless of how many begin tran/commit tran pairs appear to be nested in the code, there is only one transaction.

Note that this is not necessarily a bad thing, as it is important to maintain modularity and consistency of transactions within each module (procedure) you create.

Example:

```
begin tran
 change 1
 begin tran
 change 2
 commit tran
commit tran
```

In the previous pseudocode, there are two nested begin tran statements. Despite the fact that it appears that there are two transactions (one inside another), there is actually only one open transaction. Thus, the transaction is active until the second commit tran statement is executed.

Example:

```
begin tran
 change 1
 begin tran
        change 2
        begin tran
               change 3
        commit tran
        change 4
 commit tran
 change 5
rollback tran
```

In this example, none of the five changes would remain in the data after the rollback; again, although it looks like there are three levels of nesting, and it looks like changes 2, 3, 4, and 5 are fully bounded by begin/commit pairs, there is really only one transaction, and all work must complete in full or not at all. In fact, the transaction shown above is functionally identical to:

```
begin tran
 change 1
        change 2
               change 3
        change 4
 change 5
rollback tran
```

The nested begin/commit pairs essentially cancel each other out, leaving only the outermost pair of statements to have any effect. This behavior is more easily understood with the aid of a counter.

@@trancount

Adaptive Server Enterprise keeps track of transaction nesting through a global variable called @@trancount. This counter is available for use in normal T-SQL code, and determines whether or not a transaction is still alive. The rule for interpreting @@trancount is very simple: If the value of @@trancount is greater than zero, the transaction is still open, and the work is neither committed nor rolled back.

Example:

```
select @@trancount
go

@@trancount
0

begin tran
go
select @@trancount
go

@@trancount
1

commit tran
go
select @@trancount
go

@@trancount
0
```

At login time, the value of @@trancount for a session is set to zero. When running in unchained mode (the default), the value will change in response to the execution of the transaction control commands:

Command	Value of @@trancount
begin tran	Increment @@trancount by 1
commit tran	Decrement @@trancount by 1
rollback tran	Reset @@trancount to zero (regardless of previous value)

With this understanding, we can re-examine the earlier example, listing the value of @@trancount next to each control statement:

Example:

```
begin tran                          @@trancount set to 1
     change 1
     begin tran                     @@trancount set to 2
          change 2
          begin tran                @@trancount set to 3
               change 3
          commit tran               @@trancount set to 2
          change 4
     commit tran                    @@trancount set to 1
```

```
    change 5
rollback tran                              @@trancount reset to 0; work
                                           reversed
```

A slight change produces the same pattern of values in @@trancount, but a very different outcome:

```
begin tran                                 @@trancount set to 1
    change 1
    begin tran                             @@trancount set to 2
        change 2
        begin tran                         @@trancount set to 3
            change 3
        commit tran                        @@trancount set to 2
        change 4
    commit tran                            @@trancount set to 1
    change 5
commit tran                                @@trancount set to 0; work preserved
```

Save tran

Adaptive Server Enterprise also supports creating savepoints within a transaction; these savepoints permit some of the pending work within a transaction to be rolled back, without ending the transaction. Savepoints have no effect on @@trancount and must be named.

Example:

```
begin tran                                 @@trancount set to 1
    change 1
    begin tran                             @@trancount set to 2
        change 2
        save tran savepoint_a              @@trancount still 2
        change 3
    commit tran                            @@trancount set to 1
    change 4
rollback tran savepoint_a                  @@trancount still 1; changes 3 and 4
    change 5                                     reversed
```

At this point, changes 1, 2, and 5 are still pending — if a regular rollback tran is issued, those changes will be reversed. However, if a commit tran is used, changes 1, 2, and 5 will be preserved. Regardless of which outcome results, the transaction is still open and must be explicitly ended.

It is important to note that transaction control statements only affect whether or not work is preserved — they have no effect on the program flow. That is, rolling back a transaction does not cause ASE to return to some earlier point in the code and repeat instructions; following a rollback (or a rollback to a savepoint), ASE proceeds to execute the next statement in the code.

Commit

When the database is being modified, all changes are stored in the transaction log before being stored in the actual data table. But before any changes are written to disk, they are stored in memory, or *cache*. Adaptive Server may be configured for very simple or very elaborate combinations of caches (both dedicated to particular structures and general-purpose), but will always maintain certain cache structures.

Each user connection is given a small amount of memory (default size is 2K, or the size of the server database pages if they are in fact configured larger) known as a *user log cache*. These ULCs are used to gather together several transaction and data-change statements together, so when the transaction needs to be written to the log, multiple trips to the log pages aren't necessary for multiple commands. This has the effect of reducing crowding and contention for access to the transaction log.

Additionally, there will be cache space set aside for data and log pages. Any time a page is read from disk, it is copied into cache, and whenever changes are made to a page (data or log), the change is first recorded in the cached copy and later written to disk. When the cached pages are written to disk is different for log and data.

In general (this explanation is artificially simple; we'll fill in more details later), all of the log pages for a given transaction are written to disk when the transaction commits; if the pages were allowed to stay in cache without writing to disk, a finished transaction could be lost if the server were to unexpectedly fail. To prevent this possibility, the commit is not considered final until ASE receives confirmation that the transaction has been successfully written to disk. Additionally, log pages may be written to disk on an as-needed basis if the cache becomes too full; in this case, there is no guarantee that an entire transaction is written, but it is guaranteed that when the transaction commits, all log entries for the transaction will be on disk.

Data pages, on the other hand, will tend to stay in cache until the space they occupy is needed for some other use. If the data page is *dirty* (that is, changes have been recorded on the cached page but not yet copied to disk), the page will be written to disk before it is discarded from memory.

When the database is modified, the following steps are taken:

1. A begin tran is written into the log (in user log cache).
2. Records of data modification are added to the log (in user log cache).
3. Data modifications are made to data pages (in user log cache).
4. Acommit tran is written to the user log cache, then the ULC is flushed to the transaction log in cache.
5. Log pages for the transaction are copied from cache to the transaction log on disk.

Figure 5-1

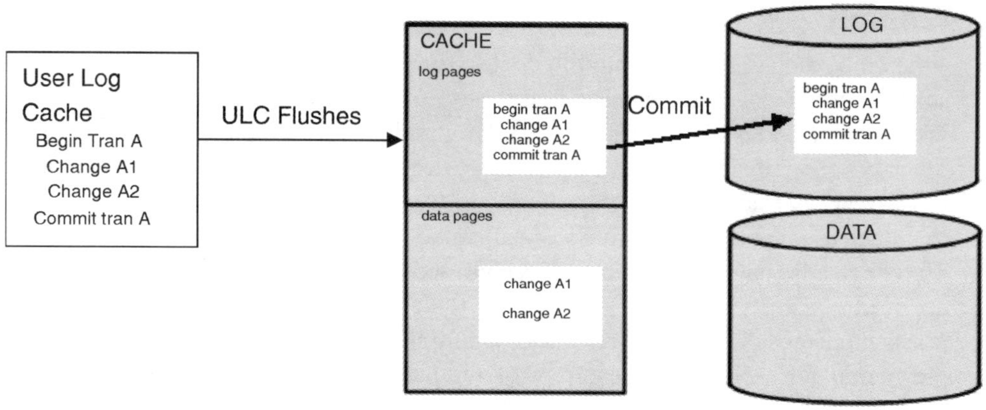

However, there is a fact that cannot be avoided from the steps described above: the data changes aren't written to disk unless their cache space is required. If cache were to remain relatively empty and the data space did not need to be recycled, the pages might not ever write to disk, and the changes could conceivably "die" in cache if the server were to fail.

Ensuring that data makes it to disk is the job of two other processes: checkpoint and recovery.

Checkpoint

A *checkpoint* is an event that causes all of a database's dirty pages (both data and log) to be copied from cache to disk. Checkpoints may be issued by the server (at intervals determined by database activity), or the dbo of a database may use the checkpoint command to force a checkpoint to occur (some option changes cannot take effect in a database until a checkpoint occurs).

A checkpoint exists primarily to reduce the work of the server at recovery time. In other words, it brings the server up faster.

When a checkpoint occurs, the follow events take place:

1. Any dirty log pages are copied to disk.
2. Any dirty data pages are copied to disk.
3. A checkpoint record is written to the log.

It should be noted that just because the data in log and disk have been copied, the data is still not final until a commit statement for the transaction is recorded in the transaction log on disk; if there were transactions that were still open (not committed at the time of the checkpoint), they would be permitted to continue. The checkpoint records in the transaction log help identify these incomplete transactions so they may be dealt with as necessary by the recovery process.

It is also important to realize that flushing all dirty pages to disk guarantees that (at least at the instant that a checkpoint finishes) data and log agree.

Figure 5-2

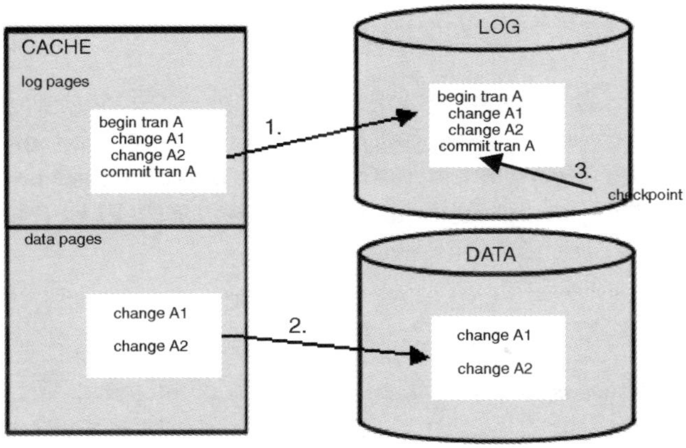

Recovery

The term *recovery* is used very precisely in ASE, and does not imply that anything has failed or had to be repaired. It is the process by which the server reconciles the data in the transaction log with the data that is actually stored in the database; when changes are found in the log that are not found in the data, the data is made to agree with the log. If there are any completed transactions that are not reflected in the database, Adaptive Server will add those changes to the data (or roll forward). If there are any incomplete transactions reflected in the database, or transactions that were interrupted by client or server failure, Adaptive Server will roll those transactions back. This will be done for every database each time the server is started, and for a single database at certain other times (including transaction log loads).

The recovery process performs the following tasks:

1. Locates the most recent checkpoint in the transaction log.
2. Builds a list of transactions that were active at the time of the checkpoint.
3. Applies all necessary changes for unrecovered transactions (both commits and rollbacks).
4. Identifies transactions that did not complete prior to shutdown and issues rollbacks.
5. Writes a checkpoint to the log (indicating that the next recovery can start from this point, rather than the beginning of the log).

As we can see, checkpoints and recovery are closely related. Recovery places a checkpoint, which indicates that recovery no longer needs to reconcile the entire log, only the portion since the most recent checkpoint. Likewise, since a checkpoint flushes all dirty data and log pages to disk, it in essence "catches up" the data to the log; in other words, it acts as a single-database recovery.

Checkpoints may also occur in conjunction with backup commands (see Chapter 8, "Backing Up and Restoring"), during periods of high transaction load (see the following section, "Recovery Interval"), and sometimes during periods of very low activity. If the server is sufficiently quiet (no pending tasks in the CPU queues), ASE may opt to get ahead by individually writing dirty pages from memory to disk. The theory is, if they have to be written to disk eventually, and there are no other demands on the server right now, it can only be helpful to write them to disk now when we can, rather than later, when we must.

If all dirty pages are written in this fashion and if there are at least 100 log records since the most recent checkpoint, the server issues a *free checkpoint*. This acts as a normal checkpoint would, but since it is done at times of very low server activity, its overhead does not impact processing in a noticeable fashion. This process can be identified as HOUSEKEEPER in the sp_who output. Most often, this process is in "checkpoint sleep."

Recovery Interval

The time it takes to recover a database is proportional to the number of unrecovered transactions in the log; if there were few changes since the last checkpoint, the database will recover almost instantaneously. If there are many thousands (tens of thousands, millions) of unrecovered log records, then recovery may be a very lengthy process. This can be troublesome at startup time, as databases are offline until they have successfully completed recovery (by default, databases are recovered by the order of their database ID, but the SA may configure a custom order to let the most important databases recover first).

The server will automatically issue checkpoints to databases that require them based on the value of the configuration option recovery interval in minutes.

Approximately once a minute, a background task will briefly examine the log of each database in the server and estimate how long it would take to recover if the server were to restart. If the estimate exceeds the value of recovery interval in minutes, ASE checkpoints the database (essentially "pre-recovering" it) and moves on to examine the next database. Please note that the recovery interval is estimated for each database individually, and it's still possible for a server to require a lengthy period of time for startup.

To configure the option use the following command:

```
sp_configure "recovery interval in minutes", 10
```

In general, the smaller the interval, the faster the recovery of the databases. However, if the recovery interval is too small, the server may generate more I/O because the server will be performing checkpoints too frequently.

When the Transaction Log is Full

Because the transaction log is the repository of all changes to the database, it is vital that the log never get full. If the log is full, it is not possible to record further changes to the log; since changes must be recorded in the log in order to succeed, all modifications to the database will be suspended until space is made available in the log. When the transaction log is nearly full, the last chance threshold is activated. This process should dump the log (and clean it out). If the log does completely fill, standard transaction log maintenance routines (dump tran and extending the log) will also fail. It is one of the primary duties of the SA to ensure that the log has adequate growth space, and does not ever completely fill.

To prevent filling, it will be necessary on a regular basis to *truncate* the log. Under normal circumstances, this occurs in the course of making regular backups of the log (see Chapter 9); after the log is copied, fully recovered transactions are identified and removed to free up space in the log. The *truncation point* that determines the amount of space that may be removed will depend on several factors, but most importantly on current transactions. Under normal circumstances, the last-chance threshold ensures that you do have room to dump the transaction log.

Put simply, the oldest open transaction determines the truncatable portion of the log. No log record that has been added since a still-running transaction may be truncated. Given the following log entries:

```
                         <beginning of log records>
                                    ...
begin tran 1
                 begin tran 2                                    truncation
                                  begin tran 3                      point
                commit tran 2
commit tran 1                                                         ↓
                                                begin tran 4
                                                                 begin tran 5
                                commit tran 3
                                               commit tran 4
                              <truncate log>
```

The truncation point is determined by the oldest, still-open transaction. Transactions 1 through 4 have all committed, leaving only transaction 5 open at the time of the truncation request. All log records preceding "begin tran 5" could be removed to free up space in the log. The example also underscores the fact that ASE is intended to be a multi-user, multi-transaction environment: transactions are interleaved in the log, and one transaction will not necessarily finish before another starts. Now, consider one small change:

```
                         <beginning of log records>
                                    ...
begin tran 1
                 begin tran 2
                                  begin tran 3
     ↑          commit tran 2
 truncation
   point                                        begin tran 4
                                                                 begin tran 5
                                commit tran 3
                                                                commit tran 5
checkpoint
                                               commit tran 4
                              <truncate log>
```

In this case, the truncation point is closer to the beginning of the log records because an early transaction, transaction 1, is still open. Even though transactions 2 through 5 have completed, they may not be truncated even if a checkpoint has recovered them (in this example, transactions 2, 3, and 5 are fully recovered since they finished before the checkpoint; transactions 1 and 4 are not, since they did not finish before the checkpoint).

If there were only a few records in the log preceding "begin tran 1," it's possible that the truncation would free very little space and require truncation again almost immediately. If the log were to fill at this point, a standard truncation request might actually be counterproductive, since the process of truncating the log is itself a logged action and will add log records. If there is plenty of free log space remaining, this is a minor issue, but if we are approaching full, it can be disastrous. As a result, it is necessary to impress upon users that leaving long-running transactions open is a bad practice. If a transaction log is near to full and a long-running transaction would prevent an effective truncation, consider using the kill command to end the transaction and permit a more effective truncation:

```
kill spid
```

The spid (server process id) of a connection is a unique identifier, assigned at login time; no two connections will have the same value of spid at the same time (although a user may log out, relinquish the spid, and find it reassigned to another user at login time).

If you must kill a user in this fashion, it is really only helpful if you kill the right user; killing any spid other than the one holding the oldest open transaction will not move the truncation point. The oldest open transaction (and its associated spid) can be determined by querying the table master..syslogshold:

```
select * from master..syslogshold
```

This table doesn't really exist; it's created out of various system information when queried. It contains no more than two rows per database, with several important columns: database id value (compare to master..sysdatabases), the time the transaction began, and the spid holding the transaction. If any spid for a database has a value of zero, do not kill it without consulting your Replication Server administrator; spid 0 represents an internal process related to replication, and killing it will cause the RepAdmin to regard you with undisguised loathing.

Let us also consider a slight variation to the preceding example; instead of finishing with a truncate request, assume it finishes like this:

<beginning of log records>
...
begin tran 1
begin tran 2
begin tran 3
↑ truncation point
commit tran 2
begin tran 4
begin tran 5
commit tran 3

```
                                                          commit tran 5
                              checkpoint
                                              commit tran 4
  < transactions 6 — 873; most commit, some roll back, trans 325 and 571 incomplete>
                              < server crashes>
```

What would happen at restart time? Our earlier discussion indicated five steps would be necessary: locate the most recent checkpoint; build a list of unrecovered transactions; apply recovery to uncommitted transactions; identify incomplete transactions; and write a new checkpoint. Following through this example, we would do the following:

1. Locate the most recent checkpoint in the transaction log (between commit tran 5 and commit tran 4); each checkpoint record contains a pointer to the oldest begin tran at the time of the checkpoint. In this case, we start recovery from transaction 1, and may ignore all prior log records (they have definitely been recovered before now).
2. Build a list of transactions that have not been through recovery; starting from the oldest open transaction (transaction 1), read forward, looking for transactions that have not finished by the time of the checkpoint, in this case, transactions 1, 4, and the many transactions after the checkpoint.
3. Apply all necessary changes for unrecovered transactions (both commits and rollbacks); transactions 2, 3, and 5 may be ignored, since they were fully recovered by the checkpoint.
4. Identify transactions that did not complete prior to shutdown and issue rollbacks; in this case, transactions 1, 325, and 571 fall into this category. These transactions will have rollbacks written for them, since they can't commit after a server crash.
5. Write a checkpoint to the log (indicating that the next recovery can start from this point, rather than the beginning of the log); since there are no active transactions at this time, the truncation point moves up to the checkpoint marker.

After recovery, the log will look like this:

```
                          <beginning of log records>
                                     ...
begin tran 1
                  begin tran 2
                                 begin tran 3
                 commit tran 2
                                                  begin tran 4
                                                                begin tran 5
                                commit tran 3
                                                               commit tran 5
                                 checkpoint
                                                 commit tran 4
  < transactions 6 — 873; most commit, some roll back, trans 325 and 571 incomplete>
                               <server crashes>
```

<server restarts>
rollback tran 1
rollback tran 325
rollback tran 571
checkpoint
<new records start here>

If truncation were necessary, almost the entire contents of the log are removable (a small amount of data must remain in the log to ensure it lines up properly with the next log in load situations). Even if truncation were not necessary at this time, the checkpoint record will speed up the process of locating the truncation point, and the next recovery.

The syntax for truncating the log (both under normal circumstances, and in emergencies like a full log) is fully discussed in Chapter 8, "Backing Up and Restoring."

Thresholds

Thresholds are a useful tool to help prevent the database log from completely filling to the point where the database becomes completely non-functional. Thresholds may be defined in any segment of your database, but are commonly added to the logsegment; when a threshold is crossed, a designated stored procedure is called, which may be designed to take corrective action (such as notifying the SA of current free space or truncating the log). The "last-chance" threshold is provided for the log of each database, and sits a short distance from the completely full mark of the log (in fact, the LCT marks the point of the log where suspension will occur). This threshold will execute a stored procedure called sp_thresholdaction (this stored procedure is not provided with Adaptive Server and must be written by the SA). sp_thresholdaction could print messages to the administrator (note that all print statements called by threshold procedures will be sent only to the errorlog), execute dump database commands or send pages/e-mails/voicemails. There may be many sp_thresholdaction procedures on a server. As with any stored procedure, Adaptive Server will first look for the procedure in the local database, then in sybsystemprocs.

All threshold procedures are aware of certain defining characteristics of their corresponding thresholds: name of the database the threshold occupies; segmentname the threshold is installed in; threshold location (measured in remaining free space); and status (is the threshold specifically the last-chance threshold or not?). These characteristics may be used as input parameters for the threshold procedure:

```
Create procedure sp_thresholdaction
@dbname varchar(30),
@segmentname varchar(30),
@space_left int,
@status int
As
Dump tran @dbname to lastchancedump
Print "Warning: Last-Chance threshold crossed"
Print "Transaction log for %1! Dumped to lastchancedump device", @dbname
Return
```

Adaptive Server will pass the sp_thresholdaction to accept four parameters:

Parameter	Description
@dbname varchar(30)	Name of the database
@segmentname varchar(30)	The name of the segment that crossed the last-chance threshold; usually the logsegment
@space_left int	Number of pages remaining in the segment
@status int	A flag that indicates whether or not the last-chance threshold has been crossed. If the threshold has been crossed, the value will be 1; otherwise @status will be 0.

This procedure will perform a dump tran for the database to a predefined device called lastchancedump. Remember that the print messages notifying the administrator will be directed to the errorlog, not to any client app or connection.

Suspended Transactions

As discussed, when a transaction log fills, Adaptive Server will suspend all processes that add entries to the log. The suspended processes will appear to hang until more space becomes available in the log (their status may be confirmed with sp_who: these processes will display as being in *log sleep*). These suspended processes should awaken when the transaction log frees some space (either by successfully truncating the log, or by adding space with alter database). If for some reason processes do not awaken, Sybase Technical Support should be notified.

Summary

Every database has a transaction log which guarantees the integrity and consistency of data changes. Changes to the database are recorded in the log before being recorded in tables or indexes, and these changes are reconciled via the process of recovery. Preserving and maintaining the log are crucial aspects of administration, and will be among the most important ongoing tasks for any SA.

Chapter 6

Security

More and more organizations are acknowledging that their data is the most important asset they own. To this end, these corporations go to great lengths to ensure that data is safe from all sorts of threats including environmental, hardware/software failure; corruption; and unauthorized access.

Unauthorized access to data has become so recognized as a threat to corporate assets that it is making national news.

ASE offers a rigorous approach to securing data, and in enabling you to protect data down to a very fine layer of granularity, including column-level security through grant and revoke options, and row-level security through views.

ASE Security Levels

There are four security levels:

- Operating system
- Server
- Database
- Database object access

Figure 6-1

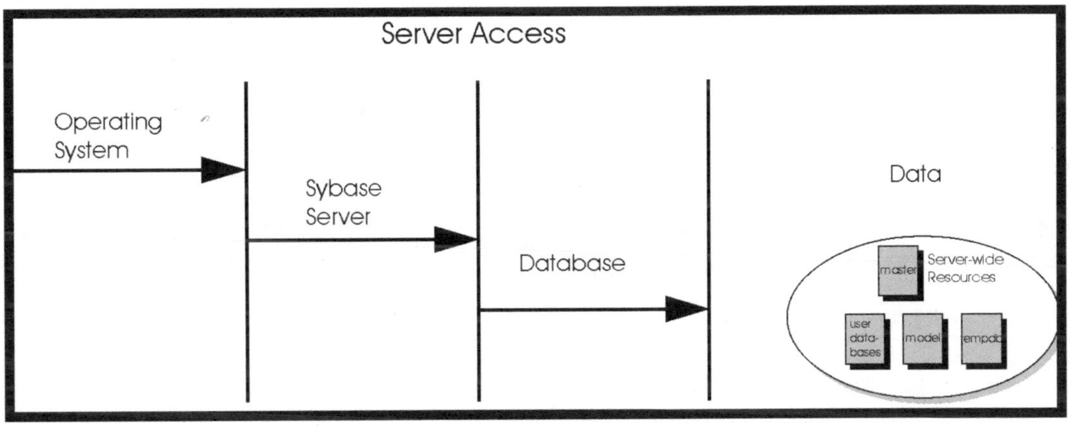

You can't access data if you cannot gain access to the server operating system. ASE handles this by bypassing the operating system; it listens to an operating system handle, or port, or node (depending on your own OS terminology). In UNIX, this means that you define a numbered port, and the server listens on that port. Queries are transmitted from the client to this port.

Once you have access to (through!) the operating system, you need access to the database server; ASE handles this through a traditional login/password combination. This is performed using the sp_addlogin procedure, and will have the effect of adding a row to the syslogins table in the master database.

Access to the database server does not guarantee access to the database(s). You need to have explicit access to the database(s). This is normally performed (there are other ways to do this, which we will discuss later) with the sp_adduser procedure, which will add rows to the sysusers table in the database to which you are granting access.

Once you have explicit access to the database, you do not necessarily have explicit access to data in the tables, to run stored procedures, or to create objects. Users gain access to the database objects through grant and revoke statements. These statements add rows to the sysprotects table.

Operating System-Level Security

Accessing the server through the operating system is managed without having direct access to the operating system. That is, you do not have to have explicit permissions in the operating system of the machine in which ASE is installed; you may connect via a client program running on another machine (but you must have permissions on <u>that</u> machine to run the client program). Connection information defined in the client application (see Chapter 3) provides the capability to communicate to the server through a network port.

Security at the operating system level is the responsibility of the operating system administrator.

The only other thing you need to know (as an ASE administrator) about the operating system has to do with file permissions. The sybase user (OK, the OS user who starts ASE, but who should be sybase) must have permission to the devices upon which you will be placing data, as well as the location for the errorlog.

Server-Level Security

Server-level security is managed via a login ID and password combination as shown below:

```
sp_addlogin login_name, password
[, default_db [, default_language
[, full_name [,pass_expiration
[,min_pw_length [, max_failed_logins ]]]]]]
```

In the following example, we are adding a user with the login garbusj who has a password garbusj1:

```
sp_addlogin garbusj, garbusj1, userdb, null, "Jeffrey Garbus",90,6,3
```

By default, this user will be current in the *userdb* database. No default language is supplied, so it will be the server default. The password will expire in 90 days, it must have a minimum of six characters, and has a "three strikes and you're out" policy in case of incorrect password entry. (This protects against somebody trying to guess a password.)

Logins and passwords have a maximum character length of 30. When you enter a password, if it contains a character outside of the basic character set (a-z, A-Z, 0-9) or starts with a number, you will need to enclose the password in quotes.

For example:

```
sp_addlogin changa,"&&alvin"
```

Note that adding logins to the server is an SSO-only privilege.

sp_addlogin Parameters

login_name	Name user connects with
password	Password user enters
default_db	Database user enters when accessing server
default_language	Language for user
full_name	Documentation only
pass_expiration	Password expiration in days (default 0)*
min_pw_length	default min 6 characters*
max_failed_logins	default 0 (never), number of times a user can enter an incorrect pw before being locked out*

* New for 12.0, so don't expect these if you're running on an older version of the server.

Require Digits in Password

Some shop standards require a user to put a digit in his password. Version 12 and later allow a new configuration option that instructs the server to check this when a login is added and when passwords are changed.

Syntax:

```
Exec sp_configure "check password for digit",{0|1}
```

If you set this value to 0, no digit is required. If you set it to 1, the server will require a digit in the password.

> **NOTE:** Access to the Adaptive Server does not guarantee access to any database other than master (the default default database). By default, you also have access to tempdb, but otherwise you need to grant access to the other databases.

Special Logins/Users

There are a variety of special cases of logins and users that you'll see reference to in documentation, and of which you'll make use while administering security. These are discussed in this section.

sa

It's important to distinguish between the sa and an SA. The sa is a specific login, created at installation time, that initially holds all super-user privileges (known as *roles*; see the following section). An SA is any individual in the ASE that acts in the capacity of a systems administrator, and has overall control of all server functions, resources, and environment. The sa login is locked (disabled) by most shops, after granting the administrator privileges (or *sa_role*) to the person(s) who will be performing administrative job functions.

There are two reasons to not use the sa login as originally installed: initially the password is *null* (that is, no password at all!), and using a single login does not allow for accountability. We recommend that you immediately either:

Create a password for the sa login

or

Create a new login (or logins) with the sa_role and lock the sa login (we'll cover locking logins in a little while).

Initially, the sa login is assigned the sa_role (administrative privileges), the sso_role (security privileges), and the oper_role (backup/load privileges). In other words, the sa login has the power after installation to do nearly anything on the server. Whether you want this login to retain this power is subject to a shop standard. The best thing to do is probably to give each SA a personal login with the appropriate roles, and to disable the original sa login. In shops where all the DBAs use the same login, there is no accountability. (We suppose that in some shops, that is the idea, but from a practical standpoint, it's nice to know who dropped the database.)

When in a database, the sa (or a login with the sa_role assigned) is automatically treated as dbo (the database owner).

TIP You can verify this with built-in functions:

```
Select suser_name()
Select user_name()
```

This gives the login the ability to control access to the database and its objects. Ultimately, the SA is responsible for all server resources.

dbo

The database owner has overall control and responsibility for each database. dbo is not a login; it is the user name within the database of the login who has control of the database access and its objects.

By default, the owner of a database is the login that creates it. As you remember from the database creation chapter, by default only a login with the sa_role can create databases, as creating the database immediately allocates server resources. The ownership of the database can be transferred later, either by an SA or by whomever happens to be the dbo at the time.

The dbo controls the database in the way that the SA controls the server. The dbo decides who has access to a database and who has which privileges within the database. In a production environment, the dbo generally creates all of the objects (we'll see why shortly, but in short it simplifies user permissions).

The dbo may load or dump the databases (there is also a role, oper_role, which is permitted to dump and load all databases), checkpoint the databases, and use the database consistency checker (dbcc) within the database.

The dbo also has the exclusive permission to run the setuser command, which allows him to dynamically alias to another user within the database. The setuser command (discussed at length later) is frequently used when a user who owns objects has left the company. Even the dbo does not have permission to access that user's objects directly; he has to alias himself to that user using the setuser command.

Object Owner

The owner of an object controls access to the object (e.g., who can access a table, execute a procedure, etc.). As just mentioned, even the dbo does not have direct access to these objects.

The owner of an object is the person who creates the object. Again, in the production environment, this is usually the dbo, but this is a standard, not a requirement. Once the object is created, the object ownership is not transferable.

The object owner controls access to his own objects and exclusively has the right to modify the schema of those objects (for example, adding indexes, columns, or rules to a table).

NOTE: A login with the SA role will also be able to access these objects.

The Three Standard Roles

A *role* is a mechanism for assigning groups of privileges to one or more logins. There are both system roles (they come with the server at install time) and user-defined roles (created by administrative staff after installation). A login may hold any combination of roles.

There are eight system roles, but only three that we ordinarily use: sa_role, sso_role, and oper_role.

Figure 6-2

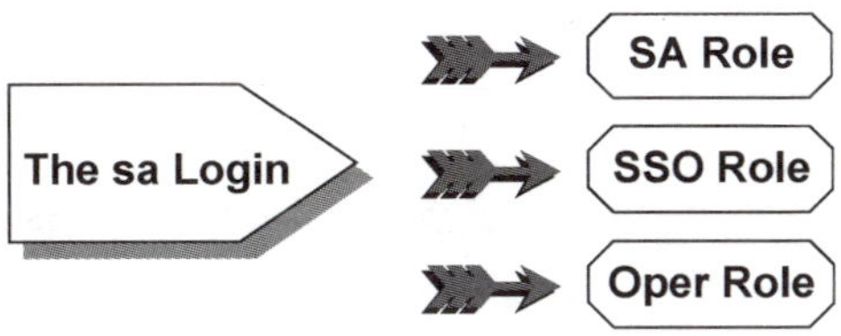

These, initially, are all assigned to the sa login, which owns these roles exclusively. In the next section, we'll talk about how to assign these roles to other logins. As previously mentioned, we recommend that one of the first tasks you assume after installing the server is to disable the sa login and assign these roles to other logins as appropriate to job functions.

The Systems Administrator Role

The sa login, in versions past, was the exclusive controller of server-wide privileges. As time passed (and sophistication of users and Sybase customers grew), it became necessary to allow more than one user to have this level of access and control. From this, the need for roles arose, and the sa_role is now granted to anyone who will take on these responsibilities:

- Manage disk resources (device definition, database creation, etc.)
- Grant or revoke the sa_role
- Execute the documented dbcc commands
- Configure server parameters (that is, control memory at the server level)
- Shut down server
- Administer the server

The System Security Officer Role

This role may have been an offshoot of combining secure SQL Server (required years ago so that Sybase could sell to DOD clients) with the base product. It allows somebody other than the SA to control access to the server. The System Security Officer (SSO), sometimes referred to in documentation as the Site Security Officer, has security responsibility for:

- Creating server login accounts, which includes assigning initial passwords
- Changing the password of any account
- Granting and revoking the System Security Officer and Operator roles
- Creating, granting, and revoking user-defined roles
- Granting the capability to impersonate other logins throughout the server
- Setting the password and security-related configuration options
- Managing the audit system

The sso_role is different from the sa_role in that the sa administers the server, and the sso regulates access to the server.

The SSO has overall responsibilities for all server security, including server configuration privileges for security-related activity.

To change a password expiration date, use:

```
sp_configure 'password expiration', n
```

This changes the number of days between required password changes (unless a different value is specified when creating a login or role). n is the number of days until a changed password expires again.

Example:

```
sp_configure 'password expiration',90
```

Here, we are forcing users to change their passwords every 90 days.

Note that ASE does not provide a means to force password change at the next login.

The SSO can keep a login from server access without actually dropping it. This is useful when you want to disable a login without removing it (perhaps an employee is under investigation, or is taking a leave of absence). Or, if a login that you want to remove owns objects (and so cannot be dropped), the easiest solution would be to lock a login, as follows:

```
sp_locklogin login_name,"lock" | "unlock"
```

Example:

```
sp_locklogin jgarbus,"lock"
```

To change a password, you can use the sp_password stored procedure:

```
sp_password caller_pw, new_pw [, login name]
```

Any login can change his own password. Only an SSO can change another user's password.

TIP: There is a startserver option that will generate a new SSO password, in case passwords are lost or forgotten. The new password will be written to the server errorlog. To use this option, include the parameter –p in the runserverfile, followed by the name of a login with the sso_role. The SSO can modify other user's login options. This will be covered in detail later.

The Operator Role

A login with the Operator (OPER) role has permission to dump and load all of the databases. The database's owner (dbo) can still dump and load the database and logs.

Remember that loading a database is a destructive process, and as such should not be granted lightly. Many shops uncleverly give their operators the sa login and password; while this gives the operators dbo status in every database (so they can dump and load the databases), it also gives them all of the other privileges of the SA. It's a much better idea to give the oper_role to the login who is responsible for the backups; this way, that login cannot inadvertently cause damage (apart from loading the wrong database!).

The OPER can dump and load all databases and transaction logs, but not create databases or do disk initializations. Note that this means that at restore time, the operator must work in conjunction with an SA.

NOTE: A login with the OPER role may dump and load databases even if he lacks permission to use a database or its objects.

Dropping Logins

Logins are removed with the sp_droplogin stored procedure:

```
sp_droplogin login_name
```

Example:

```
sp_droplogin jgarbus
```

You cannot drop logins that own a database or database objects; use the sp_locklogin (covered earlier) instead. You also cannot drop the last unlocked login with an SSO or SA role. This protects you from accidentally rendering your system inaccessible to somebody with authority to control it. Finally, you cannot drop a login if it is currently logged in.

The syslogins Table

syslogins is a server system table (hence it is only in master), which contains a row of data for each login that has been created. Passwords are stored in this table in an encrypted manner. You may optionally require that passwords are encrypted/decrypted as they travel over the network.

sp_displaylogin

The sp_displaylogin command will show information about a specific login. With no parameter it will list information about the current login:

```
sp_displaylogin [login_name]
```

Example:

```
exec sp_addlogin john,'xxxxxx',pubs2,NULL,'John Q. Doe'
```

(We add a login)

```
exec sp_displaylogin john
```

(Now we display the information)

```
Suid: 6
Loginame: john
Fullname: John Q. Doe
Default Database: pubs2
Default Language:
Configured Authorization:
Locked: NO
Date of Last Password Change: Apr 18 2001 4:40PM
```

NOTE: sp_displaylogin uses print statements, so all information goes to the message handler.

sp_modifylogin

The SSO can change information about an existing login using the sp_modifylogin stored procedure:

```
sp_modifylogin login_name, option, value
```

The available options are given below:

Option	Definition
defdb	User's default database
deflanguage	User's default language
fullname	User's full name
add default role	Assigns default roles
drop default role	Removes default roles
min passwd length	Minimum valid password length
passwd expiration	Password expiration interval, in days
max failed_logins	Failed attempts before login is locked

Example:

```
sp_modifylogin jgarbus, defdb, productiondb
```

In the above example, the login jgarbus will have a new default database, productiondb, assigned. This option, like all sp_modifylogin options, will take effect the next time the user logs in.

Permissions to use this procedure are a little tricky; users can change the first three options for their own logins; an SA can change non-role-related options for any login, and an SSO can change any of the options for any login. Note that changing the default database does not grant access to that database, and connecting to a default database to which you do not have permission can give you cryptic error messages. Also note that the value parameter takes a character data type, so when setting the last three options, you must quote the integer value, as follows:

```
sp_modifylogin jgarbus, 'min passwd length', '10'
```

sp_who

You (or any user) can use the sp_who procedure to display a list of current server connections, as shown in the following sample output:

```
exec sp_who
go
fid spid  status  loginame   origname  hostname  blk_spid  dbname   cmd               block_xloid
--- ----  ------  --------   --------  --------  --------  ------   ----------------  -----------
    0      2      sleeping   NULL      NULL      0         master   NETWORK HANDLER   0
    0      3      sleeping   NULL      NULL      0         master   DEADLOCK TUNE     0
    0      4      sleeping   NULL      NULL      0         master   MIRROR HANDLER    0
    0      5      sleeping   NULL      NULL      0         master   HOUSEKEEPER       0
    0      6      sleeping   NULL      NULL      0         master   SHUTDOWN HANDLER  0
```

```
0   7    sleeping  NULL  NULL    0  master  ASTC HANDLER       0
0   8    sleeping  NULL  NULL    0  master  CHECKPOINT SLEEP   0
0   9    sleeping  NULL  NULL    0  master  DTC COMMIT SVC     0
0   10   sleeping  NULL  NULL    0  master  AUDIT PROCESS      0
0   11   running   sa    SOLO_1  0  master  SELECT             0
```

TIP: A version of sp_who can easily be rewritten to show additional or different information. For example, you can replace hostname with engine number to verify effectiveness of multiprocessing. There are various freeware versions of sp_who on the web.

The status values in the sample output are explained in the following table:

Status Value	Explanation
alarm sleep	Waiting for alarm to wake process
background	An Adaptive Server process, IE threshold, not a user process
infected	Server detected a serious error condition
lock sleep	Waiting for lock acquisition
running	Current process if not SMP server
log sleep	Process suspended by a last-chance log threshold
recv sleep	Waiting on a network read
runnable	Waiting for a engine to free up
send sleep	Waiting on a network write
sleeping	Waiting on disk I/O or other resource
stopped	Stopped process
sync sleep	Waiting for a synchronization message from another process in the process family (fid)

The Kill Command

You can use the kill command to terminate a process in any state. At least, that's what the documentation says; the kill command is not perfect, and you sometimes have to wait for a process to wake up before it dies.

An infected process may be killed, but since a server bug frequently causes it, it is often best to restart Adaptive Server instead. Does the server always have to be recycled? If the kill does successfully terminate the process, watch closely. If no other infected processes occur, and nothing else looks unusual, you probably don't need to. The kill might have cleaned up the mess.

Except for sleeping processes, kill will take effect immediately, although it might take a while for any running transactions to roll back. This is a frequent misunderstanding, and sometimes causes folks to restart a server when only a few moments more of patience would have killed the errant process. Sleeping processes will die when they next wake up.

Occasionally sleeping processes will not die, but each release of Adaptive Server does a better job of killing processes.

Database-Level Security

Adding a login creates a new row in the syslogins table, and grants a process access to the server. This process does not necessarily have access to a user database; it will always have access to master and model, and we'll see why shortly.

Database access is managed through a user ID, which may be obtained in a variety of ways. The most common is by adding the user directly to the database with the *sp_adduser* procedure.

Syntax:

```
sp_adduser      login_name
[, name_within_database
[, group_name]]
```

Example:

```
sp_adduser jgarbus
```

Here, we add a user, jgarbus, to the database. You could, if you wanted, give him another name within the database, but this convention is not often used.

Note that with Adaptive Server Enterprise 11.5 and later, Sybase (and your authors!) strongly recommend using user-defined roles instead of groups. Groups are database specific, and are less easy to manage globally. User-defined roles can be used in a specific database or set of databases.

Users are removed from the database with the sp_dropuser stored procedure.

Syntax:

```
sp_dropuser user_name
```

Example:

```
sp_dropuser jgarbus
```

Adding a user to the database also adds a row to the sysusers table, in the way that adding a login to the server adds a row to the syslogins table. The user ID is mapped back to the login by adding the login ID of the user to the sysusers table.

The user ID does not usually match the login ID. If, for example, you are the sa login (who always has a login ID of 1) and also the database owner (who always has a user ID of 1), then you will match. But, as logins are added sequentially, and unique per server, and the user IDs are added per database, and are unique per database, there is not necessarily a correlation.

Adding users to the database is a dbo privilege (exception: an SSO may add users to any database). The database owner controls database-level resources in the same way that the SA controls server-level resources.

A login with the sa_role can add users to databases, because when in the database, the SA is treated as dbo. The server will not allow you to drop a user who owns any objects in the database.

Guest User

If a login tries to issue a "use" statement, and the database does not contain an entry for the user, the user may still gain access if the dbo has created a guest user.

Syntax/Example:

```
sp_adduser guest
```

If you attempt to use a database, and the database has a guest user, you automatically have access to the database and assume the privileges of public (discussed with object permissions, shortly). This is how logins automatically get access to the master and tempdb databases; there is a guest user in master and tempdb that cannot be removed.

If there is a guest user in model, all databases created subsequently will contain a guest user. Note that the user ID (UID) for guest is 2.

> **TIP:** In general, it is recommended that you not add a login called "guest," as it could conflict with the guest users. As of version 12, all ASE platforms have the ability to use network-based security services (see "Integrated Security Overview" later in this chapter for supported services), which allow for "default secure logins" (if a user is validated by the operating system, there is an automatic access to ASE, via various login names). In this situation, there may legitimately be a login named "guest."

Aliases

An *alias* is a mechanism within a database to permit multiple users to look like the same user. This is useful in a development environment for object and permission purposes.

Syntax:

```
sp_addalias login_name, user_within_database
```

Example:

```
use user3db
go
sp_addalias John, dbo
go
```

There are two important tips in this example. First, aliases are database specific. Be sure that you are in the database in which you want to assign the alias. You can do this with a simple select statement:

```
select db_name()
```

This will return the name of your current database context. Next, notice that John is being aliased to dbo. Anybody aliased to dbo will assume dbo privileges while within the database. This is a useful mechanism to enable developers to share resources within a development database. It is a bad idea to give away this type of privilege in a production database.

Using the sp_addalias stored procedure, login_name must not be a user of the database (or the dbo); it must be a login currently registered in the syslogins table. New aliases will be added in rows to the sysalternates table. They are removed with sp_dropalias.

Syntax:

```
sp_dropalias login_name
```

Example:

```
sp_dropalias John
```

This drops the alias we just created.

Information on Users and Aliases

The sp_helpuser command will display information about a specific user or a list of all users.

Syntax:

```
sp_helpuser [user_name]
```

Example:

```
exec sp_helpuser dbo
go
Users name      ID in db       Group Name      Login Name     Default db
dbo             1              public          sa             master
Users aliased to user
Login Name
Fred
John
Sally
```

Access Sequence

What does the server check first when determining database access?

If the login has the sa_role activated, or is the sa login, access is automatic.

Next, the server checks to see if there is a row in sysusers: have we added the user to the database? If yes, then the user gets database access. If not, the server looks for an entry in sysalternates. If there is an entry, the user gets database access. If not, the server looks for a guest user. If there is a guest user in sysusers, then the user gets access; if not, it is denied. Finally, if the login has the sso_role, access will be granted to the database.

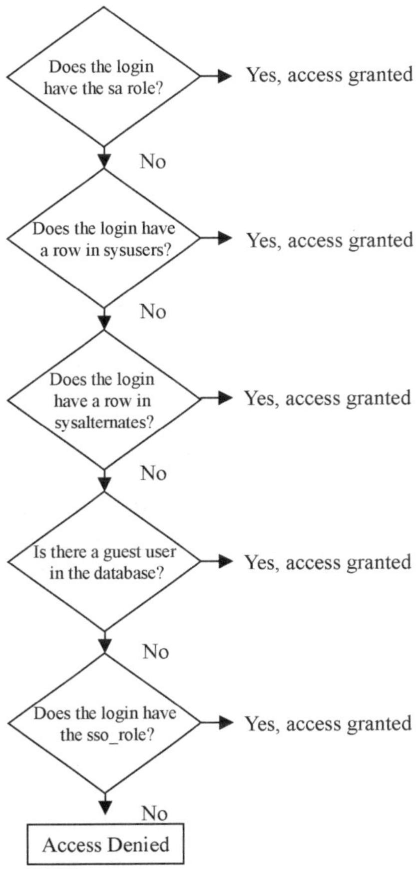

Figure 6-3

Database Access

There are six ways to give a login access to a database.

- sp_adduser login
- sp_adduser guest
- sp_addalias login, user
- sp_changedbowner
- grant the login sa_role
- set proxy

We've already looked at the first three. The sp_changedbowner stored procedure changes the owner of the database (make sure you're in the right database when you issue this command!). Of course, the database owner has access. In most production systems, the databases are all owned by the SA. Later on, we'll see how to add roles to logins; if we add the sa_role to the login, that login will have dbo access to the database (just as SA logins do). Finally, we'll see the set proxy statement, which is a server-level alias.

Groups

Remember, for Adaptive Server Enterprise 11.5 and later, user-defined roles are preferable to groups. There's a good chance, though, that you will see a system that uses groups, and as such, we present the topic for completeness.

A *group* is a logical organization of users who will be granted common permissions. This simplifies the addition of users to databases. You can set up the permissions one time, then add users directly to the groups. Although groups are useful, they have some limitations that may lead you to use roles instead (see the section "User-Defined Roles" later in this chapter).

Groups are database specific. If you need to create groups that cross databases, we recommend you use server-level roles (discussed later) instead.

Also, a user can be placed in only one group (except that a user is always in the public group). A login can have multiple roles, so again, if you need to make a login a member of multiple groups, consider server-level roles instead.

Prior to 12.5, groups were entries in sysusers with UIDs greater than 16383. In 12.5 and later, the groups are identified as being between @@mingroupid and @@maxgroupid. So, you can get a list of groups by selecting from sysusers (note that there is not a sysgroups table). For example:

Pre-12.5

```
Select "group name" = name from sysusers
where UID > 16383
```

12.5

```
Select "group name" = name from sysusers
where UID between @@mingroupid and @@maxgroupid
```

GID of public, the default group, is 0.

Syntax/Examples:

```
exec sp_addgroup marketing
exec sp_dropgroup accounting
exec sp_changegroup marketing, user1
exec sp_changegroup "public", user2
```

Here, in order, we're creating a group called marketing; dropping a group called accounting; placing user1 in the marketing group; and removing user2 from all groups but public. There is no way to remove a user from a group explicitly; this is the only way we can get user2 out of accounting and leave him in the database. In the example, the group name public is in quotes because "public" is a reserved keyword in ASE. Changing a user to the public group (of which all users are members) removes the user from whichever other group the user belongs to.

sp_help_group

The sp_helpgroup stored procedure will list information about all groups or a specific group. sp_helpgroup with no parameters will list all groups.

Syntax:

```
sp_helpgroup [group_name]
```

Example:

sp_helpgroup

```
Group Name              Group ID
public                  0
marketing               16384
accounting              16385
```

sp_helpgroup with a group name will list all users in a group.

Example:

sp_helpgroup marketing

```
Group Name      Group ID       Users in Group        Userid
marketing       16384          user1                 5
```

The sysusers Table

As an SA, you don't need to know the contents of all the system tables, but it's a good idea to know where to find this information, and, you'll find over time that the more experienced the DBA or SA you meet, the better they'll know the system tables.

sysusers is the database system table that contains information about users in a database, one row for each user, role, or group added to the database.

- UID 1 is the dbo.
- UID 2 is guest.
- Groups have a UID > 16383.

Example:

```
select * from sysusers
```

Output:

```
suid      uid     gid     name               environ
----      ---     ---     ----------------   -------
16389     16389   16389   replication_role   NULL
-16388    16388   16388   navigator_role     NULL
-16387    16387   16387   sybase_ts_role     NULL
-16386    16386   16386   oper_role          NULL
-16385    16385   16385   sso_role           NULL
-16384    16384   16384   sa_role            NULL
-2        0       0       public             NULL
-1        2       0       guest              NULL
1         1       0       dbo                NULL
```

sysusers and syslogins

You can relate a user back to the login based on the contents of the sysusers table and the syslogins table, joining them on the server user ID of the user in question.

Figure 6-4

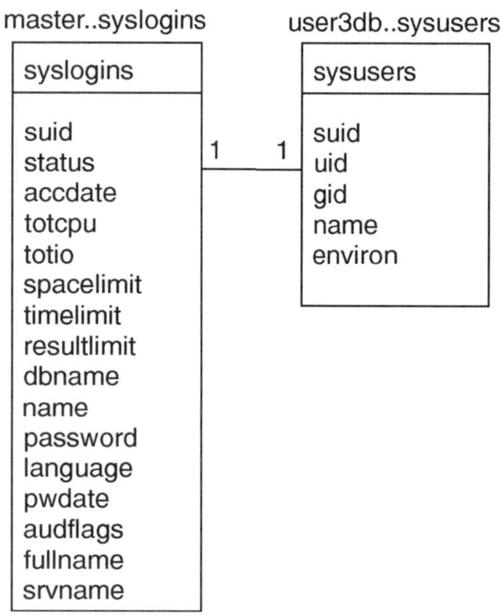

Transporting Databases

Now that we understand what happens in the system tables, we can envision what happens when databases are dumped and loaded from one server to another. Since the user IDs map directly back to the logins, and the logins are server specific, we can guess that the chances that logins match on different servers is negligible (and in fact, from personal experience, trying to keep them matching on multiple servers is an exercise in frustration).

Example:

master..syslogins

```
name            suid
sa              1
fred            75
```

user3db..sysusers

```
name            suid            uid
dbo             1               1
```

user3db..sysalternates

```
asuid           suid
1               75
```

So, if login fred owns the database when it is dumped, who owns the database when it is loaded on a new server? From a practical standpoint, it will be whoever has server user id 75 on the other server. A practical solution is to have the sa, whose server user ID is always 1, own all the databases. If Fred needs dbo access, alias him.

> **TIP:** If this is something you need to do regularly, write scripts to keep the users up to date. Alternatively, dynamically build the scripts with code along these lines:
>
> ```
> select "exec sp_adduser " + name + , " + name + " , "
>   + user_name(group)
>   from sysusers where uid between 3 and 16382
> ```

This will generate code to perform all of the sp_adduser statements for those that exist in the database.

System Built-in Functions

There are a variety of built-in functions that allow you to use select statements to gather information on the server and its objects. Defaults (that is, you do not pass an argument) return current values.

Function	Definition
col_name (obj_id,col_id)	Column name of object
col_length ("objname", "colname")	Length of column
datalength (expression)	Length of the data value
db_id (["db_name"])	Database ID #

Function	Definition
db_name ([db_id])	Database name
curunreservepdgs	Returns the number of free pages in a disk space
host_id ( )	Host process ID #
host_name ( )	Current host computer name
index_col ("objname", index_id, key #)	Indexed column name
isnull (expression, value)	Substitutes the specified value for NULL entries
object_id ("objname")	Database object ID #
object_name (obj_id[, database_id])	Database object name
proc_role	Checks to see if the invoking user possesses the correct role to execute the procedure
rowcnt	Returns the number of rows in a table (estimate)
show_role ( )	Returns the user's current active roles.
suser_id (["login_name"])	Adaptive Server user's ID #
suser_name ([server_user_id])	Adaptive Server user's login name
tsequal	Compares timestamp values
user_id (["name_in_db"])	User's db ID number
user_name ([user_id])	User's db name
used_pgs	Returns the total number of pages used by a table and its clustered index
valid_user	Returns 1 if the specified ID is a valid user or alias in at least one database on this Adaptive Server

Examples:

select user_id ( )

Returns current user ID.

select suser_name (10)

Returns login name of the login whose ID is 10.

select object_name (123456789)

Returns the name of the object specified by the object ID.

This last example is great when you're performing a procedure like sp_lock and want to identify the object that is identified in the sp_lock output.

Command Security

Permission to execute the following commands may be granted by the dbo (you cannot grant permission to grant these commands).

- create default
- create procedure
- create rule
- create table
- create view

Syntax:

```
grant {all | command_list} to user_list
revoke {all | command_list} from user_list
```

NOTES: user_list can be any combination of user names, group names, or roles.

create database can be granted only by a login with the sa_role to a user who has already been added to master.

Examples:

```
grant create rule, create default to jsmith
revoke dump database from mdoe
```

Note that we can grant lists of permissions to lists of users, groups, or roles.

Object Access

Access to the database does not guarantee access to the data. You need permission on the individual database objects to select or modify rows of information in the tables, or to execute a stored procedure.

Object Permissions

The user who creates the object owns it. Not even the database owner can directly modify an object's schema (remember the setuser command).

NOTE: A login with the sa_role can modify an object's schema as this role effectively has a no-limits security access to data and server resources.

The object owner may grant the following permissions:

- select
- insert
- update
- delete

- execute (only applies to stored procedures)
- references

Syntax:

```
grant all | permission_list on object [column_list]
to user_list
[with grant option]
```

Examples:

```
grant exec on check_procedure to public
```

NOTE: User_list maybe a user, role, group, public, or any combination thereof.

Object security is similar to command security, but in addition to granting and revoking, permission to grant permission may be delegated by use of the with grant option.

The optional column_list allows permissions to be granted or revoked not on the entire table, but only on specific columns.

All of the permissions listed here apply to tables except for execute, which applies to stored procedures.

With Grant Option

The with grant option enables the users specified in the user_list to grant the same privileges to other users in the database. with grant option undermines the control an object owner has; other users may grant permissions they hold in conflict with the owner's desired security scheme!

Example:

```
grant exec on check_procedure
to fred with grant option
```

In this example, the user Fred could pass around permission to execute check_procedure to whomever he wishes. Granting permissions to public allows any user that can log in to the server to use the object in question.

NOTE: The with grant option can only be granted to users, not groups or roles.

Revoking Object Access

The revoke command removes permissions. Note that by default, there are no permissions that are not explicitly granted, so if you revoke a permission, there is the presumption that the permission had previously been granted.

Syntax:

```
revoke [grant option for] all | permission_list on
object [column_list] from user_list
[cascade]
```

Example:

```
revoke update on authors (last_name) from mdoe
```

The cascade option is used when revoking the grant option from an individual who had granted access to other users. If grant option for is not specified, the grant option and permissions are revoked from the specified user(s) and any permissions granted by that user to other users are also revoked.

Permissions may be revoked from a single user, or from any other users that user granted permission to, or both. Likewise, a single user may have grant option for revoked without losing the actual object permission.

The combinations of grant option for and cascade can be confusing. It's fairly easy to revoke more or fewer permissions than intended. The default is to revoke a permission and grant option from a user, and from all users that received permission from the revokee.

public is a special group, and refers to anybody who has access to the database.

Column names may be specified in permission lists, so that you may grant or revoke permission on only parts of your table. A user will either have no permissions, permissions granted, or permissions revoked.

Granting Vast Permissions

It is easier to grant vast permission and then limit it.

Example:

```
grant select on employees to public
revoke select on employees (salary) from public
```

Now, everyone may select from employees, as long as the query does not request the salary column. This is easier than granting permission to each column individually.

Example:

```
grant select on customers to public
revoke select on customers from fred
```

Now, everybody may select from customers except fred. This is simpler than granting permissions to other logins individually.

Ownership Chains

What happens when one user owns a procedure that accesses a table owned by another user, and that table has a trigger which updates a second table owned by a third user? It is important to understand how object security works and how the server manages it.

Multiple Owners

Users only have access to objects to which they've been explicitly granted permission.

Figure 6-5

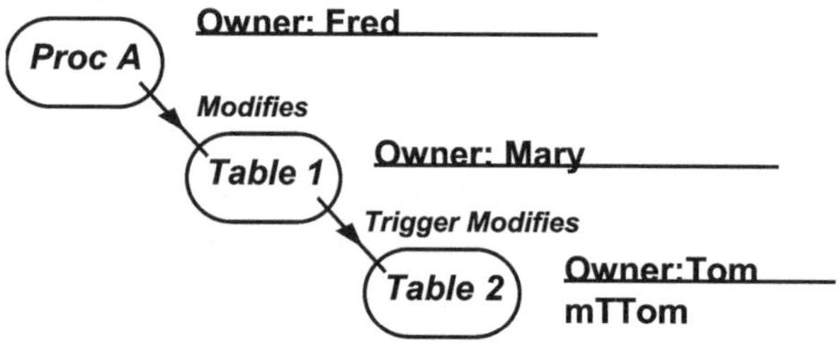

In this example, Fred owns proc A, Mary owns Table 1, and Tom owns Table 2. Fred's proc modifies table1. It has a trigger on it which modifies Table 2.

If Fred runs his own proc, it will fail unless he has explicit permission to access table1. Even then, it will fail unless he also has the appropriate permissions on table2. The same problem occurs if Mary or Tom try to execute the proc. Users need explicit access to the proc, and to the objects that the proc accesses.

Single Owners

If there is only one owner, the server automatically validates as it travels down the ownership chain.

Figure 6-6

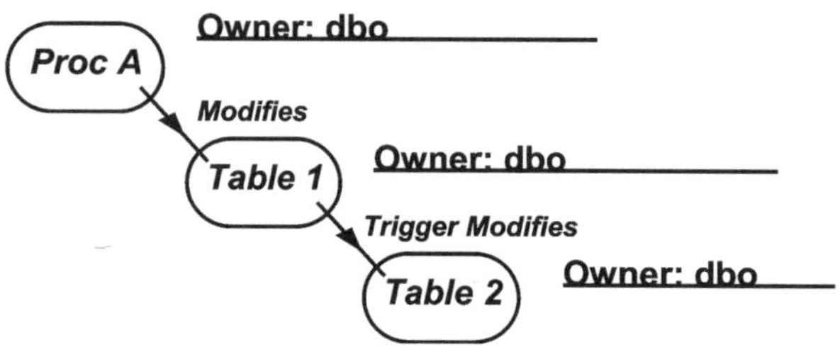

In other words, Adaptive Server automatically validates permissions on dependent objects of the same owner. Therefore, if the dbo grants execute permission on Proc A to user 1, user 1 will be able to modify Table 1 without explicit permission, and the trigger will modify Table 2. This is the usual way of assigning permissions in a production environment.

> **TIP:** Note that this is a great way to force all database access to be through stored procedures. You can grant access to the procedures without granting access to the underlying tables.

Displaying Permissions

The sp_helprotect command will show permissions on an object or for a user/group/role.

Syntax:

```
sp_helprotect [user_name | object_name]
```

Example:

```
sp_helprotect ethel
```

Output:

```
grantor   grantee   type    action         object   column   grantable
-------   -------   -----   ------------   ------   ------   ---------
dbo       ethel     Grant   Create Table            All      FALSE
```

Setuser Command

The dbo can become another user using the setuser command. This allows the dbo to become another user, and assume that user's permissions. This is commonly used to either test permissions or, if someone besides the dbo is the object owner, to change object permissions or remove an object.

Using the setuser command with no username changes the user back to dbo.

Syntax:

```
setuser ['user name']
```

Fine-Grained Access Control (FGAC)

In a new feature for 12.5, object owners can restrict access at a row level by defining access rules and binding those rules to the table. Access to data can be further controlled by setting application contexts and creating login triggers.

This row-level access control enables the database owner or table owner to control the rows in a table that users can access, based on their identification or profile and the privileges the user has from the application level. Adaptive Server enforces row-level access control for all data manipulation languages (DMLs), which prevents users from bypassing the access control to get to the data.

Access Rules

Domain rules allow table owners to control the values that users can enter into a particular column that is using a base data type, or any column that is using a user-defined data type. Rules are enforced during inserts and updates. Adaptive Server Enterprise enables row-level protection through access rules. Access rules are enforced on select, update, and delete operations. Adaptive Server enforces the access rules on all columns that are read in a query, even if the columns are not included in the select list. In other words, for a given query, Adaptive Server enforces the domain rule on the table that is updated and the access rule on the tables that are read.

Using access rules is similar to using views or an ad hoc query with where clauses, and does not cause performance degradation. The query is compiled and optimized after the access rules are attached. Therefore, if there are indexes on the columns that have access rules, the queries may perform better.

Access Rules Using Java Function and Application Contexts

Application developers can write flexible access rules using Java and application contexts. For example, you can write a rule that is hierarchical. If table T contains all the employees' schedules, the president can see all employees' schedules. Individual VPs can see their own schedules and their direct reports' work schedules, but not the president's schedule. Access rules can be bound to user-defined data types as are other types of rules, using sp_addtype. Adaptive Server enforces the access rule on user tables that use these user-defined data types. This relieves the database owner and table owner from the task of binding access rules to columns in their normalized schema.

For example, there can be a user-defined data type named username for which the base type is varchar(30). The database owner or table owner can create an access rule and bind it to username. The owners can then use username in any tables that their application will use. Adaptive Server enforces the access rule on the tables that have columns of the username data type.

Syntax for Access Rules

The access parameter is used in the create rule syntax to allow creation of access rules. For example, a table owner creates and populates table T (username char(30), title char(20), classified_data char(1024)) with the following:

AA, "Administrative Assistant","Memo to President"
AA, "Administrative Assistant","Tracking Stock Movements"
VP1, "Vice President", "Meeting Schedule"
VP2, "Vice President", "Meeting Schedule"

The table owner creates a default and a domain rule on the username column. The domain rule ensures that the column is updated with correct values. If the default and domain rules are not created, there is a potential security problem in which the user can insert a row into the table with arbitrary data that will not be qualified by the access rule.

The table owner then creates an access rule and binds it to the username column using sp_bindrule:

```
create default uname_default
as suser_name()
go
sp_bindefault uname_default, "T.username"
go
*/
create accessrule uname_acc_rule
as @username = suser_name()
go
sp_bindrule uname_acc_rule, "T.username"
go
```

A user issues the following query:

```
select * from T
```

Adaptive Server processes the access rule that is bound to the username column on T and attaches it to the query tree. The tree is then optimized and an execution plan is generated and executed as if the user had executed the query with the filter clause given in the access rule. In other words, Adaptive Server attaches the access rule and executes the query as:

```
select * from T where T.username = suser_name().
```

The result of an Administrative Assistant executing the select query is:

AA, "Administrative Assistant","Memo to President"

AA, "Administrative Assistant","Tracking Stock Movements"

The where T.username = suser_name() part of the query is enforced by the server. The user cannot bypass the access rule.

Extended Access Rule Syntax

Two kinds of access rules can be created: the AND access rule and the OR access rule. The access rule can be bound to a column, username, or a user-defined data type. Multiple access rules can be bound to the different columns of a table or different data types of a table. When the table is accessed, several access rules go into effect and those access rules interact with each other. OR access rules are used together and if any one of the OR access rules on the table is satisfied, the row can be accessed. AND access rule are used together and only if all of the AND access rules are satisfied can the row can be accessed.

NOTE: If there is only one access rule on a row of the table and it is an OR access rule, it behaves as an AND access rule.

To create an access rule:

```
create rule [ [ and | or ] access]
[owner.]rule_name
as condition_expression
```

To bind data types:

```
sp_bindrule rule_name, data type -
```

To bind to columns:

```
sp_bindrule rule_name, column
```

To unbind only accessrule if it exists:

```
sp_unbindrule data type, null, "accessrule"
```

or:

```
sp_unbindrule column, null, "accessrule"
```

To unbind both accessrule and domain_rule if they exist:

```
sp_unbindrule data type, null, "all"
```

or

```
sp_unbindrule column, null, "all"
```

To unbindrule only accessrule for futureonly if it exists:

```
sp_unbindrule data type, futureonly, "accessrule"
```

To unbindrule both accessrule and domain rule for futureonly if it exists:

```
sp_unbindrule data type, futureonly, "all"
drop rule rule_name
```

Example:

```
create access rule empid1_access
as @empid = 1
create access rule deptno1_access
as @deptid =2
/*
** create OR ACCESS rule by
** "create or access rule rule_name as ..."
*/
create or access rule name1_access
as @name = "smith"
create or access rule phone_access
as @phone ="9999"
create table testtab1 (empno int, deptno int,name char(10), phone char(4))
/* Bound access rule to the columns */
sp_bindrule empid1_access, "testtab1.empno"
Rule bound to table column.
(return status = 0)
sp_bindrule deptno1_access,"testtab1.deptno"
Rule bound to table column.
(return status = 0)
sp_bindrule name1_access,"testtab1.name"
Rule bound to table column.
(return status = 0)
sp_bindrule phone_access,"testtab1.phone"
Rule bound to table column.
(return status = 0)
insert testtab1 values (1,1,"smith","3245")
(1 row affected)
insert testtab1 values(2,1,"jones","0283")
(1 row affected)
insert testtab1 values(1,2,"smith","8282")
(1 row affected)
insert testtab1 values(2,2,"smith","9999")
(1 row affected)
insert testtab1 values(3,2,"smith","8888")
(1 row affected)
insert testtab1 values(1,2,"jones","9999")
```

```
(1 row affected)
insert testtab1 values(2,3,"jones","9999")
(1 row affected)
/** return rows when empno = 1 and deptno = 2
* and ( name = "smith" or phone = "9999" )
*/
select * from testtab1
empno    deptno   name     phone
-----    ------   -----    -----
1        2        smith    8282
1        2        jones    9999
(2 rows affected)
/* unbound accessrule from specific column */
sp_unbindrule "testtab1.empno",NULL,"accessrule"
Rule unbound from table column.
(return status = 0)
/** return rows when deptno = 2 and ( name = "smith"
* or phone = "9999" )
*/
select * from testtab1
empno    deptno   name     phone
-----    ------   -----    -----
1        2        smith    8282
2        2        smith    9999
3        2        smith    8888
1        2        jones    9999
(4 rows affected)
/* unbound all rules from specific column */
sp_unbindrule "testtab1.deptno",NULL,"all"
Rule unbound from table column.
(return status = 0)
/* return the rows when name = "smith" or phone = "9999" */
select * from testtab1
empno    deptno   name     phone
-----    ------   -----    -----
1        1        smith    3245
1        2        smith    8282
2        2        smith    9999
3        2        smith    8888
1        2        jones    9999
2        3        jones    9999
(6 rows affected)
```

Access Rules and the alter table Command

When the table owner uses the alter table command, Adaptive Server disables access rules during the execution of the command and enables them upon completion of the command. The access rules are disabled to avoid filtering of the table data during the alter table command.

Access Rules and bcp

Adaptive Server enforces access rules when data is copied out of a table using the bulk copy utility (bcp). Adaptive Server cannot disable access rules as with alter table, because bcp can be used by any user who has select permission on the table.

For security purposes, the database owner should lock the table exclusively and disable access rules during bulk copy out. The lock disables access to other users while the access rules are disabled. The database owner should enable the access rules and unlock the table after the data has been copied.

NOTE: If access rules are enabled, bcp out only retrieves as much data as the user who is running bcp has permissions on. If the entire table is to be copied, you must lock the table, drop the access rules, bcp out the data, and then reapply the access rules and unlock the table.

The Set Proxy Command

Other users can impersonate other logins with the set proxy command or set session authorization command. SSO must first explicitly grant the commands to a user list. The set proxy and set session authorization commands behave identically; set session authorization is the ANSI standard command name. Users that have been granted proxy privileges can then use the set commands.

You can only grant set proxy to logins that are valid users in the master database.

Syntax:

```
Grant set proxy to userlist
Grant set session authorization to userlist
```

The syntax for the set proxy command is as follows:

```
set proxy login_name
set session authorization login_name
```

Login_name is any valid login. Your suser_name() becomes the login_name. Your user_name() becomes the login_name's user name in the database. If a login is granted set proxy permissions, he can become any login, including the systems administrator!

The System Roles

There are some predefined server roles, shown in the following table.

Role	Definition
sa_role	performs system administration
sso_role	performs security administration
oper_role	Performs operator functions
replication_role	Used by replication processes
navigator_role	Used by navigation server

Role	Definition
sybase_ts_role	Used to perform undocumented maintenance tasks
dtm_tm_role	Used in externally-coordinated XA transactions
ha_role	controls High Availability Companion Server actions

You probably will not grant replication_role or navigator_role to a login. I will often give myself the sybase_ts_role when I go into a new shop, as it allows you to perform a variety of (officially) undocumented dbcc tasks. For example, use dbcc help (command) to get the syntax for other undocumented dbcc commands. The dtm_tm_role and ha_role will not be necessary unless you are performing distributed transactions, or have separately licensed the HA feature for warm standby.

Initially, the SA login has the SA, SSO, and OPER roles. These may be assigned to other users, and the sa login subsequently locked.

System Role Definitions

The sp_role command can be used to grant roles to and revoke roles from logins (though grant and revoke are recommended).

Syntax:

```
sp_role {"grant" | "revoke"} , role_name,   login_name
```

Example:

```
sp_role "grant", sa_role, jgarbus
```

The SSO and OPER roles are granted by the SSO; the SA role is granted by the SA. The last remaining SA and SSO roles cannot be revoked. Roles granted will take effect the next time the user logs in, or the user can invoke it immediately using the set role command. You cannot revoke a role from a login when it is currently logged in.

Alternately, you may use the same grant and revoke commands discussed previously to assign or remove roles; the chief advantage to the grant/revoke is that you may use lists of roles and logins.

Syntax:

```
grant role role_name [, role_name … ] to grantee [, grantee …]
revoke role role_name [, role_name … ] from grantee [, grantee …]
```

Example:

```
grant role sa_role, sso_role to jgarbus, gtyrrell, achang
revoke  role sa_role, sso_role, oper_role from blefevre
```

syslogins, sysloginroles, and syssrvroles

Figure 6-7

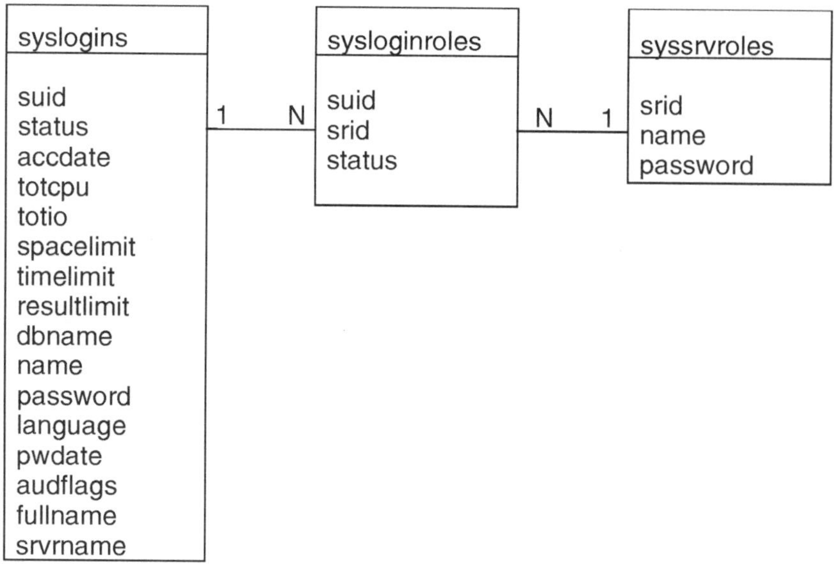

Roles (and new roles that you create) are added to the syssrvroles table. Since a login may have many roles, sysloginroles resolves the many-to-many relationship, and manages the instances of roles for each login.

Figure 6-8

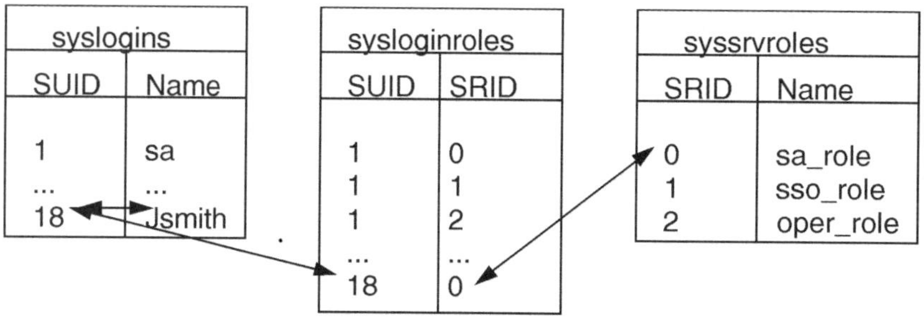

Here you can see the relationship; the sa login, which has a server user ID of 1, is assigned the sa_role, sso_role, and oper_role. Jsmith, who has a SUID of 18, also has the sa_role.

System Role Functions

Adaptive Server provides two built-in functions to see what roles a user has:

show_role()	list a login's roles
proc_role()	used to see if a login has a specific role

Example:

```
select show_role()
```

Lists all of the roles that are currently enabled for a login.

Example:

```
if (proc_role("sa_role") = 1)
 print "The role is SA"
```

This will print the message "The role is SA" if the sa_role is enabled for the login.

These can be used to display current roles, or to verify that procedures are executed only by those who have specific roles.

Turning System Roles Off

If you have specific roles, you may disable them for a session by using a set statement; this might be useful in a testing environment. If you have your own user ID and wish to test with it (rather than, say, sa) this is a good way to accomplish that without having to have two separate logins.

Syntax:

```
set role "role_name" {on | off}
```

This enables or disables a role immediately.

User-Defined Roles

In addition to the system-defined roles, ASE allows you to define your own roles. This effectively gives the SSO the ability to create groups at the server level. For those of you who are interested, this is an ANSI SQL 3 standard feature.

Permissions granted to a role take precedence over permissions granted to a user or group.

Planning User-Defined Roles

In order to facilitate user-defined roles, it is important to consider:

- The roles you want to create
- The responsibilities for each role
- The position of each in the role hierarchy
- Which roles in the hierarchy will be mutually exclusive
- Whether such exclusivity will be at the membership level or activation level

Creating Roles

Roles are created with the create role statement by users in the master database with the sso_role.

Syntax:

```
create role role_name [with passwd "password"]
```

Example:

```
create role clerk_rl
```

role_name is the server-wide name of the role. The only real restriction right now is that login names and role names must be mutually exclusive.

Optionally you can assign a password which must be supplied to enable the role. Note that the same password will be used by every login that holds the role; it's not meant to be secret, it's only intended to keep a login from automatically (or accidentally) enabling a role.

A server may contain up to 1,024 roles. The first 32 roles are set aside for system roles, leaving (of course) 992 user-defined roles.

Dropping Roles

User-defined roles can be dropped with the drop role command by a login with the sso_role who is in the master database. You cannot drop system roles.

Syntax:

```
drop role role_name [with override]
```

If the role has permissions assigned, you must use with override to drop the role or revoke all permissions first.

You need not drop memberships before dropping a role. Dropping a role automatically removes any user's membership in that role, regardless of whether you use the with override option.

Mutually Exclusive Roles

You can enforce separation of duties by forcing the roles to be mutually exclusive. Think of this as declarative referential integrity for roles.

You can configure this separation so that two roles cannot be active at the same time (activation), or so that two roles can not be assigned to the same login (membership).

Exclusive roles are assigned using the alter role command:

Syntax:

```
alter role role_name1 {add | drop} exclusive {membership | activation}
role_name2
```

If you configure roles to be membership exclusive and the roles are both already assigned to a login or role, alter role command will fail. If you configure roles to be activation exclusive and a login has both roles active, the login will receive an error message.

Assigning Passwords to Roles

You can force additional passwords to be role specific. Typically, this is used only when a login comes through an application. The application user would have to supply the password to enable the role. This also gives you the ability to, for example, disable a role temporarily by changing its password. You can assign a role a password at role creation time with the create role statement, or add or remove one afterwards, with the alter role statement.

To create a role with a password, use:

```
create role hr_rl with passwd 'HumanResources'
```

Above, we are creating a role called hr_rl which will have HumanResources (case-sensitive passwords) as a password.

The following is the syntax for adding and removing passwords:

```
alter role role_name add passwd 'password'
alter role role_name drop passwd
```

Example:

```
alter role test_rl add passwd 'mypassword'
alter role test_rl drop passwd
```

Passwords may be subject to minimum length, failed attempt, expiration interval, and required digit limitations just as logins are. The encrypted password is stored in syssrvroles.

WARNING: If a role is altered to have a limitation on failed attempts, and a login attempts to enable the role and fails the required number of times, the role is locked for all holders of the role. If the role in question were sa_role or oper_role, the consequences could be disastrous. Likewise, while you cannot explicitly lock the last unlocked login with sa_role or sso_role, it is possible for failed login attempts to indirectly lock that login.

In order to resolve this, ASE provides a parameter for the runserverfile that will allow the unlocking of a single login or role at startup time. The parameter is –u, and is followed by the name of a login or role that is presently locked.

Assigning Roles to Users

User-defined roles may be assigned to logins with the grant statement, just like system roles. Typically, you'll do this after setting up whatever hierarchy you've chosen for the roles. In other words, the grantee can be a role or a login.

If the grantee has not been granted the role being revoked, an error will be generated. Remember, creating, granting, and revoking roles is an SSO-only task.

Role Hierarchy

A role hierarchy is implemented when a role is granted to another role. It can be indirectly included in a hierarchy twice. Hierarchies cannot be recursive.

For example, you can grant both support_role and developer_role to su_role.

```
create role support_role
create role developer_role
create role su_role
grant support_role, developer_role to su_role
```

Now, you have a super user role (su_role) which contains all permissions assigned to both developers and support personnel.

Activating Roles

A role may be activated at the hierarchy level at which it is granted. They are enabled or disabled with the set role command.

Syntax:

```
set role role_name {on|off}
```

If the role has a password, you must supply the password when enabling a role:

```
set role role_name with passwd 'password' on
```

Default Roles for Logins

By default, user-defined roles assigned to a user are not enabled at connection time. You can enable the roles at login time by using the sp_modifylogin stored procedure. The only exception is that if there is a password on the role, it may not be automatically enabled at login time.

Syntax:

```
sp_modifylogin login, "add default role", role_name
sp_modifylogin login, "drop default role", role_name
```

Granting Permissions to Roles

Set permissions for roles using the normal grant and revoke statements. When setting up permissions with the grant/revoke commands, the sysusers table is checked to see if the name exists. If it does not, the master..syssrvroles is checked to see if the name is a a role that has no current permissions in the database. If it is a role, the role gets added to sysroles and sysusers. Permissions on the role take precedence over permissions assigned to users or groups.

Displaying Information about Roles

Adaptive Server provides functions and system procedures to display information about roles.

Function/System Procedure	Explanation
mut_excl_role('role1', 'role2')	[membership | activation] returns 1 if the exclusive relationship has been configured
proc_role('role')	Used in a stored procedure to see if the login has been assigned the role
role_id('role_name')	A function that returns the server id of the role
role_name(role_id)	A function that returns the server of the role
role_contain('role1', 'role2')	Returns 1 if role1's hierarchy contains role2
show_role()	Shows what system roles are active
sp_displayroles	Displays role hierarchy
sp_activerole	Displays the active roles for the current login
sp_displaylogin	Displays roles assigned to a login
sp_helprotect	Displays permissions granted to a role

sp_displayroles

The sp_displayroles stored procedure displays roles assigned to a login or to a role.

Syntax:

```
sp_displayroles [grantee_name [,{expand_up | expand_down}]]
```

grantee_name can specify a login or role to display information.

expand_down shows all the roles that the grantee has been granted.

expand_up shows the hierarchy of the roles that have been granted the grantee.

By default the current login's roles are expanded up. When expanding down, a role can show up multiple times if it is in the hierarchy multiple times.

Example:

sp_displayroles test

```
go
Role Name
---------
su_role
```

sp_displayrole test, expand_down

```
go
Role Name       Parent Role Name        Level
---------       ----------------        -----
su_role         NULL                    1

Role Name       Parent Role Name        Level
---------       ----------------        -----
sa_role         su_role                 2
dba_role        su_role                 2
dev_role        su_role                 2
tech_role       su_role                 2
dba_role        dev_role                3
dba_role        tech_role               3
```

sp_activeroles

Similar to sp_display roles, the sp_activeroles stored procedure only shows the active roles for the current login. Again, by default, the procedure performs an "expand up" to show all active roles. The expand_down parameter will cause it to display the hierarchy for all active roles.

Syntax:

```
sp_activeroles [expand_down]
```

sp_helprotect

The sp_helprotect stored procedure shows all permissions assigned to a login or on a table.

Syntax:

```
sp_helprotect [name [, username [, "grant"
[,"none"|"granted"|"enabled"|role_name]]]]
```

Parameter	Explanation
Name	Table, view, stored procedure to check permission on
Username	User name to check against
Grant	Display privileged granted with grant option
None	Do not use roles in checking procedure
Granted	Check roles granted to the username when checking permission
Enabled	Checks roles enabled to the username, when checking permissions
Role_name	Check an individual role for permissions

sp_displaylogin

The sp_displaylogin stored procedure will also display roles granted to a user:

Example:

sp_displaylogin test

```
Suid: 3
Loginame: test
Fullname:
Default Database: master
Default Language:
Configured Authorization:
        su_role (default OFF)
Locked: NO
Date of Last Password Change: Feb 13 1998  9:04PM
```

sp_configure

You use the sp_configure stored procedure to set the "max roles enabled per user" configuration parameter to the maximum number of roles that can be enabled by one user.

Example:

```
Exec sp_configure "Max roles enabled per user", 30
The default is 20. Valid values are between 10 and 127.
```

Integrated Security Overview

Adaptive Server lets you integrate ASE security with other security packages. On NT you can integrate with NT security; on UNIX platforms you can use OSF/DCE and CyberSafe Kerberos.

Use of integrated security varies with the platform and security service, but in general, the SSO must configure a mapping where logins outside ASE are associated to ASE logins. Additionally, integrated security allows all network traffic to be encrypted, and a message integrity schema can be set up to guarantee messages have not been tampered with.

Summary

Understand ASE security before you start implementing it.

There are several layers of security, from the operating system down to the data columns themselves.

If your users are going to be doing most of their work in multiple databases, consider server roles instead.

Chapter 7

Auditing

This chapter on auditing for Sybase ASE 12.5 will answer the following questions:

- What is auditing?
- Why use auditing?
- How do I set up auditing?
- What are some tips for successful auditing?
- How do I keep the audit system functioning?
- What can I audit?
- What are the components of the auditing system?

Auditing Overview

Auditing has been part of ASE since Version 10 was released. It has since been revised and refined in recent versions, receiving the most significant revision in Version 11.5. Even though auditing has changed through the releases, the main purpose of auditing remains the same: to provide accountability. Additionally, auditing can be used to help administer and secure ASE, protect data integrity, and answer many performance questions. In practice, auditing will prove to be a very helpful tool for the productive SA.

If you are considering using auditing, or are not familiar with the ASE auditing process, ponder the following questions and scenarios:

- What objects are being accessed in the database?
- How long are users staying connected to the database?
- How is the data being manipulated? What DML is being issued against the database? Are users issuing mostly selects as they claim, or are they issuing inserts, updates, or deletes?
- Is there someone trying to gain unauthorized access to the database server?
- A significant amount of data is missing in a table, and no one is admitting to deleting it. Did someone delete or truncate the data?
- The user is submitting ad hoc query requests to the server through a report generator and the results are taking forever to return. Since the user is using a GUI, we can't see the SQL. What SQL is actually being passed to the server?

- The human resource department is planning to lay off employees. Your manager is concerned that a particular employee might try to sabotage the system. How can we monitor this employee's activity?
- The application developers say they are only accessing the database with stored procedures, but unexpected changes are happening to the data. What is the application doing?

All of the above questions can be answered using the audit system. Both historical and point-in-time analysis questions can be answered with the auditing system.

This chapter will answer the above questions by covering all aspects of the auditing system. First you need to know the general uses of the auditing system. Auditing is generally used for:

- Securing Adaptive Server
- Monitoring logins
- Monitoring access to databases or objects
- Gathering usage information
- Debugging the application

Installation of Auditing

NOTE: Auditing is not required to be installed during the initial installation of ASE. Be aware this might not be good practice; you do not want to be forced to schedule downtime on a 24x7x365 production installation of ASE to enable auditing.

Installation of auditing in Sybase ASE can be accomplished by two methods: with installsecurity or with auditinit. Since the *System Administration Guide* of the documentation set provides detailed information on the installation steps involved, this chapter will focus on an overview of the installation, along with tips and recommendations for the audit system.

The auditinit method of audit installation invokes a menu-driven question and answer session to guide you through the configuration and installation of auditing.

The installsecurity method of audit installation requires more manual intervention. The installsecurity script (instsecu on NT) is stored in the $SYBASE/$SYBASE_ASE/scripts directory, but before running the script, the SA needs to perform some pre-installation tasks:

- Determine the size of the audit tables.
- Decide on using single-table or multi-table auditing. It is recommended to use multi-table for reasons outlined later in this chapter.
- Use of raw devices or file systems for the auditing database.
- Create additional devices for each table in the audit trail (if using multi-table auditing).
- Creation of the auditing database, sybsecurity.

After completion of the pre-installation tasks, use isql (or any query editor):

```
isql -Usa -Ppassword -Sserver_name -i installsecurity
```

After executing the script, you will have one table, sysaudits_01, created on its own segment, aud_seg_01. Shutting down and restarting the server will permit auditing, but it is recommended that additional audit tables be created on their own physical devices.

To enable auditing, use the sp_configure system stored procedure. Since the default configuration for auditing is off (disabled), the configuration value is 0. Auditing is either disabled or enabled for the entire server.

```
/*** enable auditing ***/
sp_configure "auditing", 1

/*** disable auditing ***/
sp_configure "auditing", 0
```

NOTE: Enabling auditing as a configuration parameter takes the place of the "sp_auditoption" stored procedure available in pre-11.5 releases of ASE.

The Sybsecurity Database and Tables

Regardless of the method of audit installation used, a common component will always be the sybsecurity database. The sybsecurity database manages auditing, and consists of several objects:

- The sybsecurity tables (sysaudits_01 – sysaudits_08)
- The sysauditoptions table
- Auditing stored procedures
- The audit queue
- All database-level system tables present in the model database

When installing the sybsecurity database, it is recommended you place the database and log on their own devices. It is further recommended you place each sysaudit_0x table on its own device, if possible. Setting up the audit database in this manner, along with thresholds, will allow for the audit data to be written to the sysaudit_0x tables in a continuous series when the present audit table reaches the threshold value. When sybsecurity is set up for single-table auditing, the administrator is required to pause auditing to archive audit records from the audit table when the device fills up. Setting up the audit database with at least two sysaudit tables on their own devices will help to prevent the loss of audit information.

NOTE: Users can create objects within the sybsecurity database, but this is not recommended. Additional user objects that are placed in the sybsecurity database interfere with the space management, and will impact the ease of administration of the database.

The sysauditoptions table is created in the sybsecurity database upon setup; it contains a single row for each server-wide audit option, along with the current option setting. Like other system tables, changes to sysauditoptions are made by calling a stored procedure (in this case, sp_audit). Unlike most configurational routines, auditing is primarily the province of the System Security Officer, not the SA. The sysauditoptions table is outlined in the following table:

Name	Data Type	Description
num	smallint	Server-wide audit option number.
val	smallint	Current setting, initially 0, or off. Values: 0 = off 1 = pass 2 = fail 3 = on
minval	smallint	Minimum valid value for this option.
maxval	smallint	Maximum valid value for this option.
name	varchar(30)	Name of option.
sval	varchar(30)	String equivalent of the current value: for example, "on", "off", "nonfatal".
comment	varchar(255)	Description of the option.

At installation time, this table already contains one entry for each server-wide audit option setting (all options are set to "off" by default). This table can be queried directly, or you can use the sp_displayaudit stored procedure to view the server-wide option settings.

Below is an example of setting server-wide audit options (sp_audit requires the sso_role to execute). The first command will enable auditing of all dbcc commands on any object, by all users, in all databases; the second command will audit all access attempts of the inventory database; the final command enables auditing of all commands issued for the login BTaylor. Since the following commands are global options, the SSO can reside in any database to activate the audit option.

```
sp_audit "dbcc", "all", "all", "on"
go
sp_audit "dbaccess", "all", "inventory", "on"
go
sp_audit "cmdtext", "all", "BTaylor", "on"
go
```

The following audit commands are database specific; they enable the auditing of specific objects in the database. The SSO must be in the database where the objects are stored.

```
use inventory
go
sp_audit "delete", "all", "parts", "on"
go
sp_audit "exec_procedure", "all", "bill_customer", "on"
go
```

Issuing the sp_displayaudit stored procedure, as shown below, will verify the global and database options that are turned on, when issued from the inventory database. Notice the last section of this output corresponds with entries in the sysauditoptions table.

```
sp_displayaudit
go

Procedure/Trigger    Audit Option      Value    Database
-----------------    --------------    -----    --------
dbo.bill_customer    exec_procedure    on       inventory

(1 row affected)
No databases currently have default sproc/trigger auditing enabled.

Table/View           Audit Option      Value    Database
----------           ------------      -----    ---------
dbo.parts            delete            on       inventory

(1 row affected)

Database Name        Audit Option      Value
-------------        ------------      -----
inventory            dbaccess          on

(1 row affected)
No databases currently have default table/view auditing enabled.

Login Name           Audit Option      Value
----------           ------------      -----
ASmith               cmdtext           on
BTaylor              cmdtext           on
CKing                cmdtext           on
DMacey               cmdtext           on
FDuvall              cmdtext           on
GHunt                cmdtext           on
IMiller              cmdtext           on
KWood                cmdtext           on
LOrdonez             cmdtext           on
MJohnson             cmdtext           on
NChicollo            cmdtext           on
SDavanzo             cmdtext           on
WBrown               cmdtext           on

(1 row affected)
No databases currently have auditing enabled.

Option Name          Value
adhoc                off
dbcc                 on
disk                 off
dtm_tm_role          off
errors               off
login                off
logout               off
navigator_role       off
oper_role            off
replication_role     off
```

```
rpc                 off
sa_role             off
security            off
sso_role            off
```

Sybsecurity Transaction Log

When setting up the sybsecurity database, the transaction log should be set up on a separate physical device. When the sybsecurity database is installed, the truncate log on checkpoint option is enabled by default; it is permissible to turn this database option to off with the sp_dboption procedure.

Leaving the database set to automatically truncate the transaction log on a checkpoint will eliminate the need to manage the transaction log. If this feature is disabled, you will need to add threshold management to the logsegment of the database. See Chapter 6, "Logging and Recovery," for a complete discussion of thresholds.

One difference does exist between the transaction log of sybsecurity and other databases. The abort transaction when log full option is disabled upon installation, and cannot be enabled. If you attempt to enable the option, ASE will return a message indicating the option cannot be set to true for the sybsecurity database. Since this option is always disabled, any transaction that is active when the log fills will go into a suspended state until free space is made available in the transaction log.

Sybsecurity Stored Procedures

There are two additional stored procedures added to the server upon the installation of auditing which, like sp_audit and sp_displayaudit, require the SSO role to execute. The following table summarizes the auditing stored procedures:

Procedure Name	Function
sp_audit	Enables or disables all auditing options
sp_displayaudit	Displays the auditing options enabled
sp_addauditrecord	Writes a user record to the audit trail
sp_addaudittable	Adds a sysaudits_0x table to the audit system

sp_audit

The sp_audit stored procedure is used to set the auditing options. This is the only system procedure required to establish the events to be audited. See the following table for a complete listing of sp_audit parameters.

The syntax for sp_audit is:

```
sp_audit option, login_name, object_name [,setting]
```

Parameter	Allowed Values
Option	adhoc, all, alter, bcp, bind, cmdtext, create, dbaccess, dbcc, delete, disk, drop, dump, errors, exec_procedure, exec_trigger, func_dbaccess, func_obj_access, grant, insert, install, load, login, logout, reference, remove, revoke, rpc, security, select, setuser, table_access, truncate, unbind, update, view_access
login_name	all, server_login_name, server_role_name
object_name	all, default (table, view, procedure, trigger), object_name
setting	off, on, pass, fail

The following are a few examples of enabling auditing using sp_audit. A complete listing of the auditable events can be found in the *Reference Manual* of the documentation set.

To enable the audit of update on the authors table:

```
sp_audit "update", "all", "authors", "on"
```

To turn off the audit of update actions on the authors table:

```
sp_audit "update", "all", "authors", "off"
```

To audit all attempts to use the drop command in the accounting database:

```
sp_audit "drop", "all", "accounting", "on"
```

To audit all failed attempts to delete from the *customer* table by all logins:

```
sp_audit "delete", "all", "customer", "fail"
```

To audit any executions of the "sp_bill_customer" stored procedure:

```
sp_audit "exec_procedure", "all", "sp_bill_customer","on"
```

To audit all successful inserts to the *invoice* table by any login:

```
sp_audit "insert", "all", "invoice", "pass"
```

sp_displayaudit

Upon execution, the sp_displayaudit stored procedure displays the auditing options enabled.

The syntax for sp_displayaudit is:

```
sp_displayaudit ["procedure" | "object" | "login" | "database" | "global" |
"default_object" | "default_procedure" [, "name"]]
```

The sp_displayaudit procedure, when called by itself, will list all audit options that are enabled server wide. Passing an object type from the allowed list of procedure, object, login, database, global, default_object, and default_procedure will list all the audit options enabled for that audit type.

Execute sp_displayaudit to see what procedures have auditing enabled:

```
sp_displayaudit "procedure"
go

Procedure/Trigger    Audit Option      Value    Database
-----------------    --------------    -----    --------------
dbo.sp_lock          exec_procedure    on       sybsystemprocs
dbo.sp_who           exec_procedure    on       sybsystemprocs

(1 row affected)
(return status = 0)
```

According to the output of sp_displayaudit, the sp_lock and sp_who stored procedures in the sybsystemprocs database are presently being audited for execution.

If the DBA needs to target the audit setting for only the sp_who stored procedure, execute sp_displayaudit as follows:

```
sp_displayaudit "procedure", "sp_who"
go
Procedure/Trigger    Audit Option      Value    Database
-----------------    --------------    -----    --------------
dbo.sp_who           exec_procedure    on       sybsystemprocs

(1 row affected)
(return status = 0)
```

sp_addauditrecord

The sp_addauditrecord stored procedure is executed to write a user-defined entry (comment) to the audit trail. Only users with the SSO role can enter comments into the audit trail, unless the SSO enables ad hoc auditing with the sp_audit procedure. Executing the sp_displayaudit stored procedure with the argument "global" passed as the first parameter will verify the status of the ad hoc global audit setting.

NOTE: In practice, it is advisable not to enable users to enter records into the audit trail. If this is permitted, you risk compromising the most important objective of auditing: accountability.

Syntax:

```
sp_addauditrecord [text] [, db_name] [, obj name]
[, owner_name] [, dbid] [, objid]
```

Option	Description and Mapping
text	Text of the message inserted to the audit trail. Maps to the extrainfo column of the sysaudits_0x table.
db_name	Name of the database. Maps to the database name in sysaudits table.
obj_name	Name of the object referenced in the audit record. Maps to the object name column of the audit table.
owner_name	Owner of the referenced object. Maps to objowner column in sysaudits.
dbid	Database ID number. Maps to dbid column in sysaudits table.
objid	Object ID number of the obj_name. Maps to the objid column in sysaudits.

The following adds a message to the audit trail to indicate the accounting database was down for four hours due to an upgrade, and no audit records should be expected for this time period.

```
sp_addauditrecord "Database was unavailable on 5/4/2001 due to upgrade,
audit records will not exist from 1:00am to 5:00am",
"accounting","","dbo",8
```

sp_addaudittable

The sp_addaudittable stored procedure is executed by the SSO to add another audit table to the audit trail. The audit table added follows the same table naming convention as the audit table(s) added in the initial installation (sysaudits_0x).

Syntax:

```
sp_addaudittable devname
```

To add another audit table to the audit trail on the audit_dev2 device, execute as:

```
sp_addaudittable audit_dev2
```

Use the devname parameter to specify the device on which the audit table should be placed. Executing sp_addaudittable with the parameter of default will cause the new audit table to be placed on the same device as the sybsecurity database.

> **NOTE:** Before adding another sysaudits_0x table to the audit trail, be sure you have enabled the sp_thresholdaction stored procedure on that segment. You do not want to accidentally let the new sysaudits table fill.

The Audit Queue

ASE collects audit records, but does not store these records directly into the sysaudit tables. Auditing records are temporarily stored in the audit queue, which will hold auditing records until they are flushed to disk. Unfortunately, if there is a system crash, any records in the audit queue will be lost since it is memory resident. To help reduce the number of records that could be lost as a result of system crash, the DBA can adjust the size of the audit queue with sp_configure.

NOTE: In previous releases of ASE, the server needed to be rebooted to activate the changes made with sp_configure to the audit queue size; ASE 12.5 permits dynamically changing the audit queue size.

When attempting to configure the size of the audit queue, the DBA should consider the trade-offs. Adjusting the audit queue to be too large could result in losing more audit records in the event of a system crash. Adjusting the audit queue to be too small can negatively impact system performance, since the audit queue will repeatedly fill up. When the audit queue is full, a process that has generated an audit record will sleep until space becomes available within the audit queue.

Therefore, it is your job as the SSO to decide upon the correct size of the audit queue. By default, the audit queue is set to 100 records. In order to properly set the size of the audit queue, you might want to start small and attempt to determine if the audit process is a bottleneck from the frequent flushing of the audit queue. Keep increasing until the performance reaches an acceptable level while balancing against the number of records lost in event of system failure. Generally, if security is your main concern, keep the audit queue smaller; if performance is your main concern, set the audit queue larger.

The syntax for altering the size of the audit queue:

```
sp_configure 'audit queue size', <num_of_audit_records>
```

An example of configuring the audit queue to store 20 audit records:

```
sp_configure 'audit queue size', 20
```

Audit Database Storage Requirements

The number of audit records that can be kept in the sysaudits tables is limited by the size of the sybsecurity database. Audit records will continue to fill the sysaudits tables until the SSO disables auditing; each audit record requires between 32 and 424 bytes. As you can expect, the higher the amount of activity on your system, combined with the number of events being audited, the faster the sybsecurity database will fill.

To help size the database, the DBA needs to know the number of audit records that will be generated, the size of the audit records, and the amount of time until audit records will be purged or archived from the database. The general formula is:

```
sybsecurity size = Audit record size * number of audit records * time in DB
for the recorded event
```

Of course, in order to correctly size the database, you need to take a sample of the auditing activity. However, this is impossible before you set up the database and install auditing. One recommendation would be to set up an auditing database, save all configuration settings in script format, take several samples of audit activity, then alter the size of the database to reflect your volume of auditing information and time between truncation or archiving.

Be careful not to configure the database too large for a system without much activity, because you cannot easily shrink a database! If you find that the database size is too large, and you need to allocate the devices associated with your sybsecurity database to other resources, then make sure to follow the above recommendation and save all audit configuration settings to a script before dropping the database and rebuilding.

The volume of activity in your audit database can be determined by following the steps outlined below:

1. Install Auditing.
2. Configure audit options.
3. If you already have run an audit, ensure that the audit table(s) have zero records by truncating the table(s), or make note of the space already used.
4. Enable audit options with sp_audit.
5. Enable auditing for selected time period.

   ```
   sp_configure "auditing", 1
   ```

6. Disable auditing after selected time period.

   ```
   sp_configure "auditing", 0
   ```

7. Evaluate the space usage of the audit tables with sp_spaceused or the doampg function.

   ```
   sp_spaceused sysaudits_01
   go
   name           rowtotal   reserved   data     index_size   unused
   ------------   --------   --------   ------   ----------   ------
   sysaudits_01   979        142 KB     130 KB   0 KB         12 KB

   (1 row affected)
   (return status = 0)
   select data_pgs(sysindexes.id, doampg)
   from sysindexes
   where sysindexes.id=object_id("sysaudits_01")
   go

   -----------
   65

   (1 row affected)
   ```

8. Determine the row counts of audit records and make note of the duration auditing was enabled:

```
1> select count(*) from sysaudits_01
2> go

-----------
979

(1 row affected)
```

9. The difference between the first space measurement and the last will give you the space used in the audit.

   Since the audit table initially had no records, we can see from the sp_spaceused output that 130K of data, or 652K pages (using the doampg function) were generated into the audit trail.
10. Divide the space used by the number of records to determine the row size:

    130K (133,120 bytes) / 979 records = 136 bytes per record
11. Divide the space used by the duration of the audit to get the rate at which the database will fill:

    130K (133,120 bytes) / 10 minutes = 13,312 bytes per minute
12. Determine the necessary database size. For this example, archiving is performed every 48 hours.

    13,312 bytes per minute * 48 hours(2880 minutes) = 38,338,560 bytes (~38 Megabytes)

> **NOTE:** It is recommended to perform the above iteration more than once (Steps 3 and beyond) and at different peak operating periods throughout the day in order to achieve the most accurate volume measurement of the audit trail.

> **NOTE:** Usage levels can, and often do, change. As with any user database, it is advisable to set up a process that will monitor the space used by the sybsecurity database. In UNIX environments, set up a simple script that will execute the sp_spaceused procedure against the susaudits_0x tables and report these results to the system administrator. The same can be done in NT or other environments with various job schedulers.

Creating Audit Tables

Up to eight sysaudits_0x tables can be added to sybsecurity. Audit tables are added to sybsecurity with the sp_addaudittable stored procedure. The audit tables can all be added to the one default device; however, it is recommended that each audit table be added to its own physical device.

It is recommended to place each audit table on its own device to allow the administrator to set up threshold procedures on each device. The threshold procedures can then either redirect auditing to another audit table or suspend auditing. The ASE *System Administration Guide* contains an example of setting up a threshold procedure for the audit threshold. Of course, the administrator can set up custom threshold procedures on the threshold; however, they will likely contain similar logic to change the target audit table and to archive the filled audit table to another archive database.

It is recommended that the DBA add a threshold procedure to all audit tables before activating auditing. To add the threshold procedure, first create the procedure in the sybsystemprocs database, then add the procedure to all devices where audit tables reside. The threshold procedure should be designed to move the audit trail to the next available audit table with the sp_configure system procedure. The second component of the audit segment's threshold procedure should be select into statements to archive the audit records to an archive database.

Single-Table Auditing

Single-table auditing is still achievable in ASE 12.5. However, it is difficult to justify single-table auditing with the added features of using multiple audit tables on different devices, combined with threshold procedures to automatically archive and move the audit trail to empty tables.

It is not recommended to use single-table auditing for several reasons. Depending on the configuration setting of suspend audit when device full, the following consequences will arise when using single-table auditing:

- If suspend audit when device full is configured on and the audit table fills, auditing will be suspended and any user processes that trigger the addition of an audit record will be suspended.
- If suspend audit when device full is configured off and the audit table fills, the audit table will automatically be truncated, and you will lose all audit records.

If you must set up single-table auditing, it is recommended you add a procedure to a free space threshold that will configure auditing to off. Combine this with an OS-level script that will search your errorlog and automatically notify the SSO of the configuration change and status of the audit table. Any audit records that occur after this point will not be logged to the audit trail, but you will not lose the audit records that already exist in the audit trail. User processes will not be affected as they would be when suspend audit when device full is enabled.

It is also a good idea to place further free space thresholds on the audit device when using single-table auditing. Place the thresholds at a fill level that will allow the SSO to receive notice of the problem and remedy the situation before the database fills.

> **NOTE:** With single-table auditing, the DBA can still incorporate logic into the threshold procedure to archive the audit trail to another database with the select into statement, and truncate the near-full audit table.

For non-production systems, the single-table setup might be acceptable. Other reasons for implementing single-table auditing might be systems where there are not enough disk resources to configure multiple audit tables, or on systems where no more available devices exist.

The Audit Table is Full, Help!

As mentioned in the previous section on single-table audit setups, it is possible to fill the audit table, thus placing the entire server in an undesired state. In this situation, the sso_role automatically becomes exempt from auditing. Any action performed by the SSO that would otherwise generate an audit record will instead write a message to the errorlog indicating an auditable event was missed.

The SSO still has the ability to archive the audit tables to another database, and truncate the audit trail. The SA may then recycle the server and the auditing procedure should resume once the server is running again.

Archiving Audit Records

The archiving of records can be crucial to a successful audit strategy. As already mentioned, it is essential to periodically purge records from the sysaudits_0x tables. The audit trail can be archived into tables placed into the sybsecurity database; however, it is recommended that you create a separate database to hold archived audit records. Be sure to create the database on a different devices than the sybsecurity database.

To archive the audit records from the audit table to a separate database, use a combination of the select and insert statements. First, create a blank table in the archive database with the same structure as the sysaudits_0x tables:

```
use audit_archive_db
go
select *
  into audit_archive_20010503
  from sybsecurity..sysaudits_01
  where 1 = 2
```

Adding the clause "where 1 = 2" creates a blank table, since the where clause is false for every record. The next step is to insert the audit records into the archive table:

```
insert audit_archive_db..audit_archive_20010503
select * from sybsecurity..sysaudits_01
```

> **NOTE:** It is helpful when returning to the audit trail's archive database to use "smart" table names to differentiate between time periods as in the above example. Of course, balance the need to individually name all of the archive tables with how you will query the audit trail. Too many small audit archive tables could be trouble when trying to search the audit trail for specific events.

Another option to archive the audit tables is to bcp the records to operating system files, as follows:

```
$SYBASE/bin/bcp sybsecurity..sysaudits_01 out audit_archive_db -c
-Usso_login
```

Querying the Audit Trail

What good would it be to collect the audit information if an analysis were not performed upon the records? This section outlines how to query the audit trail.

The sysaudits_0x tables can be queried directly, or if you have configured a method to archive the audit records, the archived audit records can be queried directly.

When audit options are enabled with the sp_audit stored procedure, a designated event is selected from the allowable options and provided as the first parameter of the sp_audit procedure. When auditing is enabled, and one of these auditable events occur, it is stored with a code that corresponds to the audit option (a list of these audit options and codes can be found in the *Reference Manual* of the documentation set). Columns in sysaudits_0x contain information about the dbid, database name, object name, and audited action, just to name a few.

The following example is a simple select statement issued against the sysaudits_0x table after auditing has been enabled and the sp_audit procedure has been issued to track all selects against the customer table in the accounting database. The event code of 62 corresponds to select:

```
select event, spid, eventtime, loginname, dbname, objname, extrainfo
from sysaudits_01
where event = 62
```

event	spid	eventtime	loginname	dbname	objname	extrainfo
62	36	May 9 2001 3:59:21:396PM	user1	accounting	customer	SELECT;
62	57	May 9 2001 3:59:45:321PM	user1	accounting	customer	SELECT;

The following determines who executed the sp_addcustomer stored procedure in the customer database and when, and limits the output to users with the sa_role. The event code of 38 corresponds to exec_procedure.

```
select eventtime, loginname, dbname, objname, extrainfo
from sysaudits_01
where event = 38
and objname = "sp_addcustomer"
and extrainfo like "%sa_role%"
/*** Event 38 corresponds to the execute event ***/
```

eventtime	loginname	dbname	objname	extrainfo
5/9/2001 4:14:19 PM	sysadmin	customer	sp_addcustomer	sa_role; ; ; ;
5/9/2001 4:14:20 PM	btaylor	customer	sp_addcustomer	sa_role; ; ; ;

Determine who truncated the product table on the inventory database, and when the user truncated the table. Event 64 corresponds to the truncate table event.

```
select eventtime, loginname, dbname, objname, extrainfo
from sysaudits_01
where event = 64
```

```
and dbname = "inventory"
and objname = "product"
```

eventtime	loginname	dbname	objname	extrainfo
5/17/2001 2:24:17 PM	user1	inventory	product	oper_role; ; ; ; ; ; ;

Notice that each query against the audit trail has used an event code to search for the individual audit event. As opposed to looking up the event code each time the audit trail is queried, create an event table, and join it to the audit query. This will keep the SA from having to look up or memorize the events corresponding with each code. Since here are 78 auditable events, the table will require one create table statement and 78 insert statements.

```
Create table audit_event
(
event_code int,
event_action varchar(50)
)

insert audit_event
values(1, "adhoc")
insert audit_event
values(2, "alter database")
insert audit_event
values(3, "alter table")
etc...
```

Issuing the first select query utilizing the additional audit_event table:

```
select a.event_action, s.spid, s.eventtime, s.loginname, s.dbname,
s.objname, s.extrainfo
from sysaudits_01 s,
   audit_event a
where a.event_code = s.event
and a.event_action = "select"
```

event_action	spid	eventtime	loginname	dbname	objname	extrainfo
select	36	May 9 2001 3:59:21:396PM	user1	accounting	customer	SELECT;
select	57	May 9 2001 3:59:45:321PM	user1	accounting	customer	SELECT;

Auditing Interaction with Third-Party Software

Many applications or third-party products are sometimes not very user friendly when trying to figure out the interactions with the database.

The Sybase audit system can help gain an understanding of this type of system's interaction with the databases by auditing the cmdtext with the sp_audit procedure. Enable the cmdtext option using sp_audit for any login that will access ASE through the application. The audit trail will then capture the SQL from these logins into the extrainfo column of the sysaudits_0x table.

Be aware that any large entry (over 255 characters in length) into the extrainfo field will cause another corresponding entry into the audit trail. The new row's extrainfo field will contain the characters over 255 characters in length; with the exception of the sequence number, the other columns will repeat. For each incremental audit record required to hold the information in the extrainfo column, the sequence column will increment by one. Large queries can take up more than two audit records. When reporting on the audit trail's extrainfo column, and searching for cmdtext entries, the SSO needs to be aware of this storage method.

The following is an example of how to build a select that will keep together the SQL captured in the extrainfo field. In this example, the SSO would like to know the SQL issued against the customer, billing, and sales tables:

```
select s1.extrainfo from sybsecurity..sysaudits_01 s1
where s1.eventtime in
(select s2.eventtime
 from sybsecurity..sysaudits_01 s2
 where s2.extrainfo like "%customer%"
   or s2.extrainfo like "%billing%"
   or s2.extrainfo like "%sales%")
```

The above example searches the extrainfo column for the table names. It would be more efficient to search the objname field in the sysaudits_01 table, but when auditing for the cmdtext commands, the objname field is left null. If your audit tables contain audit information from many databases, or you are looking for a specific login, the search could be narrowed by including those columns as SARGs in the SQL statement above.

Additional Tips for Effective Auditing

Auditing can impact performance if heavily utilized. Only audit what is necessary.

Put the system tables to good use in order to generate records and auditing options you would like to use. If you have hundreds of logins in the database, this will save much time. The following select statement will generate a script to audit the command text for all the logins that are added to a user database as an alias:

```
select "exec sp_audit " +"'cmdtext'" + ",'" + l.name +"',"
    + "'all', 'on'" + char(10) + "go"
 from master..syslogins l, pubs2..sysalternates a
 where a.suid = l.suid
 go
```

Example of output:

```
exec sp_audit 'cmdtext','JSmith','all','on'
go
exec sp_audit 'cmdtext','BTaylor','all','on'
go
```

Take advantage of the sp_addauditrecord stored procedure. Use it to document audit option changes into the audit trail, and to mark time periods in the audit trail, as shown below:

```
sp_addauditrecord "Began the audit of all DML actions and cmdtext
on the customer table on 5/9/2001 at 8:00AM.",
"accounting", "", "dbo", 8

sp_addauditrecord "Completed the audit of all DML actions and
cmdtext on the customer table on 5/12/2001 at 5:00PM.",
"accounting", "" , "dbo", 8
```

Summary

The audit system is an invaluable tool in ASE 12.5. Used properly, the audit system can help the SSO understand the interactions with the database system. Most importantly, the audit system can be used to achieve accountability.

The audit system provides two alternative installation methods, one menu driven, the other a manual setup combined with a setup script. Both multiple-table and single-table auditing are supported by the audit system.

The audit system has several components: the sybsecurity database, the audit tables (sysaudits_01 – sysaudits08), the audit queue, and a few specialized stored procedures (sp_audit, sp_addaudittable, sp_displayaudit, and sp_addauditrecord).

Chapter 8

Backing Up and Restoring

Backing up your databases periodically is perhaps the most mundane task you'll perform, and perhaps the most important.

A *database backup* (dump) is a copy of all the used pages in a database. This is your basic unit of recovery in case of a disaster; when properly verified (via dbcc utilities), we know that all transactions and work within the database are consistent, and that the backup will allow us to return the database to this consistent state.

Additionally, we will always back up or restore an entire database. ASE has no mechanism to back up or restore tables, indexes, or individual data components (though there are third-party tools that will do this).

It does take some time and energy to create a backup and restore plan, but it is worth the effort. When a database or hardware starts to fail, it is a great relief to have a disaster recovery plan that you can refer to; when the alarms are still ringing and the boss is looking over your shoulder, you won't need to worry about data loss or re-creating structure. The backups and the plan will return you to working order quickly and efficiently.

Above all, your plan should be two things: tested and available. If you've never done a "dry run" under simulated disaster conditions, you don't know if your plan will work the way that it's supposed to, or in the allotted time. Additionally, the tested plan has the advantage of familiarity — if you have to repair your systems following a disaster at 3 a.m., it's much better to be running through the plan for the 23rd time (or at least the second) instead of the first. And regardless of how bulletproof and tested your plan is, if you can't find it in an emergency, it's no good to you. Is the plan all in one binder? Near the evacuation route? Copy stored off-site with the backup media? The scariest answers that we've gotten from clients are in response to the question, "Do you know where your backup plan is right now?"

Your plan should detail what media device(s) you are going to use for your dumps, a schedule for performing full backup and/or incremental backups, and where you will store them (off-site). In your plan you must consider naming conventions, define necessary resources, determine who is responsible for each step of the restoration, and calculate estimates of potential loss (both processing time while the plan is being followed, and loss of data that didn't make it to backup).

Keep a record of this plan for further reflection and reference. As time goes by, it must be revisited, reevaluated, and revised to reflect changes in your shop; keep a history of these tests and changes with the rest of the plan.

Roles and Responsibilities

By default, the dbo has the responsibility and permission to execute the commands that dump and load a database. These permissions are not grantable by the dbo to other users, but any user aliased as the dbo (including all logins with sa_role) will be able to use these commands within the database.

Any logins granted the oper_role have permission to dump and load any database on the server (see Chapter 6, "Security," for a discussion of oper_role); note that the OPER need not be a user of any of these databases. Granting the oper_role permits your organization to assign an individual or group the responsibility for performing backups throughout the server, rather than relying on individual dbos. The oper_role may be granted to a login by any SSO:

```
sp_role "grant", oper_role, login_name
```

or

```
grant role oper_role to login_name [, login_name, …]
```

How Often Should You Back Up a Database?

You need to back up a database to guard against table corruption, database corruption, media failure, disk failure, and environmental catastrophes. Since a database dump can be performed while the database is in use, you can back up as often as you think is necessary.

Recent benchmarks on systems with ample CPU and disk space have shown that backups can hit performance as little as 5%. Not a lot, but dumping during low-utilization time is still recommended.

Most shops back up their databases once a day, and back up their transaction logs several times a day. The backup of a transaction log is a style of incremental backup, which has the added bonus of truncating recovered transactions from the log (see Chapter 5, "Database Logging and Recovery," for more). Even if you determine that incremental backups are not necessary for disaster recovery, it is necessary to truncate the log on a regular basis.

The total time it will take to restore a database is the sum of new database creation time plus database load time plus transaction log load time for each transaction log. Note that when you do this, you should use the for load option of the create database statement, as it is significantly faster.

If you dumped your database once a year, and you have dumped the transaction log daily, and your database fails on day 365, then you will have to load the database and also load 364 transaction logs in sequence. Therefore, it makes sense to perform a full database backup frequently, so that the restore process will be a less irritating process. Additionally, it would be less prone to error, both procedurally from so many steps, and from media failure due to more and older media. Restoring tends to be a stressful time, as it typically occurs after a disaster; making it less irritating is a Good Thing.

For an OLTP or production system, a combination of full and incremental backups is essential in maintaining an up-to-the-minute recovery backup plan. However, in a development environment, up-to-the-moment recovery may not be needed; in such cases, you may opt to skip incremental backups. Some shops will not perform backups at all in development, preferring to re-create databases and test data from script. This is not recommended because developers' time is worth money to the company, too.

Backup Types

Adaptive Server Enterprise has two database backup types: database dumps and transaction dumps. A *database dump* is the complete backup of both the database and the transaction log, and uses the dump database command. A *transaction dump* is a backup of the transaction log only, and uses the dump transaction command. Remember that the transaction is a copy of changes to the database.

NOTE: A database dump does <u>not</u> truncate the transaction log. To truncate the transaction log you must use the dump tran syntax. If you do not dump the transaction log (one way or another), ongoing updates will fill up and transaction processing will stop.

Backup Scenario

Take into account the following scenario:

Figure 8-1

As you can see in this diagram, the 3 a.m. to 11 a.m. dumps were successful, but at 9 a.m. and 11 a.m. only a dump transaction was performed. How do you restore the database now, after a lunchtime disk crash? What happens to transactions completed from 11 a.m. through lunchtime?

NOTE: Is it more likely that a disk will crash, or a database will become corrupt? Database corruption is unusual, but so are disk crashes. Hardware vendors are claiming 300,000 thousand hours mean time between failures; mathematically, you'd think a database corruption is more likely. From a practical standpoint, at the last shop I was at, over a three-year time period, we had one major database corruption, and a half dozen disk failures (there were about 250 GB on mostly 9 GB storage units).

Restore Scenario

Figure 8-2

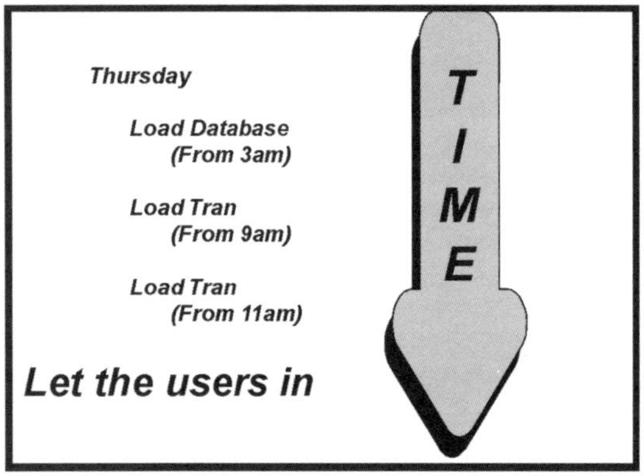

At lunchtime after replacing the bad disk, you simply need to restore the database from 3 a.m. using the load database command. Subsequently, you restore the rest of the data by loading the transaction log from 9 a.m. and then 11 a.m., using the load tran command. After the successful completion of the entire restore you let your users in. What happens with subsequent transactions, though?

If you have designed the database properly (data and transaction log on separate devices), then you can dump the transaction log from lunchtime and apply it to the restore sequence (see "Up-to-the-Minute Recovery," later in this chapter). Before we can follow through these scenarios with syntax, we need to understand the mechanism that performs the dumps and loads.

Backup Server

Backup Server is a separate Open Server application within your host machine that bypasses the Adaptive Server process and accesses the database devices directly for the purposes of dumping and loading; this allows data processing to continue with little degradation of performance. Prior to System 10, dumping was performed directly by the database server; this caused substantial contention.

NOTE: There must be a Backup Server running on the machine that the database server resides on, even if you are dumping to media on a remote machine.

The following list details the advantages of using Backup Server:

- Adaptive Server instructs the Backup Server, via remote procedure calls, to back up a specific database.
- The backup server handles I/O, rather than using Adaptive Server resources.
- Backups can be striped, enabling the operator to specify up to (initially) 32 separate devices for dumping or loading a database. The backup server breaks the database into fairly equal portions and dumps those portions in parallel.
- With additional configuration and memory, Backup Server is capable of handling hundreds of parallel devices for dumping and loading (the actual limit is platform dependent).
- Backups can be handled remotely, enabling the operator to dump the database or stripe the database to a device on separate hardware.
- Several backups can be recorded on the same tape. A successive reload locates only the file it needs to restore.
- Messages can be sent to the session initiating the dump or load, or to an operator console.

Since Backup Server is a separate process from Adaptive Server, remote access must be enabled before the commands to the Backup Server can be effective (remote access is enabled by default at installation). There must be a local Backup Server available on the same host machine as the Adaptive Server. This local backup server listens on a different port number from the Adaptive Server (as defined in the interfaces file), and may coordinate backups/loads for any Adaptive Server running on the same machine. You can dump to media on the local machine, a remote machine, or both. Because dumping to a remote machine can be network-resource intensive, we recommend consulting with your network folks (or architecting a separate network backbone) if you are going to choose that option.

Remote Backup Server

A remote Backup Server is used when dumps and loads access media on separate hardware; any Backup Server can only access disk or tape drives physically installed in the same machine that it runs on. Even though you may intend to dump or load solely using this remote media, all communication to remote Backup Servers must be coordinated by the local Backup Server. Using remote procedure calls, the local Backup Server passes backup and load requests, as well as data, to the remote Backup Server(s), which will write database and log contents to dump media. Alternately, the remote Backup Servers retrieve from dumps and forward the data back to the local Backup Server for reinsertion on devices.

Remote backup is an easy way to get the data off-site, for safety and other standard backup protocols. There are also other challenges that the remote backup server can help overcome.

Server Identification

Adaptive Server looks for a SYB_BACKUP entry in the master..sysservers table to identify the local Backup Server name. The entry for the Backup Server is added to the system table and interfaces file during Backup Server installation. If you wish to designate a different local Backup Server (or add a reference to a remote Backup Server), the server name must be added to interfaces, and identified to Adaptive Server with the sp_addserver stored procedure, as shown:

```
sp_addserver remote_backup_name, null, network_name
```

> **NOTE:** In order for the remote Backup Servers to work, they must be added to the interfaces file for the local Backup Server.
>
> Changing null to local will allow you to add the local server to sysservers; this makes the Adaptive Server recognize its own name, and populates the system variable @@servername.
>
> Network name is as it appears in the interfaces file.

Starting a Backup Server

Starting a Backup Server is similar to starting the Adaptive Server, except the startup script doesn't invoke a dataserver. The startup script is automatically created by installation and is named RUN_SYB_BACKUP by default. From the operating system command you execute this syntax:

```
startserver -r RUN_SYB_BACKUP
```

In order to shut down a Backup Server, you use the regular shutdown command within Adaptive Server with the Backup Server's name (normally done using isql):

```
shutdown {backup_servername}] [with {wait | nowait}]
```

Example:

```
shutdown SYB_BACKUP with nowait
```

The default is the with wait option. The option with wait brings down the Backup Server elegantly by allowing all current dumps or loads to complete before the server goes down; however, no new backup requests are allowed. The with nowait option immediately shuts down the Backup Server even if there is a dump or load in progress. Therefore it should be noted that the use of the with nowait option should be used only when absolutely necessary.

Dump Devices

Adaptive Server can dump to either tape devices or disk files; if you don't wish to refer to these devices by an absolute path name, you can assign a logical name to a local dump device using the sp_addumpdevice procedure. You can dump one database to one tape, one database to many tapes, many databases to one tape, or many databases to many tapes. You may also dump a single database to a combination of disk files, but may not dump multiple databases to a single file.

There are several issues to be aware of when using tape backup. Among these are the following:

- Tend to be more secure.
- Tend to be less sensitive to changing data size.
- You never know if a tape is good or bad until you test it (this has caused numerous panic attacks at horrible times in folks' lives… you must test your restore periodically).
- Should eventually be taken and stored off-site for disaster preparedness purposes.

Likewise, disk backup has the following issues:

- Tend to be significantly faster.
- Need to be archived to a more secure medium eventually.
- You can tell that a disk file is there.

Our recommendation: Dump to disk (fastest). Leave the dump on disk, but sweep it off to tape. Keep the most recent dump on disk, but get the tapes off-site, aging them as per your shop standards (for example, reuse the tape after three months).

sp_addumpdevice

On most platforms, installation automatically creates some sample dump devices; these point to nowhere, and should be dropped or redefined. You can create your own with *sp_addumpdevice.* Remember when naming the device to fully qualify the physical name of the device.

Syntax:

```
sp_addumpdevice {"tape" | "disk"},
"logical_name", "physical_name",
[cntrltype [, skip|noskip], size]
```

Example:

```
sp_addumpdevice "disk","diskdev","/sybase/dmp.dmp"
```

> **NOTE:** Logical dump devices may not be created for remote dump devices; you must use fully qualified physical names in the dump command.

You do not need to define a dump device. You can, if you like, dump directly to a filename. We recommend that you take the time to create dump devices, however, because it is easier at restore time (when presumably too many eyes are watching and waiting) to specify the dump device name.

Dumping the Database

The dump database command will make a physical copy of all used pages of a database to any defined dump device(s). In other words, if you are using only 1 GB of a 20 GB database, you will only dump the 1 GB you are using, and only take up 1 GB on the tape. However, the dump volume will contain a record of the size of the original database, and regardless of how large the dump is, it may only be loaded into a database at least as large as the original. You may not use dump and load commands to shrink the size of a database.

The dump database command looks like this:

```
dump database user3db to diskdev
```

This command is appropriate for all environments. There are many other options that you can choose from when dumping the database. Following is an example of the full syntax used to dump a database representing some of those options:

```
dump database database_name to [compress::[compression_level::]]
stripe_device
[at server_name]
[, stripe on stripe_device [ at server_name]]...
[with dumpvolume = volume_name, [dismount |
nodismount [, nounload | unload] [, noinit | init]]]
```

There is an initial limit of 32-stripe devices; reconfiguring the Backup Server's startup settings can allow it to use additional memory and process threads, and increase the stripe limitation into the hundreds. Each stripe device can be on a different machine.

NOTE: If one striped output device is bad, the whole dump is bad! You can't restore a database with 31 of 32 tapes.

This table describes parameters that can be used within the dump database syntax.

Parameter	Description
database name	The name of the database that is being dumped.
stripe_device	For a local dump, this is either the logical or physical name of the dump device. If it is a remote dump, the physical name must be specified.
backup_server_name	This option is used when specifying a remote dump device.
Densityblocksizecapacity	All of these parameters relate to the physical characteristics of the tape device; use the defaults.
retaindays = #_of_days	This is a UNIX option that can be used for any type of dump device. This option prevents the dump on the tape from being overwritten until the specified number of days has passed.

This table describes options that only apply to tape devices:

Option	Description
dumpvolume	This option descriptively labels the dump. For example, if you have more than one dump on a tape, you may label each dump (CustomerDB_January 7) through (CustomerDB _January 10). Thus you will be able to reload any of those database dumps easily by naming them in the load command.

Option	Description
dismount | nodismount	This option is only valid on platforms that support logical dismounts (OpenVMS). This parameter determines whether the tape will be available for future dumps. The dismount option is the default.
nounload | unload	This option controls the rewinding of the tape. The nounload option should be used unless this is the last dump you wish to have on the tape.
noinit | init	This option determines whether the dump will be appended to the tape or reinitializes the entire tape volume. Use init when dumping to a tape for the first time or if reusing a tape. The noinit option is the default.
file = file_name	This option allows the use of a filename of up to 17 characters. This option is not normally used. By default, Adaptive Server names the file with a concatenation of the last seven characters from the database name, the two-digit year, the Julian day, and a hex representation of the year.
notify = {client | operator_console}	By default, messages are sent to the operator console. If the operator console is not available, the messages are sent to the client initiating the request.

The following examples show different ways of using the dump database command.

Example 1: Multiple databases to a single tape

```
dump database bailey to dumpdev with init

dump database jeff to dumpdev
dump database fred to dumpdev with unload
```

Example 2: One database to multiple dump devices

```
dump database   alvin to dumpdev1,
                stripe on dumpdev2,
                stripe on dumpdev3
```

Example 3: Remote Backup

```
dump database penny to "/dev/rmt01" at B_dump_host,
stripe on "/dev/rmt02" at B_dump_host,
stripe on "/dev/rmt03" at B_dump_host
```

NOTE: B_dump_host is the name of a remote Backup Server; it must be defined in the local interfaces file, running on the remote machine, and added as a remote server.

Dump Compression

ASE 12.5 gives you the ability to compress your dumps. This offers a significant storage savings to you for your backups, at the cost of additional CPU at dump time.

Backup Server version 12.5 supports dump compression, which will allow the database dump file to take up much less space than it ordinarily would; as with all server capabilities, there are tradeoffs. In general, the greater the compression, the longer it will take to perform the dump (although compressed dumps take less time to load than uncompressed).

Field testing indicates:

- Dump files may be compressed by up to (approximately) 70% in large databases.
- Dump times will increase by a factor of 2 to 4, depending on the compression ratio (but sometimes low ratios may be faster to dump than uncompressed).
- Compression is better than third–party tools by about 30%.
- Higher compression levels may not save much space over lower levels for modestly sized databases.

Normal dumps do not perform any compression (other than the fact that the dump file will probably be smaller than the allocated space of the database, due to the fact that only used pages are dumped). In order to compress a dump, you must use the following syntax:

```
dump database <dbname> to [compress::[compression_level::]] <stripe_device>
```

Where <> indicates the *compression level*; the higher the compression level (an integer value from 1 to 9), the smaller the dump file (and the greater the dump time). If you specify compression, but do not specify the level, the compression defaults to level 6.

In order to load from a compressed dump, use the following load command:

```
load database dbname from "compress::/filename"
```

You do not have to specify the compression level in the load command, only in the dump command.

It is important to note that the relative speed and compression of your dump and load will vary, and so you will have to experiment to determine what level of compression you find most useful. The relationship between database size, available hardware, stripes used, speed, and compression may not always be linear! More than likely, level 1 compression will provide the greatest marginal benefit for the least increase in dump times.

Take a look at the following compression examples:

	Uncompressed	Default (6)	Level 3	Level 1
Dump File Size	493 MB	111 MB	128 MB	128 MB
Dump Time	2 min	6 min	2.5 min	110 sec

Database: approximately 430 MB used space
Tested on a 4 x 450 MHz Ultra Sparc

As we can see, the difference between level 1 and level 6 is not great, and requires more time. If we just compare uncompressed vs. level 1 compression for progressively larger databases:

	Uncompressed	Level 1
Dump File Size	5.6 GB	1 GB
Dump Time	18 min	12 min
4.9 GB used space		
Dump File Size	46 GB	13 GB
Dump Time	3 hours	1.5 hours
40 GB used space		

Changing the specs of the machine from 4 x 450 MHz to 2 x 150 MHz has an effect on the dump performance:

	Uncompressed	Level 1
Dump File Size	50 GB	15 GB
Dump Time	1.5 hours	5 hours
44 GB used space		

Dump Database Summary

On an Adaptive Server it is very easy for an SA or operator to perform backups, so there is no excuse not to do this as often as necessary for your business needs. Remember to back up the master database as well as all user databases. You do not have to take your production databases offline; any database can be dumped while in use. The ASE dumps capture the state of the database near the end of the dump; if pages have changed during the dumping process, log pages containing the changes will be written. There is a small impact of less than 5% on system performance during a dump. If any of the pages in a database are offline, the dump database command will not run.

When striping a local dump you may use either a physical or logical name, but you must name the physical device when striping for a remote backup.

TIP: There is nothing more important than getting a copy of your dump into an environmentally secure location. You don't want to get into a situation where you are vulnerable to a complete disaster. For example, if a fire takes out your server and your backups, what can you do?

Automatic Backups

Adaptive Server does not provide any utility to automate or schedule database backups. This is typically handled by operating system-level utilities running scripts or third-party programs. A threshold can automatically dump the log based on space usage, as we will see later.

Load Database Command

The load database command is used to restore a database from a backup into an existing database. The load will replace everything in a database with the contents of the dump, and destroy all data that was residing in the database prior to the load. Permission to load is not delegated since the process is so destructive; only operators and the database owner (including SAs, who are aliased as dbo) have the permissions to load a database. The structure of the dump and load commands are parallel. If necessary, you may load from fewer devices than were used in dumping, at the expense of a greater load time.

Take a look at the following example:

```
load database db3 from dumpdev
load database db3 from dumpdev1, stripe on dumpdev2
load database db3 from "/sybase/backups/dumpdev1.dmp" at B_dump_host,
stripe on "/sybase/backups/dumpdev2.dmp" at B_dump_host
```

In the example, database db3 is restored from dumpdev, or from the stripeset of dumpdev1 and dumpdev2, or from the stripeset at the remote Backup Server B_dump_host.

> **NOTE:** Unlike a backup, the database being loaded cannot be used by anyone, including the person performing the load operation; typically, load commands are issued from master. Following a load, the database is in an offline state,and may not be used until brought online with the online database command. In order for a load to run, the destination database must exist and must be at least as large as the database that had been dumped.

The load database command loads all used pages from the dump into the target database and runs recovery of syslogs to ensure consistency. The load process also initializes the unused pages in the database (i.e., individually writes to each page, zeroing out any data that may be located in that physical region of the disk). This is the primary reason why a load can take significantly longer than a dump. The time required to dump a database is proportional to the used pages in the database; the time required to load a database is proportional to the overall number of pages in the database, because every page must be initialized, even if it is empty. Therefore, a 5 GB database with 20 MB of data may take only a few seconds to dump but the load could take several minutes. In general, with full databases, a load will take 1.5 to 2.5 times longer than a dump.

Loading a Corrupted Database

If the database has been corrupted, use the following to drop it before recreating and loading it. Alternatively, rename it, dump it, and send it to Sybase tech support for analysis.

To restore a corrupted database, first try to drop the database (you may have to force it online first). If this doesn't work, try to run the database consistency checker database repair tool to remove the database. Once the database is dropped, you may recreate it and load from your backup set.

Syntax:

```
sp_forceonline_db database_name, sa_on
go
drop database database_name
-- or
dbcc dbrepair (database_name, dropdb)
```

Online Database

With System 11 and later, a database is left offline after being loaded. This prevents users from accessing the database until all the transaction dumps are loaded (any change to the database would prevent a subsequent load transaction from executing).

You may bring the database online using the online database command as long as there are not corrupt pages in the database.

Syntax:

```
online database database_name
```

There is not a corresponding offline database command (see "Quiesce Database," later in this chapter for similar functionality).

Load Database Summary

The nature of a load database causes it to take longer than a dump. The load command initializes all pages in the database prior to restoring data, since every page in the database must be accessed regardless whether or not it holds any data, the speed of a load is proportional to the database size. Only an SA or operator can load a database because of the destructive nature of a load.

To ensure data consistency the load runs recovery. In order for the load database command to work, the destination database must be created and the size of the destination database must be equal to or larger than the dump database. No one can be using the database, including the user performing the load.

If a database is corrupted you must repair and drop the database, then re-create a database to load into. In ASE System 11 and later the database will stay offline until the transaction dumps have been loaded.

Creating a Database for a Restore

Creating a database for load allocates the storage, but does not initialize the pages. Using this option takes significantly less time than a normal create. The only catch is that the database will not be usable except for running a load. The new database must be created with a structure just like the dumped database. For example, if you initially created the productiondb with 1 GB for data and 100 MB for log and later altered the database by 500 MB for data, you must execute the following commands:

```
use master
go
create database productiondb on DataDevice1 = 1000,
 log on LogDevice1 = 100
 for load
go
alter database productiondb DataDevice2 = 500 for load
go
load database productiondb from productiondb_dump

go
```

It would not be sufficient to create the new database with a single command. Even though the new database might be the same size (or larger) than the old, the order of commands (create then alter vs. a single create) would be different. This would result in a different mapping of the order of data and log pages on the disk (with the create/alter, we would get a range of data pages, then log pages, then more data; with a single create, we would get all data pages before log pages). In these cases, the dumped pages are loaded into the "wrong" location, and we can lose the separation of data and log.

The easiest way ensure the correct order is to save each create and alter command in a single create script as the commands are executed. If you have not saved your scripts, you can retrieve this information from the sysusages table in the master database:

```
select segmap, "Size in MB" = size/512
from sysusages
where dbid = db_id ("database_name")
```

Segmap	Size in MB
3	1000
4	200
3	500

The segmap column refers to the segments defined in your database. Initially, there are three segments in your database: system, default, and logsegment. If you convert the segmap number to binary, you can determine how the segmap relates to segment names:

```
2^0 = system segment
2^1 = default segment
2^2 = logsegment
2^3 = first user-defined segment

                log     data    sys

segmap  2^3     2^2     2^1     2^0     size
3       0       0       1       1       1000
4       0       1       0       0       200
3       0       0       1       1       500
```

Therefore, a segmap of 3 indicates a data device (default + system), and a value of 4 indicates a log device (logsegment only).

If you have added user-defined segments (and possibly dropped the default and system segments from a fragment), there will be indicators in the 2^3 column and greater. These fragments should be created as data fragments. Because segments are database specific, the database system tables containing the user-defined segment definitions are loaded in the load process, which resolves the segment mapping within the database.

Dump Transaction Command

The dump transaction command copies the contents of the system table syslogs to the dump device(s). In addition, it is the only command that cleans out the transaction log of unneeded rows (that is, all recovered transactions before the last open transaction, or the replication point). It also updates the row in sysdatabases setting the dumptrdate to the current date and time, and normally writes a checkpoint record to the database. In a production environment, this is the only way the log should be cleaned out.

Syntax:

```
dump tran[saction] database_name [to dump_device]
  [at server_name]
  [, stripe on stripe_device [ at server_name]]
  ...
  [with dumpvolume = volume_name, [dismount
  | nodismount
  [, nounload | unload] [, noinit | init]
[with {truncate_only | no_log | no_truncate}]
```

The transaction log may be dumped while the database is in use, and is normally much faster than a database dump. A dump tran will normally have less than a 20% impact on performance. Dump tran to a device will not work after select into, bcp in, or a dump tran with truncate_only, or on any database that did not separate the data and log allocations.

Dump Transaction Options

A transaction dump may be more intrusive than a database dump, since syslogs are targeted instead of the disk. Dump tran has four options available for different types of problems: dump tran dbname with truncate_only, dump tran dbname with no_log, dump tran dbname with no_truncate, and dump tran dbname with standby_access.

Dump tran dbname with truncate_only

The statement dump tran dbname with truncate_only is used when you want to truncate the transaction log without actually creating a dump. This command is used to clean out the log without a backup process; it should be used only when the data are unimportant, such as in a test environment. Since no backup is made, no device is needed in the command.

```
dump tran dbname with truncate_only
```

TIP: This is not a good thing to do in a production database! Also, it is essential to subsequently dump the database, because attempts to dump the transaction log will fail!

Dump tran dbname with no_log

The dump tran dbname with no_log syntax is to be used to truncate the log without writing a checkpoint record to the log; this is necessary when the log fills up. Always attempt a dump tran with truncate_only before trying this. Since this command interrupts the chain of backups, it is imperative to dump the database after this command. As with the truncate_only option, dump tran with no_log does not require a device name.

Syntax:

```
dump tran dbname with no_log
```

Dump tran dbname with no_truncate

In case of media failure on the data device, this will dump the log without touching the data disk in any way. Since a normal dump tran will checkpoint the database, it may not be used if the data portion of the database has suffered any kind of failure; the no_truncate option does not write a checkpoint, and so may be used to retrieve the log from an otherwise failed database. The master database must be available for this command to work. Unlike the other special dump tran commands, dump tran with no_truncate makes a copy of the log and requires a device be referenced. Sybase engineering recommends that this never be performed when users have access to the database.

Syntax:

```
dump tran dbname to devicename with no_truncate
```

Dump tran dbname with standby_access

Adaptive Server Enterprise release 12 incorporated a warm standby process which enables the SA to create a secondary environment for failover purposes. Adaptive Server Enterprise 12.5 has eliminated some minor issues, and this is now a Sybase-supported mechanism intended to support large-scale environments (described a bit later). Dumping with standby_access enables the standby environment to bring up the dumped transaction logs properly.

Syntax:

```
dump tran dbname to devicename with standby_access
```

Dump Transaction Activities

Remember that in addition to copying the contents of the log, the dump tran command will also checkpoint the database, record the checkpoint in the log, and truncate all recovered transactions in the inactive portion of the log (records preceding the oldest open transaction and the replication marker). Note that on some earlier versions of Adaptive Server Enterprise, some aborted transactions could cause "clogs" in the cleanup process, which cannot be resolved until the server cycles. (That is, it would be impossible to truncate the log prior to the abort point.)

Dump transaction is the only way to clean out the log other than setting the trunc. log on chkpt. option for the database. In general, "trunc log" is not recommended for production databases. It makes disaster recovery less functional.

Special care should be taken not to permit long-running transactions in the log. This is a bad thing. A long transaction that is too large for the log will cause its process to suspend and become stuck. This causes any attempts to dump the log to be ineffective because there is no inactive portion of the log to deallocate. Cleaning out the log is not permitted because there is nothing that is truncatable. There is no way to commit the transaction without writing additional log records to an already-full log.

You have a couple of alternatives to try. Killing the process should write the rollback record, thus ending the transaction, and allowing the pages to be deallocated. Alternatively, increase the size of the log with alter database. Note that if the log is full beyond the suspend point, even cycling the server may not help — the database must be recovered at startup, and the recovery process must write a checkpoint, which the log may be too full to accept. If recovery does not complete, the database remains offline, and you cannot dump an offline database. In such cases, consult Sybase Tech Support for instructions on bypassing recovery (a last resort).

Load Transaction

A load transaction can only follow a load database or another load transaction. The load transaction statement takes the dumped log and runs recovery to apply it to the database. Transaction dumps must be loaded in the same order in which they were dumped; the server will tell you if they are out of sequence. With optional syntax, load transaction can perform *point-in-time* restoration, which allows the partial application of log records to recovery. In this situation, you may be able to prevent undesired data changes that took place before backup (say, dropping the wrong table) from being applied during the load.

During a load database, the data in the dump is copied over the database. After the load is complete, the database contains all the data in the database at the time of the dump. By contrast, a transaction log load copies the contents of the dump over the current syslogs definition. Each load tran runs the recovery process. The online database command will roll back any incomplete transactions. The server marches through the log applying changes in the log that are not reflected in the database (normally, all records in the log are new transactions). Note that unlike some earlier versions of Adaptive Server (pre-11.5), a database should not be brought online if you expect to load further logs; recovery will write records to the tran log and interrupt subsequent loads.

The simplified syntax for the load database command is:

```
load transaction <databasename> from <devicename>
```

This command is valid in all environments. Most options available to the dump command can be used in the load. The full syntax for load transaction is:

```
load tran[saction] database_name from dump_device
[stripe on stripe_device] [at remote_bkup_server]
with dumpvolume = volume_name, [dismount | nodismount
[, nounload | unload] [, noinit | init]]]
[until_time = datetime]
```

Loading a transaction log takes significantly less time than loading a database because the log is normally much smaller than the database itself. You cannot bring the database online until you have finished loading all of the transaction logs.

Up-to-the-Minute Recovery

Most shops would have a problem with missing transactions. With Adaptive Server Enterprise, up-to-the-minute recovery is possible as long as the log is on a device that is unaffected by the initial disk crash.

Load Transaction

In the following diagram, it is lunchtime, and the database device has crashed. First, you will restore the database dump, then the subsequent logs before letting the users back in.

Figure 8-3

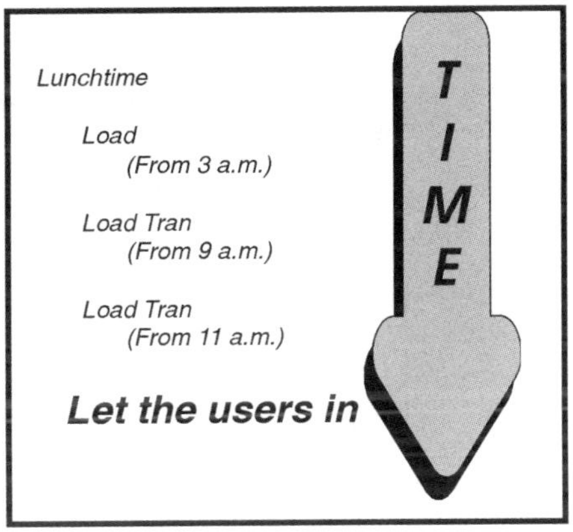

Question: What about 11 a.m. through lunchtime's transactions?
Answer: Up-to-the-minute recovery is possible in ASE.

If the transaction log is on a separate physical device from the data, you may be able to capture the committed data if the log device is still accessible. This is accomplished with the no_truncate option of dump tran. Because this option uses information in master to determine the location of the log, the master database must still be accessible. It may sound obvious, but remember to dump the final transaction log before dropping the database or loading something else on top of it.

Steps

If your database has suffered a failure that leaves the log (and master!) intact:

1. Dump the transaction log with the no_truncate option.
2. Drop the failed database (and devices, if necessary).
3. Re-create the database with the for_load option.
4. Load the most recent database dump.
5. Load the chain of tran log dumps in order, ending with the no_truncate log dump.
6. Use the online database command to complete recovery.

You will still find some minor amount of data loss; any transactions that were in progress at the time of failure will be rolled back, but you should find all pre-failure committed transactions in the database. Depending on how much time had elapsed since the previous scheduled dump, this may be a large amount of salvaged data.

If the log for a database fails, up-to-the-minute recovery is not possible. You will lose all database changes since the last transaction log dump unless the log device is mirrored. This is why it is recommended that you mirror the log device (either with ASE syntax or some hardware solution) for production databases in OLTP environments.

Point-in-Time Recovery

Adaptive Server can perform point-in-time recovery using the until_time clause of the load transaction. In such cases, only transactions committed before the until_time will be rolled forward into the database. To do point-in-time recovery, database and log must be on separate devices and the log must not have been truncated without backup (using dump tran with no_log or truncate_only). A point-in-time recovery restarts the whole transaction log sequence, and you may not subsequently dump or load the tran log until you perform a full database dump.

The format of the until_time parameter is: month day, year hh:mm:ss:ms [am|pm], as shown below:

Jul 11, 1996 09:45:00:001

While the until_time parameter will allow you to avoid undesired changes, it will also prevent desired changes from being applied during the load. If a user dropped a table at 9:45 this morning but didn't tell you until 3:45 this afternoon, using until_time may not be the best solution if critical processing took place in the six hours after the mistake.

sp_volchanged

Backup Server will sometimes require the Operator to perform media changes during dumps and loads. Once the Operator has performed the requested operation (remove a full tape and mount an empty one, for example), the sp_volchanged system procedure is used to confirm the change so that Backup Server may proceed.

Syntax:

```
sp_volchanged session_id, devicename, action [filename [,volumename]]
```

The values of session_id and devicename will be provided in the notification message from Backup Server; the same values should be used in sp_volchanged. The action parameter can take the values "abort", "proceed", or "retry"; the Operator should choose as appropriate to the situation (most cases will use "proceed"). The filename and volumename arguments are used during loads, and default to the filename and volumename specified in the load command (which are almost certainly the desired values).

Example:

```
sp_volchanged 14, "/dev/nrmt2", proceed
```

In nearly every case, the Operator will merely type in the same sp_volchanged syntax as displayed in the notification message.

Monitoring the Log

If the transaction log fills up, all data modification transactions will freeze or fail, depending on the value you've set the database option abort tran on log full to (default is "freeze"). To prevent this from occurring, you can either monitor the log by hand or set up *thresholds*. The threshold facility can be used to set indicators to monitor available space in the log. To monitor by hand, use sp_helpdb.

Last-Chance Threshold

The last-chance threshold is automatically created for every log. Before the log completely fills, there is a certain amount of space available, which is held as an emergency reserve (the exact size varies with the size of the log and whether or not the log and data are on separate devices). When the threshold is crossed, transactions in progress are aborted or suspended (definable per database), with messages for each transaction appearing in the errorlog. Additionally, crossing the last-chance threshold causes the system to execute a stored procedure named sp_thresholdaction (see Chapter 5, "Database Logging and Recovery" for more on sp_thresholdaction).

Syntax:

```
sp_thresholdaction
```

There is no default sp_thresholdaction stored procedure; it must be created. The procedure is considered to be executed by the dbo, and may contain any commands that the dbo may perform. Remember that if you perform actions in sp_thresholdaction (dump tran with truncate_only; alter database … log on …), you will have to make sure you notice (perhaps have yourself paged) and perform necessary maintenance later (dump database; update device usage records and scripts).

There is only one last-chance threshold for each database (which refers to syslogs failure) but other thresholds may be set by the SA or dbo to trigger other events.

In the the following example, four parameters are being passed: dbname, segmentname, space_left, and status. These are passed automatically.

```
use sybsystemprocs
go
create proc sp_thresholdaction
@dbname varchar(30),
@segmentname varchar(30),
@space_left int,
@status int
as
if @status = 1 /* last-chance threshold */
begin
dump tran @dbname to emergency_device
print "Warning! The '%1!' database was dumped",
@dbname
end
go
```

NOTES: Print messages will go to the errorlog, and if you are running NT, the NT event log
Space_left is in pages.

Status is 1 for the last-chance threshold, 0 for other thresholds.

Thresholds could dump the transaction log, expand it, send messages, or anything else the dbo could do.

Remember that the server looks first in its own database for a procedure.

If the procedure is not written by the dbo, be sure to grant dbo execute permission.

Free-Space Thresholds

In addition to the last-chance threshold, free-space thresholds can be created on any segment in your database. There is no limit to the number of free-space thresholds that may be placed on a segment other than the *hysteresis* distance required and the size of the device. The hysteresis distance is used to ensure that thresholds are not continuously executing stored procedures; no two thresholds may be closer than twice the hysteresis distance, and if a segment crosses a threshold and then empties slightly (falling below the threshold), it will not re-trigger the threshold unless it has fallen by at least the hysteresis distance.

The hysteresis distance is set by the system and stored in the global variable @@thresh_hysteresis. In the present version, it is set to 64 pages, so adjacent thresholds in a segment may not be any closer than 128 pages.

Use the sp_helpthreshold command to list threshold information

Aborting vs. Suspending Transactions

By default, when the last-chance threshold is crossed, all transactions within a database are suspended until after sp_thresholdaction is executed. This may be modified, at the discretion of the dbo, to abort instead. Some applications, like bcp, do not understand being suspended and the application will abort. As with other database options, the abort tran on log full option is set with the sp_dboption procedure (see Chapter 4, "Databases").

Restoring the Master Database Step by Step

The processes and commands that we've discussed for restoring databases apply in all cases but one: master. If the master database fails, the server cannot start, but if the server doesn't start, we have no way to communicate with the Backup Server or access our dumps. Restoring master is much easier when you have an up-to-date backup (that is, no changes recorded in master since the backup was made).

To restore a failed master database:

1. Run dataserver with the -b option to create a new master device.

```
dataserver -b /dev/rsd1b
```

2. Start Adaptive Server in single-user mode.

```
startserver -f RUN_SYBASE -m
```

We may use the master database, but presently it does not have any references to any user databases or sybsystemprocs.

3. If master was expanded beyond its default size, run alter database to extend it.
4. Update Backup Server name in sysservers if it is not SYB_BACKUP.

```
begin transaction
update sysservers set srvnetname = "PROD_BACKUP"
   where servname = "SYB_BACKUP"
commit transaction
```

   Note that since sybsystemprocs is unavailable, we don't have access to the usual sp_addserver procedure.

5. Load backup of the master database; once the load completes, it will shut down Adaptive Server automatically.

```
load database master from masterdump
```

6. Start Adaptive Server in single user mode and check that all databases/devices/logins appear to be restored correctly.

If everything appears okay, you are nearly done. Shut down and restart Adaptive Server normally, and skip to item 7.

If everything does not appear okay, you have more work to do. If additional devices, databases, logins, or users of master were created after the last backup of master, you will need to re-create them.

Adaptive Server provides two commands to recover existing devices and databases to a restored master database: disk reinit and disk refit.

Use *disk reinit* to recover devices created since the last dump of master; disk reinit restores information to sysdevices without re-initializing the device, retaining the data that is on the device. Values supplied to disk reinit should match values supplied to the original disk init command.

> **CAUTION:** If the wrong values are supplied to disk reinit, you can permanently corrupt your databases!

Syntax:

```
disk reinit name = logical_device_name,
   physname = physical_device_name,
   vdevno = virtual_device_number,
   size = number_of_pages
   [, vstart = virtual_address,
   cntrltype = controller_number]
```

Disk refit is used after running disk reinit to rebuild the sysusages and sysdatabases tables in master from the database fragments found on the restored devices.

```
disk refit
```

7. After executing disk refit, shut down and restart Adaptive Server in single-user mode and verify that all databases are properly restored and are the correct sizes. Run dbcc checkalloc() on all recovered databases. If everything appears okay, shut down and restart Adaptive Server normally.

Any changes or additions to logins, configuration options, remote servers, remote logins, and roles will still need to be re-created.

Moral: Keep frequent backups of the master database!

Quiesce Database

There are situations when you may wish to supplement the regular ASE solutions for ensuring data (mirroring, dump, and load) with hardware-level solutions. In many shops, operating systems or third-party tools permit the manipulation of entire sections of disk (or *partitions*) for copying or archiving. In some cases, this may be the most time-effective form of backup; for example, very large databases may require either such a large number of stripe devices or such a large amount of time that dumping the database would not be practical (or even possible).

Depending on the method of making such copies, it may be necessary to render entire devices quiet — that is, disallow change anywhere on the device until the partition operation is complete. Naturally, one of these partitions may contain multiple devices, which in turn can contain multiple databases (or portions of databases); therefore, we may need to set an entire series of databases into a no changes state very quickly.

Though you might think that we could do this with the sp_dboption "read only," the system may still make changes. Also, it is only from a user perspective; an sa could make changes. Additionally, that requires a separate execution for each database, as well as a checkpoint for the change to take effect. An easier option is to *quiesce* the databases. A database that has been quiesced may not be updated, but permits data retrieval. Without the quiesce database statement, you would have to shut the server down for a device copy.

Syntax:

```
quiesce database tag_name hold dbname [,dbname …] [for external dump]
```

Example:

```
quiesce database hold_set_1 hold sales_oltp_db, sales_dss_db, personnel_db
```

The tag_name argument provides a logical name for a set of databases, all of which are held. The chief advantage of the quiesce database command is that it can hold up to eight databases at once (multiple instances may exist concurrently with different tag names). When the necessary disk-level operations are done and the databases no longer need to be held, the quiesce database command provides the release.

The for external dump option allows the backup process to gain access to the database for copying purposes.

Syntax:

```
quiesce database tag_name release
```

Example:

```
quiesce database hold_set_1 release
```

The entire set must be released as a unit, and databases may not be dumped while they are held (if a hold request is issued while a database or log is being dumped, it will not take effect until the dump is finished).

> **NOTE:** Prior to Adaptive Server Enterprise release 12.0.1, quiesce database could only be issued against a database that had been previously dumped at least once. It is possible to quiesce master, but this should only be done after all other desired quiesces are active (and master should be released first). In Adaptive Server Enterprise release 12.5, there are no ordering dependencies.

After releasing the database, you can bring up the secondary server with the -q parameter if you used the for external dump clause. Recovery makes the databases transactionally consistent, or you can wait to bring the database online and then apply the transaction log.

Warm Standby

The following diagram illustrates the warm standby scenario.

Figure 8-4

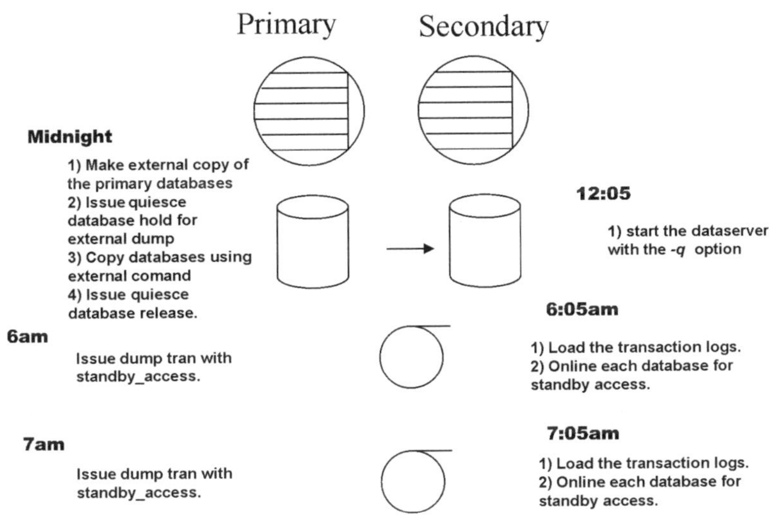

With the warm standby scenario, we have made a decision to use OS utilities to migrate the majority of the data.

The only way we can make this copy while the server is up, and still maintain transactional integrity, is to stop the transactions while the devices are being copied.

In this scenario, we are starting our warm standby copy at midnight. (See "Midnight" in the above diagram.) In order to effect the change, we first make copies of our primary databases. When this is done, we will tell the server to stop making changes to the databases on the devices we are stopping by issuing the quiesce database command for each appropriate database. After the OS utilities have completed, we release the quiesce state.

At 5 minutes after midnight, we start the secondary database with the -q option. The databases are already in place.

At 6 a.m. when transactions have begun to accumulate (and at other times of day subsequently), we will dump the transaction log with standby_access, which puts the log into a state that the secondary understands. After the dump completes (see 6:05 in the above diagram), load the transaction logs into the secondary environment. After putting the database online for standby_access, these databases are accessible for read only. This may be repeated as needed (see 7 a.m., for example).

In order to take the secondary into primary mode (make it modifiable), simply use the online database command without the standby_access parameter.

Database Recovery Scenarios

Take a look at a few possible scenarios. Here are some potential disaster situations, and what you should do to recover from them.

Scenario 1

What is the data loss? What steps are required to recover from this device failure?

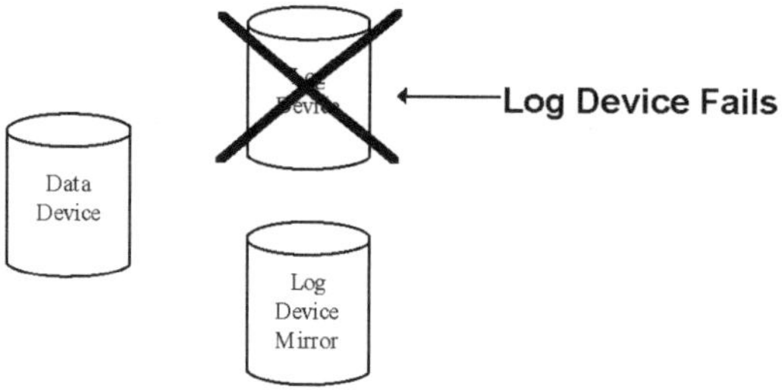

Scenario 2

What is the data loss? What steps are required to recover from this device failure?

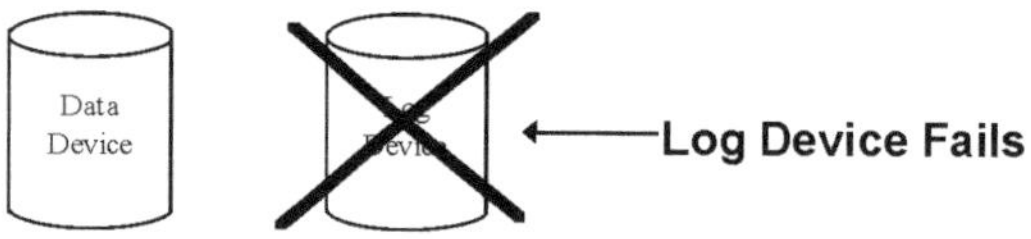

Scenario 3

What is the data loss? What steps are required to recover from this device failure?

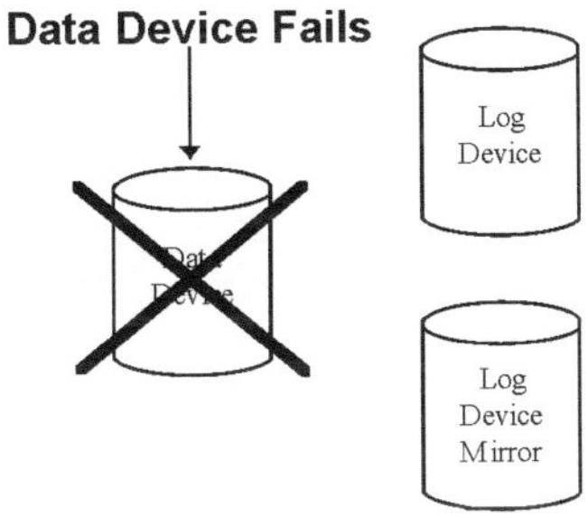

Scenario 4

Database dump performed nightly at midnight.

Log dumps performed every four hours.

Database device failure occurs at 2 p.m.

During the load, the 8 a.m. transaction log dump is found to be bad.

To what point can this database be recovered if the data device failed? If the log device failed?

Scenario 5

Database dump performed at midnight and noon with log dumps performed every four hours.

Database device failure occurs at 6 p.m.

During the load, the 12 p.m. database dump is found to be bad.

To what point can this database be recovered if the data device failed? If the log device failed?

Answers for the Scenarios

Scenario 1 — The log device is still mirrored, and the database is still up and running. No data is lost. To restore the primary log device, replace the failed log device and run the disk remirror command to reinitialize and copy the contents of the mirror back to the new device.

Scenario 2 — The database is unusable because there is no log. To restore, restore the last database dump and all log dumps since. Any data modifications since the last log dump will be lost.

Scenario 3 — The database is unusable because the data device failed. Dump the log with no truncate. To restore, restore the last database dump and all log dumps since, including the up-to-the-minute log dump. No committed data modifications up to the point that the data device failure will be lost.

Scenario 4 — The database can only be recovered up to the last transaction log dump prior to the bad log dump. This would include all changes up to 4 a.m. You cannot skip over a bad log dump and load any subsequent log dumps because that would create a gap in the restore sequence, which would make subsequent loads meaningless.

Scenario 5 — Because the dump database command does not truncate the log, the database can be fully recovered up to the last transaction log dump performed. This would be all changes up to 4 p.m., if the log device failed, or up to 6 p.m. if the data device failed and the log can be dumped with no_truncate.

If the log were truncated and not dumped (e.g., dump tran with truncate_only), prior or subsequent to the database dump, the database could only be recovered to the last previous log dump.

Summary

The database is backed up by making a physical copy of all used data pages, including the log pages, using the dump database command.

The database may be incrementally backed up with a dump of the transaction log.

The database may be subsequently loaded with the load database and load transaction statements.

Database backup is imperative in production databases, and a very good idea in development and quality assurance environments.

Chapter 9

Resource Governor

Some environments are simple. Queries are predefined and predictable. Updates affect few rows. Ad hoc queries aren't permitted. Procedures that use tempdb have limited growth.

But not many people get to administer simple environments.

What happens when we have runaway queries? Ad hoc users who repeatedly fill tempdb? Demographical research that inadvertently returns 4,000,000 rows?

For less predictable environments, we have the Resource Governor. The Resource Governor exists to provide the systems administrator the ability to set limits on precious, limited server resources.

The Resource Governor can limit runaway queries at the application level (for example, all users running CT-ISQL), login level (for example, user "bob", regardless of what app is running), or as a combination of the two.

You can limit the following resources:

- I/O costs (estimated or actual)
- Elapsed time
- Number of rows returned
- Amount of space used in tempdb

For example, if you set a limit of no more than 1,000 rows to be returned, then you can exceed your limitation based on estimated rows returned (the optimizer estimates rows returned anyway), or actual rows (when 1,000 rows have been returned), or both (we hit our limitation if either estimated or actual rows exceed 1,000). Elapsed time (in seconds) and number of rows returned may not be limited on estimated costs, only actual.

Or, if a sort (from an order by clause) will use up too much space, we can terminate a query (at many shops, tempdb is a very limited resource).

When the resource limit is crossed, the Resource Governor will perform the action defined by the sa. This action can be to:

- Issue a warning message
- Abort the transaction
- Abort the batch
- Terminate the login

You may also choose to have many resource limits active.

Once resource limits are enabled, you can define limits as well as time periods during which the limits will be active.

Note that limits are enforced on a per-spid basis; if a query is performed in parallel, unless a single worker process exceeds a limit, the Resource Governor will take no action, even if the query as a whole exceeded the limit.

Enabling Resource Limits

If you want the server to test and adhere to resource limits, the first thing you need to do is instruct the server to pay attention. You do this by enabling resource limits at the server level as follows:

```
exec sp_configure "allow resource limits",1
```

The allow resource limits configuration parameter controls the use of resource limits. When the value is set to 1, the server allocates internal memory for time ranges, resource limits, and internal server alarms. Because memory allocation is involved, this option is static, meaning that it does not take effect until the server is cycled. The server also internally assigns applicable ranges and limits to user sessions. To disable resource limits, set allow resource limits to 0.

Enabling resource limits changes the output of showplan and statistics i/o, as follows:

showplan displays estimated I/O cost information for DML statements. The information displayed is the optimizer's cost estimate for the query as a unitless number. The total estimated I/O cost is displayed for the query as a whole.

statistics i/o includes the actual total I/O cost of a statement according to the optimizer's cost formula. This value is a number representing the sum of the number of logical I/Os multiplied by the cost of a logical I/O, and the number of physical I/Os multiplied by the cost of a physical I/O.

Note that you can use the output from these statements to begin to determine what useful limits would be by running queries that approach your performance limits and setting server-wide limits accordingly.

Time Ranges

A *time range* is a named, contiguous block of time across one or more contiguous days of the week for which the limit will be enforced. Adaptive Server provides a default time range called at all times, which includes every day of the week from 00:00 to 23:59. This default time range cannot be dropped or modified.

Time ranges may overlap. For example,

```
Monday to Friday, 8:00 a.m. to 5:00 p.m.
Tuesday to Wednesday, 4:00 p.m. to 8:00 a.m.
```

Here we have two time ranges, which we might label "Normal office hours" and "Ad hoc query permitted", respectively, with ad hoc queries permitted during this narrow time frame on our production box. Note that the ranges are not necessarily single blocks of time. The "Normal office hours" range falls between the hours of 8 a.m. and 5 p.m. on each of the days Monday through Friday. It does not start Monday morning and run for 105 hours until Friday afternoon.

Adding Time Ranges

New time ranges are added with the sp_add_time_range stored procedure.

Syntax:

```
sp_add_time_range name, startday, endday, starttime, endtime
```

Parameters:

Name

May be any string (spaces are permitted if the name is quoted).

Startday and endday

Fully typed-out days of the week.

Starttime and endtime

Times to the minute using the 24-hour clock. Note that endtime must be later than starttime.

To set a time range to include the whole day, you must set the start time and end time to 00:00:

```
sp_add_time_range business_hours, Monday, Friday, '08:00', '17:00'
```

In this example, we are creating a time range named business_hours. It is valid from Monday through Friday, from 8 a.m. to 5 p.m. each day.

Simplifying the Creation of Time Ranges

Use a chart like this one to help set up time ranges. You can draw your time ranges across it, and use it for reference while creating resource limits.

	Monday	Tuesday	Wednesday	Thursday	Friday	Saturday	Sunday
0:00							
1:00							
2:00							
3:00							
4:00							
5:00							
6:00							
7:00							
8:00							
9:00							
10:00							
11:00							
12:00							
13:00							

	Monday	Tuesday	Wednesday	Thursday	Friday	Saturday	Sunday
14:00							
15:00							
16:00							
17:00							
18:00							
19:00							
20:00							
21:00							
22:00							
23:00							

Modifying Time Ranges

Sometimes, after you have been using a time range, and you have limits set for the time ranges, the business rule that drove the time range changes. For example, normal business hours may extend to 5:30. It is easier to change the valid times for the existing named time range than it is to drop it from all of your limits, and then reassign a new one.

sp_modify_time_range can change a time range. Any parameter that is set to null is not changed.

Syntax:

```
sp_modify_time_range name, startday, endday, starttime, endtime
```

Example:

```
sp_modify_time_range business_hours, NULL, NULL,NULL, '17:30'
```

The above example ignores all parameters in the time range except the last one, endtime, and sets that parameter to 5:30 p.m. This change takes effect immediately, but not for active processes. In other words, if this change is made when you sign in, it does not take effect for your process until you disconnect and reconnect.

Removing Time Ranges

You can remove a time range that you are no longer using with the sp_drop_time_range stored procedure. As with most things Sybase, you cannot drop this if it is actively in use. You also cannot drop the default time range.

Syntax:

```
sp_drop_time_range name
```

Example:

```
sp_drop_time_range business_hours
```

This example removes the named time range business_hours that we created earlier.

Creating a Limit

The resource limit applies across a time range you've selected. Use the sp_add_resource_limit stored procedure to create the limit.

Syntax:

```
sp_add_resource_limit login, appname, rangename, limittype, limitvalue
[,enforced [,action[,scope]]]
```

Parameters:

login

The login name to which the limit applies. To create a limit to apply to all users of an application, set login to NULL.

appname

The application name to which you want the limit applied. To create a limit for all apps that a login uses, set appname to NULL. Note that the application name is whatever value is passed in by the client application, and may not necessarily be the familiar name of the executable. If the wrong appname is used, the limits will not apply! You may supply login, appname, or both; they may not both be NULL.

rangename

The name of the time range for which the limit is active.

limittype

Specifies whether the limit will be based on rows, I/O, or time.

limitvalue

The value applied to the limit type; this is an integer, with a minimum value of 1.

enforced determines if the limit is enforced before or during query execution (I/O limits only).

action

Determines what action to perform (warning, abort, etc.).

scope

Specifies across what domain the limit applies (for example, for a single SQL statement or an entire batch).

Choosing a Limit Type

An individual resource limit can restrict your user's resources by:

- Row count (number of rows returned)
- Elapsed time (how long the query runs)
- I/O cost (how much I/O must be performed to retrieve the results)
- Tempdb_space

row_count

row_count limits the number of rows a query can return to the requested process. When you select row_count, value is the maximum number of rows to be returned before the specified action is taken. If the row_count limit is exceeded, the user will still get whatever rows have already been sent.

elapsed_time

elapsed_time limits the number of seconds that a query batch or transaction can run. When you select elapsed_time, value is the maximum number of seconds the query batch or transaction can run before the specified action is taken. Note that time waiting for I/O to complete, for locks to be obtained, and other processing delays all count towards the elapsed_time limit.

io_cost

io_cost limits the actual or estimated I/O cost of a query. The value is unitless, and is based on the optimizer's costing formula (for example, does the optimizer use 2 K I/O or 16 K I/O for this query?).

tempdb_space

This limits the amount of space in the tempdb database that can be taken up by the process. This is only valid during execution, not prior. Units are in logical pages. In other words, if you have 2 K pages, it will be the 512 pages per megabyte.

Choosing the Type of Enforcement

Enforcement type defines when the limit is identified. Valid values for enforcement type are:

Value	Description
1	Action is taken prior to execution.
2	Action is taken during execution.
3	Action is taken both during and prior to execution.

Note that row_count, tempdb_space, and elapsed_time can only be enforced during execution; io_cost can be enforced prior to execution, during, or both.

This is a wonderful way of deciding how aggressive your enforcement actions are going to get. You have the ability to enforce limits based on (1) estimated, (2) actual, or (3) either.

Unless you have a reason not to, we recommend you choose 3; that gives you the best of both worlds — performance of the action if the optimizer estimates that it will exceed, as well as performance if the optimizer guesses wrong, and it actually does exceed the limits.

Choosing an Action

Once the limit is exceeded, the server needs to perform the selected enforcement action. Valid enforcement actions are:

Value	Description
1	Issue a warning to the calling application.
2	Aborts the query batch.
3	Aborts the transaction.
4	Kills the session.

The default value is to abort the query batch. If you have multiple front ends accessing the data, be careful when using option 1, because different message handlers handle the warning messages differently. Regardless of enforcement action, a notification is written to the errorlog every time a limit is exceeded.

Choosing a Scope

Scope is the domain within which the server determines whether to take action. In other words, do you want to limit the number of rows to 10,000 within the scope of the individual SQL statement, the batch, or a transaction? Another way to think of scope is to ask the question, at what point does the Resource Governor start counting again?

Value	Domain	Definition
1	Query	A single SQL statement
2	Batch	A group of SQL statements
4	Transaction	The complete transaction
6	Query batch and transaction	

A scope of 1 is only valid for limit types io_cost and row_count. Scopes of 2, 4, and 6 are only valid for limit type elapsed_time.

Limit Hierarchies

Limit hierarchies are created by assigning login and application limits separately. In case of multiple or conflicting resource limits, Adaptive Server Enterprise checks limits in the following order:

1. Check limits for a login/application combo
2. Check limits for an application
3. Check limits for a login

If a limit is found, then the server applies the limit, and no further checking is performed. If no limit is found at any level, then no limit is applied.

If you want to set limits so users can only access known applications, set the following limits:

- Limit each user for the time range named at all times on each limit type to abort the transaction for the minimum value (0).
- Turn on the acceptable applications for all users on each limit type setting to the limits you want (or the maximum value).
- Specifically turn on limits for user and application.

Examples of Limits

Create a limit for all logins that run an isql session, application isql, during normal business hours. Abort the batch if the actual or estimated I/O cost is greater than 1,000.

```
sp_add_resource_limit NULL, isql, business_hours, io_cost, 1000,3,2
```

Create a limit for all systems administrators and all applications during normal business hours, to issue a warning if the actual or estimated I/O cost is greater than 100,000.

```
sp_add_resource_limit sa, NULL, business_hours, io_cost, 100000,3,1
```

Note that this second example assumes that all systems administrators share the sa login; the Resource Governor does not apply limits to roles. Also, be careful in setting limits on systems administrators ... the limits could hamper their ability to oversee the server, or even to remove the limit!

Viewing Limits

Limits can be displayed by using the sp_help_resource_limit stored procedure:

Syntax:

```
sp_help_resource_limit [name [,appname[, limittime [, limitday [, scope
[,action ]]]]]]
```

The parameters are listed in the following table:

Parameter	Description
Name	The name that the limit applies to. Only the SA can specify other logins. If it is left NULL, the current login is used.
Appname	The name of the application. If NULL, it will show all application limits.
Limittime	Time that the limit is enforced. If NULL, all times.
Limitday	Day of the week that the limit is enforced. If NULL, every day.
Scope	Scope of the limit. Follows standard scope numbers. If NULL, all scopes.
Action	Action of the limit. If NULL, all actions.

Changing Limits

Once limits are defined, you might want to modify them rather than dropping and re-creating them.

Syntax:

```
sp_modify_resource_limit name, appname, time range,limittype, limitvalue,
enforced, action,scope
```

No surprises here; these parameters are all self-explanatory based upon prior definitions.

NOTE: You can only modify the action of the limit and the limit value. All other values must match the initially created values. To change the other values you must drop and re-create the limit. If you do not want to modify either the action or the value, use either the existing value or NULL for the parameter.

Removing Limits

You can remove limits with the sp_drop_resource_limit stored procedure.

Syntax:

```
sp_drop_resource_limit name, appname, rangename, limittype, action, scope
```

The parameters are the same as they were when you created the limit.

System Tables

There are three system tables involved in resource limits:

- spt_limit_types (stored procedure table)
- systimeranges (system table)
- sysresourcelimits (system table)

spt_limit_types Table

The table spt_limit_types tells us what resource is covered by the resource governor:

```
select * from spt_limit_types
go
name           id  enforced   object_type  scope   units
------------   --  --------   -----------  -----   -----
io_cost        1      3            1         1     derived from optimizer's
                                                   costing formula
elapsed_time   2      2            1         6     in seconds
row_count      3      2            1         1     # of row returned to
                                                   client
tempdb_space   4      2            1         1     in pages

(4 rows affected)
```

We can see that tempdb_space is added, and that it is enforced during execution, in the server level and for the query scope.

systimeranges Table

The System table systimeranges has all the time ranges defined:

```
1>select * from systimeranges
2> go
name   id   startday   endday   starttime  endtime
----   --   --------   ------   ---------  -------
at all times 1 1 7 00:00 00:00

(1 row affected)
```

Shown here is the default at all times definition.

sysresourcelimits Table

The system table sysresourcelimits has all the resource limits defined so far by the user. It may not be as useful to the user as the previous two tables since it has pretty much the same information given by sp_help_resource_limit.

Summary

The resource governor gives you the ability to limit precious server resources when users or applications have the potential to usurp too much of the resources available. It has a performance hit of less than 1%, so if you are running a server at 95% of CPU you might want to worry about the impact, but otherwise, don't. Interestingly, if you are running at 95% and turn on the resource governor, you might end up limiting some of the queries that are causing the 95% CPU.

You can limit:

- I/O
- Elapsed time
- Number of rows
- tempdb space used

Actions taken upon exceeding a resource limit may be:

- Warning
- Abort the query
- Abort the transaction
- Kill the user's session

Chapter 10

Logical Process Manager

Most production environments have sufficient resources for all the users, applications, and queries that are running on the server. Other environments are more limited in available capacity. Some have higher priority applications; some have sets of users with lower priority. Some have uses which are mixed, where some of the applications have the potential to strangle server resources (for example, an ad hoc query that fills tempdb, or returns 4,000,000 rows to the front end).

This chapter discusses prioritization of work in an SMTP environment. If you are looking for a way to restrict these activities (rather than prioritize them), go back to Chapter 9, "Resource Governor."

One warning before you get seriously into this chapter: It is possible to over-tune a server, thus restricting its operation when it is able to manage resources on its own. This is a bad idea. Worse, the Logical Process Manager is an easy place to do this. Using the Logical Process Manager is something you should do only upon determining that you have a specific problem that you want to resolve, and only after you have achieved a stable mix of transactions. Using Logical Process Manager too soon is like trying to fine-tune a TV before you're on the right channel.

What is the Logical Process Manager?

Until recently (release 11.5), all processes ran with the same priority on ASE. Any process would go into the queue, and would be assigned to a CPU on a first-come, first-served basis. Once a task reached the top of the queue, it would be assigned to run on the first engine that was available, and continue to run until it exhausted its allotted time (or until the task finished, whichever was less). All tasks had equal access to the same amount of server resources, and no task was more important than another.

For example:

SPID 1
SPID 99
SPID 155
SPID 21
SPID 321
SPID 2

The above figure represents the *run queue*. If your process needs work done, it is added to the bottom of the list. Above, SPID 2 was the last added to the list. When an ASE engine is ready to perform a task, it grabs the process at the top of the queue. In this case, it takes SPID 1, not because of the number, but because of its position in the queue.

ASE version 11.5 introduced the Logical Process Manager, which allows the SA to assign execution attributes to a process, and permits you to create engine groups which may exclusively run (or not run) these processes. This gives you the ability to create high- and low-priority jobs. It also allows you to set aside processors for the exclusive use of the high-priority jobs, or to limit low-priority jobs to few CPUs.

This can be useful for:

- Mixed workload environments
- Multi-application systems
- Ad hoc users who need real-time access to data during business hours, but whose work cannot (or should not) conflict with OLTP (online transaction processing) users.

For example:

SPID 321	SPID 99	SPID 1
	SPID 155	SPID 21
	SPID 2	
LOW	MEDIUM	HIGH

In this case, different tasks have been assigned to different run queues with different priorities; both SPIDs 1 and 21 must be assigned to engines before SPID 99 may be assigned; likewise, until SPID 2 is assigned to an engine, SPID 321 will be waiting for resources to become available. Note that if only a few engines are available, it's possible that more tasks could be added to the High and Medium queues before the Low has a chance to place SPID 321 on an engine. Such *task starvation* may have serious negative consequences for your performance.

The engine that a task is assigned to is independent of its run queue priority. In the above example, it may be that SPID 1 is permitted to run on any engine, but SPID 21 (which shares the High priority) is only permitted to run on a subset of the engines. Likewise, each of the three SPIDs in the medium priority queue may have a different *affinity* towards engines. If a task is at the top of its queue but all of the engines that it has an affinity for are busy, it will not be able to run right away.

Finally, the time that a task is permitted to run on an engine (or *timeslice*) is independent of its priority or its engine affinity. In the example above, SPID 1 may be able to run on any engine, but it may be assigned to a less-than-standard amount of run time; SPID 21, by contrast, could be assigned to extra run time to make up for not being able to run on any engine.

Note that although the Logical Process Manager gives you a great deal of control in assigning priority, engine affinity, and run times, it is possible to have too much of a good thing. Trying to find the optimal balance of all three properties for each task is likely to be impossible.

Logical Process Manager Execution Classes

The three properties listed above — base priority, engine affinity, and timeslice — may be grouped together under a descriptive name known as an *execution class*. Once defined, execution classes may be assigned (or *bound*) to Logical Process Manager objects (see below), which will determine which tasks are assigned to which queues, engine groupings, and timeslices.

Base Priority

Base priority is the initial priority of any task that is assigned to this class; the priority may change (increase or decrease) for a variety of reasons during processing. There are three user-assignable priorities: Low, Medium, and High; you may not create other priorities.

Engine Affinity

Engine affinity (or engine group) specifies the numbers of engines upon which a process is eligible to run. There are two predefined engine groups, known as Anyengine (the process may run on any available engine when it gets to the top of its queue) and Lastonline (the process is restricted to using only the highest-numbered engine). You may create your own engine groups, in any combination that you wish.

Timeslice (Quantum)

Timeslice is the amount of CPU time a task can run before it offers to "schedule out" of the CPU. The default value is 100 milliseconds.

ASE provides three execution classes, EC1, EC2, and EC3, defined in the following table:

Name	Priority	Engine Affinity
EC1	High	Anyengine
EC2	Medium	Anyengine
EC3	Low	Lastonline

You can use these execution classes, create your own, or use any combination.

Logical Process Manager Objects

The Logical Process Manager allows you to define objects that may be bound to execution classes. These objects might be client applications, user logins, or stored procedures. The tasks undertaken by the application, login, or procedure will be assigned the queue, affinity, and timeslice of the object's execution class. Any object not specifically bound to an execution class defaults to EC2.

Logical Process Manager Procedures

Logical Process Manager has a host of stored procedures associated with it, for the purpose of defining execution classes, binding objects to the execution classes, and showing the results of the settings.

Stored Procedure	Description
sp_addexeclass	Adds execution classes
sp_dropexeclass	Drops unused execution classes
sp_bindexeclass	Binds objects to execution classes
sp_unbindexeclass	Unbinds objects to execution classes
sp_setpsexe	Lets users set execution class attributes dynamically
sp_clearpsexe	Clears attributes that were set dynamically
sp_addengine	Creates an engine group, or adds an engine to an existing engine group
sp_dropengine	Drops an engine from an engine group or removes an unused engine group
sp_showcontrolinfo	Displays information about engine groups and bound objects
sp_showexeclass	Displays execution class attributes and the engines in the execution class
sp_showpsexe	Shows execution class, priority, and affinity for all client sessions

sp_addexeclass

To add an execution class, use the sp_addexeclass stored procedure:

Syntax:

```
sp_addexeclass class_name, base_priority, timeslice, engine_group
```

Example:

```
sp_addexeclass executive, high, 200, ANYENGINE
```

This example creates an execution class called executive, which will run assigned tasks at high priority, on any engine, with a timeslice value of 200.

If the class already exists, this stored procedure will modify the execution class (note there is no modify stored procedure).

Example:

```
sp_addexeclass executive, high, 100, ANYENGINE
```

This example changes the execution class called executive, reducing its timeslice value from 200 back to 100.

Parameters:

class_name
: class_name is the logical name you give to the class you are creating.

base_priority
: base_priority is the priority which the execution class will have when a process running within that class starts.

timeslice
: timeslice is the amount of time (in milliseconds) to which the process is entitled before scheduling out.

> **NOTE:** This parameter is actually ignored, at least through Adaptive Server Enterprise 12.5.

engine_group
: The name of the engine group on which the execution class will run. You may use one of the predefined engine groups, or define your own engine groups using the sp_addengine stored procedure (covered later).

Predefined system classes cannot be modified.

sp_dropexeclass

To drop a class, use sp_dropexeclass.

Syntax:

```
sp_dropexeclass classname
```

Example:

```
sp_dropexeclass executive
```

This removes the class we defined earlier. System classes may not be removed. Also, you cannot remove classes that are presently bound to Logical Process Manager objects.

sp_bindexeclass

The sp_bindexeclass stored procedures binds objects to the defined execution classes.

Syntax:

```
sp_bindexeclass object_name, object_type, scope, class_name
```

Example:

```
sp_bindexeclass sa, LG, isql, EC1
```

This specifies that whenever the sa login runs isql, it will run in execution class 1 (high priority).

Parameters:

object_name

object_name is the name of the object that we are going to bind.

object_type

object_type is the type of object that we are binding, as follows:

Type	Description
AP	Object type is an application.
LG	Object type is a login.
PR	Object type is a stored procedure.

scope

The scope parameter allows you to indicate that an assigned execution class will only apply to a given object in combination with an additional detail. In the example above, the login sa runs its tasks at EC1 only if the tasks are submitted through isql; if the sa login were using another application, the assignment would not hold, and the tasks would default to EC2. If no value of scope is specified (use NULL value), the execution class applies regardless of detail or circumstance.

If an object is of type application or login, then scope is the name of a client application or login or NULL.

If the object type is stored procedure, then scope is the stored procedure owner.

You must be in the database in which the stored procedure exists to bind to a stored procedure.

class_name

class_name is the name of the class to which the object will be bound, including the system classes (EC1, EC2, EC3), and any user-defined class.

sp_unbindexeclass

This is the stored procedure that removes object bindings from an execution class.

Syntax:

```
sp_unbindexeclass object_name, object_type, scope
```

Example:

```
sp_unbindexeclass sa, LG, isql
```

Note that you must unbind stored procedures before you can drop them from the database.

sp_setpsexe

Users can use this procedure to set execution attributes dynamically.

Syntax:

```
sp_setpsexe spid, exeattr, value
```

Example:

```
sp_setpsexe 3, priority, HIGH
```

This sets the priority to High for the person running spid 3.

Parameters:

Spid

Spid is the system process id for which you want to change the execution attribute.

exeattr

This is the execution attribute that you will change. This will be "priority" or "engine group."

Values

If exeattr is priority, valid values are Low, Medium, or High.

If exeattr is engine group, the only valid value is the name of an existing engine group.

NOTES: The only system process you can change attributes for is the housekeeper task.
Any user can lower his own priority.
Only the sa can raise priorities or change other users' priorities.

sp_clearpsexe

If you have dynamically reset execution classes, and wish to reset them, you may do this with sp_clearpsexe.

Syntax:

```
sp_clearpsexe spid, exeattr
```

Example:

```
sp_setpsexe 3, priority
```

This resets the priority attribute for SPID 3 to whatever value it would normally have. This can be performed by the user or by the sa.

Engine Groups

E0	E1	E2	E3	E4	E5	E6

If you have an eight-processor box, and have configured ASE to start up with seven engines, you will get a list of engines like the one above. Engine numbers start at zero, and work their way up to the number of "max online engines" less one. In other words, a seven-engine server will have a highest engine number of 6.

There are two system-provided engine groups: ANYENGINE and LASTONLINE. If you select ANYENGINE (or fail to select a group, for this is the default), you will be referring to all ASE engines. If you select LASTONLINE, you will be referring only to the highest-numbered engine (in this case, engine 6).

Remember, this is a great way to bollix up your system by overconfiguring it, so be sure you measure the performance effects of your box before and after you do this.

sp_addengine

You create your own engine groups with the sp_addengine procedure. This will add an engine group or modify an engine group (other than system-provided groups).

This procedure must be run from the master database.

Syntax:

```
sp_addengine engine_number, engine_group
```

Example:

```
sp_addengine 0, new_group
```

This creates a group called "new_group" which runs only on engine 0. If new_group previously existed, it now also includes engine number 0.

Parameters:

engine_number

engine_number is any number between 0 and max number of engines –1. In the example preceding this section, seven engines would yield a highest engine number of 6.

engine_group

engine_group is the name of an existing group to which an engine will be added, or a new group that will be created.

sp_dropengine

Once you have created an engine group, or added engines to the engine group, you have the ability to drop the group or engines from the group. You do this with the sp_dropengine stored procedure.

Like the sp_addengine stored procedure, this must be run from the master database.

Syntax:

```
sp_dropengine engine_number, engine_group
```

Example:

```
sp_dropengine 0, new_group
```

This drops the engine from the group we've defined previously. If we have not placed another engine in this engine group, then this will additionally remove the engine group (but you may only remove groups that are not used in execution classes).

More Examples

Let's try a more practical example. You have the eight-processor box described above, and have assigned seven processors to ASE.

Problem: You have three basic classes of users/applications. The first is the online group. This group is taking orders online, and performance is important because if we can't take orders fast enough, we lose customers. The second class is the shipment group, which needs real-time access to the system to set up deliveries, but who can wait a bit for results, as they are typically printed reports. The third class is the overnight reporting, which also can wait for results, as the reports run around midnight and do not need to be completed until morning.

Proposed solution: We will define three execution classes and three engine groups, and assign the applications accordingly.

First, we will define a new engine group. We will use ANYENGINE for the OLTP users who need the fast performance, and LASTONLINE for the group of overnight reporting. The third group, the shipment folks, will get an engine group that is using only three of the seven available, and at that, will share one with LASTONLINE:

```
exec sp_addengine 4, SHIPMENT_GROUP
exec sp_addengine 5, SHIPMENT_GROUP
exec sp_addengine 6, SHIPMENT_GROUP
```

Now we have three groups defined, which are making use of engines as follows:

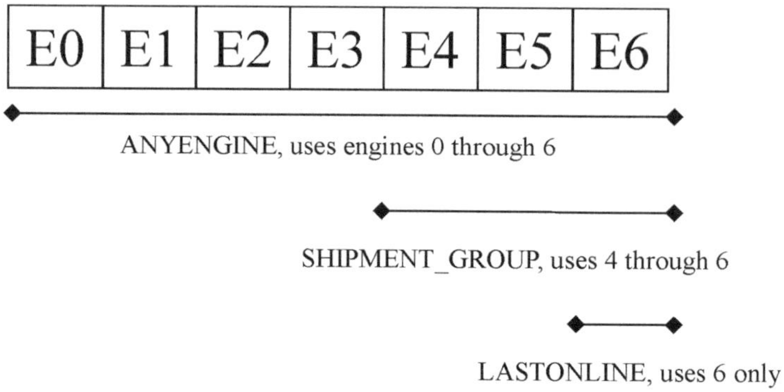

SHIPMENT_GROUP now exists, which can be verified with sp_showcontrolinfo:

```
1> sp_showcontrolinfo
2> go
type     engine_group       engines
----     --------------     -------
EG       SHIPMENT_GROUP     4, 5, 6
```

Note that the default engine groups are not displayed by sp_showcontrolinfo, only those created by the user. The value EG in the type column indicates that the output row refers to an engine group; other valid values of type are AP, LG, PR, and PS (for application, login, proc, and process). Not all types will have values in all columns of the output, so the output shown is abbreviated for clarity. The allowed parameters in sp_showcontrolinfo vary, so check the documentation set for full syntax.

The execution class may now be created (using sp_addexeclass), verified (using sp_showexeclass), and bound to the three applications (using sp_bindexeclass); after binding, sp_showcontrolinfo can be used again to double-check the outcome:

```
1> sp_addexeclass SHIPMENT_CLASS, medium, 100, SHIPMENT_GROUP
2> go
(return status = 0)
1> sp_showexeclass
2> go
classname          priority     engine_group       engines
--------------     ---------    --------------     -------
EC1                HIGH         ANYENGINE          ALL
EC2                MEDIUM       ANYENGINE          ALL
EC3                LOW          LASTONLINE         6
SHIPMENT_CLASS     MEDIUM       SHIPMENT_GROUP     4, 5, 6

1> exec sp_bindexeclass "online app", AP, null, EC1
2> exec sp_bindexeclass "shipment app", AP, null, SHIPMENT_CLASS
3> exec sp_bindexeclass "reporting app", AP, null, EC3
4> go
(return status = 0)
```

```
1> sp_showcontrolinfo
2> go
type    object_name        scope     exec_class
----    -------------      -----     ----------
AP      online_app         NULL      EC1
AP      shipment_app       NULL      SHIPMENT_CLASS
AP      reporting_app      NULL      EC3
```

If you are uncertain as to what privileges a given session has, you may examine it with sp_showpsexe; it will show the current values of priority and engine group (which may have been changed by sp_setpsexe) associated with a given spid.

```
1> sp_showpsexe
2> go
spid   appl_name      login_name   ...     current_priority  task_affinity
----   ------------   ----------   ...     ----------------  --------------
1      shipment_app   bob                  MEDIUM            SHIPMENT_GROUP
9                     NULL                 LOW               NULL
14     isql           sa                   HIGH              NULL
```

In this example, the value of NULL under task_affinity indicates that the task is not restricted to using only certain engines; that is, it is permitted to use any engine. Most system tasks will not display in the output of sp_showpsexe, but that of the Housekeeper task (here, spid 9) will.

Note that our choice of engine groups, priorities, and timeslices represented only an initial guess as to what would actually improve the load balancing on the server. Extensive testing (and further tuning) will be required to prove that our use of the Logical Process Manager didn't cause unforeseen performance problems.

Logical Process Manager Conflicts and Precedence

Because we have the ability to bind execution classes to different objects, there is the possibility that different ECs may overlap on a running process. For example, what happens if a login assigned to use EC3 executes a stored procedure that is assigned to EC1? Should the task use High priority or Low? Many engines, or only one? And can we say with certainty that many engines (which may be shared among many applications) are necessarily better than one (which may be reserved for only a single application's use)?

In order to settle potential conflicts not covered by the scope parameter of sp_bindexeclass, there is a *precedence rule* that determines what priority a task will run at, given conflicting execution classes. This rule will not attempt to decide what engine group or timeslice value to use (they will stay at their initial values), since it is not always clear that a given group or timeslice is better than another. With priorities, High is always better than Medium, which is always better than Low.

The precedence rule states that if a Logical Process Manager object calls another LPM object, the priority of the task may be changed if:

- The called object has a higher precedence.
- The called object is a procedure, which has a higher priority.

The precedence of LPM objects (from low to high) is:

- Application
- Login
- Stored Procedure

For example, if a login assigned to EC2 (Medium priority) calls a stored procedure assigned to EC3 (Low priority), we can see that while the called object (procedure) has a higher precedence than the calling object (login), it does not also have a higher priority. As a result, the priority of the original object (login/EC2/Medium) will be used for the entire task. The login does not lose its place in the Medium priority queue as a result of this conflict.

Likewise, if a login assigned to EC2 (Medium) called a stored procedure assigned to EC1 (High), the higher precedence and priority of the procedure would override the settings for the login, and the entire task would run at High priority. Here, the login has had its priority boosted to higher than expected levels.

Important Exception to the Precedence Rule

The precedence rule only applies to objects that have specifically been assigned to execution classes. Whenever an object at default EC2 (Medium) calls another object, the called object automatically overrides the priority of the calling object.

What if we repeated our first example, but the login was at EC2 not due to an explicit binding but merely because EC2 is the default? In this case, the proc's priority of Low would be used for the entire task, effectively lowering the login's expected Medium priority.

General Recommendations

Each new object assigned to an execution class that uses High priority essentially slows down all of the existing objects at High priority. In an extreme case, you could assign all procedures, all logins, all apps to use the High priority queue, and find that nothing runs any faster than when everything used the (default) Medium priority queue.

As a result, it's probably best to leave the High priority queue clear for those few circumstances when it's really needed — using sp_setpsexe for emergencies. Those apps that are less important than average may be assigned to Low priority, and the bulk of operations can be left at Medium priority (of course, this still leaves engine grouping for finer control).

As a result of the possibilities for priorities to end up far removed from their intended values, it is probably best that most Logical Process Manager controls be done at the application level. If individual logins and stored procedures are not assigned to specific execution classes, there will not be any conflict to worry about. The exception to this recommendation is that administrative logins should be assigned to EC1, so that their tasks are done as quickly as possible.

Chapter 11

Configuring and Tuning the Server

Memory is a finite resource. Configuring memory properly can improve the performance of your server. Configuring memory poorly (or overconfiguring memory) can create a maintenance nightmare, or it can degrade performance by giving precious physical memory to server resources that do not need it, while starving others. I have certainly seen systems that were running smoothly perform significantly less well after memory reconfiguration by an inexperienced administrator.

So, here we discuss what ASE does with memory, how it is divided up, and what control you have over it. Additionally, we cover server configuration options that are at least marginally memory-related but do not completely fit within the boundaries of this section.

Pre-12.5 Memory Management

Of total physical memory available on your box, the operating system acquires some, the server executable acquires some, and you configure what is done with the rest. Prior to 12.5, this is the total memory configuration parameter that you will set. Of the memory, some would be taken up by the server executable, some used by ASE kernel and internal structures, and the rest used by cache.

Figure 11-1

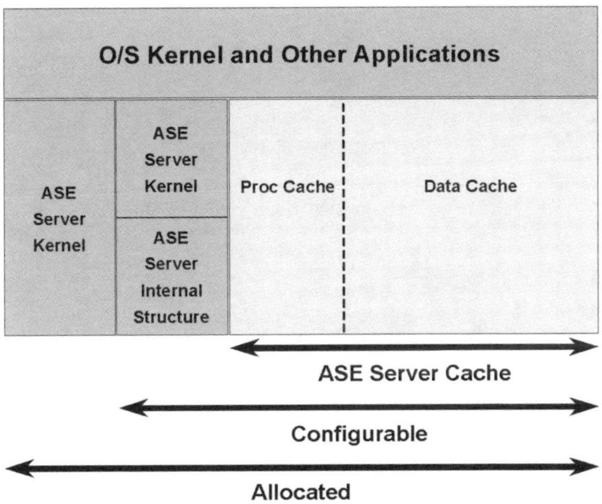

ASE has two types of cache: procedure cache and data cache. Procedure cache is used to contain stored procedure plans and trees, trigger plans and trees, and view trees. Data cache is used to contain pages read from disk, and is used to try to minimize physical I/O (which is the slowest operation a DBMS performs).

12.5 Memory Utilization

With the implementation of 12.5, Adaptive Server Enterprise has moved from a paradigm of a shared pool of memory that all server resources are fighting to subdivide. Now, for each of the memory configuration parameters, you instruct the server how much of the system resources to acquire, and it does.

In many ways, this is easier — and harder.

For example, when you want to increase data cache size, you no longer have to add memory to total memory (this parameter no longer exists), and then look to see its rippling effect on other resources. Instead, you reconfigure data cache only.

On the other hand, when your system administrator tells you that you have an extra 2 GB of memory to play with due to the prior weekend's system upgrade, instead of adding the memory to total memory, you have to decide what to do with the memory.

You can think of the model in ASE 12.5 as follows: You cannot specify the size of the container; instead you can specify the size of individual contents. ASE figures out the size of the container as the sum of the sizes of all the individual contents. However, the SA can control how large the container can grow up to (that is, the maximum amount of shared memory ASE can allocate during boot time and run time). This can be done through the new configuration parameter, max memory.

Logical, Physical, and Max Memory

Figure 11-2

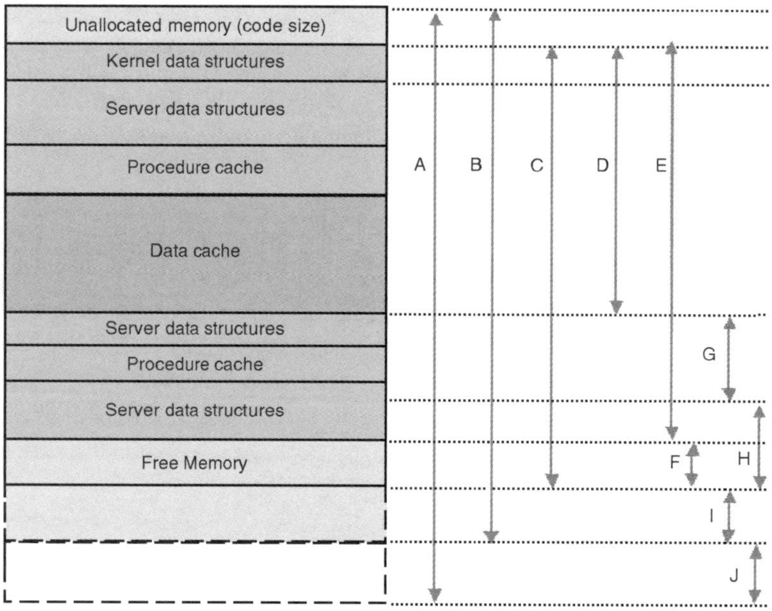

In this diagram, we can see the different boundaries of shared memory allocation. The values A-J are of interest from a shared memory allocation perspective. The following are the descriptions of the boundaries, some of which represent the new configuration parameters: total logical memory, total physical memory, and max memory.

A: max memory is a new, dynamic configuration parameter. As you have seen in the earlier sections, ASE 12.5 allocates shared memory during boot time and may allocate more shared memory during run time. Unlike pre-12.5 ASE, the SA cannot specify the size of shared memory to allocate during boot time. ASE calculates this as a sum of all memory requirements. System administrators, however, can use the parameter max memory to control the maximum amount of shared memory ASE is allowed to allocate. This parameter can be set to any value greater than the memory required for the current configuration. For more information on setting this parameter, see the "Recommended Configuration Settings" section later in this chapter.

In the figure, max memory is indicated by the boundary A. Note that max memory takes the ASE executable (code) size into account. This behavior is consistent with the total memory parameter in a pre-12.5 ASE taking executable size into account. Hence, the actual shared memory allocated will be less than the value specified by the parameter. For example, if '*max memory*' is set to 200 MB and if the code size is 10 MB, then the maximum shared memory allocated will be (200 – 10) 190 MB.

B: total logical memory is a new, read-only configuration parameter. This parameter indicates the total memory required for the current configuration. The Config Value of the parameter indicates the memory requirement during boot time. The Run Value indicates the memory requirement at any instant of time based on the current configuration. The difference between these two values should give you an idea about how the total memory requirement has changed after the boot.

Total logical memory increases and decreases when you change a configuration parameter and if that change causes memory requirement to increase or decrease. Note that total logical memory takes the ASE executable size into account as seen in boundary B of the figure.

C: total physical memory is a new, read-only configuration parameter. This parameter indicates the total amount of shared memory that is allocated at any instant of time. The Config Value is unused and always set to zero. The Run Value always increases, as ASE does not deallocate shared memory once it is allocated until you shut down ASE. The following are the relationships between total logical memory, total physical memory, and max memory.

total logical memory <= max memory

total physical memory <= max memory

The SA does not need to keep track of total logical memory and total physical memory as these are for informational purposes only and cannot be modified. The SA needs to determine the maximum size of shared memory that ASE will be allowed to allocate and set max memory to that value. Any configuration parameter can be changed as long as the memory requirement does not go beyond the max memory boundary.

D: This indicates the amount of shared memory allocated during boot time.

E: This indicates the amount of shared memory being used by ASE actively. This value includes both the memory allocated during boot time and also during run time due to reconfiguration, if any.

F: This indicates the amount of *allocated* shared memory that is available to ASE for any reconfiguration.

G, H: These two boundaries indicate two shared memory segments allocated during run time possibly due to a reconfiguration by SA.

I: This indicates the unallocated shared memory that may be required by ASE. Note that ASE requires a certain amount of memory for the current configuration, known as total logical memory. Due to lack of demand, ASE may have not allocated all the shared memory required.

J: This is the room for additional increase in configuration parameters or caches. The SA has determined the maximum amount of memory that can be allocated by ASE and set the max memory configuration parameter. However, the current configuration may not require all the memory. This additional room for growth is the difference between max memory and total logical memory.

Configuration System Tables

Adaptive Server uses the following system tables to manage the Adaptive Server configuration:

Table	Description
sysconfigures	Master table containing all assigned configuration values
syscurconfigs	Memory-only table containing current configuration values
spt_values	Master table containing valid value ranges

The sysconfigures table contains any changes that you make to the system configuration; in contrast, syscurconfigs contains current values that are assumed at server startup, and any dynamic changes. spt_values is a table that is referenced in many of the system stored procedures, to manage lists (for example, type names). It is also used to manage some value ranges on the server.

Adaptive Server also stores the configuration in a configuration file, which can be edited with a text editor. To run Adaptive Server with its built-in default values:

1. Rename, move, or delete your configuration file.
2. Shut down and restart Adaptive Server; Adaptive Server will then create a configuration file (called server_name.cfg) in the Adaptive Server directory, configuration variables are set and read using the sp_configure command. The following section gives a sample output of an unqualified sp_configure (which lists the options divided into groups; many of the options are repeated several times throughout the list for reading convenience).

sp_configure Output

We're going to depart a bit from normal procedure here, and discuss the example inline. This book is a tool, not a manual; as a result, we're not going to try to identify every single option. We will, though, identify some of these options as things you might want to try for memory management or tuning purposes.

Note that a pound sign (#) in the memory used column indicates a number of units rather than a number of bytes.

```
Group: Configuration Options

Group: Backup/Recovery

Parameter Name                Default  Memory Used  Config Value  Run Value
----------------------------  -------  -----------  ------------  ---------
allow remote access           1        0            1             1
print recovery information    0        0            0             0
recovery interval in minutes  5        0            5             5
tape retention in days        0        0            0             0

(1 row affected)
```

allow remote access must be enabled (1 is enabled, 0 is disabled) in order for the Backup Server to work, or to access any CIS applications or remote stored procedures to be executed on or from this box. print recovery information creates voluminous output in your errorlog; in a production environment, I like to turn it on, so that if there is a problem at startup, I have information immediately.

recovery interval in minutes is the amount of time you want to wait for the server to recover any given database at server startup. The shorter this is, the more frequently the server has to checkpoint (this can be a performance hit). The longer this is, the less work the server does while up, but the longer it can take to recover when the server needs to be restarted. This is a good time to point out that tuning is often a balancing act. When you have limited resources, giving more resources to one aspect of the server takes away resources from another.

```
Group: Cache Manager

Parameter Name                 Default  Memory Used  Config Value  Run Value
------------------------------ -------  -----------  ------------  ---------
global async prefetch limit    10       0            10            10
global cache partition number 1        0            1             1
memory alignment boundary      2048     0            2048          2048
number of index trips          0        0            0             0
number of oam trips            0        0            0             0
total data cache size          0        8722         0             8722
```

number of index/oam trips control the number of trips that index or OAM (Object Allocation Map) pages take before they may be aged out of cache. If you have applications that frequently wash all the pages out of cache with (for example) big table scans, try setting these up to 5 or 10; this may improve overall performance by keeping these structures in cache when they might otherwise be aged out. On the other hand, if you set this too high (or if your caches are too small), you may end up filling your caches with pages that aren't eligible to be flushed out, which means that cache must cycle excessively before the pages may be aged out.

total data cache size is now (with 12.5) a parameter that you will configure directly, either with sp_configure or with sp_cacheconfig.

CIS is the Component Integration Services feature of ASE; introduced in version 11.5, it permits the administrator to set up a logical data space that spans servers. By creating a series of proxies, the administrator can make it possible for a user to refer to database objects that are actually stored in different servers, but not have to add such references into the query code.

```
Group: Component Integration Services

Parameter Name               Default  Memory Used  Config Value  Run Value
---------------------------  -------  -----------  ------------  ---------
cis bulk insert array size   50       0            50            50
cis bulk insert batch size   0        0            0             0
cis connect timeout          0        0            0             0
cis cursor rows              50       0            50            50
cis packet size              512      0            512           512
cis rpc handling             0        0            0             0
enable cis                   1        0            1             1
max cis remote connections   0        80           0             0

Group: DTM Administration

Parameter Name               Default  Memory Used  Config Value  Run Value
-------------------------    -------  -----------  ------------  ---------
dtm detach timeout period    0        0            0             0
dtm lock timeout period      300      0            300           300
enable DTM                   0        0            0             0
enable xact coordination     1        0            1             1
number of dtx participants   500      146          500           500
strict dtm enforcement       0        0            0             0
txn to pss ratio             16       686          16            16
xact coordination interval   60       0            60            60
```

The enable DTM configuration parameter (Note: This is a licensed option!) enables Adaptive Server Enterprise to participate in distributed transactions coordinated by third-party products like BEA Systems, Tuxedo, Microsoft's Distributed Transaction Coordinator (MSDTC), etc. Adaptive Server Enterprise supports industry-standard protocol, the XA protocol, and the MSDTC protocol.

Enable xact coordination enables Adaptive Server Enterprise to manage transactions across more than one Adaptive Server Enterprise (that is, it acts as its own transaction coordinator).

```
Group: Diagnostics

Parameter Name               Default  Memory Used  Config Value  Run Value
-----------------------      -------  -----------  ------------  ---------
average cap size             200      0            200           200
caps per ccb                 50       0            50            50
dump on conditions           0        0            0             0
maximum dump conditions      10       0            10            10
number of ccbs               0        0            0             0
```

```
Group: Disk I/O

Parameter Name              Default  Memory Used  Config Value  Run Value
--------------------------- -------  -----------  ------------  ---------
allow sql server async i/o  1        0            1             1
disable disk mirroring      0        0            0             0
disk i/o structures         256      40           256           256
number of devices           10       #16*         30            30
number of large i/o buffers 6        102          6             6
page utilization percent    95       0            95            95

*A pound sign (#) in the Memory Used column indicates a number of units
rather than a number of bytes.
```

A handy new behavior in ASE 12.5 allows you to reconfigure the maximum allowed number of devices dynamically. Previously, a server reboot was required for this to take effect. In fact, over 40 previously static options are now dynamic, enabled by the new memory management mechanism (the complete list is below).

```
Group: Error Log

Parameter Name          Default     Memory Used Config Value Run Value
----------------------- ----------- ----------- ------------ -----------
event log computer name LocalSystem 0           LocalSystem  LocalSystem
event logging           1           0           1            1
log audit logon failure 0           0           0            0
log audit logon success 0           0           0            0

Group: Extended Stored Procedure

Parameter Name          Default     Memory Used Config Value Run Value
----------------------- -------     ----------- ------------ ---------
esp execution priority  8           0           8            8
esp execution stacksize 34816       0           34816        34816
esp unload dll          0           0           0            0
start mail session      0           0           0            0
xp_cmdshell context     1           0           1            1

Group: General Information

Parameter Name          Default     Memory Used Config Value Run Value
------------------      -------     ----------- ------------ -----------
configuration file      0           0           0            D:\SYBASE12

Group: Java Services

Parameter Name               Default Memory Used Config Value  Run Value
---------------------------- ------- ----------- ------------  ---------
enable enterprise java beans 0       0           0             0
enable java                  0       0           0             0
number of java sockets       0       0           0             0
size of global fixed heap    150     0           150           150
size of process object heap  150     0           150           150
size of shared class heap    1536    0           1536          1536
```

```
Group: Languages

Parameter Name                  Default  Memory Used  Config Value  Run Value
------------------------------  -------  -----------  ------------  ---------
default character set id        2        0            2             2
default language id             0        0            0             0
default sortorder id            50       0            50            50
disable character set conversi  0        0            1             1
enable unicode conversions      0        0            0             0

Group: Lock Manager

Parameter Name                  Default  Memory Used  Config Value  Run Value
------------------------        -------  -----------  ------------  ---------
deadlock checking period        500      0            500           500
deadlock retries                5        0            5             5
```

ASE checks for deadlocks (by default) every 500 milliseconds. Deadlock retries are for deadlocks that occur in index pages.

```
lock address spinlock ratio     100          0        100           100
lock hashtable size             2048         51       2048          2048
lock scheme                     allpages     0        allpages      allpages
lock spinlock ratio             85           0        85            85
lock table spinlock ratio       20           0        20            20
lock wait period                2147483647   0        2147483647    2147483647
number of locks                 5000         938      5000          5000
```

The default is almost never a sufficient number of locks long term. Again, this requires a guess. If you are using row-level locking, this will have to be significantly higher than if you use allpages locking. For a starting place, you can try configuring about 25 locks per active user connection, and add a fudge factor of about 5,000 to 10,000. Use at least double that if you have row-level locking configured on more than a few tables.

```
page lock promotion HWM         200          0        200           200
page lock promotion LWM         200          0        200           200
page lock promotion PCT         100          0        100           100
print deadlock information      0            0        0             0
read committed with lock        0            0        0             0
row lock promotion HWM          200          0        200           200
row lock promotion LWM          200          0        200           200
row lock promotion PCT          100          0        100           100
```

Lock promotions can be confusing. LWM (Low Water Mark) is the number of locks that the server must have before it will consider lock promotion (that is, trying to obtain a table lock instead of page or row locks for resource purposes). HWM (High Water Mark) is the threshold at which the server must attempt to escalate. In between these numbers, the lock promotion PCT is the percentage of the table that must be locked in order to escalate. The easiest way to figure escalation is to multiply the PCT value against the number of pages/rows (as appropriate) in the table, and to arrange this number with the HWM and LWM values, from low value to high value. Whichever number falls in the middle of the range is the escalation point.

So, for example, LWM is set to 100; HWM is set to 200; and PCT is set to 50. This means that until there are 100 locks, the server may not consider lock escalation. When the process obtains 200 locks, the server must consider lock escalation. If the number of locks falls between these numbers, the server will only consider lock escalation if that number of locks represents 50 percent or more of the table.

Remember that these lock escalations may be set on a server, database, or table level.

print deadlock information can be used in conjunction with server trace flags 3604 and 1204 to get detailed information out of the server to help track down deadlocking problems. Theoretically there is some system overhead involved in turning these options on, but I've never been able to measure it, even on busy servers.

```
Group: Memory Use

Parameter Name                 Default  Memory Used  Config Value  Run Value
------------------------------ -------  -----------  ------------  ---------
additional network memory      0        0            0             0
allocate max shared memory     0        0            0             0
allow resource limits          0        #4           0             0
audit queue size               100      2            100           100
average cap size               200      0            200           200
caps per ccb                   50       0            50            50
deadlock pipe max messages     0        0            0             0
default network packet size    512      #136         512           512
disk i/o structures            256      40           256           256
dynamic allocation on demand   1        0            1             1
enable rep agent threads       0        0            0             0
errorlog pipe max messages     0        0            0             0
event buffers per engine       100      #10          100           100
executable codesize + overhead 0        669167       0             669167
lock hashtable size            2048     51           2048          2048
lock spinlock ratio            85       0            85            85
max SQL text monitored         0        4            0             0
max number network listeners   5        4405         5             5
max online engines             1        97320        1             1
```

max online engines is where you configure your server to use multiple processors. Until recently, the recommendation has been to configure this to the number of physical processors minus one; recently, I've gotten reports that setting this to the number of engines is even more effective. Benchmark this on your system to find out what your best results are prior to going production. Since it is possible to introduce performance problems by overconfiguring, always start with the max online engines value low, and gradually increase it (benchmarking as you go).

```
max memory                     23552    0            23808         23808
memory per worker process      1024     2            1024          1024
number of alarms               40       4            40            40
number of aux scan descriptors 200      #206         200           200
number of ccbs                 0        0            0             0
number of devices              10       #16          30            30
number of dtx participants     500      146          500           500
number of java sockets         0        0            0             0
number of large i/o buffers    6        102          6             6
```

```
number of locks                  5000    938      5000      5000
number of mailboxes              30      6        30        30
number of messages               64      6        64        64
number of open databases         12      1368     12        12
```

Make sure you configure number of open databases to at least the number of databases on your system. Otherwise, as you add more databases and try to access them simultaneously, you can get messages that are difficult to interpret.

```
number of open indexes           500     582      500       500
number of open objects           500     651      500       500
number of remote connections     20      33       20        20
number of remote logins          20      22       20        20
number of remote sites           10      911      10        10
number of user connections       25      2273     25        25
```

Note that you may require the value of number of user connections to be greater than the number of simultaneous users. User applications may take up more than one connection each; communications with devices (and ASE-defined mirrors), the errorlog, other servers, and standard output all consume connections as well.

```
number of worker processes       0       0        0         0
open index hash spinlock ratio 100       0        100       100
open index spinlock ratio        100     0        100       100
partition groups                 1024    860      1024      1024
partition spinlock ratio         10      0        10        10
permission cache entries         15      #156     15        15
plan text pipe max messages      0       0        0         0
procedure cache size             3271    6542     3271      3271
```

The procedure cache size is changed from previous versions of ASE. In the past, this was expressed as a percentage of overall cache size, but it is now expressed as an absolute measure in units of 2 K blocks. See "Calculating Procedure Cache" later in this chapter for more on cache configuration.

TIP: 1 MB contains 512 blocks of size 2 K.

```
process wait events              0       0        0         0
remote server pre-read packets 3         #32      3         3
size of global fixed heap        150     0        150       150
size of process object heap      150     0        150       150
size of shared class heap        1536    0        1536      1536
size of unilib cache             0       118      0         0
sql text pipe max messages       0       0        0         0
stack guard size                 16384   0        16384     16384
stack size                       41984   0        41984     41984
statement pipe max messages      0       0        0         0
total data cache size            0       8722     0         8722
txn to pss ratio                 16      686      16        16
user log cache size              2048    0        2048      2048
user log cache spinlock ratio  20        0        20        20
wait event timing                0       0        0         0
```

```
Group: Meta-Data Caches

Parameter Name                 Default Memory Used Config Value Run Value
------------------------------ ------- ----------- ------------ ---------
number of open databases       12      1368        12           12
number of open indexes         500     582         500          500
number of open objects         500     651         500          500
open index hash spinlock ratio 100     0           100          100
open index spinlock ratio      100     0           100          100
open object spinlock ratio     100     0           100          100
partition groups               1024    860         1024         1024
partition spinlock ratio       10      0           10           10

Group: Monitoring

Parameter Name                 Default Memory Used Config Value Run Value
----------------------------   ------- ----------- ------------ ---------
Q diagnostics active           0       0           0            0
SQL batch capture              0       0           0            0
deadlock pipe active           0       0           0            0
deadlock pipe max messages     0       0           0            0
errorlog pipe active           0       0           0            0
errorlog pipe max messages     0       0           0            0
max SQL text monitored         0       4           0            0
object lockwait timing         0       0           0            0
per object statistics active   0       0           0            0
plan text pipe active          0       0           0            0
plan text pipe max messages    0       0           0            0
process wait events            0       0           0            0
sql text pipe active           0       0           0            0
sql text pipe max messages     0       0           0            0
statement pipe active          0       0           0            0
statement pipe max messages    0       0           0            0
statement statistics active    0       0           0            0
wait event timing              0       0           0            0

Group: Network Communication

Parameter Name                 Default Memory Used Config Value Run Value
------------------------------ ------- ----------- ------------ ---------
additional network memory      0       0           0            0
allow remote access            1       0           1            1
allow sendmsg                  0       0           0            0
default network packet size    512     #136        512          512
max network packet size        512     0           512          512
max number network listeners   5       4405        5            5
number of remote connections   20      33          20           20
number of remote logins        20      22          20           20
number of remote sites         10      911         10           10
remote server pre-read packets 3       #32         3            3
syb_sendmsg port number        0       0           0            0
tcp no delay                   0       0           0            0
```

When you are sending large amounts of data across the network frequently, you can get a significant performance benefit by matching up the ASE default network packet size (default 512 bytes) with the physical network packet size (example: 1,536 bytes). In order to make this happen, you need to increase the max network packet size to accommodate the size you want your packet to be. In addition, you need to set up additional network memory for the packets to draw upon. Each connection gets a read buffer, a write buffer, and a write overflow buffer; in other words, you need three of those 512-byte packets, or three of the larger-sized buffers. The tcp no delay parameter can also be useful; it instructs the server to begin sending the packet to the client before building the entire result set. As always, consult with your network administrator before making changes that will affect network loads.

```
Group: O/S Resources

Parameter Name              Default     Memory Used  Config Value  Run Value
-------------------------  -------     -----------  ------------  ---------
max async i/os per engine  2147483647  0            2147483647    2147483647
max async i/os per server  2147483647  0            2147483647    2147483647
o/s file descriptors       0           0            0             100000
tcp no delay               0           0            0             0

Group: Parallel Query

Parameter Name              Default     Memory Used  Config Value  Run Value
--------------------------  -------     -----------  ------------  ---------
max parallel degree         1           0            1             1
max scan parallel degree    1           0            1             1
memory per worker process   1024        2            1024          1024
number of worker processes  0           0            0             0
```

max parallel degree is the number of parallel processes that may be used for a single query; max scan parallel degree is the largest number of parallel processes that can be used against a single table, if not using a partition-based scan. The number of worker processes parameter is the total number of processes available, server-wide, for parallel processing.

Beware of configuring too many worker processes, as you may overload your CPUs. Also, be aware that additional worker processes will consume a greater number of locks, and may contribute to lock blocking and deadlocking. Think of it this way: If 10 processes are all running, and use parallelism to a degree of 10 each, you suddenly have 100 processes running. I have seen loads on boxes go from 25% busy to 100% by configuring this too high.

```
Group: Physical Memory

Parameter Name                  Default Memory Used Config Value  Run Value
------------------------------  ------- ----------- ------------  ---------
additional network memory       0       0           0             0
allocate max shared memory      0       0           0             0
dynamic allocation on demand    1       0           1             1
lock shared memory              0       0           0             0
max memory                      23552   0           23808         23808
shared memory starting address  0       0           0             0
total memory                    23552   33188       16594         16594
```

```
Group: Processors

Parameter Name                  Default Memory Used Config Value Run Value
----------------------------    ------- ----------- ------------ ---------
max online engines              1       97320       1            1
number of engines at startup    1       0           1            1

Group: Rep Agent Thread Administration

Parameter Name                  Default Memory Used Config Value Run Value
------------------------        ------- ----------- ------------ ---------
enable rep agent threads        0       0           0            0

Group: SQL Server Administration

Parameter Name                  Default Memory Used Config Value Run Value
------------------------        ------- ----------- ------------ ---------
SQL Perfmon Integration         1       0           1            1
abstract plan cache             0       0           0            0
abstract plan dump              0       0           0            0
abstract plan load              0       0           0            0
abstract plan replace           0       0           0            0
allow backward scans            1       0           1            1
```

allow backward scans lets the server walk page chains in reverse, for example while performing a descending sort. Unfortunately, I've seen this cause deadlocks while configured on in some applications.

```
allow nested triggers           1       0           1            1
allow resource limits           0       #4          0            0
allow updates to system tables  0       0           0            0
```

When you directly modify system tables, you need to allow updates to system tables (set this parameter to 1). Note that you should only modify system tables with great care. It is easy to cause irreparable damage (for example, corrupting a table or database) unintentionally (not understanding the repercussions of the change) or accidentally (perhaps modifying too many rows of data). If you must change system tables directly, be sure to set allow updates to system tables back to 0 as soon as you are done with your changes.

WARNING: It is very unusual to do this without tech support on the line walking you through it, or a Sybase tech manual in hand with a process that requires it.

```
cpu accounting flush interval   200     0           200          200
cpu grace time                  500     0           500          500
deadlock retries                5       0           5            5
default database size           2       0           2            2
default exp_row_size percent    5       0           5            5
default fill factor percent     0       0           0            0
enable DTM                      0       0           0            0
enable HA                       0       0           0            0
enable housekeeper GC           1       0           1            1
enable sort-merge join and JTC  0       0           0            0
event buffers per engine        100     #10         100          100
housekeeper free write percent  1       0           1            1
```

```
i/o accounting flush interval   1000    0       1000      1000
i/o polling process count       10      0       10        10
identity burning set factor     5000    0       5000      5000
identity grab size              1       0       1         1
license information             25      0       25        25
number of alarms                40      4       40        40
number of aux scan descriptors  200     #206    200       200
number of large i/o buffers     6       102     6         6
number of mailboxes             30      6       30        30
number of messages              64      6       64        64
number of open databases        12      1368    12        12
number of open objects          500     651     500       500
number of pre-allocated extent  2       0       2         2
number of sort buffers          500     0       500       500
page lock promotion HWM         200     0       200       200
page lock promotion LWM         200     0       200       200
page lock promotion PCT         100     0       100       100
print deadlock information      0       0       0         0
procedure cache size            3271    6542    3271      3271
row lock promotion HWM          200     0       200       200
row lock promotion LWM          200     0       200       200
row lock promotion PCT          100     0       100       100
runnable process search count   2000    0       2000      2000
size of auto identity column    10      0       10        10
sql server clock tick length    100000  0       100000    100000
text prefetch size              16      0       16        16
time slice                      100     0       100       100
upgrade version                 1100    0       12500     12500
```

Examining the upgrade version value is a quick way to find out what version of the server you're running. Alternatively, select the @@version global variable for even more information.

```
Group: Security Related

Parameter Name                  Default Memory Used Config Value Run Value
------------------------        ------- ----------- ------------ ---------
allow procedure grouping        1       0           1            1
audit queue size                100     2           100          100
auditing                        0       0           0            0
check password for digit        0       0           0            0
```

It's worth noting that most of the options in sp_configure may only be changed by an SA, but the security related options are restricted to the SSO. The check password for digit option will force all passwords on the server to incorporate at least one digit.

```
curread change w/ open cursors  1       0           1            1
current audit table             1       0           1            1
enable ssl                      0       0           0            0
maximum failed logins           0       0           0            0
```

Use the maximum failed logins option with care; it will lock logins that have entered a password incorrectly some fixed number of times (the default, 0, means that the password will not be disabled). This can affect any login, so if a troublemaker were to sit down and try to guess the password of your only SA/SSO login and fail the required number of times, you might have a server without a usable administrative login! In such cases, it is possible to unlock a given login at server restart time; see the discussions of the –u flag in Chapter 2, "Adaptive Server Installation," and Chapter 6, "Security."

```
minimum password length              6       0       6       6
msg confidentiality reqd             0       0       0       0
msg integrity reqd                   0       0       0       0
secure default login                 guest   0       guest   guest
select on syscomments.text           1       0       1       1
```

Note that since version 12.0, it has been possible to configure the minimum password length to less than the default value of 6 bytes. In fact, it may be set to 0 bytes, which will permit the use of null passwords. This is not necessarily a good idea. The select on syscomments.text option allows you to disable the ability of users to see the code that is associated with stored procedures.

```
suspend audit when device full       1       0       1       1
systemwide password expiration       0       0       0       0
unified login required               0       0       0       0
use security services                0       0       0       0
use ssl client cert auth             0       0       0       0

Group: Unicode

Parameter Name Default         Memory   Used   Config Value   Run Value
----------------------------   -------  ----   ------------   ---------
default unicode sortorder      binary   0      binary         binary
enable surrogate processing    1        0      1              1
enable unicode conversions     0        0      0              0
enable unicode normalization   1        0      1              1
size of unilib cache           0        118    0              0

Group: User Environment

Parameter Name Default         Memory   Used   Config Value   Run Value
---------------------------    ------   ----   ------------   ---------
default network packet size    512      #136   512            512
number of user connections     25       2273   25             25
permission cache entries       15       #156   15             15
stack guard size               16384    0      16384          16384
stack size                     41984    0      41984          41984
user log cache size            2048     0      2048           2048
user log cache spinlock ratio  20       0      20             20
(return status = 0)
```

The sp_configure stored procedure can be run without parameters, to display the output above, or you can pass parameters, either to change the output or to change the value of a parameter.

Syntax:

Command	Effect
sp_configure	Displays all configuration parameters by group, their current values, their default values, the value to which they have most recently been set, and the amount of memory used by this particular setting.

Command	Effect
sp_configure "parameter"	Displays current value, default value, most recently changed value, and amount of memory used by setting for all parameters matching parameter.
sp_configure "parameter", value	Resets parameter to value.
sp_configure "parameter", 0, "default"	Resets parameter to its default value.
sp_configure "group_name"	Displays all configuration parameters in group_name, their current values, their default values, the values to which they were recently set, and the amount of memory used by each setting.
sp_configure "configuration file", 0,"sub_command", "file_name"	Sets configuration parameters from the configuration file.

Example:

```
sp_configure "number of locks", 8000
```

Displaying Configuration Values

The sp_displaylevel procedure allows the level or amount of information displayed by sp_configure to be configured for an individual user. The settings can be basic, intermediate, or comprehensive. The initial default is comprehensive.

Configuration File

Adaptive Server maintains its configuration in an ASCII text file that Adaptive Server reads at startup. This file also contains information about data caches.

The default location is the $Sybase home directory and the default name of the file is servername.cfg. If you do not want to use the default, the configuration file to be used on Adaptive Server startup can be specified on the dataserver command line with the -c option. Certain sub-commands of sp_configure allow you to directly read, write, or validate the configuration file.

The following reads in a set of dynamically configurable values from a configuration file:

```
sp_configure "configuration file", 0, "read", "file_name"
```

The following verifies a set of dynamically configurable values in a configuration file.

```
sp_configure "configuration file", 0, "verify", "file_name"
```

This is used to ensure that values modified with a text editor are correct and valid (that is, they are within the theoretical range of the option; the values may be incorrect in that there may not be enough memory or other resource to support the new value). The verify subcommand does not modify any run-time configuration values.

The 0 is used as a placeholder for when you are using sp_configure to set values. Use sp_configure "configuration file", 0, "write", file_name to write out the current set of configuration variables (dynamic and static) to a configuration file. This file can then be used for configuring other like servers, or for archive purposes.

If the configuration file gets corrupted or otherwise lost, it can be rebuilt:

1. Shut down the server and restart the server with no configuration file. The server will write out a configuration file with default values and use those values for the configuration.
2. As part of the boot process, if there is no configuration file, the server in addition to servername.cfg will also write servername.bak. This is the backup file, which contains the values in sysconfigures.
3. If you want to use your old configuration file instead, shut down the server, copy servername.bak to servername.cfg, and restart.

The configuration file contains all of the configuration parameters that will take effect when the server comes up. If you see "Default," that means that the server-defined default for your version and platform will be applied. Otherwise, the server will use the value that you supply.

Sample Configuration File

```
##############################################################################
#
#       Configuration File for the Sybase SQL Server
#
#       Please read the System Administration Guide (SAG)
#       before changing any of the values in this file.
#
##############################################################################

[Configuration Options]

[General Information]

[Backup/Recovery]
 recovery interval in minutes = DEFAULT
 print recovery information = DEFAULT
 tape retention in days = DEFAULT

[Cache Manager]
 number of oam trips = DEFAULT
 number of index trips = DEFAULT
 memory alignment boundary = DEFAULT
 global async prefetch limit = DEFAULT
 global cache partition number = DEFAULT

[Named Cache:default data cache]
 cache size = DEFAULT
 cache status = default data cache
 cache replacement policy = DEFAULT
 local cache partition number = DEFAULT

[Meta-Data Caches]
 number of open databases = DEFAULT
 number of open objects = DEFAULT
 open object spinlock ratio = DEFAULT
 number of open indexes = DEFAULT
 open index hash spinlock ratio = DEFAULT
 open index spinlock ratio = DEFAULT
 partition groups = DEFAULT
```

```
 partition spinlock ratio = DEFAULT

[Disk I/O]
 disk i/o structures = DEFAULT
 number of large i/o buffers = DEFAULT
 page utilization percent = DEFAULT
 number of devices = 30
 disable disk mirroring = DEFAULT
 allow sql server async i/o = DEFAULT

[Languages]
 disable character set conversions = 1

[Unicode]
 enable unicode normalization = DEFAULT
 enable surrogate processing = DEFAULT
 enable unicode conversions = DEFAULT
 size of unilib cache = DEFAULT

[Network Communication]
 default network packet size = DEFAULT
 max network packet size = DEFAULT
 remote server pre-read packets = DEFAULT
 number of remote connections = DEFAULT
 number of remote logins = DEFAULT
 number of remote sites = DEFAULT
 max number network listeners = DEFAULT
 tcp no delay = DEFAULT
 allow sendmsg = DEFAULT
 syb_sendmsg port number = DEFAULT
 allow remote access = DEFAULT

[O/S Resources]
 max async i/os per engine = DEFAULT
 max async i/os per server = DEFAULT

[Parallel Query]
 number of worker processes = DEFAULT
 memory per worker process = DEFAULT
 max parallel degree = DEFAULT
 max scan parallel degree = DEFAULT


[Physical Memory]
 max total_memory = 23808
 additional network memory = DEFAULT
 shared memory starting address = DEFAULT
 allocate max shared memory = DEFAULT
 dynamic allocation on demand = DEFAULT
 lock shared memory = DEFAULT

[Processors]
 max online engines = DEFAULT
 number of engines at startup = DEFAULT

[SQL Server Administration]
 procedure cache size = DEFAULT
```

```
 default database size = DEFAULT
 identity burning set factor = DEFAULT
 allow nested triggers = DEFAULT
 allow updates to system tables = DEFAULT
 default fill factor percent = DEFAULT
 default exp_row_size percent = DEFAULT
 number of mailboxes = DEFAULT
 number of messages = DEFAULT
 number of alarms = DEFAULT
 number of pre-allocated extents = DEFAULT
 event buffers per engine = DEFAULT
 cpu accounting flush interval = DEFAULT
 i/o accounting flush interval = DEFAULT
 sql server clock tick length = DEFAULT
 runnable process search count = DEFAULT
 i/o polling process count = DEFAULT
 time slice = DEFAULT
 cpu grace time = DEFAULT
 number of sort buffers = DEFAULT
 size of auto identity column = DEFAULT
 identity grab size = DEFAULT
 housekeeper free write percent = DEFAULT
 enable housekeeper GC = DEFAULT
 allow resource limits = DEFAULT
 number of aux scan descriptors = DEFAULT
 SQL Perfmon Integration = DEFAULT
 allow backward scans = DEFAULT
 license information = DEFAULT
 enable sort-merge join and JTC = DEFAULT
 abstract plan load = DEFAULT
 abstract plan dump = DEFAULT
 abstract plan replace = DEFAULT
 abstract plan cache = DEFAULT
 text prefetch size = DEFAULT
 enable HA = DEFAULT

[User Environment]
 number of user connections = DEFAULT
 stack size = DEFAULT
 stack guard size = DEFAULT
 permission cache entries = DEFAULT
 user log cache size = DEFAULT
 user log cache spinlock ratio = DEFAULT

[Lock Manager]
 number of locks = DEFAULT
 deadlock checking period = DEFAULT
 lock spinlock ratio = DEFAULT
 lock address spinlock ratio = DEFAULT
 lock table spinlock ratio = DEFAULT
 lock hashtable size = DEFAULT
 lock scheme = DEFAULT
 lock wait period = DEFAULT
 read committed with lock = DEFAULT
```

```
 print deadlock information = DEFAULT
 deadlock retries = DEFAULT
 page lock promotion HWM = DEFAULT
 page lock promotion LWM = DEFAULT
 page lock promotion PCT = DEFAULT
 row lock promotion HWM = DEFAULT
 row lock promotion LWM = DEFAULT
 row lock promotion PCT = DEFAULT

[Security Related]
 systemwide password expiration = DEFAULT
 audit queue size = DEFAULT
 curread change w/ open cursors = DEFAULT
 allow procedure grouping = DEFAULT
 select on syscomments.text = DEFAULT
 auditing = DEFAULT
 current audit table = DEFAULT
 suspend audit when device full = DEFAULT
 check password for digit = DEFAULT
 minimum password length = DEFAULT
 maximum failed logins = DEFAULT
 enable ssl = DEFAULT
 use ssl client cert auth = DEFAULT
 unified login required = DEFAULT
 use security services = DEFAULT
 msg confidentiality reqd = DEFAULT
 msg integrity reqd = DEFAULT
 secure default login = DEFAULT

[Extended Stored Procedure]
 esp unload dll = DEFAULT
 esp execution priority = DEFAULT
 esp execution stacksize = DEFAULT
 xp_cmdshell context = DEFAULT
 start mail session = DEFAULT

[Error Log]
 event logging = DEFAULT
 log audit logon success = DEFAULT
 log audit logon failure = DEFAULT
 event log computer name = DEFAULT

[Rep Agent Thread Administration]
 enable rep agent threads = DEFAULT

[Component Integration Services]
 enable cis = DEFAULT
 cis connect timeout = DEFAULT
 cis bulk insert batch size = DEFAULT
 max cis remote connections = DEFAULT
 cis packet size = DEFAULT
 cis cursor rows = DEFAULT
 cis bulk insert array size = DEFAULT
 cis rpc handling = DEFAULT
```

```
[Java Services]
 enable java = DEFAULT
 size of process object heap = DEFAULT
 size of shared class heap = DEFAULT
 size of global fixed heap = DEFAULT
 number of java sockets = DEFAULT
 enable enterprise java beans = DEFAULT

[DTM Administration]
 enable DTM = DEFAULT
 enable xact coordination = DEFAULT
 xact coordination interval = DEFAULT
 number of dtx participants = DEFAULT
 strict dtm enforcement = DEFAULT
 txn to pss ratio = DEFAULT
 dtm lock timeout period = DEFAULT
 dtm detach timeout period = DEFAULT

[Diagnostics]
 dump on conditions = DEFAULT
 maximum dump conditions = DEFAULT
 number of ccbs = DEFAULT
 caps per ccb = DEFAULT
 average cap size = DEFAULT

[Monitoring]
 Q diagnostics active = DEFAULT
 sql text pipe active = DEFAULT
 sql text pipe max messages = DEFAULT
 plan text pipe active = DEFAULT
 plan text pipe max messages = DEFAULT
 statement pipe active = DEFAULT
 statement pipe max messages = DEFAULT
 errorlog pipe active = DEFAULT
 errorlog pipe max messages = DEFAULT
 deadlock pipe active = DEFAULT
 deadlock pipe max messages = DEFAULT
 wait event timing = DEFAULT
 process wait events = DEFAULT
 object lockwait timing = DEFAULT
 SQL batch capture = DEFAULT
 statement statistics active = DEFAULT
 per object statistics active = DEFAULT
 max SQL text monitored = DEFAULT
```

Dynamic vs. Static Options

There are two kinds of configuration variables: dynamic and static. Dynamic parameters take effect immediately after the sp_configure command is executed, like recovery interval, password expiration interval, default language and nested triggers.

Static parameters do not take effect until the server is next started. These parameters (generally) are ones that affect memory allocation.

Note that ASE 12.5 is edging closer to dynamic allocation of memory with every release of the server. In fact, with 12.5, the following (formerly static) configuration parameters are now dynamic:

additional network memory
audit queue size
cpu grace time
deadlock text pipe max messages
default database size
default fill factor percent
disk i/o structures
errorlog text pipe max messages
max cis remote connections
memory per worker process
number of alarms
number of aux scan descriptors
number of devices
number of dtx participants
number of java sockets
number of large i/o buffers
number of locks
number of mailboxes
number of messages
number of open databases
number of open indexes
number of open objects
number of pre-allocated extents
number of user connections
number of worker processes
open index hash spinlock ratio
open index spinlock ratio
open object spinlock ratio
partition groups
partition spinlock ratio
permission cache entries
plan text pipe max messages
print recovery information
process wait events
size of global fixed heap
size of process object heap
size of shared class heap
size of unilib cache
sql text pipe max messages
statement text pipe max messages
tape retention in days
timeslice

Memory-Related Variables

All of the following variables use memory. Run sp_configure and look at the memory used section to see how much they are taking up.

```
sp_configure 'Memory Use'
```

Additional network memory
Allow resource limits
Audit queue size
Default network memory
Disk i/o structures
Enable rep agent threads
Event buffers per engine
Executable codesize plus overhead
Number of alarms
Number of aux scan descriptors
Number of devices
Number of languages in cache
Number of large i/0 buffers
Number of locks
Number of mailboxes
Number of messages
Number of remote logins
Number of remote sites
Number of user connections
Number of worker processes
Partition groups
Permission cache entries
Procedure cache percent
Remote server pre-read packets

Max cis remote servers	Number of open databases	Stack guard size
Max number network listeners	Number of open indexes	Stack size
Max roles enabled per user	Number of open objects	
Memory per worker process	Number of remote connections	

Recommended Configuration Settings

CAUTION: Do not overconfigure these parameters, as you will be wasting memory.

Setting	Description
User connections	Maximum number of concurrent connections required by applications, tools, systems processes, plus devices, mirrors, and other servers, then round up to next multiple of 10
Devices	One plus the number of configured devices
Open databases	Number of rows in sysdatabases
Open objects	Total database objects existing on Adaptive Server
Locks	Leave the default unless you are getting "Out of available locks" error, then figure out if that is an expected result
Audit queue size	Max number of audit records to hold in memory (see Chapter 7, "Auditing")
Default network packet size	Leave at 512 to support db-lib applications
User log cache	If you have short transactions (and you should) leave this alone

Cache Configuration

In any high-performance system, you will need adequate memory to manage I/O (cache). In fact, the more memory you have, the better. For Adaptive Server Enterprise 12.5, rather than a pool of storage, memory is allocated for the specific use to which it will be put. This dramatically simplifies the decisions about configuring memory.

Sizing Cache

Cache should contain sufficient memory for user data and procedures. In data cache, it is useful to contain index levels, system tables, and as much data as feasible. The next chapter talks about creating separate, named data caches, but even if you are not going to use named data caches, be sure to read about buffer pools. All caches will have a 2 K I/O buffer pool (or a buffer pool corresponding to the page size for the server), and most should have large I/O buffer pools (size depending on the purpose of the pool).

Procedure cache should contain enough space for each concurrent process to execute your biggest stored procedure. By turning set statistics io on, you can watch physical vs. logical access; the more logical access, the better your performance.

For more information on tuning cache, see the next chapter, "Named Caches."

Memory Guidelines

On some platforms, adding more memory is a common and easy performance tuning technique.

Note that for 12.5, adding more memory is not sufficient; you need to determine which area of server processing will receive the boon of additional memory.

The principle advantage of adding memory to a physical server (and reconfiguring the Adaptive Server to make use of that memory) is to increase the size of data cache, and therefore increase the likelihood of finding a given page of data in cache when it is time to look for it.

In an OLTP environment, it is easier to see that there is a point of diminishing returns because pages must be written out to disk frequently anyway. In very large databases (VLDBs), it is harder to justify the "more memory, better performance" thinking. Even with 4 GB of memory, it's hard to estimate in a 100 GB database whether or not a randomly requested page is likely to be in cache.

It is a good idea to try to leave at least enough room in cache for frequently used index levels. As you add memory, measure the impact and stop when adding memory has no effect (or a negative effect). On some SMP platforms, you may find that after configuring for more engines you find frequent occurrences of message 701 ("There is not enough procedure cache …") in the log. If you do, you'll need to increase the amount of memory allocated to proc cache.

Calculating Procedure Cache

Typically, you will identify how much memory you need for cache. A good formula is enough space for each concurrent user connection to use your largest procedure, plus a fudge factor.

The following is a general formula:

45 K (stored procedure size) *
400 (user connections) *
1.25 (fudge factor) = 22,500 K

In this case, 22,500 K = 11,520 2Kb blocks, which would be procedure cache size parameter for sp_configure.

Bear in mind that often, the largest stored procedure is a system proc, typically used only by the administrative staff. You may wish to use the largest commonly used procedure in your calculations, and may still end up overestimating the necessary procedure cache size.

TIP: You can use the dbcc memusage command to determine largest query plan size, but you should do this in development, not production.

Sample Server Configuration

Based upon the previous configuration examples, we need approximately 26 MB for Adaptive Server Kernel, 80 MB of data cache, and 22.5 MB of procedure cache. Assuming the Adaptive Server executable requires 4 MB, we need to configure Adaptive Server for 133 MB of memory.

A sample configuration session would appear as follows:

```
sp_configure 'procedure cache, 11520 — 22.5 MB * 512 pages/meg
sp_configure 'data cache, 40960 — 80 * 512
sp_configure 'number of user connections', 400
sp_configure 'number of locks', 10000
sp_configure 'number of devices', 100
```

```
sp_configure 'number of open databases', 15
sp_configure 'number of open objects', 1000
```

A number of options that previously would have required a server reboot (including number of locks and number of user connections) can now change their values within a certain range from their startup value without rebooting. This makes it difficult to estimate the size of one of these structures, since the Memory Used column of sp_configure's output indicates not only the cost of the allocated structures, but also some "wiggle room" in case you need to increase the amount later on.

It is possible to come up with some rough estimates of the cost of a given resource (and this may vary from platform to platform). Experimentation on the beta of ASE 12.5 gives a per-lock cost of approximately 160 bytes, and a per-user connection cost which is platform dependent:

NT	96 K
32-bit	140-175 K
64-bit	200-240 K

Summary

Configure memory based upon identified needs. Don't overconfigure. In most cases, it's probably best to start with a lower number of resources, and increase as the need arises, rather than to overconfigure initially and end up paying for resources that aren't required.

Chapter 12

Named Cache

Data cache is the area of memory that Adaptive Server Enterprise uses to load pages from disk. It is also used to reduce I/O by retaining memory pages that might otherwise have to be shipped to disk.

In general, ASE manages memory very well, as we've described in the previous chapter. If you are using only the default data cache, the server can use this area of memory for any data that it needs to bring in off of the disk.

When you create named caches, you are carving memory into tiny chunks that will be used only as you specify. If you carve your memory into 50 tiny chunks, when the server needs a large fragment of memory, it may not be available, and one of the tinier chunks of memory will churn.

So, only use named caches if you have analyzed and identified positive performance benefits from doing this; otherwise it can turn around and bite you. On the other hand, if access to cache is a bottleneck (which you've identified with sp_sysmon), a little time spent configuring named caches can improve performance very quickly (especially on servers using multiple engines). As with all administration, cache configuration is a balancing act.

We've made this recommendation/warning a few other times in this book already, but here it is again: This is an area where you can overconfigure your server.

Data Cache

The data cache holds all data (including system table data), indexes, and log pages currently in use. Adaptive Server permits the data cache to be partitioned into separate named caches; memory assigned to a named cache will only be used by objects bound to the cache. "Objects," in this case refers to whole databases, or data objects within the database (tables, system tables, and indexes).

Tuning Cache

Cache should contain sufficient memory for user data and procedures; procedure cache sizing was addressed in the previous chapter, so we can concentrate on data cache sizing here. The question that gets asked the most often is, how much memory do I need? The second most-asked question is, how much memory can the server use?

The answer to the first question can be broken down into a precise, exact answer: probably. But we recommend getting the answer via an inexact method instead. In other words, pick a number that you think works. Then, analyze the Data Cache Management section of sp_sysmon output to see if you are getting information that shows that the cache has become a bottleneck, or you have hard disk bottlenecks that you think can be resolved by placing data in cache. Based on your testing, increase or decrease cache, and repeat. This is inexact, but it usually requires only a few iterations to come to a reasonable value.

The following shows an example:

```
Data Cache Management
---------------------

Cache Statistics Summary (All Caches)
                              per sec  per xact count  % of total
                              -------  -------- -----  ----------

Cache Search Summary
   Total Cache Hits           560.1    32.6     33606   97.9%
   Total Cache Misses          12.1     0.7       723    2.1%
---------------------         -----    ----     -----  ------
Total Cache Searches          572.2    33.3     34329

Cache Turnover
   Buffers Grabbed            1.5      0.1      92       n/a
   Buffers Grabbed Dirty      0.0      0.0      0        0.0%

Cache Strategy Summary
   Cached (LRU) Buffers       554.4    32.3     33266  100.0%
   Discarded (MRU) Buffers    0.0      0.0      0        0.0%

Large I/O Usage
   Large I/Os Performed       0.8      0.0      46     100.0%
   Large I/Os Denied          0.0      0.0      0        0.0%
------------------------      ---      ---      --     ------
Total Large I/O Requests      0.8      0.0      46

Large I/O Effectiveness
   Pages by Lrg I/O Cached    0.0      0.0      0      n/a

Asynchronous Prefetch Activity
                              0.0      0.0      0      n/a

Other Asynchronous Prefetch Statistics
   APFs Used                  0.0      0.0      0      n/a
   APF Waits for I/O          0.0      0.0      0      n/a
   APF Discards               0.0      0.0      0      n/a

Dirty Read Behavior
   Page Requests              2.3      0.1      139    n/a
-------------------------     ---      ---      ---    ---
Cache: default data cache
                              per sec  per xact count  % of total
                              -------  -------- -----  ------------
Spinlock Contention           n/a      n/a      n/a    %

Utilization                   n/a      n/a      n/a    100.0%
```

```
Cache Searches
 Cache Hits                    560.1    32.6   33606    97.9%
    Found in Wash              2.2      0.1    130      0.4%
 Cache Misses                  12.1     0.7    723      2.1%
--------------------           -----    ----   -----    -----
Total Cache Searches           572.2    33.3   34329

Pool Turnover
 2 KB Pool
    LRU Buffer Grab            1.5      0.1    92       100.0%
    Grabbed Dirty              0.0      0.0    0        0.0%
--------------------           ---      ---    --       ------
Total Cache Turnover           1.5      0.1    92

Buffer Wash Behavior
 Statistics Not Available — No Buffers Entered Wash Section Yet

Cache Strategy
 Cached (LRU) Buffers          554.4    32.3   33266    100.0%
 Discarded (MRU) Buffers       0.0      0.0    0        0.0%

Large I/O Usage
 Large I/Os Performed          0.8      0.0    46       100.0%
 Large I/Os Denied             0.0      0.0    0        0.0%
------------------------       ---      ---    --       ------
Total Large I/O Requests       0.8      0.0    46

Large I/O Detail

Large I/Os Performed           0.8      0.0    46       100.0%
Large I/Os Denied              0.0      0.0    0        0.0%
------------------------       ---      ---    --       ------
Total Large I/O Requests       0.8      0.0    46

Large I/O Detail
 4 KB Pool
    Pages Cached               0.0      0.0    0        n/a
    Pages Used                 0.0      0.0    0        n/a
 16 KB Pool
    Pages Cached               0.0      0.0    0        n/a
    Pages Used                 0.0      0.0    0        n/a

Dirty Read Behavior
 Page Requests                 2.3      0.1    139      n/a
```

Note that "spinlock contention" is bad; it means that the CPUs in an SMP environment are fighting over a cache. It is an indicator that you need to split up your caches.

In the data cache(s), it is useful to have enough room to store index pages (as many levels as possible), system tables, and as much data as feasible; too often, administrators try to cache the data first — but you probably won't have enough memory for all of it. However, by carefully assigning the structures needed to find the data (indexes, system tables), you can achieve a pretty high hit rate for your caches (that is, the ratio of pages found in cache vs. those that require a slow read from physical disk). You can look at the sp_sysmon output for cache hit rate, which even in large environments with limited memory can reach into the high 90s.

Buffer Pools

Within each cache, you have at least one set of hash buffers (buffer pools), whose purpose is to provide entry into an I/O pool of a particular size (one, two, four, or eight pages… or, for a 2 K page, that would be 2 K, 4 K, 8 K, or 16 K per read/write). Every cache will require that some of its space (at least half a megabyte) support the 2 K I/O size; for performance purposes, you will probably choose to include other I/O sizes in many (most?) of your caches. On caches holding tables that engage in large retrievals, the 16 K I/O size will reduce the number of reads; caches that are assigned to hold transaction logs will find 4 K I/O to be the most efficient. The *default data cache* (which all objects not specifically assigned to a given cache will use) will typically be given both 4 K and 16 K buffer pools (the 8 K size isn't really helpful for logging, and not as useful as the 16 K size for large operations, so you'll probably leave it out).

The precise size of each buffer pool in each cache will (like the cache sizes themselves) best be determined by a trial-and-error process: sp_sysmon will indicate if a given I/O size in a given cache is being used or not. Based on the degree of overuse/underuse, the buffer pools may be expanded or reduced to most efficiently use the memory allocated to the cache.

Benefits of Named Caches

Named caches give you the ability to place critical tables or indexes in memory and/or give them the ability to get a higher priority in memory, by assigning areas of memory for the exclusive use of these objects.

Caches with large I/O can improve table scan and large query performance. Active tables can be placed in separate caches from their indexes to increase concurrency.

Contention in the cache space can be reduced between:

- A database and its log
- User databases and tempdb
- Multiple processes in an SMP environment

The idea here is that you have identified areas where you think you can make better educated guesses about how to use the memory than the server has.

Creating a Named Cache

As much space as possible should be configured in data cache before creating any named caches. Make sure that the default data cache is not too small, as it is the only cache used at server startup, and a tiny cache could have a negative performance impact.

Named caches are created with sp_cacheconfig or you can add them into the server configuration file by hand (although you must be very careful to get the configuration file formatting correct if you do so; it's probably best to use the stored procedure).

Syntax:

```
sp_cacheconfig [cachename
[, "cache_size {P|K|M|G}"]
[,{logonly | mixed}] [,{strict | relaxed}]]
[, "cache_partition=[1|2|4|8|16|32|64]"]
```

Example:

```
sp_cacheconfig "fred cache", "3M", mixed
```

CAUTION: As with most memory configuration parameters, the Adaptive Server must be cycled for the cache configurations to take effect.

Parameter	Description
cachename	The name assigned to the data cache; it must be unique within the Adaptive Server, but does not need to follow other naming restrictions.
cache_size	Size of the cache. Units may be expressed in Pages, Kb, Mb, or Gb, defaulting to Kb. Minimum cache size is 512 Kb, and fractional Kb sizes are not allowed.
logonly|mixed	Specifies the type of cache; default is mixed (any kind of data may be assigned to this cache).
strict|relaxed	Cache replacement strategy; leave at the default (strict) except under very special circumstances (engines > 4, hit rate > 97%).
cache_partition	Specifies the number of partitions to create in the cache. Each pool in the cache must be at least one-fourth the logical page size.

To drop a cache, set its cache_size to "0" or delete it from the configuration file. There is no "drop cache" command.

We strongly recommend you change cache configurations slowly, and carefully benchmark results between changes.

Without parameters, sp_cacheconfig reports on all configured caches within Adaptive Server, and their current status (cache exists/will exist at server restart/will be dropped at server restart). Alternatively, use sp_helpcache.

Specifying only the cachename reports on the current configuration of that cache. Only the SA may configure caches (it is a server-wide resource); any user may use sp_cacheconfig to view cache information.

Results Before Cycling the Server

```
sp_cacheconfig
go
Cache Name              Status     Type      Config Value    RunValue
------------------      --------   -------   ------------    --------
default data cache      Active     Default   0.00 Mb         8.75 Mb
fred cache              Pend/Act   Mixed     3.00 Mb         0.00 Mb
                                             ------------    --------
                                   Total     3.00 Mb         8.75 Mb
=======================================================================
Cache:  default data cache, Status: Active, Type: Default
        Config Size: 0.00 Mb, Run Size: 8.75 Mb
        Config Replacement: strict LRU, Run Replacement: strict LRU
        Config Partition: 1, Run Partition: 1
IO Size     Wash Size     Config Size     Run Size     APF Percent
-------     ---------     -----------     --------     -----------
2 Kb        1792 Kb       0.00 Mb         8.75 Mb      10
(return status = 0)
```

Results After Cycling the Server

```
sp_cacheconfig
go
Cache Name              Status     Type      Config Value    RunValue
------------------      --------   -------   ------------    --------
default data cache      Active     Default   0.00 Mb         5.68 Mb
fred cache              Pend/Act   Mixed     3.00 Mb         3.00 Mb
                                             ------------    --------
                                   Total     3.00 Mb         8.68 Mb
=======================================================================
Cache: default data cache, Status: Active, Type: Default
      Config Size: 0.00 Mb, Run Size: 5.68 Mb
      Config Replacement: strict LRU, Run Replacement: strict LRU
      Config Partition: 1, Run Partition: 1
IO Size     Wash Size     Config Size     Run Size     APF Percent
-------     ---------     -----------     --------     -----------
2 Kb        1162 Kb       0.00 Mb         5.68 Mb      10
=======================================================================
cache:  fred cache, Status: Active, Type: Mixed
        Config Size: 3.00 Mb, Run Size: 3.00 Mb
        Config Replacement: strict LRU, Run Replacement: strict LRU
           Config Partition: 1, Run Partition: 1
IO Size     Wash Size     Config Size     Run Size     APF Percent
--------    ---------     ------------    --------     -----------
2 Kb        614 Kb        0.00 Mb         3.00 Mb      10
return status = 0)
```

Creating Buffer Pools

By default, all I/O is performed in 2 K units. Named caches may perform I/Os as large as an extent (16 K). In order for a cache to perform large I/Os, a buffer pool must be created to support it. Each buffer pool is for a specific size in a specific cache.

NOTE: These are based on 2 K pages; ASE 12.5 allows larger page sizes.

To create a buffer pool, use sp_poolconfig or edit the configuration file (as before, it is more reliable to use the stored procedure than to directly edit the file). Unlike cache creation, buffer pool creation or removal does not require a server restart.

Syntax:

```
sp_poolconfig cachename,
"memsize{P|K|M|G}",
"poolK"
[, "affected_poolK"]
```

Example:

```
sp_poolconfig "fred cache", "1M", "16K"
```

Unless otherwise specified, creating pools pulls memory away from the 2 K pool. So, this moves 1 MB from the 2 K pool and adds it to the 16 K pool.

cachename
: Name of the data cache being configured.

memsize
: Amount of memory within this cache which will be reserved for the buffer pool.

poolK
: I/O size of the buffer pool.

affected_poolK
: Buffer pool which will lose space to create this buffer pool; default is the 2 K buffer pool.

To remove a buffer pool, set its memsize to 0.

Using Buffer Pools

Creating (or resizing) a buffer pool carves up an existing resource; changing one buffer pool reduces or increments the available memory for another buffer pool (or pools).

```
sp_cache_config 'fred cache'
go

Cache Name            Status      Type      Config Value    Run Value
----------            ------      -----     ------------    ---------
fred cache            Active      Mixed     3.00 Mb         3.00 Mb
                                            ------------    ---------
                                  Total     3.00 Mb         3.00 Mb
```

```
==========================================================================
Cache:   fred cache, Status: Active, Type: Mixed
         Config Size: 3.00 Mb, Run Size: 3.00 Mb
         Config Replacement: strict LRU, Run Replacement: strict LRU
         Config Partition: 1, Run Partition: 1
 IO Size    Wash Size      Config Size      Run Size     APF Percent
 --------   ---------      -----------      --------     -----------
2 Kb         408 Kb        0.00 Mb          2.00 Mb      10
16 Kb        192 Kb        1.00 Mb          1.00 Mb      10
(return status = 0)
```

Buffer pools (specifically including the mandatory 2 K buffer pool) cannot be made smaller than 512 K. Large I/Os will not be used if there are not enough buffers within the pool; if a buffer pool of a given size is unavailable, Adaptive Server will use the 2 K pool.

NOTE The query optimizer automatically accounts for buffer pools. If a table or an index is bound to a named cache which is configured for buffer pools, the optimizer will determine if large I/O will improve performance.

Wash Area

Caches may be modeled as a page chain: pages are added to one end of the chain when read from disk, then fall out of cache when they have traversed the entire chain. The end of the chain where pages are added is the *MRU* (most recently used) end, and pages are removed from cache at the *LRU* (least recently used) end. If a page is needed and is found in cache, it will be moved back to the MRU end of the chain to begin its aging process again. The *wash area* is the section of a buffer pool past the *wash marker*; when pages cross the wash marker, they are written (washed) to disk if they are dirty. Following the write, the pages are marked as clean and made available at the LRU end of the cache chain.

The wash area serves a useful purpose: if a page has made it "most of the way" to the LRU end of the chain, and is nearly ready to be removed from cache, there is less chance that it will be needed again. Although the page has not yet hit the LRU end (and thus must be written to disk before removing from cache), it's nearly there, and it probably won't hurt anything to write the page(s) to disk ahead of time. This way, if many pages are added to cache in a rush, the pages in the wash area may be removed from cache quickly, without having to wait to write them before accepting new pages into cache.

But there is a downside to this model: queries that require pages could find them in the wash area. In this case, a page might be in the act of writing to disk, which means that what should have been a fast retrieval (pages already in cache) gets slowed down by the interference of washing the pages. This is likely to occur if the wash area is not correctly sized.

Figure 12-1

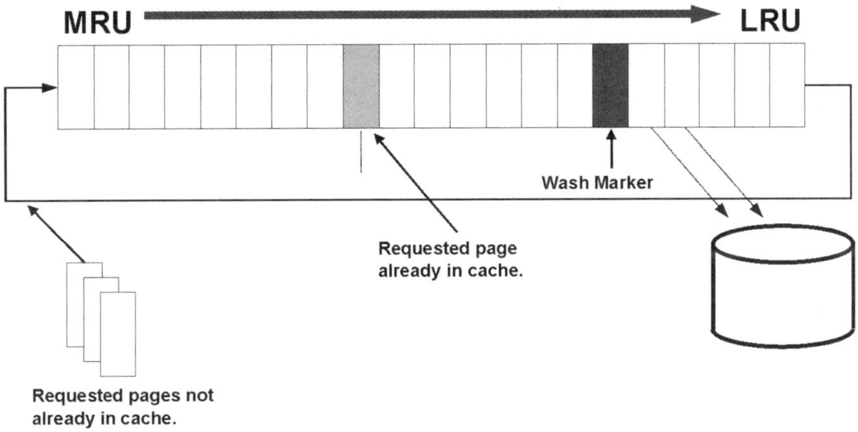

Wash Area Size

In most cases, the default size of the wash area will provide the best performance for a named cache; tune all other aspects of the system before adjusting the wash area size. If the wash area is too small, operations requiring clean pages may have to wait for dirty pages to be written to disk before proceeding; these "dirty buffer grabs" can seriously degrade performance. If the wash area is too large, operations that change a page past the wash marker will force it to be written to disk again (or have to wait for a page already being washed to finish).

Note that if you do choose to modify the wash area size of a buffer pool, there is a lengthy set of rules that determines valid sizes for a given buffer pool (minimum/maximum in absolute terms and number-of-buffers-terms, and valid/invalid sizes within the min-max range).

If the wash area size of a buffer pool is specifically suspected as a bottleneck, you may check the effects of washing with sp_sysmon.

If the Buffers Grabbed Dirty section shows a non-zero value in the Count column, check the Grabbed Dirty row for each pool and increase the size of the wash area for the affected pool. If the percentage of buffers Found in Wash is high and dirty buffer grabs are not a problem, reduce the size of the wash area.

To change the size of a buffer's wash area, use sp_poolconfig. This change takes effect immediately.

Syntax:

```
sp_poolconfig cachename, "poolK", "wash = sizeK"
```

Example:

```
sp_poolconfig "fred cache", "16K", "wash = 256K"
```

NOTE: To remove an override size for a wash area, it's probably easiest to locate the buffer pool in the configuration file and change its value back to the keyword DEFAULT.

Binding

When a page corresponding to a bound object is read in, it gets placed into that named cache. Initially, all objects are bound to default data cache. Creating a named cache is pointless unless you actually bind something to it.

Binding assigns a database or object to a particular cache. Objects (tables and indexes) may only be bound from the database in which they are stored; databases may only be bound from the master database. To bind an entire database (probably only tempdb needs this treatment) or system table, the database must be in single-user mode. Only syslogs (the transaction log) may be bound to a logonly cache. Objects may only be bound to caches that exist (that is, the server must have cycled since cache creation).

Both binding and unbinding of objects are dynamic, and will take immediate effect. Please note that binding an object will not read all of the object's pages into cache; it merely flips a value in a system table that indicates that the next time a page from that object is read from disk, it will be sent to the designated cache. By contrast, unbinding an object from a cache will flush all currently cached pages for that object. An object may only be associated with a single cache, and as soon as the unbind is requested, the pages must be removed; as a result, we know that following an unbind, the next read of an object will be from disk. Unbound objects automatically revert to using default data cache.

Binding to a Named Cache

To bind an entity to a cache, use sp_bindcache. These bindings are not stored in the configuration file. Since text and image data types are actually stored in a separate data structure, it is this object that is being bound to a cache, not an individual column. "text only" is used when binding a text or image data type to a named cache.

Syntax:

```
sp_bindcache cachename, dbname
[,tablename [,indexname | "text only"]]
```

Example:

```
sp_bindcache "fred cache", pubs2
sp_bindcache "fred cache", pubs2, titles
sp_bindcache "fred cache", pubs2, titles, titleind
```

Dropping Cache Bindings

To drop a bound entity from a cache, use sp_unbindcache. When unbinding an object from a cache, any dirty pages with the object on it will be flushed to disk and all pages will be removed from the cache. Note that since a given object may only be bound to one cache, it is not necessary to give the cache name when using sp_unbindcache.

Syntax:

```
sp_unbindcache dbname [,tablename
[,indexname | "text only"]]
```

Example:

```
sp_unbindcache pubs2, titles
```

To drop all bound entities from a cache, use sp_unbindcache_all <cache name>.

Retrieving Information on Bindings

To get information on specific objects bound to a named cache, use sp_helpcache. Omitting the cachename parameter reports on all configured caches in the Adaptive Server and all entities bound to them.

Syntax:

```
sp_helpcache [cachename]
```

Example:

```
sp_helpcache "fred cache"
```

Transaction Performance and Named Caches

When you add named data caches, your transaction performance might benefit. Some of these benefits include:

- Available large cache size for freer server activity
- Bind a "hot" table (in high user-application demand) to cache to increase concurrency
- Hold "hot" pages (portion of table in high query-reference demand)
- Multi-processor systems with high transaction rates or request DSS (decision support system) benefit the most
- Improved memory usage and reduced I/O can yield increased single CPU performance
- Greater number of spinlocks allows greater access to the caches if there are multiple CPUs since each named cache is governed by its own spinlock

Spinlocks

Caches may form a hotspot on multiengine servers; no matter how many tasks are running on multiple engines, each cache (by default) can only accept one process at a time. Access to the caches is regulated by a structure known as a spinlock; imagine a revolving door with only one triangular section instead of the usual three or four, and you've got the idea. A task needs to access a cache, so it enters the spinlock (rotating the door behind it) and has exclusive rights to the cache for the moment.

If another task on another engine wants into the same cache, it's stopped — there's no way to enter the doorway, since the only open section has already rotated to the inside. When the task in the cache exits (rotating the door), the queued task may now enter through the spinlock. Although this spinlock prevents interference between running tasks, it can also cause unwanted contention and bottlenecking; the two tasks in our example may have been trying to access completely different pages (even belonging to different tables or databases), and still end up blocking.

Fortunately, there are ways to resolve this contention. Each cache gets its own spinlock, so if multiple popular tables live in the same cache, it is a simple thing to rebind them to different caches. More caches = more spinlocks = (probably) less contention. Note that sometimes just splitting a cache in two and rebinding objects may clear up contention without requiring any more memory.

However, multiple caches may not always clear up the contention. If different tasks are trying to acquire different pages of the same object, it is not an option to use multiple caches — each object may only be bound to one cache. To deal with this situation, a new caching feature was introduced in ASE 12.0: *cache partitioning* (popularly known as "cachelets").

A cache may be divided into multiple subsections, each of which gets its own spinlock; an internal hashing process determines which pages go to which subsection. Creating a partitioned cache may still lead to contention if two tasks want two pages that happen to be in the same subsection, but the odds that the pages are in different subsections (and therefore protected by different spinlocks) are improved as the number of subsections increases.

Cachelets may be set either globally (by sp_configure) or on a per-cache basis (using sp_cacheconfig). It's much more useful to use sp_cacheconfig, as it is unlikely that all of the caches you create in the server will require the same number of cachelets.

Sybase recommends trying cachelets prior to named caches because cachelets are easier to tune.

Syntax:

```
sp_cacheconfig cache_name, "cache_partition = value"
```

Values may be the word "default" (use the server-wide setting, which should be left at 1), or some power of 2, from 2 to 64 inclusive.

Example:

```
sp_cacheconfig "fred cache", "cache_partition = 4"
```

Following a server reboot, fred cache will be subdivided into four sections, each of which has its own spinlock, and each of which contains all of the buffer pools previously configured in the cache. Actually, we'll get an error from this attempt.

Remember that all buffer pools have a minimum size of 512 KB; when you configure cachelets, each buffer pool must have a minimum size of 512 KB * number of cachelets; this is because each buffer pool spans each of the cachelets. In our prior examples, fred cache was configured to 3 MB total, with 1 MB of that set to the 16 K buffer pool.

Figure 12-2
fred cache

However, each of the buffer pools must meet its minimum required size (512 KB) across each of the cachelets. In our example, we created four such cachelets, as shown in the following figure.

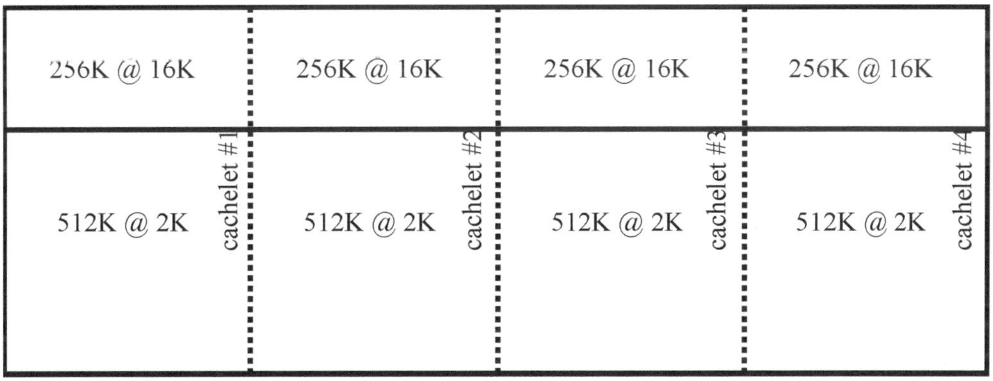

Figure 12-3
fred cache after partitioning

Each cachelet gets an equal amount of space from each buffer pool, so we see that the 2 K buffer pool meets its minimum size requirements (512 KB per cachelet), but the 16 K pool does not. In order to create cachelets in fred cache, we would either have to increase the size of the 16 K pool to 2 MB (which would require the cache be increased to 4 MB), or reduced the number of cachelets to two (which would allow 512 KB/cachelet in the 16 KB pool).

As with sizing caches and buffer pools, it's best to take an iterative approach to reducing spinlock contention in caches. The contention may be measured with sp_sysmon, in the Cache Management section; any spinlock contention value greater than 10% should be dealt with immediately. If you cannot reduce the spinlock contention, it is recommended that you do not increase the number of engines, as you will only make the contention worse (in fact, with bad spinlock contention, you may find that you improve performance by decreasing your engine count).

Example:

```
sp_sysmon "00:02:00", dcache

Data Cache Management
---------------------
```

```
  Cache Statistics Summary (All Caches)
  -------------------------------------
<output skipped>
---------------------------------------------------------------------------
  Cache: default data cache
                             per sec    per xact     count    % of total
  -------------------------  -------    --------     -----    ----------
    Spinlock Contention      6          0.8          59       0.6 %
<output skipped>
---------------------------------------------------------------------------
  Cache: fred cache
                             per sec    per xact     count    % of total
-----------------------      -------    --------     -----    ----------
    Spinlock Contention      2          0.3          17       0.2 %
<output skipped>
```

Cache Notes

Size the cache or pool for the transaction log so as to reduce the number of times Adaptive Server processes need to re-read log pages that must go to disk because the pages have been flushed from the cache.

In general, you want heavily scanned pages to have access to a 16 K pool; you want the indexes and random access data to have access to a 2 K pool; and you want the log to have access to a 4 K pool.

Adaptive Server Processes Need to Re-read Log Pages

Certain processes need to re-read log pages. These include:

- Triggers that use the inserted and deleted tables built from the transaction log when the trigger queries the tables.
- Deferred updates, inserts, and deletes that require a re-read of the log to apply changes to tables or indexes.
- Transactions that are rolled back, since log pages must be accessed to roll back the changes.

Sizing a Cache for a Transaction Log

1. Time the processes that need to re-read the log pages.
2. Time how long the longest triggers and deferred updates last.
3. Time the long-running transactions that are rolled back.
4. Size the growth rate of the log during the first three items listed here.

   Use sp_spaceused at regular intervals to estimate how fast the log grows.

Example:

Size the log for maximum length of time:

(Deferred update: 5 min.)(Log growth: 125 pp/min.)
= (Pages allocated while transaction executes = 625 pp)

Or

Size the log for average length of time if few transactions or queries run for a long period of time.

Choosing the I/O Size

Group commit holds partially filled transaction log pages of 2 K for a very brief span of time so that records of several transactions can be written to disk simultaneously.

Create a 4 K pool for the transaction log:

- To reduce log writes in environments with high transaction rates or transactions that create large log records
- If your database is using 2 K log I/O
- If the number of log writes per second is high
- If the average number of writes per log page is slightly above one

sp_sysmon

This stored procedure reports on the ratio of transaction log writes to transaction log allocations.

```
                             per sec    per xact   count     % of total
Transaction Log Writes       22.5       458.0      1374      n/a
Transaction Log Alloc        20.8       423.0      1269      n/a
Avg # Writes per Log Page    n/a        n/a        1.08274   n/a
```

Benefits of Assigning tempdb to Its Own Data Cache

Assigning tempdb to its own data cache reduces heavy use of the data cache when temporary tables are created, populated, and then dropped. If tempdb is heavily in use, and you are experiencing memory contention, you can split off a lot of the work of the hash buffers by separating tempdb I/O from the other I/O by binding tempdb to its own named cache.

Creating and Configuring Caches and Pools

The cache binding commands for the SA are:

- sp_cacheconfig
- sp_poolconfig

To bind tempdb to its own cache, follow these steps:

1. Configure the caches.
2. Restart the server.
3. Bind tempdb to the new cache.

```
sp_bindcache "tempdb_cache", tempdb
```

Guidelines for Cache Configuration

To configure named caches in Adaptive Server properly, analyze the following to determine whether there are situations that will benefit from named caches and cache binding:

- Databases
- Database objects
- I/O patterns
- Queries
- Guidelines for cache configuration

Tuning Ideas

Consider these ideas when tuning:

- The size of any frequently accessed tables you want to keep entirely in cache; the bigger the object, the more of your limited memory resource you'll take up.
- Place tempdb into a separate named cache.
- On multi-CPU systems, consider spreading your busiest tables and indexes across multiple caches to minimize cache contention.
- Leave a large enough default data cache for activity on unbound tables and indexes.
- The recovery process uses only the 2 KB buffer pool in the default data cache. If this is too small, recovery will run slowly.
- Don't over-partition the cache. You'll probably end up wasting cache space and hurting performance rather than helping it.

When setting up buffer pools, follow these guidelines when deciding whether to configure for large I/Os to improve performance:

- Determine whether you have queries that can benefit from large I/Os such as table scans, leaf-level scans of large nonclustered indexes, and range queries on clustered indexes that retrieve a large number of rows.
- Don't leave too little space for the 2 KB buffer pool. Many queries and types of data do not need large I/O (for example, single-row retrievals using an index). In addition, some tasks use only 2 KB I/Os (for example, disk init, certain dbcc commands, and drop table).
- Reconfigure buffer pools to match workload requirements. For example, increase the smaller buffer pools (that is, 2 KB and 4 KB pools) during the day when performing OLTP activities. Reconfigure them for a larger 16 KB buffer pool for DSS activities run at night.

The I/O size for transaction logs is 4 KB by default. To get the best log performance, make sure that the logonly cache the log is bound to has a 4 KB buffer pool.

Summary

Only reconfigure cache when you have a specific performance need to correct. Otherwise, you may end up making your memory problems worse. Use the scientific method to determine whether your changes helped or didn't. If the changes did not help, put things back the way they were.

Chapter 13

Remote Server Management

Remote Access

ASE was conceived as a database using a network and the client/server paradigm. From the beginning, ASE has used a client program that formulated and made requests of server programs over a network. A server could act as a client and make a request of another server, usually on behalf of a requesting client; the mechanism used was a Remote Procedure Call (RPC). This was a request made via the Tabular Data Stream (TDS), and when the remote server received it, passed it to its rpc handling function to process.

> **NOTE:** Don't get Sybase's RPC term confused with other software vendors who may talk about remote procedure calls. They are different things!

Figure 13-1 shows a traditional Sybase RPC request. A client issues a request in the form of:

```
exec remote_server_name.database_name.owner.procedure_name
```

Figure 13-1

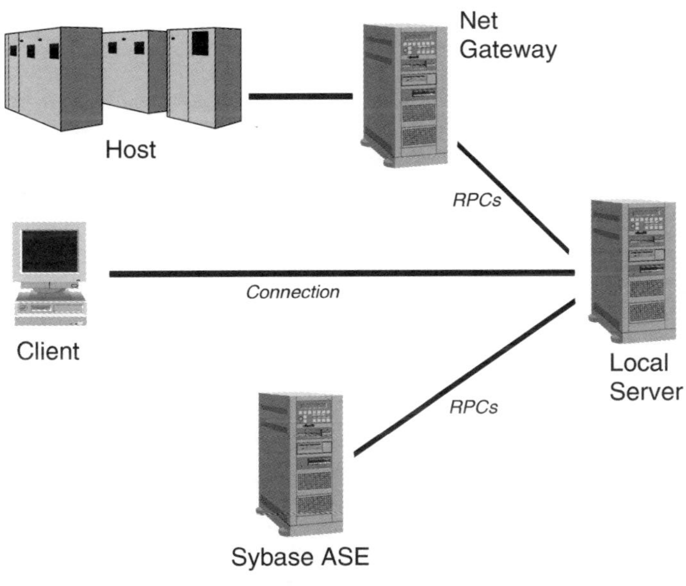

The request goes to the local server, which forwards it via an RPC call to the remote server. The remote server returns the data and then the output parameters and return code. The local server does not have a way to forward the data rows but could return the output parameters and return code to the requesting client.

In order for this to work, the following steps must be performed:

1. Ensure the server is named the same in the interfaces file and the sysservers table.
2. Reboot the server (to allow the local server name to take effect).
3. Allow remote access in both servers.
4. Map logins from originating server to remote server.

These steps are detailed in the following sections.

Server Naming

The server names may be verified by examining the interfaces file (by text editor or the dsedit utility). The server that will originate the RPC must be identified in sysservers as the local server, and the server responding to the RPC added as a non-local (remote) server. These additions to sysservers can be accomplished with sp_addserver.

Syntax:

```
sp_addserver remote_server_name [, local]
```

Example:

```
exec sp_addserver sales, local
exec sp_addserver inventory
```

In this example, the local server is identified by the name sales, and the sales server is made aware of the existence of the server namedinventory. Adding the local server name also populates the @@servername global variable. The new local servername takes effect when the server is rebooted.

Remote Access

By default, ASE permits server-to-server communications (otherwise, it would be impossible to communicate with the Backup Server). The sp_configure option allow remote access needs to be set to 1 (true) for both servers. Since this is a dynamic option, the server need not be rebooted.

Example:

```
sp_configure 'allow remote access', 1
```

Login Mapping

The login that originates the RPC on the local server needs to be equated with a login on the remote server. The sp_addremotelogin procedure enables an SA to define how these mappings work, and the sp_remoteoption procedure allows an SSO to define what (if any) password checking is enforced.

Syntax:

```
sp_addremotelogin remote_server_name [, local_login_name [,
remote_login_name]]
```

```
sp_remoteoption remote_server_name [, local_login_name, remote_login_name,
{trusted|net password encrypted|timeouts}, {true|false}]
```

Example:

```
exec sp_addlogin joe
exec sp_addremotelogin sales, joe, bob
```

In this case, both procedures are executed in the inventory server; a local login called "joe" is created in inventory, and a mapping is defined specifically between the pair of servers.

Example:

```
exec inventory...report_proc
```

If this execution is submitted by "bob" from the sales server, the procedure will be executed in the inventory server as if it had been locally executed by "joe." The results will be returned to the client connection of the "bob" login. If "joe" has no permission to execute the proc, a permissions error will result.

Example:

```
sp_addlogin mary
sp_addremotelogin customer, mary
```

In this example, both procedures are executed in the inventory server. The login "mary" is created and mapped, but there is not a specific login in the customer server for the mapping. Any remote procedure calls originating from customer that refers to procedures in inventory will be executed according to the permissions of mary. In this way, we can save the effort of creating specific login pairs between servers, but we don't get quite as much accountability; all logins in customer will have precisely the same privileges to execute procedures in inventory.

Once the mappings are established, security options may be defined for remote logins. Logins that initiate a remote procedure call may be trusted, may have encrypted passwords, and may engage in network timeouts.

Example:

```
sp_remoteoption sales, joe, bob, trusted, true
```

In this example, the remote login between sales.bob and inventory.joe is trusted: no password needs to be supplied during the RPC. The network timeouts option indicates that connections used by the RPC will be held for approximately 60 seconds before being closed (if off, this option allows the connections to be held indefinitely), and net password encrypted sends all RPC passwords in an encrypted form (more secure, but slower).

To report on the remote logins defined on a server, use sp_helpremotelogin.

CIS — Component Integration Services

An alternative to Remote Procedure Calls was introduced in ASE 11.5: Component Integration Services (CIS). Instead of requiring users to make explicit calls of procedures in other servers, the SA may set up a logical data space, where multiple servers behave as if their objects were in a single server. A user may query an object via a structure known as a *proxy* (a placeholder that substitutes for the actual object) which is in the local server.

Behind the scenes, references to the proxy are translated into references to the object's actual, physical location (server and database), invisible to the user. When the results are returned to the user, it's not apparent that they came from "somewhere else." Included within ASE are those portions of CIS that will communicate with Sybase server products (Adaptive Server Enterprise, Adaptive Server Anywhere, Adaptive Server IQ); you may add licensed additional code that will extend CIS's capabilities to talk with data servers from other vendors, allowing for transparent, heterogeneous servers (see Figure 13-2).

Figure 13-2

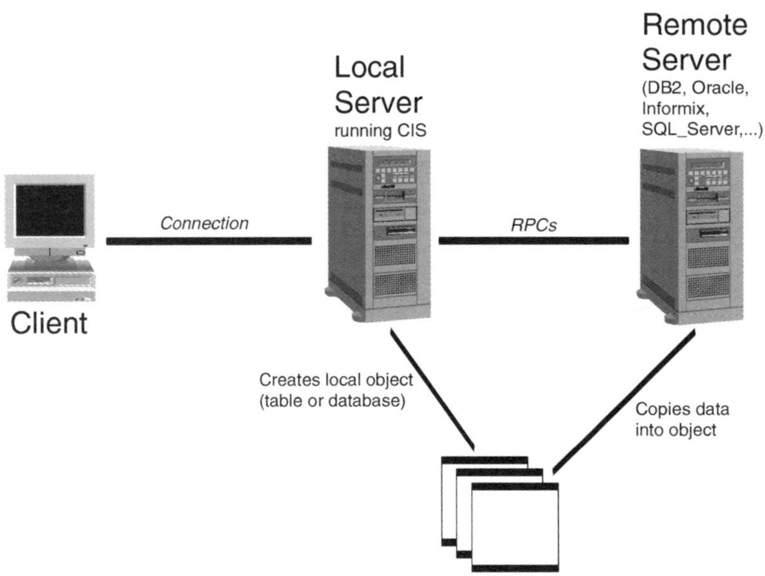

In ASE 12.5, inter-server communication is made more secure with the adoption of the *Secure Sockets Layer* (SSL) protocol. Most commonly used with web servers, SSL allows for strong, encryption of network traffic using a well-publicized standard based on public key cryptography. Additionally, Sybase has added support for the Lightweight Directory Access Protocol (LDAP), which allows a small (lightweight), centralized service to provide directory services. This can substitute for the presence of a separate interfaces file on each node of the enterprise. In Windows NT, LDAP allows the use of the registry to access servers; in UNIX, another naming service can be designated to supply server naming (but the traditional interfaces technique is still used by default).

Only ASE-native CIS is the focus of our discussion.

Using proxy tables (or proxy databases) requires some setup:

1. The remote server must be added to sysservers and CIS enabled.
2. A local storage location must be defined for the remote object and the remote table's schema must be mapped to the local server.

Remote Server

CIS has extended the definition of a server to include the idea of a *server class*. Server classes establish the access path to an external database. They are included in the pathname of the proxy tables, and defined using additional parameters in sp_addserver.

Syntax:

```
sp_addserver server_name, server_class, net_name
```

Parameters:

server_name
: The name of the external server referred to by the proxy table.

server_class
: The class name associated with the server.

net_name
: The name of the server as it appears in the interfaces file.

The supported server classes are:

ASEnterprise
: Adaptive Server Enterprise 10.0 and higher.

ASAnywhere
: Adaptive Server Anywhere version 6.0 and higher.

ASIQ
: This server class has been used when Omni is configured to stand between a client application and Sybase IQ version 11.5. With the release of ASIQ version 12, this class will now assume that the IQ database being accessed is version 12.0 or greater. This version, while based on ASA, supports expanded syntax in areas of group by and aggregate handling, and therefore requires Omni to distinguish between ASA 6/7 and ASIQ 12.

Note that support for ASIQ 11.x is no longer provided, as this version has been EOL'd at the end of 2000.

sql_server
: Sybase SQL Server version prior to System 10; also, this class can be used for Microsoft SQL Server through version 6.5 (version 7.0 needs a gateway), ASA 5.5, and OmniConnect version 10.5.

direct_connect
: DirectConnect gateways, Net Gateway 3.0.1 or higher, and OpenServer Connect 4.0 or higher.

db2
: Sybase DirectConnect/MVS TRS (TRS can be configured as a server in either direct_connect or db2 class).

sds
: Custom applications using the Sybase Standard or Enhanced Full Text Search specialty data store, or Open Server Apps written with the specialty store SDK.

ASA/CIS
: External access to relational or non-relational data through JDBC or ODBC drivers has been part of ASA since version 6.0.1. To Omni, ASA proxy tables appear no different than ordinary ASA tables and views. CIS is enabled by default in ASE, but this status should be verified with sp_configure.

Local Storage

A local storage location may be defined for the remote object with the sp_addobjectdef procedure, or by using the pathname option in the create table statement. The pathname method is recommended.

Syntax:

```
create [existing] table local_name
( <column_list> )
[ external {table | procedure}]
at "pathname"
```

The default external object type is the table. If procedure is specified, it is assumed to be read-only, and insert, update, and delete operations are not allowed. Selects against the proxy procedure will cause CIS to issue an RPC to the remote server and process the results as if it were a normal table (that is, you execute the procedure by selecting it … a syntactical fiction).

If the existing clause is used, metadata from the location identified in pathname will be imported into CIS, which will be compared with the column_list. If the data types are not compatible (convertible), the command will be rejected. The column_list syntax is the same as the standard create table syntax. An alternate form of the command is:

```
create proxy_table local_name at "pathname"
```

In this case CIS uses the metadata obtained from the remote location specified in pathname to create the column_list. Once the proxy table is created (by either means) it is then referenced using its local_name as if it were a regular table in the database. It can be used within local views, procedures, triggers, or any other T-SQL command that expects a table name.

The alternate definition method for proxies (sp_addobjectdef) is a bit more complex than create existing table or create proxy table.

Syntax:

```
sp_addobjectdef object_name, "object_loc" [,"object_type"]
```

Parameters:

object_name
: Name of the local proxy table in the format of [dbname.owner.]object.

object_loc
: Storage location of the remote object in the format of server_name.dbname.owner.object;[aux1.aux2], where object is the name of the remote table, view, or proc; Aux1.aux2 is a string of characters passed to the remote server (see below).

object_type
: Type of object the proxy refers to; default is "table"

Aux1.aux2 is a string of characters passed to the remote server during create table or create index commands to act as the segment name. The meaning of the string is dependent on the server class. For instance, if the server class is db2, then aux1 is the name of the DB2 database and aux2 is the DB2 tablespace (see the *CIS User's Guide for ASE and OmniConnect* for more details).

Proxy Databases

A proxy database is a database taken from a remote server and reproduced on the local server. When a proxy database is created, the metadata from the remote server is used to create proxy tables.

Syntax:

```
create database <dbname>
[create database options]
[[with default_location='pathname']
[for proxy_update]]
```

The for proxy_update option establishes the database as a proxy database, and the with default location clause indicates the data import location. If for proxy_update is used, with default_location must be used, or an error occurs.

Using with default location without with proxy_update establishes a default storage location for new and existing table creation. However, when using create database, no automatic importing of proxy table definitions is done.

The pathname argument is in the format of servername.dbname.owner; the servername must exist in sysservers. If the owner is specified, only objects owned by that owner are imported.

When creating the proxy database, the following steps are performed for you:

- Size of the database to be created is estimated (if no size is given in the create database command)
- All proxy tables and views created (system tables are not copied)
- All permissions on tables granted to public
- guest user added to the proxy database
- create table permission to granted to public
- Database status set to proxy

Remote Access Setup Example

By default, remote access and CIS are enabled and remote logins are untrusted. Given a local server named Loc_Server and a remote server named Rem_Server, what follows are the steps required on both servers to be able to execute a remote procedure from the local server to the remote server. On the local server we will create a login "joe_local," and on the remote server a login of "tom_remote." To allow joe_local to execute on the remote server as joe_local, we'll also add a login of joe_local on the remote server.

Local Server	Remote Server
exec sp_addlogin joe_local	exec sp_addlogin tom_remote
exec sp_addserver Loc_Server, local	exec sp_addserver Rem_Server, local
exec sp_addserver Rem_Server	exec sp_addserver Loc_Server
verify both Loc_Server and Rem_Server are in the local interfaces file	verify both Loc_Server and Rem_Server are in the remote interfaces file exec sp_addremotelogin Loc_Server exec sp_addlogin joe_local

At this point a login on the local server should be able to execute a procedure on the remote server using the following syntax, using the same login name as on the local server:

```
exec Rem_Server…myproc
```

The form of sp_addremotelogin used above assumes that every local login on Loc_Server maps to an identically-named login on Rem_Server; if desired, we could have used one of the alternate forms that mapped logins in a different fashion.

Remote logins may be removed (preventing given logins from executing remote procedures) by using sp_dropremotelogin. Information about a remote server or a remote login may be obtained using sp_helpserver or sp_helpremotelogin.

Syntax:

```
sp_dropremotelogin remote_server_name [, loginname [, remotename]]

sp_helpserver [server_name]

sp_helpremotelogin [remote_server_name [, remotelogin]]
```

Using CIS for Remote Procedure Calls

There are two approaches now possible within Adaptive Server Enterprise to make remote procedure calls. The first (and original) approach uses the ASE site handler; the second approach uses CIS. The CIS approach is used if the configuration property cis rpc handling is 1, in which case all new connections inherit the current setting, or if the session-specific command set cis_rpc_handling ON has been sent. If CIS rpc handling is enabled, then all rpc's will be sent to a remote server via CIS. This can result in improved performance, since CIS connections to remote servers are persistent.

If CIS is used to establish connections to remote servers, then you need to separately map the logins.

Enhanced Mapping of External Logins

Users of ASE that invoke the services of Omni, knowingly or unknowingly, will require login names/passwords to remote servers. By default, the username/password pair used by Omni to connect to a remote server will be the same username/password used by the client to connect to ASE.

This default mapping is frequently insufficient, and since its first release Omni has supported a one-to-one mapping of ASE login names and passwords to remote server login names and passwords. For example, using the stored procedure sp_addexternlogin, it is possible to map ASE user steve, password sybase to DB2 login name login1, password password1:

sp_addexternlogin DB2, steve, login1, password1 In the Everest release, it will also be possible to provide a many-to-one mapping so that all ASE users that need a connection to DB2 can be assigned the same name and password.

sp_addexternlogin DB2, NULL, login2, password2 One-to-one mapping has precedence, such that if user steve has an external login for DB2, that would be used rather than the many-to-one mapping.

In addition to this, it will be possible to assign external logins to ASE roles. With this capability, anyone with a particular role can be assigned a corresponding login name/password for any given remote server.

sp_addexternlogin DB2, null, login3, password3, rolename The use of the fifth argument to this procedure, containing the role name, identifies the name of a role rather than the name of a user. Whenever a user with this role active requires a connection to DB2, the appropriate login name/password for the role will be used to establish the connection. When establishing a connection to a remote server for a user that has more than one role active, each role is searched for an external login mapping, and the first mapping found is used to establish the login. This is the same order as displayed by the stored procedure sp_activeroles.

The general syntax for sp_addexternlogin is:

```
sp_addexternlogin
        <servername>,
        <loginname>,
        <external_loginname>,
        <external_password>
        [, <rolename>]
```

<rolename> is optional; if specified, the loginname parameter is ignored.

Precedence for these capabilities is as follows:

- If one-to-one mapping is defined, it will be used — this has the highest precedence.
- If no one-to-one mapping is defined, then if a role is active and a mapping for it can be found, the role mapping will be used to establish a remote connection.
- If neither of the above are true, many-to-one mapping is used if defined.
- If none of the above are true, the ASE login name and password are used to make the connection.

If role mapping is done, and a user's role is changed (via set role), then any connections made to remote servers that used role mapping will have to be disconnected. This cannot be done if a transaction is pending, therefore the set role command will not be acceptable if a transaction is active and remote connections are present that used role mapping.

The stored procedure sp_helpexternlogin will also be updated to allow viewing the various types of extern logins that have been added via sp_addexternlogin. The syntax for sp_helpexternlogin is:

```
sp_helpexternlogin [<servername> [,<loginname> [,<rolename>]]]
```

All three parameters are optional, and any of the parameters can be NULL. The stored procedure sp_dropexternlogin has also been modified to accept a third argument, <rolename>. If <rolename> is specified, the second argument, <loginname>, is ignored.

ASE Variable Page Size Issues

As part of the support for larger page sizes in ASE 12.5, it will sometimes be necessary to provide additional information regarding the maximum size of certain columns. The new limits on column sizes are:

Page Size (bytes)	Maximum Column Size (bytes)
2048	1900
4096	4000
8192	8000
16384	16000

Columns of type char(), varchar(), binary(), and varbinary() may be sized up to the maximums listed above (prior versions limited column lengths to 255; this could cause issues when dealing with non-Sybase servers with different column limits). Additionally, the limit on number of columns per table has increased from 250 to 1024, and maximum index widths have likewise been relaxed (although indexes are still limited to 31 columns).

Page Size (bytes)	Maximum Index Width (bytes)
2048	600
4096	1250
8192	2600

Page Size (bytes)	Maximum Index Width (bytes)
16384	5300

CIS still needs to know the max size of char and varchar columns of other databases, but most of this information is resolved by the server classes. For the direct_connect and sds server classes, additional information is obtained by the sp_capabilities procedure. In the case of the direct_connect server class, ASE supply the maximum acceptable column length; this is done with the procedure sp_thread_props:

Syntax:

```
sp_thread_props "maximum ASE column length", n
```

n is the value of the maximum width, based on page size.

Accounting for increased page sizes also necessitates some new CIS commands in ASE 12.5:

Command	Description
create new proxy table	Allows the new extended char lengths.
create existing proxy table	Allows columns to be over 255 bytes. Previously char, varchar, binary, and varbinary greater than 255 bytes had to be treated as text or image columns. If the column size is still too large, they must be declared as text or image.
create proxy_table	Imports metadata from the remote server, translates it into the proper syntax for a create existing table command, which it runs internally. The same rules on column size as applied to the create existing proxy table apply here.
alter proxy table	Processed locally, then on the remote server. If the remote server fails, the command is backed out of the local server.

Standard RPC vs. CIS

There are two approaches now possible for administering RPCs within ASE: the first (and original) approach uses the ASE site handler; the second approach uses CIS. The second approach is used if the configuration property cis rpc handling is 1, in which case all new connections inherit the current setting, or if the session-specific command set cis_rpc_handling ON has been sent.

If CIS rpc handling is enabled, then all rpc's will be sent to a remote server via CIS. This can result in improved performance, since CIS connections to remote servers are persistent.

NOTES: CIS rpc handling allows for long characters.
Unicode characters are supported for CIS.
Wide result sets may be broken into multiple units if unable to fit into the TDS.
The Max CIS remote servers and Max CIS remote connections properties have been dropped.
Cascading proxy tables are permitted, which can cause deadlocks.

Creating Tables from System Files

ASE 12.5 allows you to create a proxy table to refer to an underlying system file. The resulting table has predefined columns that define its size, filename, and content (as an image column), etc. Such a proxy table maps to the underlying file system directory. By using an insert statement you can create a new file in the directory, a select would obtain filename information, and writetext would change the contents of a file.

Syntax:

```
create proxy_table <table_name>
external directory at "pathname to directory[;R]"
```

With the optional ;R flag, CIS will recursively search all subdirectories for information. If traceflag 11206 is turned on, messages will go to the error log about the directory contents.

Example:

```
create proxy_table prox_dir
external directory at "/usr/local/fred_dir"
```

The above example creates a table named prox_dir with information from the fred_dir directory with the following columns:

Column	Data Type	Description
id	numeric(24)	Unique identifier
filename	varchar(n)	Fully qualified location of the file
size	int	Size in bytes for REG files
filetype	varchar(4)	DIR, REG, FIFO, CHRS(char special), BLKS, UNKN
access	char(10)	UNIX format "drwxrwxrwx"
uid	varchar(n)	Fileowner n=9 on most systems
gid	varchar(n)	Group
atime	datetime	Access time; last time data were accessed
mtime	datetime	Modified; last time file was modified
ctime	datetime	Change time of last time file status changed
content	image	Actual data

Example:

```
select filename, size, content from prox_table
where filename like 'data%'
```

This example finds all files whose names begin with "data" and report their name, size in bytes, and contents.

File Access

ASE 12.5 has the ability to access files within the file system. This allows you to:

- Back up tables to files using select into or insert/select
- Query file content
- Use in place of bcp

There are two forms of the command:

```
create proxy_table <table_name>
external file at "pathname"
```

This creates a one-column table; the column name is record, with type varchar(255). The contents of each row are the contents of the file up to a newline character. It is assumed that files are regular files in human-readable form.

The second form of this command allows you to define columns. The data is read from the file up to a new line for each row, and fields are assumed to be separated by tabs.

```
create existing table mydata
(name         varchar(50)         null,
 age          int                 null,
 ssn          char(9)             null)
external file at "/usr/local/fred_dir/name_file"
```

Summary

Sybase has a variety of mechanisms to enable you to remotely access Sybase servers, non-Sybase servers, and file system tables. Choose the method that best meets your needs.

Chapter 14

Preventative Maintenance Regimen

Like any piece of machinery, an Adaptive Server must be properly maintained to stay in good working order. In this chapter, we will discuss some common tasks that are performed to maintain the server.

Periodic Maintenance

The different types of maintenance will be described in levels based on scope. Some tasks take place at the server level, meaning that your tasks involve resources that affect the entire server; for example, memory is a shared resource among all the tasks running on an Adaptive Server. Other tasks take place at the database level. The database is the server's unit of backup and recovery, so we perform database backups (making a copy of the database) and other types of care and maintenance one database at a time. Finally, at the table level (the table is what contains your data), you do things to help ensure database performance; that is, fast access to the data.

Server-Level Maintenance

The word "server" is used in a variety of ways in IT literature, from a file server (which manages disks) to the Adaptive Server (which interfaces with each client to manage your data). Here, we focus on the Adaptive Server as a singular unit. We will try to stay focused on issues and monitors for the server as a whole.

Part of systems administration is disaster preparedness. Under some circumstances, you may need to reinstall your entire server. Given this, it becomes necessary to include scripts that can be used to rebuild the entire server as part of the server-level maintenance routine. This need not be a daily issue.

Activity Monitoring

Adaptive Server comes with various tools to monitor the activity on the server. Regular monitoring of the server can prevent situations where the system starts to perform badly because of misconfiguration, or the monitoring can be used to identify any bottlenecks in the server. The act of monitoring the server's performance on a repeated basis throughout a day can also be used to identify peak times for the server's use.

sp_monitor

The simplest tool for monitoring is the sp_monitor system stored procedure. The sp_monitor stored procedure can be used to track high-level system resource statistics. This procedure has been available on older versions of Adaptive Server, but is not especially useful in multiprocessor environments.

Example:

```
sp_monitor
go

last_run             current_run          seconds
------------------   ------------------   ---------------
May 8 2001 11:44AM   May 8 2001 11:48AM   246

cpu_busy             io_busy              idle
------------------   ------------------   ---------------
40(0)-0%             63(0)-0%             88724(246)-100%

packets_received     packets_sent         packet_errors
----------------     ------------------   ---------------
583(2)               819(3)               0(0)

total_read           total_write          total_errors       connections
----------------     ------------------   ---------------    -----------
5775(0)              4618(4)              0(0)               11(0)
```

When reading sp_monitor output, it is important to distinguish between the historical and current results. The numbers inside the parentheses indicate the number of seconds (for cpu_busy, io_busy, and idle) or the count of events (for the other results) since the last time sp_monitor was run. The numbers outside of the parentheses indicate the time or count since the server was restarted. The results are not very detailed, but may give us a top-level feel for how the server is behaving.

sp_sysmon

sp_sysmon produces lower level system utilization information than the sp_monitor procedure. This data is often more useful for identifying bottlenecks or periods of intensive server use. Unlike sp_monitor, the sp_sysmon stored procedure does take into account the existence of multiple processors. However, when the utilization percentages are combined, it is possible to see overall utilizations of greater than 100%.

The procedure actually returns a lot of information that is organized into various sections, described in the table below. The name of the section can be used to force the procedure to return information only about the section called.

Section	Name	Description
Application Management	appmgmt	Reports on user tasks
Data Cache Management	dcache	Reports on all data caches
Disk I/O Management	diskio	Reports on all disk I/O
ESP Management	esp	Reports on extended stored procedures
Housekeeper	Housekeeper	Reports on the housekeeper process
Index Management	indexmgmt	Reports on index management
Kernel Utilization	kernel	Tells how busy the kernel was
Lock Management	locks	Reports locks, deadlocks, and lock promotions
Memory Management	memory	Reports on pages allocated and deallocated
Metadata Cache Management	mdcache	Reports on the Metadata cache
Monitor Access to Executing SQL	monaccess	Reports on showplans and Monitor Server access to query plans
Network I/O Management	netio	Reports on network I/O
Parallel Query Management	parallel	Reports on parallel queries
Procedure Cache Management	pcache	Reports on procedure cache
Recovery Management	recovery	Reports on number and length of checkpoints
Task Management	taskmgmt	Reports on open connections
Transaction Management	wactmgmt	Reports on transaction management activities
Transaction Profile	xactsum	Reports on transaction related activities
Worker Process Management	wpm	Reports on the activity of worker processes

Syntax:

```
exec sp_sysmon "HH:MM:SS" [, section_name]
```

Example output:

```
DBCC execution completed. If DBCC printed error messages, contact a user
with System Administrator (SA) role.
===============================================================================
      Sybase Adaptive Server Enterprise System Performance Report
===============================================================================

Server Version:        Adaptive Server Enterprise/12.5/B/Sun_svr4/OS
                       5.8/rel125
Server Name:           olympus
Run Date:              April 08, 2001
```

```
Statistics Cleared at: 10:11:10
Statistics Sampled at: 10:12:10
Sample Interval:       00:01:00

===========================================================================

Kernel Utilization
------------------

  Engine Busy Utilization
    Engine 0                        20.0 %
```

The output of sp_sysmon is extensive, and learning to read and interpret all of its results requires a great deal of practice. Administration can be as much art as science. There may be many sets of correct values for the server configuration parameters. Precise meanings of the various sections and subsections is described in the *Performance and Tuning Guide* of the ASE documentation set.

Use of sp_sysmon contributes some overhead, but it is difficult to impossible to measure. The procedure should be run before and after changing system parameters, or adding or removing caches, disks, or engines within the server. This will allow the administrator to gather a before and after picture of any changes to the server and their effect on performance. Running the procedure before and after the installation of new applications to the server can help identify the impact the new application has on the overall server. And of course, this should be run periodically run during peak times to see what kind of load is on your systems.

NOTE: Until recently, you could only run sp_sysmon for maximum periods of 5 minutes. Today, there is no limit. As a result, you can pick any monitoring interval. It can be useful to run (for example) 5 minutes on, 5 minutes off. If you have a lot of processing you want to understand, and the processing runs 30 minutes, go ahead and run sp_sysmon for 30 minutes.

What to Monitor

When using the sp_sysmon output, keep an archive of the outputs and try to at least gather information about Engine Busy Utilization (in the Kernel Utilization section) and Disk I/O Management. Try to gauge maximum, minimum, and average values for these readings during peak and off-peak times. This will provide a frame of reference for what is "normal" on the server, and make abnormalities easier to identify. Also try to gather information on user/process connections (Worker Process Management and Task Management sections). Metrics like the total number of connections at a particular time of day, average connections per user, and the average length of time blocked by other users (some of which you will have to calculate yourself) can help gauge the normal work load attributed by users to the server.

You should only run one of either sp_monitor or sp_sysmon at a time to avoid internal counter collisions. For the same reasons, do not try to run multiple instances of sp_monitor or sp_sysmon at the same time, since that may put more information into the counters than intended.

As an alternative, Adaptive Server also comes with a Monitor Server that collects real-time data on the servers and can hold store that data to assist in discovering bottlenecks. You may write your own client tools to display and interpret these data, or you may use the monitor clients of Sybase Central.

There are also many good third-party tools that can be used to monitor Adaptive Server.

sp_who and sp_lock

Adaptive Server should also be monitored on a regular basis for locking contention, which occurs when multiple users try to lock the same data as other users. This is considered a form of bottleneck, and while unavoidable, it can be minimized through efficient query writing and proper configuration of the locking scheme for tables.

The sp_lock stored procedure will list the various locks at a point in time on the Adaptive Server. The output will include the type of lock and the spid of the user that is being blocked by the lock (if any).

The sp_lock output shows what process (spid) has a lock on what object ID, and will always list at least one lock (sp_lock itself locks data while running).

sp_lock is often used in conjunction with sp_who to diagnose locking contention; sp_who is used to identify the running processes on the server. For each connection (and certain background system processes) it will provide information including the login name, any blocking locks, and what kind of task was being performed when the procedure was run.

Syntax:

```
sp_lock [spid1 [, spid2]]
```

The optional list of spid values restricts the output to only locks held by the requested spids. Otherwise, all locks held by all spids will be displayed.

Example:

```
sp_lock
go
```

The class column will display the cursor name for locks associated with a cursor for the current user and the cursor id for other users.

```
fid  spid  loid  locktype    table_id   page  row dbname   class              context
---  ----  ----  --------    --------   ----  --- ------   -----              -------
0    8     16    Sh_intent   1          0     0   tempdb   Non Cursor Lock    NULL
0    8     16    Ex_intent   23         0     0   tempdb   Non Cursor Lock    NULL
0    13    26    Sh_intent   32000114   0     0   master   Non Cursor Lock    NULL
0    14    28    Ex_intent   32000114   0     0   pubs2    Non Cursor Lock    NULL
0    14    28    Ex_page     32000114   728   0   pubs2    Non Cursor Lock    Ind pg
0    14    28    Ex_page     32000114   776   0   pubs2    Non Cursor Lock    Ind pg

(1 row(s) affected)
```

sp_lock output is ordered by fid and then spid.

The fid column identifies the family (including the coordinating process and its worker processes) to which a lock belongs. Values for fid are:

- A zero value indicates that the task represented by the spid is executed serially. It is not participating in parallel execution.
- A nonzero value indicates that the task (spid) holding the lock is a member of a family of processes (identified by fid) executing a statement in parallel. If the value is equal to the spid, it indicates that the task is the coordinating process in a family executing a query in parallel. spid is the server process ID of the process.

The loid column identifies the unique lock owner ID of the blocking transaction. Even loid values indicate that a local transaction owns the lock. Odd values indicate that an external transaction owns the lock. Use the object_name system function to derive a table's name from its ID number.

The locktype column indicates whether the lock is a shared lock ("Sh" prefix), an exclusive lock ("Ex" prefix), or an update lock, and whether the lock is held on a table ("table" or "intent"), on a page ("page"), or on a row ("row"). A "blk" suffix in the locktype column indicates that this process is blocking another process that needs to acquire a lock. As soon as this process completes, the other process(es) moves forward. A "demand" suffix in the locktype column indicates that the process is attempting to acquire an exclusive lock.

You can use the object_name() built-in function to see the name of the object for the ID displayed in the table_id column. (Or you can modify the sp_lock stored procedure to display the name; or better yet, write your own version of the procedure.)

- page is the page being locked if the lock type is a page lock.
- row is the row being locked if the lock type is a row lock.
- dbname is the name of the database in which the item being locked resides

The class column indicates whether a lock is associated with a cursor. It displays one of the following:

- Non Cursor Lock indicates that the lock is not associated with a cursor.
- Cursor Id number indicates that the lock is associated with the cursor ID number for that Adaptive Server process ID.
- A cursor name indicates that the lock is associated with the cursor cursor_name that is owned by the current user executing sp_lock.

The context column identifies the context of the lock. Worker processes in the same family have the same context value. Legal values for context are as follows:

- NULL means that the task holding this lock is either a query executing serially or a query executing in parallel in transaction isolation level 1.
- Sync-pt duration request means that the task holding the lock will hold the lock until the query is complete. A lock's context may be Sync-pt duration request if the lock is a table lock held as part of a parallel query, if the lock is held by a worker process at transaction isolation level 3, or if the lock is held by a worker process in a parallel query and must be held for the duration of the transaction.
- Ind pg indicates locks on index pages (allpages-locked tables only).

- Inf key indicates an infinity key lock (for certain range queries at transaction isolation level 3 on data-only-locked tables).
- Range indicates a range lock (for range queries at transaction isolation level 3 on data-only-locked tables) These new values may appear in combination with Fam dur (which replaces Sync pt duration) and with each other, as applicable.

  Syntax:

  ```
  sp_who [loginname | "spid"]
  ```

The loginname or spid value (which must be in quotes) will retrieve information about a single process; otherwise, the procedure will list all current processes.

Example:

```
sp_who
go
fid spid status      loginname orignname hostname   blk_spid dbname      cmd        block_xloid
--- ---- --------    --------- --------- --------   -------- -------------------- -----------
0   2    sleeping    (null)    (null)    0          master   NETWORK     0
                                                             HANDLER
0   3    sleeping    (null)    (null)    0          master   NETWORK     0
                                                             HANDLER
0   4    sleeping    (null)    (null)    0          master   DEADLOCK    0
                                                             TUNE
0   5    sleeping    (null)    (null)    0          master   MIRROR      0
                                                             HANDLER
0   6    sleeping    (null)    (null)    0          master   ASTC HANDLER0
0   7    sleeping    (null)    (null)    0          master   CHECKPOINT  0
                                                             SLEEP
0   8    sleeping    (null)    (null)    0          master   HOUSEKEEPER 0
0   9    recv sleep  sa        sa        TEDWARDS1  0        dbccdb      AWAITING   0
                                                                         COMMAND
0   10   recv sleep  SysAdmin  SysAdmin  AYEKA      0        master      AWAITING   0
                                                                         COMMAND
0   12   recv sleep  SysAdmin  SysAdmin  C:\WINDOWS 0        master      AWAITING   0
                                                                         COMMAND
0   13   running     sa        sa        TEDWARDS1  0        dbccdb      SELECT     0
0   14   recv sleep  sa        sa        TEDWARDS1  0        pubs2       AWAITING
                                                                         COMMAND

(1 row(s) affected)
```

The references to loid and xloid (unique lock owner IDS) only apply to distributed transactions between databases or between servers. If you aren't running that sort of processing, the loid/xloid values should all be zero. Likewise, the references to fid (family ID) are only meaningful when running parallel query processing; in such cases, a user connection and internal parallel query worker processes are working together on one query when they share a value of fid.

Monitoring the System Errorlog

By default, ASE will place an errorlog file in the directory in which you started the server (usually the install directory). In addition to boot time messages identifying which resources came up, their success, and the amount of elapsed time, any major errors or anomalies from the server will be recorded in the errorlog; this can include abnormal disconnections from the server to major system halting errors. Some third-party tools will notify you of additions to the errorlog, but primary responsibility for the regular monitoring of the errorlog rests with the SA. Note that SQL error messages will list a value of severity that will indicate the relative importance of the error (the higher, the more severe). Severity levels 11-18 are classed as user errors, and severities 19+ are classed as system errors; severity level 10 is reserved for informational messages.

The following list points out things to look for.

- Monitor the server for valid startup. Any errors that occur during startup can be an indication of a misconfiguration or a hardware error. Any errors that occur during the start of the server may prevent a database from coming online or in the worst case prevent the server from starting.
- Look for any database threshold errors. Adaptive Server monitors thresholds for every database that does not set the "no free space acctng" dboption (which should probably never be set on a production database). If a threshold is crossed (either the last-chance threshold in the log, or any other user-defined threshold) the associated threshold procedure will be executed. Notification about crossing the threshold, and the output of any "print" messages from within the threshold proc will be added to the errorlog. For more on thresholds and threshold procedures, see Chapter 5, "Database Logging and Recovery."

Errorlog Example

Commentary for this example follows the output.

```
00:00000:00000:2001/04/24 09:27:12.21 kernel Use license file
/clwprod/sybase/SYSAM-1_0/licenses/license.dat.
00:00000:00000:2001/04/24 09:27:12.28 kernel Using config area from primary
master device.
00:00000:00000:2001/04/24 09:27:12.35 kernel Warning: Using default file
'/clwprod/sybase/olympus.cfg' since a configuration file was not specified.
Specify a configuration file name in the RUNSERVER file to avoid this
message.
00:00000:00000:2001/04/24 09:27:14.17 kernel Using 1024 file descriptors.
00:00000:00000:2001/04/24 09:27:14.21 kernel Adaptive Server
Enterprise/12.5/B/Sun_svr4/OS 5.8/rel125beta/1486/32bit/FBO/Tue Feb 20
15:34:55 2001

— Note here that we can see what version the server is running
00:00000:00000:2001/04/24 09:27:14.21 kernel Confidential property of
Sybase, Inc.
00:00000:00000:2001/04/24 09:27:14.21 kernel Copyright 1987, 2001
00:00000:00000:2001/04/24 09:27:14.21 kernel Sybase, Inc. All rights
reserved.
00:00000:00000:2001/04/24 09:27:14.21 kernel Unpublished rights reserved
under U.S. copyright laws.
00:00000:00000:2001/04/24 09:27:14.21 kernel
00:00000:00000:2001/04/24 09:27:14.21 kernel This software contains
confidential and trade secret information of Sybase,
00:00000:00000:2001/04/24 09:27:14.21 kernel Inc. Use, duplication or
disclosure of the software and documentation by
```

```
00:00000:00000:2001/04/24 09:27:14.21 kernel the U.S. Government is subject
to restrictions set forth in a license
00:00000:00000:2001/04/24 09:27:14.21 kernel agreement between the
Government and Sybase, Inc. or other written
00:00000:00000:2001/04/24 09:27:14.21 kernel agreement specifying the
Government's rights to use the software and any
00:00000:00000:2001/04/24 09:27:14.21 kernel applicable FAR provisions, for
example, FAR 52.227-19.
00:00000:00000:2001/04/24 09:27:14.21 kernel Sybase, Inc. 6475 Christie
Avenue, Emeryville, CA 94608, USA
00:00000:00000:2001/04/24 09:27:14.21 kernel Using
'/clwprod/sybase/olympus.cfg' for configuration information.
00:00000:00000:2001/04/24 09:27:14.22 kernel Logging ASE messages in file
'/clwprod/sybase/ASE-12_5/install/errorlog'.
00:00000:00000:2001/04/24 09:27:14.43 kernel kdcl_sess_open: connectivity
library supports master/query syntax.
00:00000:00000:2001/04/24 09:27:14.45 kernel Directory Control Layer (DCL)
using directory driver: InterfacesDriver
00:00000:00000:2001/04/24 09:27:14.56 kernel Network and device connection
limit is 1014.
00:00000:00000:2001/04/24 09:27:15.64 server Number of blocks left for proc
headers: 3232.
00:00000:00000:2001/04/24 09:27:15.73 server Proc header memory allocated
1616 pages for each per engine cache
00:00000:00000:2001/04/24 09:27:15.95 server Memory allocated for the
default data cache cachelet 1: 8192 Kb
00:00000:00000:2001/04/24 09:27:15.96 server Size of the 2K memory pool:
8192 Kb
00:00000:00000:2001/04/24 09:27:15.97 kernel Initializing virtual device 0,
'/clwprod/sybase/data/master.dat' with dsync 'on'.
00:00000:00000:2001/04/24 09:27:15.97 kernel Virtual device 0 started using
asynchronous i/o.
00:00000:00000:2001/04/24 09:27:15.97 kernel Worker Thread Manager is not
enabled for use in SQL Server.
00:00000:00000:2001/04/24 09:27:15.98 kernel Either the config parameter
'use security services' is set to 0, or ASE does not support use of
external security mechanisms on this platform. The Security Control Layer
will not be initialized. No external security mechanisms will be supported.
00:00000:00000:2001/04/24 09:27:15.98 kernel engine 0, os pid 7688 online
00:00000:00000:2001/04/24 09:27:15.98 server No active traceflags
```

This is a useful message if, for example, you have turned on trace flags to detect deadlocks.

```
00:00000:00001:2001/04/24 09:27:16.00 kernel libomni1 - Component
Integration Services loaded; version 'libomni1 - Component Integration
Services/12.5/B/Sun_svr4/OS 5.8/rel125beta/1486/32bit/FBO/Tue Feb 20
15:34:55 2001'.
00:00000:00001:2001/04/24 09:27:16.00 kernel libomni1 - Component
Integration Services: using 'Sybase Client-Library/12.5/B/SPARC/Solaris
2.8/1/OPT/Tue Oct 31 13:34:17 2000'
00:00000:00001:2001/04/24 09:27:16.01 server Opening Master Database ...
00:00000:00001:2001/04/24 09:27:16.21 server Loading SQL Server's default
sort order and character set
```

```
00:00000:00001:2001/04/24 09:27:16.21 server Loaded default Unilib
conversion handle.
00:00000:00001:2001/04/24 09:27:16.26 server Recovering database 'master'.
00:00000:00001:2001/04/24 09:27:16.39 server Checking external objects.
00:00000:00001:2001/04/24 09:27:16.46 server Database 'master' is now
online.
00:00000:00001:2001/04/24 09:27:16.47 server The transaction log in the
database 'master' will use I/O size of 2 Kb.
00:00000:00001:2001/04/24 09:27:16.48 server This installation was created
using a 12.0 or later version of buildmaster.
00:00000:00001:2001/04/24 09:27:16.48 server server name is 'olympus'
00:00000:00001:2001/04/24 09:27:16.49 server Activating disk 'DBSpace1'.
00:00000:00001:2001/04/24 09:27:16.49 kernel Initializing virtual device 2,
'/clwprod/sybase/data/DBSpace1.dat' with dsync 'on'.
00:00000:00001:2001/04/24 09:27:16.49 kernel Virtual device 2 started using
asynchronous i/o.
00:00000:00001:2001/04/24 09:27:16.49 server Activating disk 'sysprocsdev'.
00:00000:00001:2001/04/24 09:27:16.49 kernel Initializing virtual device 1,
'/clwprod/sybase/data/sysprocs.dat' with dsync 'on'.
00:00000:00001:2001/04/24 09:27:16.49 kernel Virtual device 1 started using
asynchronous i/o.
```

Note that first the server brought up the master database and the physical devices. Next, we'll recover each of the other databases. Remember, you can choose the order in which the databases recover.

```
00:00000:00001:2001/04/24 09:27:16.65 server Recovering database
'sybsystemdb'.
00:00000:00001:2001/04/24 09:27:16.78 server Boot Count: 7
00:00000:00001:2001/04/24 09:27:16.81 server Checking external objects.
00:00000:00001:2001/04/24 09:27:16.83 server The transaction log in the
database 'sybsystemdb' will use I/O size of 2 Kb.
00:00000:00001:2001/04/24 09:27:16.87 server Database 'sybsystemdb' is now
online.
00:00000:00001:2001/04/24 09:27:16.90 server Recovering database 'model'.
00:00000:00001:2001/04/24 09:27:17.01 server Checking external objects.
00:00000:00001:2001/04/24 09:27:17.03 server The transaction log in the
database 'model' will use I/O size of 2 Kb.
00:00000:00001:2001/04/24 09:27:17.07 server Database 'model' is now
online.
00:00000:00001:2001/04/24 09:27:17.07 server The logical pagesize of the
server is 2 Kb.
00:00000:00001:2001/04/24 09:27:17.07 server 0 dump conditions detected at
boot time
00:00000:00001:2001/04/24 09:27:17.07 server Resident Node id: ab484a259170
00:00000:00001:2001/04/24 09:27:17.08 server Transaction coordinator
initialized.
00:00000:00001:2001/04/24 09:27:17.09 server Clearing temp db
00:00000:00001:2001/04/24 09:27:18.64 server The transaction log in the
database 'tempdb' will use I/O size of 2 Kb.
00:00000:00001:2001/04/24 09:27:18.81 server The transaction log in the
database 'tempdb' will use I/O size of 2 Kb.
```

```
00:00000:00001:2001/04/24 09:27:18.86 server Database 'tempdb' is now
online.
00:00000:00001:2001/04/24 09:27:18.88 server The transaction log in the
database 'tempdb' will use I/O size of 2 Kb.
00:00000:00001:2001/04/24 09:27:18.93 server Recovering database
'sybsystemprocs'.
00:00000:00001:2001/04/24 09:27:19.07 server Checking external objects.
00:00000:00001:2001/04/24 09:27:19.08 server The transaction log in the
database 'sybsystemprocs' will use I/O size of 2 Kb.
00:00000:00001:2001/04/24 09:27:19.13 server Database 'sybsystemprocs' is
now online.
00:00000:00002:2001/04/24 09:27:19.14 kernel ninit:0: listener type: master
00:00000:00002:2001/04/24 09:27:19.14 kernel ninit:0: listener endpoint:
/dev/tcp
00:00000:00002:2001/04/24 09:27:19.14 kernel ninit:0: listener raw address:
\x000207ee390601e80000000000000000
00:00000:00002:2001/04/24 09:27:19.14 kernel ninit:0: transport provider:
T_COTS_ORD
00:00000:00001:2001/04/24 09:27:19.17 server Recovery complete.
00:00000:00001:2001/04/24 09:27:19.17 server SQL Server's default unicode
sort order is 'binary'.
00:00000:00001:2001/04/24 09:27:19.17 server SQL Server's default sort
order is:
00:00000:00001:2001/04/24 09:27:19.17 server       'noaccents_iso_1' (ID =
54)
00:00000:00001:2001/04/24 09:27:19.17 server on top of default character
set:
00:00000:00001:2001/04/24 09:27:19.17 server       'iso_1' (ID = 1).
```

When you see this message, the server is up.

Only the startup messages are shown in this example. Following the copyright information, we find messages concerning:

- Allocation of memory
- Opening of master device and recovery of master database
- Opening of the remaining devices
- Recovery of system databases sybsystemdb and model
- Drop and re-creation of tempdb
- Recovery of sybsytemprocs
- Recovery of user databases
- Confirmation of server sort order and character set

Any errors in this section should be considered serious; errors after the startup section concern conditions during run time, and may or may not be serious.

Managing the System Errorlog

The errorlog starts and stops with the server; if the server is up for a long period of time, the errorlog can grow quite large. If left unmanaged, the errorlog can grow large enough to fill up entire file systems if not properly maintained. On some systems, if the errorlog cannot grow any more, Adaptive Server will crash.

If your operating system will permit it (some don't), simply move the errorlog periodically (weekly, bi-weekly). If not, for example on NT 4, it is recommended that administrators periodically (weekly, bi-weekly) shut down Adaptive Server and move the errorlog to another location.

Resource Verification

Another good practice for administrators is to verify that all resources in the server are allocated properly and that all configurable parameters are optimally configured. Adaptive Server allocates memory for most resources and parameters at startup, and most of the server options require some amount of memory to maintain. If any resources are overallocated, then memory that might be better used in cache by the Adaptive Server is essentially wasted. If any options or parameters are underallocated, then Adaptive Server may not perform as well. Check resources allocated vs. in use; are any configured parameters drastically out of range? For example:

- Concurrent connections at 100, with 25 the most used at any one time?
- Device connections at 50, with only 5 devices defined?
- Remote access defined but not in use?
- Are all of your resources on line?
- Did all of the disks start up?
- Are all of the engines online?

Software Maintenance

Sybase maintains its software with releases and point releases, called "SWR" (Software Roll-Up) (known as "EBFs" on older releases of the server). These software updates are available to supported users via download.

A common approach to dealing with SWRs is:

1. Wait a couple of weeks or months before installing the upgrade. On very rare occasions, a fix will come out immediately after the SWR release.
2. Install it on the development server and test it there for a few weeks. This is often common sense in most shops. By the time anything is implemented in production, the changes should be implemented in a development environment and rigorously tested to make sure the new upgrade fixes the identified problems and also to make sure the changes do not expose any new problems.
3. Finally, after testing on your development server, install it on your production server. Be prepared to back off of your upgrade at a moment's notice. It is always advisable to hope for the best and prepare for the worst when dealing with software upgrades. Should the installation of

a software update go badly, the worst case scenario is that the database server may need to be rebuilt. Be prepared to fall back to the last known working version of the server should the upgrade process fail.

The above approach is considered appropriately conservative. Many shops generally adhere to balancing the following two axioms regarding software implementation.

- If it ain't broke, don't fix it. The various SWR releases usually come with a list of problems that have been repaired. Often, the majority of the list may not apply to the applications running on your servers. Introducing the latest SWR may cause the applications to behave differently enough that major modifications may be called for.
- If you put off upgrades long enough, eventually Sybase will not support you.

While patience is considered a virtue, waiting too long may invalidate your service contracts. The goal is to not wait too long.

Recording Run-Time Data

The sp_configure stored procedure will list all system configuration variables that are easily set by the administrators. These configuration settings are also stored in a file under the $SYBASE directory called <servername>.cfg; if multiple servers are running, there will be multiple configuration files. Adaptive Server also archives the file when changes are made; these backup files are named <servername>.bak (current version) and a series of numbered older files <servername>.### (historical configurations). Always keep offsite copies (hard and soft) of the config file. The copy can be used to start a restored server without having to manually reconfigure the server a parameter at a time. It is also a good idea to archive a good copy of the results from a run of sp_configure. If there are any problems with the configuration file, this allows the appropriate settings to be entered manually.

Database-Level Maintenance

Adaptive Server has a series of routines called dbcc, or database consistency checker. These were originally unpublished routines used to verify the supporting structures for the data stored in the database. These structures, if corrupted, can prevent the database from functioning, and if left unrepaired can potentially lead to a fatal corruption of the database. If the corruption is copied into a database backup, the backup and future restorations from that backup will also be corrupt.

We use these routines as periodic maintenance to confirm that the database's internal integrity is consistent. It is very unusual to find an error here, but if you do find one, you should correct it quickly.

Scheduling Database Maintenance

Many factors influence how often and when dbcc checks need to be made on the databases:

- Business operational requirements
- Database use
- Backup schedule
- Database and table size
- Importance of data

To summarize, we ask, what will it cost in time and resources if we need to bring the server down to resolve a database corruption? Dbcc execution scheduling is an exercise in risk management.

The overriding factor in determining the database maintenance schedule is to avoid interference with business activities. That is, pick a convenient time to run and the particular dbcc commands that will not lock out users from important business activities. For example, dbcc checkdb acquires locks on all objects in the database while it performs the check, and you cannot control the order in which it checks the objects. For example, if you are running an application that uses table4, table5, and table6, and running dbcc checkdb takes 20 minutes to complete, the users will be blocked from accessing these tables for the entire duration of the command, even when the command is not checking them.

Business Operational Requirements

The business day for an organization is a large factor in the decision of when to perform database checks. Many organizations have the heaviest usage between the hours of 8 a.m. and 5 p.m. In other organizations (with web applications, international sites, or three-shift schedules), the server could be used heavily 24 hours per day.

If your Adaptive Server is used primarily between the hours of 8 a.m. and 5 p.m., Monday through Friday, dbcc checks can run at night and on weekends so that the checks do not have a significant impact on users.

If Adaptive Server is used 24 hours a day, 7 days a week, it is possible to limit the impact by choosing which dbcc checks to run (dbcc checkstorage may be far less intrusive than dbcc checkalloc, for example), or by scheduling a cycle of checks on individual tables and indexes rather than checking entire databases.

Some sites with 24-hour, high-performance demands run dbcc checks by taking the backups and loading them on another server. This is not necessarily the best option; it is probably better to run checkstorage (the least intrusive dbcc) during a low-load time. Any inconsistencies present in the database will be reproduced on the other server, and running the dbcc checks on the copy will expose any faults. Once the faults are located, dbcc commands can be executed on the production server to repair the problems (and a post-repair backup made!).

Database Use

Most databases are almost constantly changing, as data are added, updated, and removed. It is important to check these databases periodically to make sure that the underlying logical and physical structures are intact.

Databases that contain archive data that changes infrequently, read-only databases, and small or infrequently utilized databases still require dbcc checks to ensure that the underlying disk media maintains that data correctly (for example, a new or transient disk error can introduce new, physical errors detectable by dbcc). However, checks on these types of databases can be performed a lot less frequently than on more heavily used databases.

Backup Schedule

How often the database is backed up is another factor in determining the frequency of dbcc checks on a database. The more often the database and transaction logs are backed up, the more data can be restored in case of failure; a decision must be made as to how much data loss is tolerable, and a dump schedule developed to support that decision.

After the dumps are scheduled, decide how to incorporate the dbcc commands into that schedule. It is not mandatory that dbcc checks are performed before every dump, but it is a <u>very</u> good practice.

An ideal time to dump a database is after a complete check of that database is run using dbcc checkstorage and dbcc checkcatalog (see later in this chapter for descriptions). If these commands find no errors in the database, the backup contains a clean database, and problems that occur after loading the dump can be corrected by reindexing. Other dbcc routines (such as dbcc tablealloc) may be used on individual tables and indexes to correct allocation errors reported by dbcc.

Database Size

Large databases require a longer amount of time to back up (not to mention run all the other periodic maintenance). Extremely large individual tables will experience a longer period of shared table locks for most dbcc commands. This should be considered during the scheduling of database maintenance.

If tables are not extremely large, a complete set of dbcc commands can be run fairly frequently.

How to Run dbcc

A dbcc is like any SQL command. From inside isql, issue dbcc followed by the name of the check desired. Most dbcc checks will require privileged status (such as dbo or sa_role) to run. Note that many dbcc checks require more complex combinations of arguments, and you should verify the syntax if you are not familiar with a particular dbcc.

Example:

```
use pubs2
go
dbcc checkdb ()
go
```

```
dbcc checkcatalog ()
go
dbcc checkstorage ()
go
```

The following specific checks are supported by dbcc. These are described later in this section.

- checkstorage
- checkcatalog
- checktable
- tablealloc
- indexalloc
- checkalloc
- checkdb

Each dbcc has a specific purpose, some of which overlap with other dbcc checks. For general checks of a specific database, use checkstorage, checkcatalog, and checktable. (Note that checktable should be performed for each table in the database.)

This combination covers necessary dbcc checks in the database.

dbcc checkstorage

This command is all-encompassing, and includes a host of features. It is somewhat unique to the dbcc family, and additional information will be provided about this command later in this chapter.

Syntax:

```
dbcc checkstorage [(dbname)]
```

dbname is the name of the target database (the database to be checked). If no database name is entered, it defaults to the current database.

dbcc chckstorage performs the following checks:

- Allocation of text valued columns
- Page allocation and consistency
- OAM page entries
- Pointer consistency
- Text valued columns and text column chains

This command runs fast and is very thorough. It performs no object locking. This command performs extensive I/O and may swamp the system's I/O. A dedicated cache can be used which only minimally impacts other caches. Most of the work associated with dbcc checkstorage is performed not in the database being checked, but in a separate, working database dedicated to checkstorage.

The advantages of using dbcc checkstorage include the following:

- Combines many of the checks provided by the other dbcc commands
- Does not lock tables or pages for extended periods, which allows dbcc to locate errors accurately while allowing concurrent update activity

- Scales linearly with the aggregate I/O throughput
- Separates the functions of checking and reporting, which allows custom evaluation and report generation
- Provides a detailed description of space usage in the target database
- Records dbcc checkstorage activity and results in the dbccdb database, which allows trend analysis and provides a source of accurate diagnostic information

dbcc checkstorage is different in several ways:

- This command uses the dbccdb database to store configuration information and the results of checks made on the target database.
- It uses at least two "workspaces" (designated sections of dbccdb database) during the check operation.
- It offers system and stored procedures to help you prepare your system to use dbcc checkstorage.
- It provides stored procedures that generate reports on the data stored in dbccdb.
- It does not replace the other dbcc commands, but combines most of the check functionality into a single program.
- It does not offer utilities to repair any faults; it only diagnoses faults.
- It is less likely to misdiagnose ordinary operations as flaws (so-called "spurious errors") than other dbcc checks.

dbcc checktable

Syntax:

```
dbcc checktable ({table_name | object_id} [, skip_ncindex] )
```

The first parameter is the name of the table to be checked or the object_id of the table (from sysobjects).

The skip_ncindex option allows you to skip checking the page linkage, pointers, and sort order on nonclustered indexes (resulting in a significant time savings). The linkage and pointers of clustered indexes and data pages are essential to the integrity of your tables, but non-clustered indexes are not likely to be as critical. You can drop and re-create nonclustered indexes if Adaptive Server reports problems with page linkage or pointers.

This program is exceedingly slow, but it does perform thorough checks (not as thorough as checkstorage however). It requires a shared table lock to perform its checks, and releases the locks when the check of the table is complete. This dbcc command can use large I/O and asynchronous prefetch when they are configured for the caches used by the databases or objects to be checked. The largest I/O size available is used (up to 16 K I/O may be configured).

The checks performed include:

- Index and data pages are linked correctly.
- Indexes are sorted properly.
- Pointers are consistent.

- Data rows on each page have entries in the row-offset table; these entries match the locations for the data rows on the page.
- Data rows on each page have entries in the row-offset table in the page that matches their respective locations on the page.
- Partition statistics for partitioned tables are correct.

  Example:

```
use pubs2
go
dbcc checktable (titles)
go
```

  Example output:

```
Checking titles
The total number of data pages in this table is 3.
Table has 18 data rows.
DBCC execution completed. If DBCC printed error messages, contact a user
with System Administrator (SA) role.
```

dbcc checkdb

Syntax:

```
dbcc checkdb [(database_name [, skip_ncindex]) ]
```

If no database name is specified, dbcc checkdb checks the current database.

If the option skip_ncindex is selected, dbcc checkdb does not check any of the nonclustered indexes on user tables in the database.

The dbcc checkdb command runs the same checks as dbcc checktable, but performs them on each table in the specified database. dbcc checkdb gives similar messages to those returned by dbcc checktable and makes the same types of corrections.

This program is exceedingly slow, but it does perform very thorough checks. It requires a shared table lock to perform its checks, and releases the locks when the check of the table is complete.

dbcc checkalloc

Syntax:

```
dbcc checkalloc [(database_name [, fix | nofix] )]
```

If no database name is specified, dbcc checkalloc checks the current database.

> **NOTE:** All checkalloc tasks are performed by checkstorage except the fix, so you are unlikely to need this unless you need to run the fix option.

The default option for dbcc checkalloc is nofix. When using dbcc checkalloc with the nofix option, it does not correct allocation errors. With the fix option, dbcc checkalloc can fix all allocation errors that would otherwise be fixed by dbcc tablealloc (see below) and can also fix pages that remain allocated to objects that have been dropped from the database. Before you can use dbcc checkalloc with the fix option, you must put the database into single-user mode.

Checks performed include:

- All pages are correctly allocated.
- Partition statistics on the allocation pages are correct.
- No page is allocated that is not used.
- No page is used that is not allocated.

This command runs very slowly, and it does not perform very thorough checks compared to checkstorage, but it can repair some types of corruption. It performs no object locking. Because only allocation pages are cached, checkalloc performs extensive I/O and may swamp the system's I/O. This dbcc command can use large I/O and asynchronous prefetch when they are configured for the caches used by the databases or objects to be checked. The largest I/O size available is used (up to 16 K I/O may be configured).

Note finally that it can report spurious errors if there are active users in the database.

> **NOTE:** Not all errors can be fixed. For example, if a page is allocated to an object that doesn't exist, this will not be corrected here.

Example:

```
use pubs2
go
dbcc checkalloc
go
```

Example output:

```
***************************************************************
TABLE:   salesdetail    OBJID = 144003544
INDID=0  FIRST=297       ROOT=299        SORT=0
        Data level: 0.  3 Data  Pages in 1 extents.
INDID=2  FIRST=289       ROOT=290        SORT=1
        Indid     : 2.  3 Index Pages in 1 extents.
INDID=3  FIRST=465       ROOT=466        SORT=1
        Indid     : 3.  3 Index Pages in 1 extents.
TOTAL # of extents = 3
***************************************************************
TABLE: titleauthor              OBJID = 176003658
INDID=1  FIRST=433       ROOT=425        SORT=1
        Data level: 1.  1 Data  Pages in 1 extents.
        Indid     : 1.  1 Index Pages in 1 extents.
INDID=2  FIRST=305       ROOT=305        SORT=1
        Indid     : 2.  1 Index Pages in 1 extents.
INDID=3  FIRST=441       ROOT=441        SORT=1
        Indid     : 3.  1 Index Pages in 1 extents.
TOTAL # of extents = 4
***************************************************************
TABLE: titles          OBJID = 208003772
INDID=1  FIRST=417       ROOT=409        SORT=1
```

```
        Data level: 1.  3 Data  Pages in 1 extents.
        Indid     : 1.  1 Index Pages in 1 extents.
INDID=2  FIRST=313       ROOT=313        SORT=1
        Indid     : 2.  1 Index Pages in 1 extents.
TOTAL # of extents = 3
****************************************************************

. . . . . . . . . .
```

dbcc indexalloc

Syntax:

```
dbcc indexalloc ( {table_name | table_id }, index_id [, {full | optimized |
fast | null} [, fix | nofix]])
```

The first parameter is the name of the table to be checked or the object_id of the table (from sysobjects). The identifier of the index is required. This information can be located in the sysindexes table of the specific database. For a more easily readable version, perform sp_helpindex table_name.

As with checkalloc, this command's tasks are performed by checkstorage, although this command offers a fix option.

If the fix or nofix options are specified for dbcc indexalloc, one of the report options (full, optimized, fast, or null) must also be provided. As mentioned before, it may be easier to skip any specific checks of (non-clustered) indexes; it is almost always easier to drop and rebuild an index than it is to search for index corruptions and repair them. Therefore, you will probably find yourself running dbcc indexalloc only rarely.

Note that large indexes can take a long time to rebuild, and that the table will be locked during index builds.

The dbcc indexalloc command checks the specified index to see that:

- All pages are correctly allocated.
- No page is allocated that is not used.
- No page is used that is not allocated.

dbcc indexalloc is an index-level version of dbcc checkalloc that provides the same integrity checks on an individual index.

The speed and thoroughness of dbcc indexalloc depend on the options picked. With the full option, this command can run very slowly, and performs less thorough checks than the checkstorage command. With the optimized option, it runs at a moderate speed and is moderately detailed in its checks. It requires a shared table lock. Because only allocation pages are cached, it performs extensive I/O and may swamp the system's I/O.

dbcc tablealloc

Syntax:

```
dbcc tablealloc ({table_name | table_id} [, {full | optimized | fast |
null} [, fix | nofix]])
```

The first parameter is the name of the table to be checked or the object_id of the table (from sysobjects). If the fix or nofix options are specified for dbcc indexalloc, one of the report options (full, optimized, fast, or null) must also be provided.

Dbcc tablealloc performs these checks:

- All pages are correctly allocated.
- Partition statistics on the allocation pages are correct.
- No page is allocated that is not used.
- No page is used that is not allocated.

The speed and thoroughness of the command depend on the options picked. With the full option, dbcc tablealloc can run very slowly and performs thorough checks (not as thorough as checkstorage). With the optimized option, it runs at a moderate speed and is moderately detailed in its checks. It requires a shared table lock. Because only allocation pages are cached, this command performs extensive I/O and may swamp the system's I/O.

Example:

```
use pubs2
go
dbcc tablealloc(titles, full, fix)
go
```

Example output:

```
Msg 7939, Level 22, State 1:
Line 2:
Table Corrupt: The entry is missing from the OAM for object id 144003544
indid 0 for allocation page 2560.
When the fix option is used, the following message indicates that the
missing entry has been restored:
The missing OAM entry has been inserted.
```

Example:

```
dbcc tablealloc (table5, full, fix)
go
```

Example output:

```
Information from sysindexes about the object being checked:
TABLE: table5            OBJID = 144003544
INDID=0  FIRST=337       ROOT=2587        SORT=0
Error message:
Msg 7939, Level 22, State 1:
Line 2:
Table Corrupt: The entry is missing from the OAM for object id 144003544
indid 0 for allocation page 2560.
Message indicating that the error has been corrected:
```

```
The missing OAM entry has been inserted.
        Data level: 0.  67 Data  Pages in 9 extents.
dbcc report on page allocation:
TOTAL # of extents = 9
Alloc page 256 (# of extent=1 used pages=8 ref pages=8)
EXTID:560 (Alloc page: 512) is initialized. Extent follows:
NEXT=0 PREV=0 OBJID=144003544 ALLOC=0xff DEALL=0x0 INDID=0 STATUS=0x0
Alloc page 512 (# of extent=2 used pages=8 ref pages=8)
Page 864 allocated (Alloc page: 768 Extent ID: 864 Alloc mask: 0x1)
Page 865 allocated (Alloc page: 768 Extent ID: 864 Alloc mask: 0x3)
Page 866 allocated (Alloc page: 768 Extent ID: 864 Alloc mask: 0x7)
Page 867 allocated (Alloc page: 768 Extent ID: 864 Alloc mask: 0xf)
Page 868 allocated (Alloc page: 768 Extent ID: 864 Alloc mask: 0x1f)
Page 869 allocated (Alloc page: 768 Extent ID: 864 Alloc mask: 0x3f)
Page 870 allocated (Alloc page: 768 Extent ID: 864 Alloc mask: 0x7f)
Page 871 allocated (Alloc page: 768 Extent ID: 864 Alloc mask: 0xff)
Alloc page 768 (# of extent=1 used pages=8 ref pages=8)
Alloc page 1024 (# of extent=1 used pages=8 ref pages=8)

Alloc page 1280 (# of extent=1 used pages=8 ref pages=8)
Alloc page 1536 (# of extent=1 used pages=8 ref pages=8)
Alloc page 1792 (# of extent=1 used pages=8 ref pages=8)
Alloc page 2048 (# of extent=1 used pages=8 ref pages=8)
(Other output deleted.)
Information on resources used:
Statistical information for this run follows:
Total # of pages read = 68
Total # of pages found cache = 68
Total # of physical reads = 0
Total # of saved I/O = 0
Message printed on completion of dbcc command:
DBCC execution completed. If DBCC printed error messages, contact a user
with System Administrator (SA) role.
```

dbcc checkcatalog

Syntax:

```
dbcc checkcatalog [(database_name)]
```

If a database name is not specified, dbcc checkcatalog checks the current database.

Checks performed include:

- Every type in syscolumns has a matching entry in systypes.
- Every table and view in sysobjects has at least one column in syscolumns.
- The last checkpoint in syslogs is valid.

This command is moderately fast and moderately thorough in its checks. It holds shared locks on system catalogs, which are released after the checks are done. Note that unlike the previous dbcc routines, dbcc checkcatalog does not examine the structure of a database as much as the contents of its system tables. As such, it could almost be described as a referential integrity check of the database catalog.

Example:

```
dbcc checkcatalog (testdb)
go
```

Example output:

```
Checking testdb
The following segments have been defined for database 5 (database name
testdb).
virtual start addr      size      segments
--------------------    ------    --------
33554432                4096      0
                                  1
16777216                102       2
DBCC execution completed. If DBCC printed error messages, see your System
Administrator.
```

dbcc dbrepair

Syntax:

```
dbcc dbrepair (database_name, dropdb )
```

Both parameters must be specified to drop the database.

No user can be using the database in question when this command is issued.

dbcc dbrepair drops a damaged database when the SQL drop database command fails. This command should be performed only after all other means to drop the database have failed.

This command completely locks the database during operation and physically removes the entire database. Care should be exercised to be sure that information is available about the segments and database devices to rebuild the database, and to have a clean dump of this database available to restore.

sp_plan_dbccdb

Syntax:

```
sp_plan_dbccdb [database name]
```

If no database name is supplied, this command will perform the planning report against all databases.

sp_plan_dbccdb performs these checks:

- Recommends suitable sizes for new dbccdb and dbccalt databases
- Lists suitable devices for dbccdb and dbccalt
- Suggests a cache size and a suitable number of worker processes for the target database(s) in a report format

Example:

```
use dbccdb
go
sp_plan_dbccdb master
go
```

Example output:

```
Recommended size for dbccdb is 4MB.

dbccdb database already exists with size 8MB.

Recommended values for workspace size, cache size and process count are:

dbname    scan ws    text ws    cache    process count
------    -------    -------    -----    -------------
master    64K        64K        640K     1

(return status = 0)
```

Understanding the Output from dbcc Commands

The output of most other dbcc commands includes information that identifies the object or objects being checked and error messages that indicate what problems, if any, the command finds in the object. When dbcc tablealloc and dbcc indexalloc are run with the fix option, the output also indicates the repairs that the command makes.

The dbcc checkstorage command does not display the results of the check on your computer screen. Instead, the results are stored in the dbccdb database. You can print a variety of reports from this database.

Errors Generated by dbcc

Whatever techniques are required to solve the problems, the solutions are much easier when you find the problem soon after the occurrence of the corruption or inconsistency. Consistency problems can exist on data pages that are not used frequently, such as a table that is updated only monthly. dbcc can find, and often fix, these problems for you.

Errors generated by database consistency problems encountered by dbcc commands other than dbcc checkstorage usually have error numbers from 2500 to 2599 or from 7900 to 7999. These messages, and others that can result from database consistency problems (such as Error 605), may include phrases like "Table Corrupt" or "Extent not within segment."

Some messages indicate severe database consistency problems which others are not so urgent. A few may require help from Sybase Technical Support, but most can be solved by:

- Running dbcc commands that use the fix option.
- Following the instructions in the *Troubleshooting Guide*, which contains step-by-step instructions for resolving many database errors found by dbcc.

Soft and Hard dbcc Faults

dbcc categorizes faults discovered under two categories: soft and hard faults.

A *soft fault* is an inconsistency in Adaptive Server that has not been determined to be persistent. Most soft faults result from temporary inconsistencies in the target database caused by users updating the target database during the dbcc checkstorage operation or by dbcc checkstorage encountering data definition language (DDL) commands. These faults are not repeated when you run the command a second time. Soft faults can be reclassified by comparing the results of the two executions of dbcc checkstorage or by running dbcc tablealloc and dbcc checktable after dbcc checkstorage finds soft faults. If the same soft faults occur in successive executions of dbcc checkstorage, they can be considered "persistent" soft faults. Persistent soft faults may indicate a corruption, or a hard fault. If dbcc checkstorage is executed in single-user mode, the soft faults reported are persistent soft faults. These faults can be resolved by using sp_dbcc_differential-report or by running dbcc tablealloc and dbcc checktable. If you use the latter two commands, you need to check only the tables or indexes that exhibited the soft faults.

Generally soft faults that remain after checkstorage is run are not significant and no further action need be taken.

A *hard fault* is a persistent corruption of Adaptive Server. Not all hard faults are equally severe. For example, all the following situations cause a hard fault, but the results are different:

- A page that is allocated to a nonexistent table minimally reduces the available disk storage.
- A table with some rows that are unreachable by a scan might return the wrong results.
- A table that is linked to another table causes the query to stop.

Some hard faults can be corrected by simple actions such as truncating the affected table or running a different dbcc option with the fix option. Others can be corrected only by restoring the database from a backup.

Using dbcc checkstorage

Significant preparation work is required to tune the server to optimally use resources to perform the dbcc checkstorage command. Resource planning, server tuning, constructing the dbccdb database, and configuring the workspaces are essential to successful and speedy completion of this command.

Checklist of Preparation Activities

1. Obtain recommendations for database size, devices (if dbccdb does not exist), workspace sizes, cache size, and the number of worker processes for the target database.
2. If necessary, adjust the number of worker processes that Adaptive Server uses.
3. Create a dbcc named cache (optional).
4. Configure a 16 K I/O buffer pool.
5. If dbccdb already exists, drop it and all associated devices before creating a new dbccdb database.
6. Initialize disk devices for the dbccdb data and the log.
7. Create dbccdb on the data disk device.
8. Add disk segments (optional).
9. Populate the dbccdb database and install dbcc stored procedures.
10. Create the workspaces.
11. Update dbcc configuration values.

Planning Resources

Selecting the appropriate device and size for dbccdb is critical to the performance of dbcc checkstorage operations. The system procedure sp_plan_dbccdb provides different configuration recommendations for the specified target database depending on whether or not dbccdb exists. You use this information to configure Adaptive Server and set up the dbccdb database.

If dbccdb does not exist, sp_plan_dbccdb returns the following information:

- Minimum size for dbccdb
- Devices that are suitable for dbccdb
- Minimum sizes for the scan and text workspaces
- Minimum 16 K buffer pool size
- Number of worker processes

The values recommended for the cache size are approximate because the optimum cache size for dbccdb depends on the pattern of the page allocation in the target database. Take a look at the following examples:

Example:

```
use dbccdb
go
sp_plan_dbccdb pubs2
go
```

Example output (dbccdb does not exist):

```
Recommended size for dbccdb is 4MB.
Recommended devices for dbccdb are:

Logical Device Name   Device Size   Physical Device Name
-------------------   ----------    ----------------------
sprocdev              28672         /remote/SERV/sprocs_dat
tun_dat               8192          /remote/SERV/tun_dat
tun_log               4096          /remote/SERV/tun_log

Recommended values for workspace size, cache size and process count are:

dbname    scan ws     text ws      cache      process count
------    -------     --------     -----      -------------
pubs2     64K         64K          640K       1
```

Example output (dbccdb does exist):

```
Recommended size for dbccdb database is 23MB (data = 21MB, log = 2MB)

dbccdb database already exists with size 8MB.

Recommended values for workspace size, cache size and process count are:

dbname    scan ws     text ws      cache      process count
------    -------     -------      -----      -------------
pubs2     64K         64K          640K       1
```

Example output (no database name provided):

```
Recommended size for dbccdb is 4MB.
dbccdb database already exists with size 8MB.

Recommended values for workspace size, cache size and process count are:

dbname              scan ws     text ws     cache     process count
--------------      -------     -------     -----     -------------
master              64K         64K         640K      1
tempdb              64K         64K         640K      1
model               64K         64K         640K      1
sybsystemprocs      384K        112K        1280K     2
pubs2               64K         64K         640K      1
pubs3               64K         64K         640K      1
pubtune             160K        96K         1280K     2
sybsecurity         96K         96K         1280K     2
dbccdb              112K        96K         1280K     2
```

Planning Workspace Size

Two workspaces are required for execution of checkstorage: scan and text. Space requirements for the workspaces depend on the size of the largest database that will be checked. Additional workspaces are necessary if you want to run concurrent dbcc checkstorage operations. Although we must assign the workspaces to segments within dbccdb, they do not have to use freshly-created user-defined segments; the workspaces may be built onto the default segment.

Note that the use of segments can improve performance of concurrent checkstorage operations.

Different databases can use the same workspaces. Therefore, the workspaces must be large enough to accommodate the largest database with which they will be used. Use the stored procedure sp_plan_dbccdb to obtain the largest suggested workspace sizes for all of the databases on the server.

You can set up dbccdb configuration so that you can run dbcc checkstorage concurrently on multiple databases. This is possible only when the second and subsequent dbcc checkstorage operations have their own dedicated resources. If you want to perform concurrent dbcc checkstorage operations, each operation must have its own scan and text workspaces, worker processes, and reserved cache.

The total space requirement for workspaces depends on whether the user databases are checked serially or concurrently. If dbcc checkstorage operations are run serially, the largest scan and text workspaces can be used for all user databases. If dbcc checkstorage operations are run concurrently, dbccdb should be set to accommodate the largest workspaces that will be used concurrently.

Configuring Worker Processes

If no setting is made to increase this, the Sybase Server will assign one worker process to the dbcc checkstorage command. Using the recommendations from the output of sp_plan_dbccdb, the command can conceivably support many more worker processes for concurrent access to the data.

These parameters affect dbcc checkstorage parallelism:

Parameter Name	Set With	Purpose
number of worker processes	sp_configure	Configures number of worker processes available in the server.
memory per worker process	sp_configure	Assigns extra memory to each worker process (may not be necessary).
max worker processes	sp_dbcc_updateconfig	Registers limit on worker processes used by dbcc checkstorage for target database.

Set the value for number of worker processes high enough to allow for the sum of the number of processes specified by max worker processes. A low number of worker processes reduces the performance and resource consumption of dbcc checkstorage. Cache size, CPU performance, and device sizes might suggest a lower worker processes count, but if there are not enough worker processes configured for Adaptive Server, dbcc checkstorage will not run. The configuration parameters maximum parallel degree and maximum scan parallel degree (used to limit parallel query behavior) have no effect on the parallel functions of dbcc checkstorage. As long as there are sufficient worker processes, parallelism in dbcc checkstorage is not disabled.

dbcc checkstorage requires multiple processes, so the number of worker processes parameter must be set to at least 1 to allow for a parent process and a worker process.

sp_plan_dbccdb recommends values for the number of worker processes, depending on database size, number of devices, and other factors. You can use smaller values to limit the load on your system. dbcc checkstorage may use fewer worker processes than sp_plan_dbccdb recommends or fewer than you configure.

Using more worker processes does not guarantee faster performance. The following scenario describes the effects of two different worker process configurations:

- An 8 GB database has 4 GB of data on disk A and 0.5 GB of data on each of the disks B, C, D, E, F, G, H, and I. With nine worker processes active, the time it takes to run dbcc checkstorage is 2 hours, which is the time it takes to check disk A. Each of the other eight worker processes finishes in 15 minutes and waits for the disk A worker process to finish.
- With two worker processes active, the time it takes to run dbcc checkstorage is still 2 hours. The first worker process processes disk A and the other worker process processes disks B, C, D, E, F, G, H, and I. In this case, there is no waiting, and resources are used more efficiently.

The memory per worker process parameter specifies the total memory allocation for worker processes support in Adaptive Server. The default value is adequate for dbcc checkstorage.

Checkstorage will use the minimum number of worker processes that will finish in the shortest time, so in the example, it will use two processes even if more are configured.

Setting Up a dbcc Named Cache

If you use a named cache for dbcc checkstorage, you might need to adjust the Adaptive Server configuration parameters. During a dbcc checkstorage operation, the workspaces are temporarily bound to a cache. This cache is also used to read the target database. Using a named cache that is dedicated to dbcc minimizes the impact of the database check on other users and improves overall server performance. You can create a separate cache for each dbcc checkstorage operation that will be run concurrently, or you can create one cache that is large enough to fit the total requirements of the concurrent operations. The size of the named cache required for optimum performance depends on the size of the target database and distributions of data in that database. dbcc checkstorage requires a minimum of 640 K of 16 K buffers per worker process in the named cache.

For best performance, assign most of the dedicated cache to the 16 K buffer pool. The recommended cache size is the minimum size for the 16 K pool. Since every cache requires a 2 K buffer pool, you must add the size of the 2 K pool (minimum 512 K) to the recommended value to get the true minimum cache size.

> **NOTE:** If you are using larger page sizes, that minimum pool size will match your page size.

If you dedicate a cache for dbcc checkstorage, the command does not require more than the minimum 2 K buffer pool (0.5 MB). If the cache is shared, you can improve the performance of dbcc checkstorage by increasing the 16 K pool size before running the operation, and reducing the size after the operation is complete. The 16 K pool requirements are the same for a shared cache; however, while a shared cache may meet the size requirement, other demands on the cache might limit the buffer availability to dbcc checkstorage and greatly impact the performance of both checkstorage and Adaptive Server as a whole.

For a detailed discussion of named caches and how to configure them, refer to Chapter 12, "Named Caches."

To examine the current cache setup, use the sp_cacheconfig procedure, which will provide information on the current caches setup. If there is sufficient space, create an additional named cache to provide the 16 K large I/O buffer pool previously discussed. The example here creates a 50 MB cache named large_io and dedicates 40 MB of it to a 16 K pool. The remaining 10 MB of space is, by default, set to 2 K I/O.

```
sp_cacheconfig large_io_cache, "50M"
go
<server reboot to finish cache creation>
sp_poolconfig large_io_cache, "40M", "16K"
go
1> sp_poolconfig "large_io_cache"
2> go
```

```
Cache Name        Status   Type     Config Value    Run Value
--------------    ------   -----    ------------    ---------
large_io_cache    Active   Mixed    50.00 Mb        50.00 Mb
                                    ------------    ---------
                           Total    50.00 Mb        50.00 Mb

=============================================================
Cache: large_io_cache, Status: Active, Type: Mixed
       Config Size: 50.00 Mb, Run Size: 50.00 Mb
       Config Replacement: strict LRU, Run Replacement: strict LRU

IO Size   Wash Size   Config Size    Run Size       APF Percent
--------  ---------   ------------   ------------   -----------
2 Kb      10 Mb       10.00 Mb       10.00 Mb       10
16 Kb     40 Mb       40.00 Mb       40.00 Mb       10
(return status = 0)
```

Planning the dbccdb Database

There are several steps involved in planning and creating databases. These topics are discussed in this section.

Allocating Disk Space for dbccdb

Additional disk storage is required for the dbccdb database. Because dbcc checkstorage uses dbccdb extensively, you should place dbccdb on a disk (or disks, if you plan to run multiple instances) that is separate from other database devices. Data and log devices for this database should also be on separate devices, wherever possible, to ensure that the dbcc commands operate at maximum speed. Under no circumstances should the dbccdb database be created on the master device: it abuses the device resource that you want left free.

Segments for Workspaces

By dedicating segments for the workspaces, you can control the placement of the workspaces and improve the performance of dbcc checkstorage. When new segments are added to the dbccdb database for the exclusive use of workspaces, be sure to unmap the devices attached to these segments from the default segment with sp_dropsegment.

Creating the dbccdb Database

If not already completed, plan the size of the dbccdb database with the sp_plan_dbccdb procedure. See "Using dbcc checkstorage" earlier in this chapter to obtain recommendations for database size, devices (if dbccdb does not exist), workspace sizes, cache size, and the number of worker processes for the target database.

If dbccdb already exists, drop it and re-create it using the above recommendations. The following example creates an 8 MB dbccdb database (6 MB for data and 2 MB for log). Then, the optional segments for text and scan workspaces are created too (in a larger/busier dbccdb, we might spread the database over several devices, and separate the segments).

```
use master
go
drop database dbccdb
go
create database dbccdb
      on dbccdb_dat = 6
      log on dbccdb_log = 2
go
use dbccdb
go
sp_addsegment scanseg, dbccdb, dbccdb_dat
go
sp_addsegment textseg, dbccdb, dbccdb_dat2
go
```

Adding Tables and Stored Procedures to dbccdb

After creation, dbccdb is no different from any other user database: it's empty, and it knows nothing about dbcc checkstorage. To add the tables and stored procedures required to support and perform dbcc operations, we must run an installation script. The script, installdbccdb, is placed in the directory $SYBASE/$SYBASE_ASE/install at server installation time. Submit this script to your server via isql or your preferred query editor (SA privileges will be required).

```
cd $SYBASE/scripts
isql -Usa -i installdbccdb
Password:
. . . . . . . . . . . . . .
```

Using sp_dbcc_createws

After creating the database, create the dbcc workspaces for the database. The example below creates a 10 MB scan segment and a 10 MB text segment for the newly created dbccdb database.

```
use dbccdb
go
sp_dbcc_createws dbccdb, scanseg, scan_pubs2, scan, "10M"
go
sp_dbcc_createws dbccdb, textseg, text_pubs2, text, "10M"
go
```

The sp_dbcc_createws procedure uses the following parameters:

Parameter	Description
database name	Name of the dbcc checkstorage working database where the workspace will be created
segment name	Name of the segment where the workspace will be located; may be the "default" segment
workspace name	Logical name for the workspace; should be descriptive for later reference
workspace type	"Scan" for the scan workspace; "text" for the text workspace

Parameter	Description
workspace size	Taken from the output of sp_plan_dbccdb; should not exceed the actual size of the segment it's built on

Configuring dbcc

When you have finished installing dbccdb, you must update the dbcc_config table. Use the stored procedure sp_dbcc_updateconfig to set parameters for each database which will be examined using dbcc checkstorage. You must update each dbcc parameter separately for each target database, as shown in the following example.

```
use dbccdb
go
sp_dbcc_updateconfig pubs2,"max worker processes", "1"
go
sp_dbcc_updateconfig pubs2, "dbcc named cache", pubs2_cache, "2M"
go
sp_dbcc_updateconfig pubs2, "scan workspace", scan_pubs2
go
sp_dbcc_updateconfig pubs2, "text workspace", text_pubs2
go
sp_dbcc_updateconfig pubs2, "OAM count threshold", "5"
go
sp_dbcc_updateconfig pubs2, "IO error abort", "3"
go
sp_dbcc_updateconfig pubs2, "linkage error abort", "8"
go
```

The sp_dbcc_updateconfig procedure uses the following parameters:

Parameter	Description	
database name	Name of the target database that checkstorage will work on	
type	Type of option being configured; valid values include max worker processes, dbcc named cache, scan workspace, text workspace, OAM count threshold, IO error abort, and linkage error abort. The value of this parameter will determine the valid value/necessity of the string1 and string2 parameters	
string1	for "max worker processes"	number of worker processes to use when checking the target database
	for "dbcc named cache"	name of the cache to use when checking the target database
	for "text|scan workspace"	name of the workspace to use when checking the target database
	for "OAM count threshold"	percentage of variation on OAM page counts before fault is declared
	for "IO error abort"	allowable number of disk I/O errors before checkstorage aborts checks on the disk

Parameter	Description	
	for "linkage error abort"	allowable number of linkage errors before checkstorage aborts checks on the object
string2	for "max worker processes"	not used
	for "dbcc named cache"	size of the 16 K buffer pool
	for "text|scan workspace"	name of the workspace to use when checking the target database
	for "OAM count threshold"	not used
	for "IO error abort"	not used
	for "linkage error abort"	not used

After the configuration is set up for all of the databases, all the steps required to set up the dbccdb database are completed. dbcc checkstorage can now be used to check databases.

Maintaining dbccdb

There will occasionally be the need to perform the following maintenance tasks on the dbccdb database:

- Reevaluate and update the configuration using the following system procedures
- Clean up obsolete data in dbccdb using the following system procedures
- Perform consistency checks on dbccdb itself

Reevaluating and Updating dbccdb Configuration

The original planned values from sp_plan_dbccdb assume that your database may vary in size by as much as 10%. If the characteristics of user databases change more widely than this, use the stored procedure sp_dbcc_evaluatedb to reevaluate the current dbccdb configuration and recommend more suitable values.

The following changes to user databases might affect the dbccdb configuration, as follows:

- When a user database is created, deleted, or altered, the size of the workspaces and named cache, or the number of worker threads stored in the dbcc_config table might be affected.
- Changes in the named cache size or worker process count for dbcc_checkstorage might require you to reconfigure the Adaptive Server buffer cache and worker processes.

If the results of previous dbcc checkstorage executions are available for the target database, use sp_dbcc_evaluatedb to determine new configuration values. sp_dbcc_evaluatedb assumes the existence of dbccdb and expects the results of dbcc checkstorage operations on the target database to be stored in dbccdb. If dbccdb does not exist or if the results of dbcc checkstorage operations for the target database are not available, sp_dbcc_evaluatedb reports this fact, instead of configuration parameters. sp_dbcc_configreport also reports the configuration parameters for the specified database.

Use sp_dbcc_updateconfig to add new databases to the dbcc_config table and to change the configuration values in dbcc_config to reflect the values recommended by sp_dbcc_evaluatedb.

Cleaning Up dbccdb

Each time you run dbcc checkstorage, Adaptive Server stores the data generated from that operation in dbccdb. You should periodically clean up dbccdb by using sp_dbcc_deletehistory to delete data for the target database that was created before the date that you specify.

When a database is deleted, all configuration information and dbcc checkstorage results related to that database should be deleted from dbccdb. Use sp_dbcc_deletedb to delete all database information from dbccdb.

Failure to do this can lead to great confusion when old dbcc results are attributed to a newly created database. Also, your database can fill up.

Performing Consistency Checks on dbccdb

The limited update activity in the dbccdb tables should make corruption less frequent. Two signs of corruption in dbccdb are:

- Failure of dbcc checkstorage during the initialization phase as it evaluates the work that needs to be performed, or during the completion phase when it records its results.
- Loss of information about faults resulting from corruption in the recorded faults, found by dbcc checkstorage. dbcc checkstorage can be used to check dbccdb, using dbccdb to store the results; however, a severe corruption in dbccdb may cause dbcc checkstorage to fail during this check.

To permit dbcc checkstorage to locate severe corruption in dbccdb, you can create the alternate database, dbccalt, which you use only for checking dbccdb. You create dbccalt using the same process that you used to create dbccdb as described in "Using dbcc checkstorage." If no free devices are available for dbccalt, any device that is not used by the master database or dbccdb can be used. dbcc checkstorage and the dbcc system procedures function the same with dbccalt as they do with dbccdb.

When the target database is dbccdb, dbcc checkstorage uses dbccalt, if it exists. If dbccalt does not exist, dbccdb can be checked using itself as the management database. If the target database is dbccdb and dbccalt exists, the results of dbcc checkstorage operations on dbccdb are stored in dbccalt. If dbccalt does not exist, the results are stored in dbccdb itself. Alternatively, dbcc checkalloc and dbcc checktable can be used to check dbccdb. If dbccdb becomes corrupted, you can drop it and re-create it or load an older version from a backup. If you drop it, some of its diagnostic history will be lost. Alternately, you may find it easier to drop dbccdb and re-create/reconfigure it from script should it become corrupt.

Generating Reports from dbccdb

Several dbcc stored procedures are provided with dbccdb so that you can generate reports from the data within dbccdb.

sp_dbcc_fullreport

This stored procedure runs several other stored procedures to get a full picture of the dbcc operations that occurred. It runs sp_dbcc_summaryreport, sp_dbcc_configreport, sp_dbcc_statisticsreport, and sp_dbcc_faultreport short for database..object_name on or before the specified date.

Syntax:

```
sp_dbcc_fullreport [database name [, object name [, date]]]
```

Parameters:

database name

Specifies the name of the database. If you do not specify database name, the report contains information on all databases in the dbccdb database, dbcc_operation_log table.

object name

Specifies the name of the table or index for which you want the report generated. If you do not specify object name, statistics on all objects in the target database are reported.

date

Specifies the date on which the dbcc checkstorage operation was performed. If you do not specify a date, the date of the last operation is used.

sp_dbcc_summaryreport

To report a summary of dbcc checkstorage operations, use sp_dbcc_summaryreport. This reports all dbcc checkstorage operations that were completed for the specified database on or before the specified date.

Syntax:

sp_dbc@code first = c_summaryreport [database name [, date]]

Parameters:

database name

Specifies the name of the database for which you want the report generated. If you do not specify dbname, sp_dbcc_summaryreport generates reports on all databases in dbccdb..dbcc_operation_log for which the date is on or before the date and time specified by the date option.

date

Specifies the date on which dbcc checkstorage was performed. If you do not specify a date, sp_dbcc_summaryreport uses the date of the last dbcc checkstorage operation performed on the target database. If both the date and the time are specified, summary results of all the operations performed on or before the specified time are reported. If no date is specified, all operations are reported.

Example:

```
sp_dbcc_summaryreport
go
```

Example output:

```
DBCC Operation : checkstorage
```

Database Name	Start time	End Time	Operation ID	Hard Faults	Soft Faults	Text Columns	Abort Count	User Name
sybsystemprocs	05/12/1997 10:54:45	10:54:53	1	0	0	0	0	sa
sybsystemprocs	05/12/1997 11:14:10	11:14:19	2	0	0	0	0	sa

sp_dbcc_configreport

This stored procedure generates a report that describes the configuration information used by the dbcc checkstorage operation for the specified database.

Syntax:

```
sp_dbcc_configreport [database name]
```

Parameter:

database name

Specifies the name of the database. If dbname is not specified, the report contains information on all databases in the dbccdb database, dbcc_operation_log.

Example:

```
Reporting configuration information of database sybsystemprocs.
```

Parameter Name	Value	Size
database name	sybsystemprocs	51200K
dbcc named cache	default data cache	1024K
text workspace	textws_001 (id = 544004969)	128K
scan workspace	scanws_001 (id = 512004855)	1024K
max worker processes	1	
operation sequence number	2	

sp_dbcc_statisticsreport

The sp_dbcc_statisticsreport stored procedure reports database-specific statistics information from the dbcc_counter table in the dbccdb database. This reports statistics information generated by dbcc checkstorage on or before the specified date. This data can be useful in determining how the database is utilizing the space assigned to it.

Syntax:

```
sp_dbcc_statisticsreport [database name [, object name [, date]]]
```

database name

Specifies the target database. If database name is not specified, the report contains information on all databases in dbccdb..dbcc_operation_log.

object name

Specifies the name of the table or index for which you want the report generated. If you do not specify object name, Adaptive Server reports statistics on all objects in the target database.

date

Specifies the date on which the dbcc checkstorage operation was performed. If you do not specify date, Adaptive Server uses the date of the most recent operation.

Examples:

```
use master
go
sp_dbcc_statisticsreport 'sybsystemprocs', 'sysobjects'
go
Statistics Report on object sysobjects in database sybsystemprocs

Parameter Name          Index Id       Value
-----------------       --------       -----------
count                   0              160.0
max size                0              99.0
max count               0              16.0
bytes data              0              12829.0
bytes used              0              15228.0
count                   1              16.0
max size                1              9.0
max level               1              0.0
max count               1              16.0
bytes data              1              64.0
bytes used              1              176.0
count                   2              166.0
max level               2              1.0
max size                2              39.0
max count               2              48.0
bytes data              2              3092.0
bytes used              2              4988.0

Parameter Name          Index Id       Partition      Value      Dev_name
-------------------     --------       ---------      -----      --------
page gaps               0              1              16.0       master
pages used              0              1              17.0       master
extents used            0              1              3.0        master
overflow pages          0              1              0.0        master
pages overhead          0              1              1.0        master
pages reserved          0              1              6.0        master
page extent gaps        0              1              7.0        master
ws buffer crosses       0              1              7.0        master
page extent crosses     0              1              7.0        master
page gaps               1              1              1.0        master
pages used              1              1              2.0        master
```

```
extents used           1          1          1.0        master
overflow pages         1          1          0.0        master
pages overhead         1          1          1.0        master
pages reserved         1          1          6.0        master
page extent gaps       1          1          0.0        master
ws buffer crosses      1          1          0.0        master
page extent crosses    1          1          0.0        master
page gaps              2          1          5.0        master
pages used             2          1          8.0        master
extents used           2          1          1.0        master
overflow pages         2          1          0.0        master
pages overhead         2          1          1.0        master
pages reserved         2          1          0.0        master

page extent gaps       2          1          0.0        master
ws buffer crosses      2          1          0.0        master
page extent crosses    2          1          0.0        master
```

sp_dbcc_faultreport

To report on faults located in a specific database object, use the sp_dbcc_faultreport stored procedure. It reports faults in the specified database object that occurred on or before the specified date. There are options to generate a short or long report.

Syntax:

```
sp_dbcc_faultreport [report type [, database name [, object name [, date
]]]]
```

Parameters:

report type

Specifies the type of fault report. Valid values are short and long. The default is short.

database name

Specifies the name of the target database; for example, master..sysdatabases. If database name is not specified, the report contains information on all databases in dbccdb..dbcc_operation_log.

object name

Specifies the name of the table or index for which you want the report generated. If object_name is not specified, statistics on all objects in the target database are reported.

date

Specifies the date on which the dbcc checkstorage operation was performed. If you do not specify date, Adaptive Server uses the date of the most recent operation.

Examples:

```
use sybsystemprocs
go
sp_dbcc_faultreport 'short'
go

Database Name : sybsystemprocs
```

```
Table Name        Index    Type Code   Description             Page Number
--------------    ------   ---------   --------------------    -----------
sysprocedures     0        100031      page not allocated      5702
sysprocedures     1        100031      page not allocated      14151
syslogs           0        100022      chain start error       24315
syslogs           0        100031      page not allocated      24315

use sybsystemprocs
go
sp_dbcc_faultreport 'long'
go

Generating 'Fault Report' for object sysprocedures in database
sybsystemprocs.

Type Code: 100031; Soft fault, possibly spurious
Page reached by the chain is not allocated.
page id:  14151
page header:
0x00003747000037880000374600000005000648B803EF0001000103FE0080000F
Header for 14151, next 14216, previous 14150, id = 5:1 time stamp =
0x0001000648B8, next row = 1007, level = 0 free offset = 1022, minlen = 15,
status = 128(0x0080)
```

sp_dbcc_differentialreport

To compare the results of dbcc checkstorage operations between two dates, run the sp_dbcc_differentialreport stored procedure. It compares the results of the dbcc checkstorage operations completed for the specified database object on the specified dates. It highlights the changes in I/O statistics and faults that took place between the two dates.

Syntax:

```
sp_dbcc_differentialreport [database name [, object name]], [db_op] [,
"start date" [, "end date"]]
```

Parameters:

database name

Specifies the name of the database. If you do not specify a database name, the report contains information on all databases in dbccdb..dbcc_operation_log.

object name

Specifies the name of the table or index for which you want the report generated. If object name is not specified, statistics on all objects in the target database are reported.

db_op

Specifies the source of the data to be used for the report. The only value is checkstorage. The report is generated on the data specified by db_op on date1 and date2 for the specified object in the target database. If dates are not specified, the last two operations of the type db_op are compared.

start date

Specifies the first date of a dbcc checkstorage operation to be compared.

end date

Specifies the last date of a dbcc checkstorage operation to be compared.

Example:

```
sp_dbcc_differentialreport master, sysprocedures, checkstorage, "01/01/96",
"01/02/96"

The following changes in dbcc counter values for the object "sysprocedures"
in database master have been noticed between 01/01/96 and 01/02/96.

Description              Date1         Date2
----------------         -----         -----
pages used               999           1020
pages reserved           1000          1024
page extent gaps         64            67
```

Database Dumps

Regularly dump each database, including the master, sybsystemprocs, and model databases. Since the tempdb is cleared whenever the server is started it is unnecessary to take dumps of this database. Aside from making the backups, it is also important to get a copy of the backups in a secure off-site location. Additionally, keep track and maintain a record of the dumps.

See Chapter 8 for more information on database dumps.

Disaster Recovery

It is also important to prepare a disaster recovery plan, possibly more than one. When dealing with any disaster recovery plan, always ask how each plan could go wrong. Include, as part of the plan, the physical database dumps as well as any configuration data or scripts that would be used to reconstruct the server. Test these backup plans extensively.

Log Management

As mentioned in previous chapters about transaction logging, transaction logs are the repository of changes made to the databases. But since they are limited in size, they must be watched to prevent them from filling up. A full log stops all modification to the database, and the only way to reliably "prune" the logs (remove completed, checkpointed transactions) is to dump them. Make sure that the logs are dumped on a regular basis and use threshold management to avoid "log segment full" errors.

To verify how large the logs have grown, use the sp_spaceused stored procedure or dbcc checktable (described earlier in this chapter) to monitor the log and its remaining pages.

Space Management

Another task that is left to system administrators is to ensure that the databases themselves are not completely full, or that the space in a database is not being misused. A database will grow over time as data is added to it. Eventually, it can grow to the point where it uses all its allocated space. To prevent this from happening, use the sp_spaceused stored procedure to verify the unused space in the database. When the database approaches full, more space can be added or data can be purged from the database.

It is also the administrator's job to ensure that the space is not misused. Remember, databases can be enlarged but not easily shrunk. Try to make sure that the databases are adequately sized with room to grow.

Script Maintenance

From time to time, it may become necessary to attempt a complete rebuild of an Adaptive Server. In order to re-create the server, it is essential to have scripts ready that can perform the installation, configuration, and population of the databases. Always keep up-to-date scripts with all database definition information, from disk inits through object creation. Many of these can be created retroactively with third-party reverse engineering tools or the defncopy utility. Keep the scripts on a different machine than the production database server. This way, if the production database server is ever corrupted beyond repair, the server can be duplicated on another machine.

Verifying Dumps

It is often said that almost any administrator can perform a backup but a useful administrator can perform a restoration.

This comment is not directed towards the administrators themselves but at the backups they create. When performing backups to tapes, the tapes can become worn or damaged, preventing restoration from the bad tapes. It is also possible that the backups have not been performed properly, which may also prevent restoration.

If tape striping is used, beware of any bad tapes in the stripe set; a single bad tape will invalidate an entire stripe set. The same is true of long chains of transaction log dumps — a single bad dump tran will invalidate all subsequent dump files.

Try to get a separate server set aside for testing of the database and transaction log dumps so you can verify whether or not the backups actually work. This also provides an excellent rehearsal for a real disaster. Otherwise, there are some third-party products that can verify whether a dump is valid or not.

Table-level Maintenance

Some maintenance happens at the server level, some at the database level, and some at the table level. We've covered the server-level and database-level maintenance, now we'll look at tables.

Updating Statistics

When a query is processed by Adaptive Server, the optimizer is used to make a decision as to the most effective method for retrieving the data. The data used to make these decisions is known as the *optimizer statistics*. ASE uses two system tables called systabstats and sysstatistics to store a variety of measures on each table in the database. Statistics dealing with the table as a whole (systabstats) are dynamically maintained, but those on individual columns (sysstatistics) are not, and must be updated on a regular basis. Otherwise, the data distribution of the table may change and the Adaptive Server may not know it. Updating statistics may be a very intrusive task and should be performed during off-peak times.

Statistics are updated for a table with the following syntax:

```
update statistics table_name
    [ [index_name] | [( column_list ) ] ]
    [using step values]
    [with consumers = consumers ]
```

Statistics (including time since the last update) may be observed by querying the systabstats and sysstatistics table, or by using the optdiag utility from the OS prompt.

The 255-byte Rule

A word of caution for administrators involved in database design. Adaptive Server only maintains statistics for the first 255 bytes of data. This means that if any wide columns are used in the database schemas, only the first 255 bytes of the column data are considered statistically significant. Any significant distributions of data beyond that limit are invisible to the optimizer.

Monitoring Space Utilization

For volatile tables (syslogs is a volatile table) it is essential to monitor database space taken up by the table. Threshold management is the easiest way; place the table on its own segment and put a threshold on it. Running sp_spaceused on a object will show how much space it is using. Also keep track of the rate of change, so you can add space before you reach your threshold or fill up the segment.

Summary

Especially in production systems, system health is vital to keeping the servers operational. To verify the status of the system, it is important to run basic maintenance routines to ensure that no problems have begun to develop. These tasks, depending on the size of the environment can vary from just a few steps to complex, involved routines. They can take potentially a few minutes each day to taking over the time of an administrator. Because of this and the criticality of the tasks, it is also recommended that they be automated to whatever extent is possible. Develop scripts to perform some of these tasks and page or notify administrators when a problem appears, or invest in some third-party tools that automate and perform some of these tasks.

Chapter 15

Troubleshooting

This chapter exists for the purpose of steering you in the right direction in case of trouble. By the time you've reached this chapter, you should be able to handle any problem that comes up that doesn't need direct aid from Sybase technical support.

So, based on some typical problems that you as a DBA need to solve, where would you look first? This chapter is useful for review. Read the question first, think about how you might solve it, and then look at our suggested approaches.

The Server Will Not Come Up

Where do you look first? What needs to be up?

Possible Approach:

First, check the system errorlog (or event log on NT). Usually there will be an explicit clue there. Most typically, something has happened to either file permissions or system memory, and you can discern this from the errorlog.

Other things to check:

- Is the network up?
- Are there enough resources available (e.g., memory) for the server to grab?
- Have you examined all operating system logs?
- Are you signed in as the sybase user or an OS system admin (a common mistake)? (You should be signed in as the sybase user to start the server).
- Is the server already started?

Some Users Claim the Server Stopped

Where should we start? First, don't panic.

Possible Approach:

If you can connect to the server, use sp_who and sp_lock to determine the status of the person calling. The most typical cause of "The server's hung" phone calls is locking. A blocked process causes the user to think that the whole server is down.

Is it really not working or just running very slow? Possible situations:

- The connection timed out.
- The process is blocked.
- The process is fine, but the front end is having problems.

If you cannot connect to the server, run showserver to see if the server is up. If it is up, try again in a few minutes; max connections may be reached. Finally, look at the errorlog.

Server is Up, but Some Users Cannot Gain Access

Where do you look?

Possible Approach:

If you have access, check connections. Otherwise, it is probably time to look at the network on their side, or their net-libs and Open Client. What time ranges are the users allowed to run in? It's possible that the Resource Governor is keeping them out. Can any user connect from the client machine? Or can the users complaining connect from another machine? Verify error messages.

> **NOTE:** Don't forget obvious errors such as the user forgetting the correct password!

Processing Slows Down or Stops

What are the likely culprits?

Possible Approach:

On a single-processor box, some batch process may be hogging the server. The caller's process may be blocked by another process. Many system procedures (checkpoints, transaction dumps, etc.) temporarily lock resources, which the caller may be trying to access. Your user may have a low priority, or be running outside of the normal time range. Don't forget to look at sp_who, sp_lock, and sp_sysmon output.

Some Database or Databases Cannot be Accessed

Where do you look first?

Use sp_configure and sp_who to determine if you have exceeded the maximum number of databases.

Also, sp_helpdb will tell you if the database is marked as corrupt or suspect.

Finally, if this database has just been restored, you may have forgotten the online database command.

Possible Approach:

Log in to the server, and use sp_helpdb to find out if the database is corrupt. If it looks fine, check sp_configure to see if the number of databases configured has been exceeded.

Check user access to the database. Is the database in single-user or dbo-only mode? Has the database finished recovering? Is the database online? Finally, check to see how many databases are configured; are you trying to access database 26 when you are only configured for 25?

Users Cannot Access Objects

What happens when a user cannot execute a select statement to a table you think he has access to? Or tries to run a procedure and gets permission errors?

Possible Approach:

Use sp_helprotect to check permissions not only of individual but of group and public too. Check table consistency with dbcc.

From the Troubleshooting Guide

We invited Sybase technical support to add their favorites, pet peeves, and most common calls to this list. They directed us to the troubleshooting guide, and asked us to draw information from that manual. We'd like to direct you there as well; it has a wealth of specific information.

Disaster Recovery Tasks

This section steps you through tasks necessary for recovery from various disaster situations involving Sybase system databases or the entire master device.

How to Build a New Master Device

To build a new master device, execute buildmaster, specifying the location and size of the master device. buildmaster should always be run by the operating system user who owns the Adaptive Server devices. Remember that buildmaster takes the size in 2 K blocks. For example, if you want a 14 MB master device, set the size parameter to 7168 2 K blocks.

WARNING: Never execute buildmaster while Adaptive Server is running!

To build a new 14 MB master device, use a command similar to one in the following table:

Operating System	Command
UNIX	buildmaster -ddevice_name -s7168
Digital Open VMS	buildmaster/disk=device_name/size=7168
Novell NetWare	load bldmaster -s7168
OS/2, Windows NT	bldmaster -ddevice_name -s7168

If the master database has been altered, alter it again using exactly the same commands. The master database must be re-created both logically and physically to look exactly the way it did at the time of the last dump. This includes any alterations to tempdb or model. buildmaster initializes the specified device as the Sybase master device and creates the master, model, and tempdb databases on this device. Any information existing on the device will be overwritten. Refer to buildmaster in the Adaptive Server utility programs manual for additional information.

NOTE: Be sure to execute buildmaster from the correct Adaptive Server version. Refer to "How to Determine Your Adaptive Server Version" for instructions.

How to Rebuild master Database and Leave Master Device Intact

To rebuild the master database only and leave the master device intact, run buildmaster with the -m option (on UNIX, Novell NetWare) or the /master option (on Digital OpenVMS). Be sure to specify the correct size of the master device, not the master database.

NOTE: Due to the new 6 MB master in Adaptive Server 12.0.x, an additional precaution is necessary for sites running version 12.0.x. If you installed Adaptive Server starting with version 12.0.x, use the 12.0.x buildmaster for this step. Otherwise, if you upgraded from pre-12.0.x Adaptive Server to 12.0.x, use the pre-12.0.x buildmaster. Using the correct version of buildmaster avoids potential problems due to the increased size of master in 12.0.x.

The commands in the following table build a new master database without changing the configuration block or initializing the master device. These commands also set sort order and character set values to their defaults.

Operating System	Command
UNIX buildmaster	-ddevice_name -sdevice_size -m
SCO UNIX	buildmaster -d/dev/rid001d -s5120 -m
Digital OpenVMS	buildmaster /disk=device_name /master /size=device_size
Novell NetWare	load bldmastr -ddevice_name -sdevice_size -m
OS/2, Windows NT	bldmastr -ddevice_name -sdevice_size -m

WARNING: Never run the buildmaster utility while Adaptive Server is running.

After rebuilding master, and prior to loading the backup, alter the master database on the master device as necessary to ensure that the lstart, size, and vstart values of master match up with those on the dump. Otherwise, you may see corruption following the load of master.

Refer to the Adaptive Server utility programs manual for additional information about buildmaster.

How to Start Adaptive Server in Single-User Mode

To start Adaptive Server in single-user mode, issue the following command:

```
% startserver -m -f runserver_filename
```

If this fails, do the following instead:

Edit a copy of the runserver file for the Adaptive Server and add the -m option (on UNIX) or the /masterrecover option (on Digital OpenVMS) to the end of the dataserver line. On Novell NetWare, OS/2, andWindows NT, no runserver file is used. Instead, specify the -m flag on the file server command line, as shown in the example below.

The following examples show the runserver file edited to start an Adaptive Server named TEST in single-user mode:

On UNIX:

```
#!/bin/sh
#
# Adaptive Server Information:
# name: TEST
# master device: /work/master.dat
# master device size: 10752
# errorlog: /usr/u/sybase/install/errorlog
# interfaces: /usr/u/sybase/interfaces
#
/usr/u/sybase/bin/dataserver -d/work/master.dat
-sTEST -e/usr/u/sybase/install/errorlog
-i/usr/u/sybase/interfaces
-c/usr/u/sybase/TEST.cfg -m
```

On Digital OpenVMS:

You do not need to edit the runserver file. Start Adaptive Server with the following command:

```
$ startserver /server= server_name /masterrecover
```

NOTE: Create a separate runserver file for each Adaptive Server to start in single-user mode. Refer to "How to Start Adaptive Server with Trace Flags" for information about using runserver files.

Start Adaptive Server with the following command:

Operating System	Command
UNIX	startserver -frunserver_filename -m
Digital OpenVMS	startserver/server=server_name /masterrecover
Novell NetWare	load sqlsrvr -ddevice_name -m
OS/2	sqlsrvr -ddevice_name -m
Windows NT	See directions below.

Once Adaptive Server is running and recovery is complete on all databases, review the errorlog and verify that no errors occurred. If you have successfully started Adaptive Server in single-user mode, a message like the following should appear in the errorlog:

```
00:95/12/29 13:09:53.14 server *** WARNING *****************
00:95/12/29 13:09:53.17 server Adaptive Server booted single user mode -
updates allowed to system catalogs
```

On Windows NT:

Follow these steps to start Adaptive Server in single-user mode on Windows NT:

1. Log into Windows NT using an account with Windows NT administrator privileges.
2. Double-click the Server Config icon in the Sybase for Windows NT program group.
3. Select the Adaptive Server icon.
4. Select Configure Adaptive Server.
5. Select the name of the Adaptive Server to configure, and choose Continue.
6. Enter "sa" for login name. (No password is required.)
7. If the Adaptive Server is not running, Server Config asks you to start it now; choose Yes.
8. Select the Command Line Option or the Command Line Parameters button. Server Config displays the Command Line Parameters dialog box.
9. Edit the text in the Command Line Parameters dialog box to include the start-up parameter -m.
10. Click OK.
11. Choose Save at the Adaptive Server's configuration dialog box.
12. Exit Server Config.

Returning Adaptive Server to Multiuser Mode

To start Adaptive Server in multiuser mode, use the original runserver file without the -m option.

On Novell, restart Adaptive Server without the -m flag.

On Digital OpenVMS, restart Adaptive Server without the /masterrecover option.

How to Run the installmaster and installmodel Scripts

To execute the installmaster and installmodel scripts, located in the $SYBASE/scripts directory, type the command for your platform.

Operating System	Command
UNIX	isql -Usa -Psa_password -Sserver_name>> installmasterisql -Usa -Psa_password -Sserver_name>> installmodel
SCO UNIX	isql -Usa -Psa_password -i/usr/sybase/scripts/installmaster isql -Usa -Psa_password -i/usr/sybase/scripts/installmodel
Digital OpenVMS	isql/u="sa"/p="sa password"/input=installmasterisql/u="sa"/p="sa password"/input=installmodel
Novell NetWare	load isql -Usa -Psa_password -Sserver_name-isys:sybase\scripts\instmstr.sqlload isql -Usa -Psa_password -Sserver_name-isys:sybase\scripts\instmodl.sql

Operating System	Command
OS/2, Windows NT	isql -Usa -Psa_password -Sserver_name-ic:\sybase\scripts\instmstrisql -Usa -Psa_password -Sserver_name-ic:\sybase\scripts\instmodl

NOTE: On the Novell NetWare platform, each load command must be on a single line.

The installmaster and installmodel scripts install the system procedures, set up some required Sybase internal tables, and install the privileges for the model database.

How to Load the master Database from Backup

This is a three-step procedure:

1. Put Adaptive Server in single-user mode. Refer to "How to Start Adaptive Server in Single-User Mode."
2. Start isql as sa.
3. Execute these commands:

   ```
   1> load database master
   2> from logical_dump_device_name
   3> go
   ```

   OR

   ```
   1> load database master
   2> from "physical_dump_device_name"
   3> go
   ```

Alternatively, if the database was dumped to a remote site, refer to "load database" in the *Adaptive Server Enterprise Reference Manual* for information about loading the master database.

Once the master database is loaded successfully, Adaptive Server automatically shuts itself down and the isql session exits with the following message:

```
DB-Library: Unexpected EOF from SQL Server.
```

How to Restore System Table Information in master Database

This section is divided into two parts. The first part describes how to reestablish device and database information in the system catalog, and the second part describes how to reestablish Adaptive Server logins.

Restoring Device and Database Information in the System Catalog:

If a create database, alter database, or disk init command has been issued since the last database dump of master, or if no valid dump of master exists, and no valid bcp files of system tables exist, refer to "Backing Up and Restoring the System Databases" in the *System Administration Guide* for information on the use of the disk reinit and disk refit commands. These commands restore the system tables information contained in the master database, which describes all Sybase devices and user databases.

If you kept the disk init scripts originally used to initialize the database devices, you can use them to formulate the disk reinit commands, since disk reinit uses the same parameters. If these scripts are not available, examine the contents of sysdevices before a disaster and build the necessary disk reinit command scripts for use when needed. This information is also available from the server errorlog and the operating system.

Execute disk reinit on the device on which sybsystemprocs is located if it is on a device other than master. To retrieve the correct parameters for disk reinit, check the values you saved from sysdevices. If this information is not available, check the most recent errorlog.

NOTE: The device on which sybsystemprocs resides will not be included in your disk init script, as sybinit creates that device during installation. Therefore, record the values in sysdevices for the device on which sybsystemprocs resides, even if you plan to use your disk init scripts.

After all the disk reinit commands complete, compare the current contents of sysdevices with a copy of the sysdevices table that was made before the master device was lost. Since the disk refit command is based on the contents of that table, it is crucial that the table accurately reflect all devices.

After the disk refit command is complete, manually compare the contents of the current sysdatabases and sysusages with copies of those same tables that were made prior to the loss of the master device.

Keep up-to-date copies of these tables on hand, using bcp with the -c option, to ensure the quickest recovery after a disaster. If sysdatabases and sysusages do not match your hardcopy records, contact Sybase Technical Support for assistance.

Reestablishing Adaptive Server Logins:

If you have added Adaptive Server logins since the last database dump of master, or if no valid dump of master exists, restore the syslogins table.

How you restore the table depends on what information you have on hand:

- If you saved the scripts with all sp_addlogin and sp_droplogin statements made in the correct order, run those scripts.
- If you do not have the scripts, but have a copy of syslogins saved, reconstruct the sp_addlogin and sp_droplogin commands and the corresponding suids.
- If neither the scripts nor the copy of syslogins is available, follow these steps:
    a. Query all of the user databases to determine the name and the suid of each user. The sp_addlogin system procedure assigns an suid to each login in numerical order, and this suid is mapped to the sysusers table in each user database.
    b. Once all names and suids are known, execute sp_addlogin for each user, in the appropriate order, so that newly generated logins have the same suid as the users in the user databases. You might have to enter dummy accounts for users whose logins have been dropped in order to keep current users' suid values in the correct sequence. Drop these dummy accounts when you are done.

How to Alter the number of devices Parameter Manually

This step is necessary only if you are using a virtual device number (vdevno) that is greater than the default value for the number of devices configuration parameter (in this case, some of your devices will be inaccessible until you perform this step). The default value for number of devices is 10 on most platforms.

> **NOTE:** Perform this task only if the configuration file prior to an Adaptive Server crash is lost. If the configuration file is available, use that file to start up Adaptive Server or use the number of devices from the last configuration file.

To aid in the recovery process, determine whether this step will be needed before an actual disaster. Do this by examining the device_number column in the sp_helpdevice output.

If Adaptive Server is not up and running, check the startup section of the most recent error log, which contains the device number.

If a virtual device number greater than the default is being used, increase the number of devices parameter in the configuration file before you start Adaptive Server. For example, if the highest vdevno in use is 30 and the default is 10, edit the configuration file to set the number of devices parameter to 31.

How to Alter tempdb

If tempdb has been enlarged and these changes are not reflected in your current master database, alter tempdb again to ensure that there is enough space to process your normal work load. Refer to the *System Administration Guide* for more information.

To help prevent errors from occurring during disaster recovery, record the commands you used originally to alter tempdb.

How to Alter the model Database

Because the model database is created at the same time as the master database, no action is needed to build it. If you have made any changes to model, however, you must reapply them.

If you need to alter the size of the model database, alter the size of the tempdb database so that it is at least as big as model. If you attempt to start Adaptive Server, and model is bigger than tempdb, Adaptive Server will not start.

How to Add a Sybase Dump Device

This capability was required in older versions (prior to version 10), and is still available, but it is now more common to dump to a physical device. You can specify a device by simply naming it, using syntax like the following:

```
load database master from " <physical device name>"
```

If you must use dump devices, refer to sp_addumpdevice in the Reference Manual for information. Record the exact syntax of the original sp_addumpdevice command for each Adaptive Server. This helps prevent errors from occurring during disaster recovery.

How to Reset Adaptive Server to Its Default Configuration

Whenever you make a change to your configuration values using sp_configure, Adaptive Server saves the old configuration file under the name servername.sequential_number. This means that your default configuration should exist in one of these files.

If you successfully locate the desired configuration file, do the following:

1. Name the current servername.cfg file to servername.cfg.old.
2. Rename the file you located to servername.cfg.
3. Restart Adaptive Server.

If you are unable to locate the desired configuration file, do the following:

1. Rename the servername.cfg file in your Sybase home directory to servername.cfg.old.
2. Start Adaptive Server without specifying a configuration file name.

Adaptive Server will use the default configuration and create a new configuration file if there is no servername.cfg file available at start-up time.

How to Set a Default Backup Server Manually in Adaptive Server

This procedure is needed to allow the Adaptive Server that is being recovered to access its Backup Server. If this step is not performed when needed, then Adaptive Server will not be able to process any dump or load commands. As a Sybase System Administrator (sa_role), execute the following commands in an isql session on the Adaptive Server that is being recovered:

```
1> use master
2> go
1> select srvname, srvnetname from sysservers
2> where srvname = "SYB_BACKUP"
3> go
```

There are three possible outcomes to this query. The following table matches each outcome to the steps you should take in that circumstance:

Avoiding Disaster through Good DBA Practices

This section provides a number of recommendations for keeping your Adaptive Server installation working at peak effectiveness. By maintaining these good practices, you can maximize server uptime, correct problems proactively, and be as prepared as possible to handle emergencies.

Outcome Action:

Adaptive Server returns a single row and the srvnetname column contains the correct reference for the Backup Server. No further action is needed Adaptive Server returns a single row but the srvnetname column does not contain the correct reference. Issue the following commands:

```
1> update sysservers
2> set srvnetname = "backup_server_name"
3> where srvname = "SYB_BACKUP"
4> go
```

where backup_server_name is the name of the Backup Server as it appears in the interfaces file. Adaptive Server returns 0 rows Issue the following command:

```
1> sp_addserver SYB_BACKUP, null,
2> backup_server_name
3> go
```

where backup_server_name is the name of the Backup Server as it appears in the interfaces file.

Keep Up-to-Date Backups

Maintaining current backups of your data is vital for any recovery plan. Keep multiple generations of backups, and keep some offsite as an extra precaution. Make regular database dumps of:

- the master database. To insure that your backup of master is always current, back up master after each maintenance command that affects disks, storage, databases, or segments—for example, after creating or deleting databases, initializing new devices, and creating or modifying segments.
- the model database
- the sybsystemprocs database
- user databases

Maintain Copies of System Tables and DDL

Keep the latest offline copies of the following tables:

- sysusages
- syslogins
- sysloginroles
- sysdatabases
- sysdevices
- syscharsets
- sysconfigures
- sysservers
- sysremotelogins
- sysresourcelimits (11.5 and later)
- systimeranges (11.5 and later)

Use the bcp utility to copy out these tables. In addition, maintain a hardcopy by printing the output of the following queries:

```
select * from sysusages order by vstart
select * from sysusages order by dbid, lstart
select * from syslogins
select * from sysloginroles
select * from sysdatabases
select * from sysdevices
select * from syscharsets
```

```
select * from sysconfigures
select * from sysservers
select * from sysremotelogins
select * from sysresourcelimits (11.5 and later)
select * from systimeranges (11.5 and later)
```

Also maintain:

- Copies of your configuration file.
- The first two blocks (2 pages) of the master device.
- A copy of the config block. You can generate this using Sybase Central or Power Designer. On UNIX platforms, you can obtain a copy of the config block with this command:

  ```
  dd if=master_device of=$SYBASE/config_block.bak
  bs=1024 count=8
  ```

- All Data Definition Language (DDL) scripts you use to create user objects and specially stored procedures if you elect to use sp_hidetext (11.5 and later).

> **NOTE:** Implement all changes to schema in the same way that the installmaster script is implemented.

Verify Database Consistency

Run dbcc checks on a regular basis to monitor the health of your databases. Database-wide checks are available with dbcc checkdb, dbcc checkalloc, and dbcc checkstorage (11.5 and higher). dbcc checkcatalog is also a useful tool. For a brief overview of dbcc commands, see the section titled "Useful dbcc Commands." Detailed information appears in the *System Administration Guide*.

Since dbcc checks can be resource intensive, consider adopting a strategy to take advantage of object level dbcc's. On a given day run a certain number of checktable and tablealloc commands for a portion of the database. On subsequent days, run different tables. Over a period of days you can accomplish a complete check of your databases for integrity. For example if your database has 200 tables in addition to the system tables, run dbcc's on the system tables on night one, run dbcc's on each of the first 50 of the user tables on night two, the next 50 the next night and so on, until at the end of five nights you have checked every table in the database. On the sixth night you can begin the cycle again.

> **NOTE:** Running table-level dbcc's misses the GAM page checks. Alternative strategies include: loading the database to another server, and running the dbcc's on that server; dbcc checkstorage (11.5 and higher).

Building dbcc checks into your regular backup/maintenance schedule can ensure that you have consistent, accurate backups available at all times.

Implement Mirroring

Mirroring, either at the Adaptive Server level or at the operating system level, can provide nonstop recovery in the event of media failure. The factors you need to consider, and instructions on implementing Adaptive Server mirroring, are detailed in the section titled "Mirroring Database Devices" in the *System Administration Guide*.

Perform Ongoing Maintenance

As part of a routine program of server maintenance, you should:

- Monitor the Adaptive Server errorlog for errors. Note that users may not report errors of severity 17 or 18 if their work is not interrupted. Set up a routine that browses the errorlog, searching for errors. See the section titled "Monitoring the System Errorlog" in Chapter 14. For information on the error log format and severity levels, see the *System Administration Guide*.

> **NOTE:** NT users can also monitor server messages by means of the Windows NT Event Log. For details, refer to *What's New in Sybase Adaptive Server Enterprise Release 11.5*.

  Prune the errorlog regularly as it grows constantly since Adaptive Server appends informational messages to the log during startup. A full errorlog with no space to write to may cause the server to freeze. Remember to shut down the server first, and make a copy of the log before pruning. An example of log pruning on UNIX follows:

```
% cp errorlog errorlog. date
% cp /dev/null errorlog
```

  where date is the current date.

- Monitor the operating system log to keep an eye on the health of the hardware and the server environment. Many Adaptive Server errors can be due to underlying hardware problems, and can therefore indicate hardware problems.
- Monitor space usage with system procedures such as sp_helpsegment, sp_spaceused, and sp_helpdb. By running sp_spaceused regularly, for example, you can determine if a database is running out of space for new objects.

  Alternatively, you can set up thresholds to monitor free space on database segments.

  See "Getting Information About Database Storage" and "Creating Threshold Procedures" in the *System Administration Guide* for details.
- On versions prior to 11.9.2, update index statistics. Distribution pages hold statistics on the distribution of index key values. As a table grows and changes, these statistics become old, and the server may start to choose the wrong index strategy for queries. You can address this condition by running update statistics periodically.

  Versions 11.9.2 and later do not utilize distribution pages; instead, they use a different mechanism for maintaining statistics. Refer to *New Functionality in Adaptive Server Enterprise 11.9.2* for details.

Avoid Risky Practices

Avoid moving tempdb off the master device. When Adaptive Server is installed, tempdb resides on the master device. Although it is possible to move tempdb off the master device later for space considerations, this is not advisable. Once tempdb is moved off the master device, it is difficult and time-consuming to recover if a problem occurs on the master device or the device to which tempdb is moved.

Never put anything other than master, model, and tempdb on the master device. Storing user databases on the master device may make it difficult to recover the system databases or user databases if either become damaged.

Recovery Tips, or What to Do When Things Go Wrong

Choose the correct recovery method. Your choice of methods will be dictated by the type of failure you encounter. For example, loss of a device will require restoring from backups. Network/machine failure usually has little impact on the server but could corrupt data in some situations, and recovery may fail.

If mirroring is enabled at your site, disable the mirror before loading a dump, thus preserving a copy of what you had before in case dumps are bad.

Never run buildmaster on the original master device. It may contain information you need later. Instead, do a buildmaster on a different device, and when your environment is completely restored, you can move back to your original master device.

Additional Tips

After an operating system upgrade, check permissions on your Sybase devices.

Online Recovery and Recovery Fault Isolation

Version 11.5 of Sybase Adaptive Server Enterprise introduced Recovery Fault Isolation (RFI) to enhance the granularity of recovery. This discussion surveys various recovery options and focuses on the difference between traditional online recovery and RFI. We use examples to show how RFI can be used to enhance the recovery scenarios and how it can help to avoid extensive downtime due to recovery problems.

Background

Recovery can mean several things:

- Online recovery is the process by which the database is brought into a consistent state after the server is restarted.
- Recovery from backups means restoring a corrupt database by loading a database dump, then applying transaction log dumps to the database to bring it back to a consistent state.
- Finally, although Adaptive Server does not offer this functionality, recovery can also refer to recovering specific objects from a dump or other offline storage and restoring only that object rather than the database as a whole. While this technique is outside the scope of the current discussion, it may be useful in some of the recovery processes outlined below.

Online Recovery Concepts and Pre-11.5 Recovery

Online recovery brings the database to a consistent state after you restart the server.

During routine Adaptive Server operation, all changes to the database are written first to the log, then to the data pages on disk. Log pages are written to disk when the transaction completes, that is, when the transaction commits. However, because all changed pages are written to disk whenever a checkpoint occurs, for other reasons prior to commit, changes can be written to the log or data pages as part of an as-yet-incomplete transaction. If the server fails after an uncommitted transaction is written to the log but before the transaction completes, online recovery reads the log and ensures that no uncommitted changes are reflected in the database. Likewise, online recovery ensures that any changes recorded in the log for committed transactions that have not yet been flushed to disk are updated on the data pages and written to disk.

Prior to version 11.5, online recovery was an all-or-nothing proposition. If recovery failed due to some corruption, there was no way to partially recover the database and leave the corrupt portion offline. The preferable option was to restore the database from backups. However, if backups were not available or time constraints made it difficult to go through the extensive procedures necessary to restore through backups, customers often used an undocumented and risky procedure, referred to as "suiciding the log," to skip recovery and get the database back online.

Recovery from Backups

The traditional recovery option, when online recovery fails, is to restore the database from dumps, and incrementally apply transaction logs to bring the restored database back to the most current possible state. This is the best solution for restoring to an absolutely consistent state after corruption. It often brings the database to a state of consistency to within seconds of the point of original failure.

However, the drawback with this traditional approach is that the recovery granularity is at the level of the transaction dump. If a transaction causing corruption is dumped, the traditional method means loading a database dump and applying transaction log dumps up to, but not including, the transaction dump containing the offending transaction. This can result in hours of lost transactions.

Suiciding the Log

While suiciding the log can usually bring the server back online, it also frequently results in both physical and logical corruption in the database, because it bypasses the normal process of rolling back incomplete transactions in the log (and rolling forward completed transactions) that take place during online recovery. Frequently, the resulting corruption is not encountered until a later time, and the connection with the earlier log suicide is not always recognized.

WARNING: Log suicide is highly risky, and is not recommended except in extreme cases.

Recovery with RFI

ASE version 11.5 implements Recovery Fault Isolation (RFI), a new online recovery feature that provides a level of granularity in recovery by means of partial recovery. RFI can isolate corruption, encountered during recovery, to the corrupt pages. This enables you to restore database integrity by isolating and repairing corruption on a page-by-page (and, consequently, on an object-by-object) basis without having to restore the entire database and transaction logs from backups.

> **NOTE:** While RFI can only define granularity at the page or database level, corruption is typically corrected at the object level with, for example, an entire index being recreated or an entire table being replaced.

Using RFI

> **NOTE:** RFI allows partial recovery only on user objects. If it encounters corruption on system tables, recovery fails for the entire database.

RFI allows the database administrator (DBA) to select the granularity of recovery for each user database. The choices are:

- Mark the whole database suspect on any recovery failure. This is the default behavior and it is how recovery worked in previous versions.
- Set the number of pages that can be offlined during recovery and still allow the database to be opened. The DBA can decide whether the partially recovered database is to be open for updates or for reads only. Finally, the DBA can set the database to be marked suspect on any recovery failure, then change the setting to recover all but the corrupt pages. In this mode, users cannot access the database, enabling the DBA to determine the appropriate course of action and proceed accordingly.

There is a significant difference between RFI's page-level and database-level granularity. Database granularity mandates that all transactions in the database should either be completed and rolled forward, or rolled back and all changes backed out. In either case the database is in a logically consistent state at the end of recovery. In short, recovery is all or nothing. Any interruption in recovery that makes this impossible causes recovery to fail entirely, and the only sure way to guarantee a consistent state is to restore from backups. This can be problematic, depending on how many backups are available, their validity, and how recent they are. Page-level granularity, on the other hand, allows the server to offline corrupt pages in a transaction while onlining other pages. Since recovery has not been able to complete and verify the transactions, this will leave some of the transactions only partially available and all other transactions completely recovered as usual. There is no way to determine whether transactions that involved offlined pages are complete except by manual examination. If, for example, a transaction changes rows on three pages and the changes on two pages are written to disk before the server stops, recovery would normally assure that the third page also was written to disk. If, however, recovery marks as suspect the page to which the third update is to be made, there is no way to determine whether the transaction is complete or incomplete; that is, whether all three pages are updated or only the first two. A transaction in this state is deemed to be partially available, as the changes to the first two pages are available while the change to the third page is unavailable, and it is not known whether it was changed.

At another level, consider a case where a page from a specific table is marked offline. Subsequent work is dependent on this page but only at an implicit level, meaning that it is assumed that business rules will be handled without explicitly coding referential checks. If the code were to explicitly check for the offline data, an errorwould be raised; but if this is not done and thework proceeds with only an implicit dependence on the offline pages (which cannot be restored to a consistent state), it may result in logical inconsistencies in the database. This is yet another reason we recommend that all dependencies between data be explicity coded via declared referential constraints, triggers or existence checks.

It is important to understand that while it is possible to bring corrupt pages online, doing so without first repairing the pages will result in logical and data inconsistency. When restoring a database by repairing offline pages (or by restoring objects to which the offlined pages belonged), therefore, the DBA must explicitly determine the degree to which logical consistency of the database may be suspect according to business rules and coding practices. Of course, restoring the database from a database backup and incremental transaction backups assures both the logical and physical integrity of the database through the last successful load of a transaction dump. It is also important to run dbcc tablealloc or dbcc indexalloc with the fix option on any objects with suspect pages because the allocation information for these objects is also suspect.

What to Do When Online Recovery Fails

The options for recovering from a failure in online recovery, in order from most desirable to least, are:

- Restoring from backups
- Partial online recovery using RFI
- Suiciding the log

Restoring from Backups

Prior to Version 11.5, this was the only option if recovery failed, the database could not be repaired, and suicide of the log was not desirable. It is still the preferred option for recovering the database after failure during online recovery if a) the entire database is marked suspect due to thresholds being exceeded, or b) system table(s) are corrupt. It is also the preferred method whenever the absolute need for physical and logical consistency overrides all other concerns.

> **NOTE** It is highly recommended that you run dbcc checks prior to and following a dump, to ensure that the backup is valid. Refer to Backup and Recovery in the *System Administration Guide* for details.

Partial Online Recovery Using RFI

Implementing RFI gives the DBA many more choices in the event of failure during online recovery. Before opting for log suicide, consider these advantages of RFI over log suicide:

1. Isolated pages are known and can be examined. You can thus make an informed decision on whether to repair the faults or restore from backups.
   - If the isolated pages belong to an index, the corruption can often be fixed by dropping and recreating the index.
   - If the isolated pages are data pages, the data can sometimes be recovered via other means. You can also leave the pages safely offline; transactions that explicitly depend on their presence will fail until they are made available.
   - Pages referenced in recovery that are marked suspect, but are subsequently deallocated further along in the recovery process, are assumed to have been properly written for the earlier transaction and are taken off the suspect list, thus making the corruption for that page "self-healing."
2. You can set thresholds to determine at what level page faults are unacceptable, and at which the whole database should remain unrecovered.
3. You can make the database available to users while conducting repairs. The database can be configured to allow updates or to allow read-only access.
4. Faults on system table pages cause recovery to fail for the entire database.
5. You can implement a limited form of suicide recovery by disregarding all or some of the suspect pages and onlining them even if they are corrupt. The suicide is limited in the sense that only transactions associated with those pages are suspect. Recovery rolls forward (or back) other transactions in the log properly.

Implementing Recovery with RFI

In Version 11.5 and higher, the default granularity of recovery remains at the database level. Take the following steps to implement page level granularity:

1. Check or implement page granularity on desired databases using the sp_setsuspect_granularity stored procedure:

   ```
   sp_setsuspect_granularity [dbname [,{"database" | "page"}
   [, "read_only"]]]
   ```

   If you set the granularity to page level, you have the option to set the database to read_only mode when recovery detects suspect pages. By default, all available pages are accessible for both reads and writes.

NOTE: Wherever possible, use the read_only mode. If a query attempts to access an offline page, the server raises error messages 12716 and 12717 regardless of whether the database is read-only.

2. Set the threshold for escalating page-level granularity to database granularity using the sp_setsuspect_threshold stored procedure:

```
sp_setsuspect_threshold [dbname [,threshold ]]
```

Once the number of offlined pages reaches this threshold value, recovery marks the entire database suspect. The default threshold value is 20 pages. It is unlikely that setting it much higher will be of much use since 20 corrupt pages is very likely to indicate corruption at a level than cannot be effectively repaired.

3. Bring the suspect pages or database on line. You can print a list of pages or databases that are suspect after recovery using the sp_listsuspect_db and sp_listsuspect_page stored procedures:

```
sp_listsuspect_db
sp_listsuspect_page [dbname]
```

You can bring these pages or database online using the sp_forceonline_db or sp_forceonline_page stored procedures:

```
sp_forceonline_db dbname
{"sa_on" | "sa_off" | "all_users"}
sp_forceonline_page dbname, pagenumber
{"sa_on" | "sa_off" | "all_users"}
```

sa_on and sa_off toggle the database or page online and offline, and allow access to the database or page only to those with the sa_role set on. This permits the DBA to examine and repair the suspect database or pages without other users being able to access them.

WARNING: The all_users option is irreversible and makes the database or page available to all users. If no repairs have been made, this may result in some level of logical inconsistency.

Suiciding the Log

The new RFI feature in 11.5 eliminates most of the need for suiciding the log. The two most common reasons for suiciding the log in the past were:

1. No backups are available or the backups are too old.
2. Insufficient time to restore.

There should never, of course, be a situation where backups are unavailable or are too old. Unfortunately, that is too often the case, either because the dumps are bad or due to poor planning. In such situations, suiciding the log may be the only recourse. Aside from those situations, however, you should never consider suiciding a viable option.

NOTE: DBAs should test all backup and restore procedures before relying on them. If you attempt to load a dump on the original database and it completes only partially, you will have eliminated the possibility of using that database again and may even have eliminated the final chance to recover data by suiciding the log.

RFI Example

Here is an example of recovery using RFI's page-level features:

During recovery of a database, five pages were marked suspect. The DBA examined the pages and determined that three of them are index pages on a single allpages-locked (APL) table, and that the other two marked suspect are data pages belonging to different tables. The database has been marked as read_only and while users can query the database, no changes can currently take place. First, the DBA onlines the pages with the sa_on option. The DBA then immediately dumps the transaction log to ensure the ability to recover to this point should something else go wrong. Recovery would involve loading a database dump and all subsequent transaction dumps. Before RFI, a dump of a suspect databasewas not possible. With RFI, the DBA can make a dump of the slightly corrupt database in case it is needed later. Often a recent dump with a few problems is preferable to an older dump with no problems. This is purely a safety measure as the DBA hopes to be able to repair the database, which is currently partly unrecovered.

Next the DBA runs dbcc indexalloc on the index containing the three offline pages. indexalloc reveals errors, and it is decided that the best thing to do is to rebuild the index. If the index was a nonclustered index, or a data-only-locked (DOL) clustered (placement) index, it could simply be dropped and recreated. However, this is an APL clustered index and any time the clustered index is suspect, the table is suspect as well. The DBA runs dbcc checktable to examine the integrity of the data pages. dbcc checktable always checks the data page linkage before checking the index structures. (Keep in mind that a DOL table's data and non-leaf index pages do not maintain sibling links that can be followed by dbcc pglinkage type of checks.) By looking at the output of dbcc checktable, the DBA determines that the data page linkage is intact. This means that it is safe to drop the clustered index.

NOTE: If the data page linkage also showed corruption, the DBA would have to resort to backups or find another way to restore the table (an offline bcp copy, for example).

Looking at the data pages for the other two objects, it is found that the first object is a static reference table, and an offline copy of this table's data exists. The DBA decides to truncate the table and bcp in a new copy. For the second object, an APL clustered table, the data page linkage is found to be broken, but the clustered index is still intact. With this information the DBA is able to locate all of the rows, bcp them out, truncate the table and bcp them back in. Once all of these tasks are complete, the question of possible incomplete logical changes to the tables due to incomplete transactions still remains. The only way to test for data integrity is to use user-written queries and reports that expose inconsistencies. After doing this, the DBA can determine if those inconsistencies can be tolerated, or repaired, or if backups are the best option. The final step is to detect and fix any allocation inconsistencies that may exist due to recovery having only partially completed. The DBA can run dbcc checkalloc to check the entire database, or dbcc tablealloc and dbcc indexalloc can be run on the suspect objects. From this example it is clear that Recovery Fault Isolation makes many more choices available to the DBA. With database-only granularity, the DBA has no way to examine the extent of the corruption and make a decision as to what the best solution to the failed recovery might be.

How to Manually Change Sort Order or Default Character Set

Follow these instructions to change the sort order or default character set for your Adaptive Server if errors occurred when you tried to use sybinit to do this. This writeup includes the following sections:

- Manual Process
- How to Load a Sort Order or Additional Character Set
- How to Change the Sort Order
- How to Change the Default Character Set
- How to Find a Sort Order File Name
- How to Find a Sort Order ID
- How to Find a Character Set ID
- How to View Your Existing Sort Order and Character Sets

Before deciding to use the manual process:

1. Read "Changing the Default Character Set, Sort Order, or Message Language" in the *System Administration Guide* for information about the consequences of changing the sort order and default character set.
2. Look at your Adaptive Server error log and in $SYBASE/init/logs (11.9.x and earlier) or $SYBASE/ASE-12_0/init/logs (12.0.x) for sybinit to determine why sybinit (or sybconfig) failed to change the sort order or default character set.
3. If you find errors in the error log, correct them. See below for common causes of failure.
4. Try again to use sybinit (or sybconfig) to change the sort order or default character set. If it still fails, see the section titled "Manual Process." Some common causes of the failure to change the sort order or default character set using sybinit (or sybconfig) include:
    - You are changing to a case-insensitive sort order and duplicates would exist in a system table (because "A" is now equal to "a", and so on). You should be able to determine which table(s) has this problem from information in the error log. Modify the data so that duplicates will not exist under a case-insensitive sort order.
    - There is insufficient system segment space to re-create system indexes. Use sp_extendsegment to increase the system segment space for user databases or use alter database to increase the size of the system segment for the master database. Refer to "Extending the Scope of Segments" and "A Segment Tutorial" in the *System Administration Guide* for details.
    - There is insufficient log space. Refer to "Using the Special dump transaction Options" in the *System Administration Guide* for what to do in this case.
    - A problem exists in sybinit (or sybconfig).

Manual Process

The manual process to change the sort order is:

1. Do the following steps first:
   Make sure the environment variable (or logical name) LANG is not defined.
   Set the environment variable (or logical name) SYBASE.
   Login to Adaptive Server and make sure the default database for user "sa" is master:

   ```
   1> select dbname, name from master..syslogins where name = "sa"
   2> go
   dbname name
   ----------- ------------------
   master sa
   ```

   Make the users aware that Adaptive Server will be going down.
2. If you do not already know the file name for the sort order you want to load, see "How to Find a Sort Order File Name."
3. Load the sort order or additional character set you want into syscharsets. Refer to "How to Load a Sort Order or Additional Character Set" for instructions.
4. Determine the value for sort order ID if you plan to change the sort order. Refer to "How to Find a Sort Order ID" for instructions.
5. Determine the value for character set ID if you plan to change the default character set. Refer to "How to Find a Character Set ID" for instructions.
6. If you planned to change the default character set, do it now. Refer to "How to Change the Default Character Set" for instructions.
7. If you planned to change the sort order, do it now. Refer to "How to Change the Sort Order" for instructions.
8. Before proceeding, make sure no one is actively using Adaptive Server.
9. Shut down Adaptive Server.
10. Restart Adaptive Server. If you changed the sort order, Adaptive Server will make a number of changes at this time. Refer to "Recovery After Reconfiguration" in the *System Administration Guide* for details about what Adaptive Server does during this database recovery. Look at the Adaptive Server error log to make sure no problems have occurred.
11. When Adaptive Server has finished the changes related to the changed sort order, it automatically shuts down.
12. Restart Adaptive Server.
13. Confirm the change by running sp_helpsort or looking at the end of the error log.

    For example:

    ```
    1> sp_helpsort
    2> go
    Sort Order Description
    ------------------------------------------------------------------
    Character Set = 1, iso_1
    ISO 8859-1 (Latin-1)—Western European 8-bit character set.
    ```

```
Sort Order = 50, bin_iso_1
Binary sort order for the ISO 8859/1 character set (iso_1).
Characters, in Order
-----------------------------------------------------------------------
! " # $ % & ' ( ) * + , - . / 0 1 2 3 4 5 6 7 8 9 : ; >> = > ?
@ A B C D E F G H I J K L M N O P Q R S T U V W X Y Z [ \ ] ^ _
` a b c d e f g h i j k l m n o p q r s t u v w x y z { | } ~
á â ã ä å æ ç è é ê ë ì í î ï d ñ ò ó ô õ ö / ø ù ú û ü y p
```

14. If the sort order did not change:
    - Use sp_configure to return to the old values for sort order ID and default character set ID as in steps 6 and 7 above.
    - Study the error log to determine why the change failed.
    - Fix the problem that caused the change to fail.
    - Try again, starting at step 6 above.
15. Refer to "If You Changed the Sort Order or Default Character Set" in the *System Administration Guide* and do the steps described there. It is very important that you do these steps to guarantee the integrity of your data.

You are now finished changing your sort order or default character set. The following procedures are referenced in this "Manual Process" section.

How to Load a Sort Order or Additional Character Set

Use one of the following commands to load a sort order or an additional character set into syscharsets where:

- sa_pwd is the "sa" password
- server_name is the name of the Adaptive Server
- sort_file is the appropriate sort order name from the charsets directory; to load a character set, use "charset.loc" for the value for sort_file
- char_set is the name of the character set you are loading

For example, to load the case-insensitive sort order for character set iso_1 on UNIX, the command is:

```
% $SYBASE/bin/charset -P sa_pwd -S server_name nocase.srt iso_1
```

For example, to load the cp850 character set on OpenVMS, the command is:

Operating System	Command
UNIX	$SYBASE/bin/charset -P sa_pwd -S server_name sort_filechar_set or $SYBASE/ASE-12_0/bin/charset ... in 12.0.x
Digital OpenVMS	charset /pass="sa_pwd" -/server="server_name" sort_file -/local=sybase_system:[sybase.charsets.char_set]
Novell NetWare	load $SYBASE/bin/charset -Psa_pwd -Sserver_name sort_filechar_set or load $SYBASE/ASE-12_0/bin/charset ... in 12.0.x
OS/2, Windows NT	$SYBASE/bin/charset -Psa_pwd -Sserver_name sort_filechar_set or $SYBASE/ASE-12_0/bin/charset ... in 12.0.x

```
$ charset /pass="sa_pwd" -
/server="server_name" charset.loc -
/local=sybase_system:[sybase.charsets.cp850]
```

How to Change the Sort Order

Use the following command to change the sort order:

```
1> sp_configure "default sortorder id", sort_order_ID
2> go
```

How to Change the Default Character Set

Use the following command to change the default character set:

```
1> sp_configure "default character set id", charset_ID
2> go
```

How to Find a Sort Order Filename

The charset command which allows you to load a sort order into syscharsets requires the specification of a sort order filename. In addition, you need to know the sort order filename to determine the sort order ID. This section describes two different methods for determining sort order filenames.

Method 1: If You Know the Sort Order Description

Use this method if you know the sort order description.

- Go to the appropriate character set directory and display the sybinit (or sybconfig) menu options for that character set's sort order files.

For example:

UNIX:

```
% cd $SYBASE/charsets/ char_set_dir
% grep menuname *.srt
```

OpenVMS:

```
$ set default -
sybase_system:[sybase.charsets. char_set_dir]
$ search *.srt menuname
```

For example, for character set iso_1 on UNIX:

```
% cd $SYBASE/charsets/iso_1

% grep menuname *.srt
binary.srt:menuname = "Binary ordering, for the ISO 8859/1
or Latin-1 character set (iso_1)."
dictionary.srt:menuname = "General purpose dictionary ordering."
espdict.srt:menuname = "Spanish dictionary ordering."
espnoac.srt:menuname = "Spanish case and accent insensitive
dictionary order."
espnocs.srt:menuname = "Spanish case insensitive dictionary order."
noaccents.srt:menuname = "Dictionary order, case insensitive,
```

```
accent insensitive."
nocase.srt:menuname = "Dictionary order, case insensitive."
nocasepref.srt:menuname = "Dictionary order,
case insensitive with preference."
```

- Identify the appropriate filename based on the menu description.

Method 2: If You Know the Sort Order ID

Use this method if you know the sort order ID.

- Go to the appropriate character set directory. For example:

  UNIX:

  ```
  % cd $SYBASE/charsets/ char_set_dir
  ```

  OpenVMS:

  ```
  $ set default -
  sybase_system:[sybase.charsets. char_set_dir]
  ```

- Using the sort order ID, determine the filename:

  UNIX:

  ```
  % grep sort_order_id *.srt | grep ID
  ```

  For example, to find sort order 52 on UNIX:

  ```
  % cd $SYBASE/charsets/iso_1
  % grep 52 *.srt | grep ID
  nocase.srt:id = 0x34 ; Unique ID # (52) for the sort order
  ```

  OpenVMS:

  ```
  $ search *.srt sort_order_id,ID /match=and
  ```

  For example, to find sort order 52 on OpenVMS:

  ```
  $ set default sybase_system:[sybase.charsets.iso_1]
  $ search *.srt 52,ID /match=and
  ******************************
  SYBASE1150_SYSTEM:[SYBASE.CHARSETS.ISO_1]NOCASE.SRT;1
  id = 0x34 ; Unique ID # (52) for the sort order
  ```

  For both of these examples, the filename for sort order ID 52 is nocase.srt.

How to Find a Sort Order ID

To find a sort order ID, search the sort order file for "ID". For example, use the following command if you want the sort order ID for "Dictionary order, case insensitive" for character set iso_1 (the sort order file name is nocase.srt):

UNIX:

```
% cd $SYBASE/charsets/iso_1
% grep ID nocase.srt
id = 0x34 ; Unique ID # (52) for the sort order
```

OpenVMS:

```
$ set default sybase_system:[sybase.charsets.iso_1]
$ search nocase.srt ID
```

```
******************************
SYBASE1150_SYSTEM:[SYBASE.CHARSETS.ISO_1]NOCASE.SRT;1
id = 0x34 ; Unique ID # (52) for the sort order
```

How to Find a Character Set ID

To find a character set ID, search the character set data file for id. For example, on a UNIX machine use the following command if you want the character set ID for character set iso_1:

```
% cd $SYBASE/charsets/iso_1
% grep id charset.loc
id = 0x01
```

How to View Your Existing Sort Order and Character Sets

Enter the following command to view the character sets and sort orders that are currently available in your Adaptive Server:

```
1> select id, csid, name, description from master..syscharsets
2> go
```

In the output:

- When csid = 0, the value of id represents the character set ID
- When csid = the character set ID (something other than 0), the value of id represents the sort order ID

  For example:

```
1> select id, csid, name, description from master..syscharsets
2> go
id csid name description
--- ---- ---------- ---------------------------------------------
0 0 ascii_8 ASCII-8 - 7-bit ASCII, with implementation-
defined characters for values 128-255.
1 0 iso_1 ISO 8859-1 (Latin-1)—Western European
8-bit character set.
50 1 bin_iso_1 Binary sort order for the ISO 8859/1
character set (iso_1).
```

In the example:

- For character set ascii_8, the character set ID is 0
- For character set iso_1, the character set ID is 1
- For sort order bin_iso_1, the character set ID is 1 and the sort order ID is 50

Useful dbcc Commands

This section provides an overviewof a number of database consistency checker (dbcc) commands described in this manual for diagnosing and troubleshooting Adaptive Server problems.

Standard dbcc Commands

The standard, supported dbcc commands used in this document are as follows:

dbcc Command	Purpose
tablealloc	Checks allocation information for the specified table.
textalloc	Checks allocation information in text pages for the specified table.
indexalloc	Checks allocation information for the specified index.
checkalloc	Runs the same checks as tablealloc for all pages in a database.
checktable	Checks the integrity of data and index pages in the specified table.
checkdb	Runs the same checks as checktable, for all tables in a database.
checkstorage	Combines some of the checks of the above commands, and provides additional checks.
checkverify	Checks faults identified by checkstorage to see if they are indeed hard errors.
reindex	Checks the integrity of indexes on user tables. prints a message when it finds the first index error and then drops/recreates the index.

For a complete description of these commands, see the *System Administration Guide*.

Other dbcc Commands

This document utilizes a number of additional dbcc commands. These commands, listed below, are useful in specific troubleshooting situations to gather information and diagnose problems. Use of dbcc page and many other undocumented dbcc commands requires that you have sybase_ts_role enabled.

> **WARNING:** These are undocumented and non-standard commands. Sybase Technical Support does not support them for general use. Although the command syntax is provided here for reference, you should use these commands only in the specific diagnostic situations described in this document, and with the specific syntax shown in those sections. Failure to do so could cause performance problems and/or database corruption.

dbcc page

Purpose: Prints the contents of a page within a database.

Usage:

```
dbcc page ( dbid, pageno,[printopt [,cache [,logical [,cachename]]]])
```

or

```
dbcc page ( dbname, pageno,[printopt [,cache [,logical [,cachename]]]])
```

```
dbid—database ID
dbname—database name
pageno—page number
printopt—output format:
0—print buffer and page header only (default)
1—print buffer and page headers, rows and
offset table
2—print buffer and page headers, hex dump
of data and offset table
```

```
cache—where to get the page:
0—read page from disk
1—read page from cache if present, otherwise
read from disk (default)
logical—the page type
0—pageno is a virtual page
1—pageno is a logical page (default)
cachename—the cache name
-1—all caches
```

dbcc pglinkage

Purpose: Checks the linkage of a page chain.

Usage:

```
dbcc pglinkage ( dbid, start_pg_num, number_pages,
printopt, search_for, search_order)
dbid—database ID
start_pg_num—page number at which
to start checking
number_pages—the number of pages to check:
0—check all pages
printopt—denotes which pages to display:
0—display only the number of
pages checked
1—display the last 16 pages checked
2—display all the page numbers checked
search_for—stop checks when this page number
is reached
search_order—direction of search:
0—follow previous page pointers
1—follow next page pointers
```

dbcc log

Purpose: Displays transaction log records.

Usage:

```
dbcc log ( dbid, objid, pageno, rowno, nrecs, type,
printopt)
dbid—database ID
objid—can be >> 0, zero, or > 0. Meaning of this
option depends on the values of 'pageno'
and/or 'rowno'. For example, if objid >0 and
'pageno' and 'rowno' = 0, all records for
that object are displayed.
pageno—page number (or 0)
rowno—row number (or 0)
nrecs—number of records and log scan direction
type—the type of log record to display
printopt—denotes display options
0—display header and data
1—display header only.
```

dbcc traceflags
(available with 11.0.3 and later)
Purpose: Shows what traceflags, if any, are currently active in the server.
Usage:

```
dbcc traceflags
```

dbcc traceon
Purpose: Activates the specified trace flag.
Usage:

```
dbcc traceon (trace_flag)
```

dbcc traceoff
Purpose: De-activates the specified trace flag.
Usage:

```
dbcc traceoff (trace_flag)
```

Summary

Common sense and a little experience will tell you where to start digging; what you find will tell you how to fix it.

Chapter 16

Tools

In addition to supporting the SQL language (with extensions), ASE makes use of a number of utilities to assist in administration. Each of these tools has a particular purpose, and each is run not from within an ASE user connection, but from the operating system prompt (or graphical desktop). In addition to the basic query editor isql (and its Java equivalent, jisql), provided tools include:

- bcp
  Bulk Copy Program; allows for OS flat files to be directly loaded into tables, or for tables (or views) to be copied to a flat file. Works in fast or slow modes.
- defncopy
  Creates script files for certain database objects directly from system table information; may also be used to read script files and quickly create objects.
- optdiag
  Reads the contents of sysstatistics and systabstats and displays the results in a formatted fashion. May be used to characterize the structure of tables and the distribution of data in columns; may also be used to manually update statistics or to load simulated statistics for query performance analysis.
- Sybase Central
  Plug-in based GUI tool for server administration; may be used to examine the structure of items in the server, or to create new structures via step-by-step "wizards."

bcp

The Bulk Copy Program, or bcp, copies data to or from a table, and from or to a flat file in a user-specified format. Aside from the obvious mass-insertion functionality, bcp is useful for transferring data from one server to another, load balancing partitioned tables, and keeping table-size "backups" without using the dump and load commands. Depending on the settings of the database and the structure of the table, a bcp execution that adds data to a table may run in either fast or slow mode. The chief difference between the modes (apart from speed) is the amount of logging performed. A slow bcp will log every row inserted, while a fast bcp will only log the allocation of new extents. While this makes for a much speedier process, it is not as recoverable in the event of interruption or failure.

To perform a fast bcp, the SA must ensure:

1. The database option "select into/bcp/pllsort" is set to true.
2. Triggers do not exist on the table (or the alter table … disable trigger command has been used to turn the triggers off).
3. Indexes do not exist on the table.

If any of these conditions are not met, the bcp will run in slow mode; bcp will apply any default values defined in the table, and rules and constraints will be ignored. Even if run in slow mode, bcp will not fire triggers. If bcp is used to copy data from a table to a file, the distinctions to fast versus slow do not apply. Note that both bcp-in and bcp-out require the appropriate permissions (insert permission for bcp-in, select permission for bcp-out).

Partial Syntax:

```
bcp [[database_name.]owner.][[table_name | view_name  [:partition_id]] {in
| out} datafile [{-c|-n}] [-b batchsize] [-F firstrow] [ -L lastrow] [-P
password][-r row_terminator] [-S server] [-t field_terminator] [-U
username]
```

Parameter	Description
table name | view name	Must have permission on the table|view (insert for bcp in, select for bcp out).
partition id	Specifies the page chain of a partitioned table to copy data into; only applicable to bcp in to a table.
in | out	The direction of the data flow, relative to the database table.
–c	ASCII character format (columns tab-delimited, rows ending in newline); transferable between platforms, and usually the easiest way to use bcp.
–n	Platform–specific native format; do not use if shifting data between machine types.
–b	Batch mode; specifies the number of rows to load in one batch before a commit. For fast bcp in, batch mode allows for some recoverability — all the rows of the completed batches will be present in the table if the bcp process is interrupted.
–F	Number of the first row of the file or table to be copied (default is first row in table/file).
–L	Number of the last row of the file or table to be copied (default is last row in table/file).
–P	Password of the login used to connect to the database.
–r	Row terminator character (comma, tab, etc.) used for the bcp process. Not needed in character mode; do not use with native mode or unpredictable results may occur.
–S	Name of the server to connect, if not the $DSQUERY server.
–t	Column terminator character (comma, tab, etc.) used for the bcp process. Not needed if character; do not use with native mode or unpredictable results may occur.
–U	Username (login) used to connect to the database.

Note that proxy tables (discussed in Chapter 13, "Remote Server Management") may map to files outside of the dataserver. Use of SELECT INTO commands could be used to create files from a table or retrieve information from a file into a table — mimicking the use of bcp, but permitting the use of search arguments or functions.

TIP: If you have massive amounts of data to import, run multiple BCP sessions into the same table at the same time, and onto separate partitions if possible.

defncopy

Certain objects in the database save their creation commands in the syscomments system table; these objects may have their definitions copied directly to script files using the defncopy utility. Alternately, the script files for these objects may be copied directly to syscomments, recreating them while bypassing the usual creation process.

Objects referable by defncopy include triggers, defaults, rules, views, and procedures. Note that defncopy may only be used on those objects that store their definitions in syscomments; this means that defncopy may not be used on tables, indexes, databases, or devices. It will be necessary to maintain scripts for these objects by other means (preferably, but keeping the original scripts used to create these objects).

Partial syntax:

```
defncopy dbname {in | out filename dbname [owner.]objectname
[[owner.]objectname...] [-P password] [-S [server]] [-U username]}
```

optdiag

The optdiag utility is used to display information associated with the sysstatistics and systabstats system tables — information such as size and structure of a table, its indexes, and the distribution of data within the columns. Additionally, optdiag may be used to change the contents of these tables (either for what-if analysis, or because the normal statistics update commands would be inconvenient). As a performance tuning tool, optdiag is invaluable but the information retrieved from optdiag can be complex, and its full use (especially when used to change system table data) is outside of the scope of this book.

Partial syntax:

```
optdiag [ binary ] [simulate ] statistics { -i input_file |
database[.owner[.[table[.column]]]] [-o output_file] } [-U user_name] [-P
password] [-S server] [-v version] [-h help] [-s] [-T flag_value]
```

Parameter	Description
simulate	The simulate flag allows for two sets of statistics to be maintained: the actual statistics, used for most queries, and the simulated statistics, used only when specifically requested. Helpful for performance analysis.
-I	Allows the SA to specify an input text file; contents of the file will be loaded into the system tables to supplement (or replace) existing statistics.
-o	Used to capture results in an output file; useful in many circumstances, but especially when manually overriding statistics. The output file may be edited to reflect the desired values and loaded with the -i flag.
-v	Displays the version of optdiag, but does not produce any results.
-s	Allows for system tables to be included in the output.
-T	Permits the use of trace flags to alter the behavior of the session; valid values are described in the documentation set.

Sybase Central

Sybase Central is a plug-in based GUI tool for the administration of servers; if the appropriate plug-in is installed, you may administer the corresponding type of server. ASE 12.5 distributes a Java-based implementation of Sybase Central (previous versions were specific to Win9x/NT), and it may be installed on any Java-capable machine.

To establish a connection to Sybase Central, select Connect from the Tools menu.

Figure 16-1

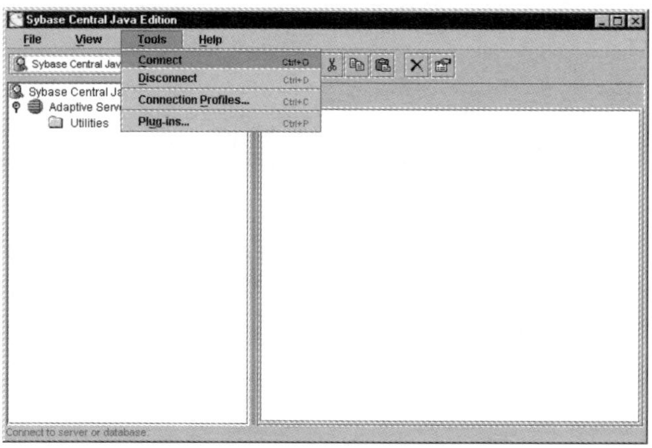

Next, specify the machine name and the port number of the server that you wish to connect to, along with login and password.

Figure 16-2

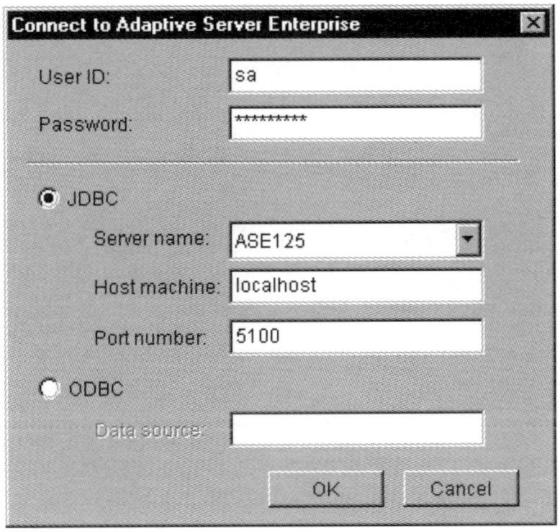

As is common in GUI programs, right-clicking with the mouse on an item in the Sybase Central window will bring up a menu of command options.

Figure 16-3

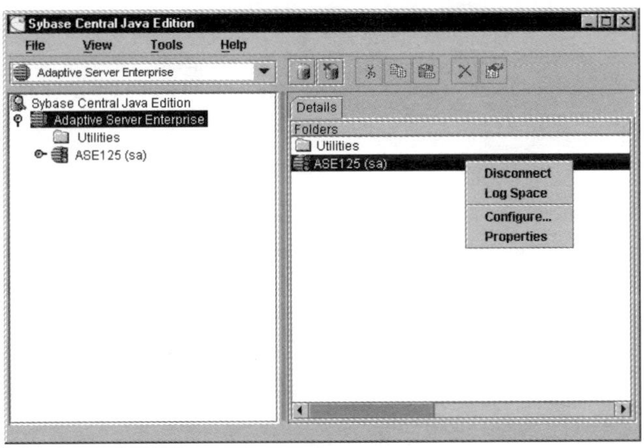

While it is potentially simpler to use Sybase Central than a regular query editor, using a script-based tool is probably preferable.

Appendix A

CSPDBA Sample Test

1. What are the default character set and sort order after installation of ASE 12.5?
2. What is the command used to determine what the current sort order and character set is?
3. What facility may optionally replace the interfaces file functionality in 12.5?
4. What is the difference between a static configuration parameter and a dynamic configuration parameter?
5. What does the command "sp_helpconfig 'number of user connections', 100" return?
6. Describe the DSLISTEN and DSQUERY environment variables.
7. List at least three pieces of information that are contained in the RUNSERVER file.
8. Name the five system databases that are used by Adaptive Server Enterprise version 12.5 and are required in order for the server to function properly.
9. Name three databases that are used by Adaptive Server Enterprise version 12.5 to increase functionality.
10. What is the sybsystemdb used for?
11. What information is stored in the interfaces file?
12. Name the graphical tool used since Sybase version 11.0 in editing the interfaces file.
13. Describe what the utility optdiag is used for.
14. JAVA classes in ASE version 12.0 can be used to define what type of database objects?
15. Give the stored procedure syntax used to estimate table and index space required for the Titles table to contain 100,000 rows.
16. Describe what can take place and some of the uses for the sp_configure procedure with the "configuration file" option.
17. High Availability Companion Server, a new feature available in ASE 12.0, is achieved by allowing what?
18. Which parameter limits the amount of memory that the server may acquire?
19. To estimate the current size of procedure cache, how would you utilize the following message written to the errorlog?

    Number of proc buffers allocated: 1635

    Number of proc headers allocated: 1680
20. Describe what a resource file is.
21. Describe the difference between the syscurconfigs and the sysconfigures tables in the master database.

22. After installation of ASE, what databases are created and initially stored on the master device?
23. Name the two different types of physical storage devices available, and which one does Sybase recommend?
24. What is the name of the automatic process responsible for periodically cleaning up memory?
25. What is the procedure used to reconfigure the Housekeeper task?
26. What type of cache, which resides in the kernel and server structures portion of memory, is used to store information on number of open databases, number of open indexes, and number of open objects?
27. Name the system table in each database where query plans are stored.
28. Name two system tables that are queried during the execution of sp_helpdevice.
29. What is the purpose of naming a default device and what is the default device used if none is named?
30. Explain the purpose of the dsync clause on the disk init command, and describe the default behavior.
31. Write the T-SQL command to create a device called data1 on the physical device /dev/data1 for a total of 10 MB. Assume the next available virtual device number is 11.
32. What syntax is used to drop a device, and what happens to the vdevno that was associated with it?
33. What happens when disk mirroring is disabled either intentionally or unintentionally?
34. What is the effect of the following commands:

```
disk mirror
      name = "data_dev1"
      physname = "New Physical device name"
disk unmirror
      name = "data_dev1"
      side = "primary"
      mode = remove
```

35. What command is used to reactivate mirroring?
36. Certain devices are more critical than others. If only certain devices could be mirrored, in which order should mirroring on these devices be enabled?
37. What steps are necessary for the master mirror to be used (if necessary) at startup?
38. Name the system tables in the master database responsible for mapping physical devices, databases, and the relationships between them, respectively.
39. What two system tables in the master database are modified when you create a new database?
40. Look at the following create database statement and explain how the database will be created:

```
eate database pubs2
```

41. To get the name, size, and owner of a database and its device fragment information, what system stored procedure would you use?

42. Look at the following create database statement and explain how the database will be created. Also, how many rows will be written to the sysusages table in the master database for the testdb database?

```
create database testdb
on data1 = 5
log on log1 = 2
```

43. Look at the following syntax and explain the difference between the two procedures.

```
sp_dboption testdb, "dbo use only", "true"
      sp_dboption testdb, "single user", "true"
```

44. What are the steps you must take to move the logsegment of a database to a new device?

45. Look at the following series of commands and explain how the database will look at the end of them:

```
create database testdb on data1 = 5
      alter database testdb on data1 = 2
      alter database testdb on data1 = 1
```

46. What is the syntax to change the owner of a database?

47. What is the effect of the system stored procedure sp_placeobject?

Questions 48 - 54 depend on the following sequence of commands:

```
disk init
              name = "data1",
             physname = "/dev/data1",
             vdevno = 11,
             size = 5120
go
disk init
             name = "data2",
              physname = "/dev/data2",
             vdevno = 12,
             size = 5120
go
disk init
             name = "log1",
             physname = "/dev/log1",
              vdevno = 13,
             size = 2560
go
create database testdb on data1 = 10
      log on log1 = 5
go
alter database testdb on data2 = 10
go
sp_addsegment seg1, testdb, data2
go
sp_dropsegment "system", testdb, data2
go
```

48. What is the total size of the database testdb?

49. What is the total size of the logsegment of the testdb database?
50. Which segments are on the data1 device?
51. Which segments are on the data2 device ?
52. What is the maximum size that seg1 can grow to?
53. What is the maximum size of the system segment?
54. If seg1 ran out of space, what series of commands do you need to run to give it additional space to grow?
55. What does the following command do?

```
alter table tableA partition 4
```

56. What is the definition of a heap table?
57. What is the system stored procedure for viewing partition information?
58. What system role is authorized to add logins and modify passwords?
59. What is the system stored procedure used to view the current login's assigned role(s)?
60. What is the effect of the -p option added to the RUNSERVER file before a server recycle?
61. What procedure can be used to view information about groups?
62. List all parameters passed to the sp_addlogin procedure and describe whether they are optional or mandatory.
63. Explain the effect of the following command:

```
grant set session authorization to user1
```

64. Who can issue the setuser command?
65. If anne was a member of the programmers group, what permissions would she have after the following commands were executed?

```
grant all on tableA to programmers
go
revoke update on tableA from anne
go
```

66. What is the effect of the following commands?

```
grant all on tableA to sam
      go
      revoke delete on tableA from sam
go
```

67. Review the following syntax and describe what permissions harry and sam have:

```
create role manager_role
go
      create role employee_role
      go
      grant select, delete on tableA to employee_role
go
      grant update, insert on tableA to manager_role
      go
```

```
grant employee_role  to manager_role
go
grant manager_role to sam
go
grant employee_role to harry
go
```

68. Describe automatic recovery.
69. When data modifications take place on pages in cache, which pages are written to disk first?
70. What is the effect of a rollback tran?
71. If a transaction was committed but not yet checkpointed and the server is recycled, would the data modification remain in the database?
72. Explain how the configuration parameter "recovery interval in minutes" affects cache.
73. What system stored procedure is used to force the order in which databases are recovered and brought online during a server recycle?
74. What dbcc command is used to check the structure of a table, and how could it be made to run faster by skipping the non-clustered index structures?
75. What is the effect of the following command?

```
dbcc tablealloc (tableA, nofix)
```

76. If a database is marked suspect, what dbcc command can be used to remove the database so it can be re-created from a backup?
77. The dbcc checkstorage command is a special dbcc command that requires the dbccdb working database, and is equivalent to what other dbcc commands?
78. Installing the dbccdb database requires several steps. Outline them.
79. What can you tell about the database dump taking place from the following command?

```
dump database testdb
      to stripe_device at backup_server_name
      stripe on stripe_device at backup_server_name
```

80. An optional parameter on the dump database command is "with [init | noinit]". Explain the difference and which of these is the default.
81. What database is the single most difficult to restore?
82. To take a backup copy of the active transaction log without truncating it, what dump command would you use?
83. To prune the active portion of the transaction log without taking a backup copy of it, what command is used?
84. Using the "with until time" parameter on the load transaction command is known as what?
85. Assume a full database backup was taken at 8 a.m. and then again at 12 p.m., and incremental transaction log dumps were taken at 9 a.m., 10 a.m., and 11 a.m. At 12:45 p.m., the system crashes and you must recover from backups. However, the full database dump file taken at 12 p.m. is corrupt. What is the latest point in time you can recover the database under this scenario?

86. From the previous question, now assume that the file from the full database backup from 12 p.m. was ok, but the file created in the 11 a.m. incremental dump was corrupt. What is the latest point in time you could recover the database to?
87. Does the dump database command prune the inactive portion of the transaction log?
88. What system table will identify the longest running transaction on a server?
89. What is the last-chance threshold and what is the system stored procedure used with it?
90. Fatal errors written to the errorlog all have severity codes higher than what?
91. Name some of the uses for the monitoring tool sp_sysmon.
92. Name the three basic types of locks that might be acquired on a row, page, or table.
93. Assume userA has an exclusive lock on pageA, but cannot complete the transaction until he can acquire a shared lock on pageB. userB, however, has an active transaction with an exclusive lock on pageB and he cannot complete until a shared lock is acquired on pageA. What is this situation called?
94. Name the three different types of locking schemes that are present in ASE 11.9.2+, and include which one of these is the installation default.
95. What type of locks are taken on index pages for DOL (Data Only Locking) scheme tables?
96. What system tables were added in 11.9.2 to manage database statistics?
97. What is a latch?
98. What system stored procedure can be used to change the default locking scheme for a server?
99. Explain the difference between a row being deleted from an APL (allpages) locking scheme table and a DOL (data only) locking scheme table.
100. What command can be used to manually collect garbage (unused space) and improve performance?
101. What type of reorg would allow you to reclaim unused space, un-forward any previously forwarded rows, and improve clustering of the placement index structure?
102. When utilizing a DOL table (data-only locking schemes), which utility should be run periodically to determine if reorg needs to be run?
103. What option can be used on the create index command of a clustered index to avoid free space fragmentation on index pages?
104. Resource limits can be set to restrict any valid login to the server from monopolizing resources, based on what three criteria?
105. What utility allows you to copy out the structure definitions of objects in the database to an operating system file?
106. What is the purpose of the -b option on the bcp utility?
107. What utility can be used to balance skewed partitions in a partitioned table?

Appendix B

CSPDBA Sample Test Answers

1. What are the default character set and sort order after installation of ASE 12.5?

   Answer: Default character set is cp850, which supports the English language, uppercase and lowercase, and any special accent characters that are used in European languages. The default sort order that goes with this character set is binary, which is the fastest of sorts when building index structures or during execution of order by clauses.

2. What is the command used to determine what the current sort order and character set is?

   Answer: sp_helpsort

3. What facility may optionally replace the interfaces file functionality in 12.5?

   Answer: LDAP (Lightweight Directory Access Protocol)

4. What is the difference between a static configuration parameter and a dynamic configuration parameter?

   Answer: When a dynamic parameter is modified, the effects take place immediately. When a static parameter is modified, the server must be rebooted for the effect to take place.

5. What does the command "sp_helpconfig 'number of user connections', 100" return?

   Answer: It returns the amount of memory that will be taken by the server if that parameter is set to that value.

6. Describe the DSLISTEN and DSQUERY environment variables.

   Answer: DSLISTEN is an environment variable set by the OS administrator and indicates which network port the server will "listen on" when commands are sent. The DSQUERY environment variable, which is also set by the OS admin, is used by the client to identify what port to connect to if no server name is specified when connecting.

7. List at least three pieces of information that are contained in the RUNSERVER file.

   Answer: the server name
   the name/location of the errorlog
   the name/location of the master device
   the name/location of the master mirror
   the name/location of the configuration file

the name/location of the interfaces file
the name of the server

8. Name the five system databases that are used by Adaptive Server Enterprise version 12.5 and are required in order for the server to function properly.

   Answer: sybsystemprocs, sybsystemdb, master, model, and tempdb

9. Name three databases that are used by Adaptive Server Enterprise version 12.5 to increase functionality.

   Answer: dbccdb, sybsecurity, and sybsyntax

10. What is the sybsystemdb used for?

    Answer: It is required for client applications implementing distributed transaction management (two-phase commit) using the SYB2PC protocol.

11. What information is stored in the interfaces file?

    Answer: The server name, protocol, and address. It also stores information such as the number of retry attempts for reconnecting after the initial connect fails, and delays (the number of seconds to wait between retries).

12. Name the graphical tool used since Sybase version 11.0 in editing the interfaces file.

    Answer: dsedit, Directory Services Editor

13. Describe what the utility optdiag is used for.

    Answer: Used to display the contents of sysstatistics and systabstats for a given database; may also be used (with some risk) to override the server's calculation of statistics.

14. JAVA classes in ASE version 12.0 can be used to define what type of database objects?

    Answer: They are used to create Java data types (for columns in tables), and may be used to invoke Java methods as user-defined functions.

15. Give the stored procedure syntax used to estimate table and index space required for the Titles table to contain 100,000 rows.

    Answer: sp_estspace titles, 100000

16. Describe what can take place and some of the uses for the sp_configure procedure with the "configuration file" option.

    Answer:
    sp_configure "configuration file", 0, write, "filename" is used to copy the original version of the configuration file to another filename.
    sp_configure "configuration file", 0, restore, "filename" is used to copy the most recent version of the configuration file to another filename.
    sp_configure "configuration file", 0, verify, "filename" is used to perform validation checking only for the configuration parameters in the filename. (Useful for validating parameters before updating the existing configuration file).
    sp_configure "configuration file", 0, read, "filename" is used to perform validation checking of configuration parameters in the filename. It then modifies any dynamic parameter values from the values in the file.

17. High Availability Companion Server, a new feature available in ASE 12.0, is achieved by allowing what?

    Answer: Two separate ASE servers can achieve HA by being allowed to communicate with the same devices.

18. Which parameter limits the amount of memory that the server may acquire?

    Answer: max server memory

19. To estimate the current size of procedure cache, how would you utilize the following message written to the errorlog?

    Number of proc buffers allocated: 1635
    Number of proc headers allocated: 1680

    Answer: ((1635 * 76) + (1680 * 2048) / 1024)
    Each proc buffer requires 76 bytes
    Each proc header requires 2048 bytes
    Divide by 1024 for number of KB

20. Describe what a resource file is.

    Answer: A resource file contains server configurations and attributes such as directory names, physical device names, and port numbers. It is created during the creation of a new ASE server. The resource file can be used to build other servers with the same or similar attributes with the use of the srvbuilders utility (sybatch on NT).

21. Describe the difference between the syscurconfigs and the sysconfigures tables in the master database.

    Answer: syscurconfigs contains the run values of configuration parameters since the last time the server was rebooted. sysconfigures contains the currently configured values of the parameters.

22. After installation of ASE, what databases are created and initially stored on the master device?

    Answer: sybsystemdb, master, model, and tempdb

23. Name the two different types of physical storage devices available, and which one does Sybase recommend?

    Answer: Raw disk partitions and operating system files. ASE previously recommended raw disk partitioned devices in prior releases. But starting with version 12.0, operating system devices are supported because we can now guarantee consistent writes for file systems (with the dsync option, not available on NT).

24. What is the name of the automatic process responsible for periodically cleaning up memory?

    Answer: The Housekeeper task. It is an automatic task that wakes up on a periodic basis and flushes dirty data pages from cache to disk, flushes new table statistics generated by data modification statements, and reclaims any unused space on Data Only Locked tables.

25. What is the procedure used to reconfigure the Housekeeper task?

    Answer: sp_configure "housekeeper free write percent", <number>. The <number> is measured in percentage in which the task can increase writes to the database. Also, sp_configure "enable housekeeper GC" allows the Housekeeper task to perform garbage collection on DOL tables.

26. What type of cache, which resides in the kernel and server structures portion of memory, is used to store information on number of open databases, number of open indexes, and number of open objects?

    Answer: Metadata cache. This type of cache is used to contain system tables related to these parameters and avoid expensive physical I/O each time this data needs to be accessed.

27. Name the system table in each database where query plans are stored.

    Answer: sysprocedures. Each query plan is stored in binary form and is equal to approximately 2 K for each row. You can determine the size of the largest query plan by running the following query:

    ```
    SELECT max(count(*)/8+1)
       FROM sysprocedures
       GROUP BY id
    ```

28. Name two system tables that are queried during the execution of sp_helpdevice.

    Answer: sysdevices and sysusages, which are both contained in the master database.

29. What is the purpose of naming a default device and what is the default device used if none is named?

    Answer: A default device is used during a create database statement if no device name is given. The master device is the default device if no other is named.

30. Explain the purpose of the dsync clause on the disk init command, and describe the default behavior.

    Answer: dsync = true means that writes are made directly to disk on UNIX file systems and nothing is buffered. This guarantees full recoverability. If no dsync value is specified, the default is set to true.

31. Write the T-SQL command to create a device called data1 on the physical device /dev/data1 for a total of 10 MB. Assume the next available virtual device number is 11.

    Answer:

    ```
    disk init
         name = "data1",
         physname = "/dev/data1",
         vdevno = 11,
         size = 5120,
         dsync = false
    ```

32. What syntax is used to drop a device, and what happens to the vdevno that was associated with it?

    Answer: The syntax to drop a device is sp_dropdevice <logical device name>. Prior to version 12.0, a reboot was required to reclaim the virtual device number but that is no longer the case.

33. What happens when disk mirroring is disabled either intentionally or unintentionally?

    Answer: I/O to the designated/faulty device is discontinued.
    A checkpoint is issued to the master database.
    An error message is written to the errorlog.
    A waitfor mirrorexit process is automatically enabled, if one exists.
    ASE continues to run normally in unmirrored mode.

34. What is the effect of the following commands:

```
disk mirror
      name = "data_dev1"
      physname = "New Physical device name"
disk unmirror
      name = "data_dev1"
      side = "primary"
      mode = remove
```

    Answer: The data is effectively moved from its current physical location to the new physical location, mirroring becomes disabled, and all new writes to disk will go to the new device.

35. What command is used to reactivate mirroring?

    Answer: disk remirror is used to resume mirroring when it has been suspended.

36. Certain devices are more critical than others. If only certain devices could be mirrored, in which order should mirroring on these devices be enabled?

    Answer: The master device, then any log devices, then any active database devices.

37. What steps are necessary for the master mirror to be used (if necessary) at startup?

    Answer: Edit the RUNSERVER file and add the -r option, which is used to specify the physical name of the mirror.

38. Name the system tables in the master database responsible for mapping physical devices, databases, and the relationships between them, respectively.

    Answer: sysdevices, sysdatabases, sysusages

39. What two system tables in the master database are modified when you create a new database?

    Answer: sysdatabases and sysusages

40. Look at the following create database statement and explain how the database will be created:

```
create database pubs2
```

    Answer: The pubs2 database will be created on the default device, using the default database size (initially 2 MB, but possibly different), populated from the model database. All three segments (system, default, and logsegment) will be created on the same device.

41. To get the name, size, and owner of a database and its device fragment information, what system stored procedure would you use?

    Answer: sp_helpdb <databasename>, from within the database in question

42. Look at the following create database statement and explain how the database will be created. Also, how many rows will be written to the sysusages table in the master database for the testdb database?

```
create database testdb
on data1 = 5
log on log1 = 2
```

    Answer: The testdb database will be created with a system and default segment on the device data1 for a total of 5 MB and a logsegment on the log1 device for a total of 2 MB. There will be two rows written to the sysusages table.

43. Look at the following syntax and explain the difference between the two procedures.

```
sp_dboption testdb, "dbo use only", "true"
      sp_dboption testdb, "single user", "true"
```

    Answer: In the first example, only the owner of the database will be allowed to use it. In the second, only one user will be allowed in the database at any given time, but it could be any user who can access the database.

44. What are the steps you must take to move the logsegment of a database to a new device?

    Answer:
    (a) Dump the log to truncate it.
    (b) Alter the database onto the new device with the "log on" syntax command.
    (c) Use the system stored procedure sp_logdevice db_name, new_device_name.

45. Look at the following series of commands and explain how the database will look at the end of them:

```
create database testdb on data1 = 5
      alter database testdb on data1 = 2
      alter database testdb on data1 = 1
```

    Answer: Initially, the database will contain a system, default, and logsegment on data1 for a total of 5 MB. The system and default segments will then be expanded onto the same device for a total of another 3 MB, first for 2MB then for 1MB. The logsegment is not expanded.

46. What is the syntax to change the owner of a database?

    Answer:

```
sp_changedbowner <new owner>
go
```

47. What is the effect of the system stored procedure sp_placeobject?

    Answer: All future allocations to the object will be written to the new device specified in the sp_placeobject procedure.

Questions 48-54 depend on the following sequence of commands:

```
disk init
              name = "data1",
                    physname = "/dev/data1",
                    vdevno = 11,
                    size = 5120
go
disk init
             name = "data2",
                     physname = "/dev/data2",
                    vdevno = 12,
                    size = 5120
go
disk init
             name = "log1",
                    physname = "/dev/log1",
                     vdevno = 13,
                    size = 2560
go
create database testdb on data1 = 10
      log on log1 = 5
go
alter database testdb on data2 = 10
go
sp_addsegment seg1, testdb, data2
go
sp_dropsegment "system", testdb, data2
go
```

48. What is the total size of the database testdb?

    Answer: The total size is 25 MB.

49. What is the total size of the logsegment of the testdb database?

    Answer: The logsegment is 5 MB.

50. Which segments are on the data1 device?

    Answer: system and default segments.

51. Which segments are on the data2 device ?

    Answer: The default and seg1 segments.

52. What is the maximum size that seg1 can grow to?

    Answer: The maximum size of seg1 could be 10 MB.

53. What is the maximum size of the system segment?

    Answer: The maximum size of the system segment can reach a total of 10 MB.

54. If seg1 ran out of space, what series of commands do you need to run to give it additional space to grow?

Answer:

```
use master
go
disk init name = "data3",   ....
go
alter database testdb on data3 = …
go
use testdb
go
sp_extendsegment seg1, testdb, data3
go
sp_dropsegment "default", testdb, data3
go
sp_dropsegment "system", testdb, data3
go
```

55. What does the following command do?

```
alter table tableA partition 4
```

    Answer: The table is partitioned into four "logical" page chains, in effect giving it four "last pages."

56. What is the definition of a heap table?

    Answer: It is a table without a clustered index.

57. What is the system stored procedure for viewing partition information?

    Answer: sp_helpartition <tablename>

58. What system role is authorized to add logins and modify passwords?

    Answer: sso_role, (System Security Officer).

59. What is the system stored procedure used to view the current login's assigned role(s)?

    Answer: sp_displaylogin

60. What is the effect of the -p option added to the RUNSERVER file before a server recycle?

    Answer: The -p<login name> option will cause the server to generate a new password for the designated login (which must have the sso_role) and write the new password to the startup connection screen.

61. What procedure can be used to view information about groups?

    Answer: sp_helpgroup

62. List all parameters passed to the sp_addlogin procedure and describe whether they are optional or mandatory.

    Answer: sp_addlogin
    loginname – mandatory
    password – mandatory
    defdb – optional
    deflanguage – optional
    fullname – optional

passwdexpiration – optional
minpwdlen – optional
maxfailedlogins – optional

63. Explain the effect of the following command:

```
grant set session authorization to user1
```

Answer: user1 is now authorized to assume the identity of any valid user in any database on the server.

64. Who can issue the setuser command?

Answer: dbo and any user who has been granted proxy authorization.

65. If anne was a member of the programmers group, what permissions would she have after the following commands were executed?

```
grant all on tableA to programmers
go
revoke update on tableA from anne
go
```

Answer: anne would have insert, delete, select, and references permissions on tableA.

66. What is the effect of the following commands?

```
grant all on tableA to sam
      go
      revoke delete on tableA from sam
go
```

Answer: sam has all permissions on tableA except delete. (This might be used in a system where an audit trail is required.)

67. Review the following syntax and describe what permissions harry and sam have:

```
 create role manager_role
go
      create role employee_role
      go
      grant select, delete on tableA to employee_role
go
      grant update, insert on tableA to manager_role
      go
      grant employee_role  to manager_role
      go
      grant manager_role to sam
      go
      grant employee_role to harry
      go
```

Answer: harry may select and delete from tableA while sam may select, delete, update, and insert to the same table.

68. Describe automatic recovery.

    Answer: Whenever the server is recycled, ASE reconciles each database against its log; if there is a discrepancy between the two as to what data should exist in the database, the log wins. If a database does not complete recovery, it is in an offline state and not available for use.

69. When data modifications take place on pages in cache, which pages are written to disk first?

    Answer: Log pages are always written before their associated data pages.

70. What is the effect of a rollback tran?

    Answer: All data modifications within the current transaction are rolled back.

71. If a transaction was committed but not yet checkpointed and the server is recycled, would the data modification remain in the database?

    Answer: Yes. The transaction log would be used to roll forward and redo the data modification. Once a transaction is committed, it can no longer be rolled back.

72. Explain how the configuration parameter "recovery interval in minutes" affects cache.

    Answer: Whenever the value in recovery interval is met in a given database, a checkpoint is issued. This causes dirty data and log pages to be flushed from cache to disk.

73. What system stored procedure is used to force the order in which databases are recovered and brought online during a server recycle?

    Answer: sp_dbrecovery_order

74. What dbcc command is used to check the structure of a table, and how could it be made to run faster by skipping the non-clustered index structures?

    Answer: dbcc checktable (tableA, skip_ncindex)

75. What is the effect of the following command?

    ```
    dbcc tablealloc (tableA, nofix)
    ```

    Answer: This command will report (but not fix) any allocation errors on tableA.

76. If a database is marked suspect, what dbcc command can be used to remove the database so it can be re-created from a backup?

    Answer: dbcc dbrepair (<dbname>, dropdb)

77. The dbcc checkstorage command is a special dbcc command that requires the dbccdb working database, and is equivalent to what other dbcc commands?

    Answer:

    ```
    dbcc checkdb (with skip_ncindex)
                  dbcc checkalloc
    ```

78. Installing the dbccdb database requires several steps. Outline them.

    Answer:
    Step 1: Plan for the necessary resources using the system stored procedure sp_dbcc_plandb.
    Step 2: Install the dbccdb database using create database and the installdbccdb script.
    Step 3: Create a named cache and configure for large I/O (16 K buffer pool size) using

sp_cacheconfig, sp_poolconfig, and sp_bindcache.
Step 4: Add workspace segments which will be utilized by dbcc checkstorage using the sp_addsegment command (optional).
Step 5: Create the workspaces using the sp_dbcc_createws system stored procedure.
Step 6: Configure for parallel processing using sp_configure number of worker processes and sp_configure max parallel degree (if necessary).
Step 7: Specify worker process and the size of workspaces and named caches to use using the system stored procedure sp_updateconfig.

79. What can you tell about the database dump taking place from the following command?

```
dump database testdb
     to stripe_device at backup_server_name
     stripe on stripe_device at backup_server_name
```

Answer: The database is being backed up onto a "remote" backup server (at backup_server) and is being striped across two devices at that server.

80. An optional parameter on the dump database command is with [init | noinit]. Explain the difference and which of these is the default.

Answer: The with init parameter will cause the tape mounted to the backup server to reinitialize (rewind) itself back to the beginning of the tape before the dump, and overwrite whatever information is currently on the tape device. The default is with noinit.

81. What database is the single most difficult to restore?

Answer: master is the most stressful by far.

82. To take a backup copy of the active transaction log without truncating it, what dump command would you use?

Answer:

```
dump tran <dbname> to backup_device with no_truncate
```

83. To prune the active portion of the transaction log without taking a backup copy of it, what command is used?

Answer:

```
dump tran <dbname> with no_log
```

or

```
dump tran <dbname> with truncate_only
```

84. Using the with until time parameter on the load transaction command is known as what?

Answer: It is known as point-in-time recovery and can be utilized to recover the transaction log up to a point in time with a resolution of plus or minus 3 milliseconds.

85. Assume a full database backup was taken at 8 a.m. and then again at 12 p.m., and incremental transaction log dumps were taken at 9 a.m., 10 a.m. and 11 a.m.. At 12:45 p.m., the system crashes and you must recover from backups. However, the full database dump file taken at 12 p.m. is corrupt. What is the latest point in time you can recover the database under this scenario?

Answer: 11 a.m. You would load the database with the full backup from 8 a.m., and then load each incremental transaction log backup—9 a.m., 10 a.m. and 11 a.m.

86. From the previous question, now assume that the file from the full database backup from 12 p.m. was okay, but the file created in the 11:00 a.m. incremental dump was corrupt. What is the latest point in time you could recover the database to?

    Answer: 12 p.m. You would simply load the database dump taken at 12 p.m.

87. Does the dump database command prune the inactive portion of the transaction log?

    Answer: No. Only the dump tran [transaction] command will prune the log.

88. What system table will identify the longest running transaction on a server?

    Answer: syslogshold

89. What is the last-chance threshold and what is the system stored procedure used with it?

    Answer: The last-chance threshold, or LCT, represents the suspend point in a transaction log; if the log fills up to the point of the LCT, all changes in the database will be suspended until space is made available in the log. The LCT calls the system stored procedure sp_thresholdaction if it exists (it is the responsibility of the SA or DBO to create sp_thresholdaction).

90. Fatal errors written to the errorlog all have severity codes higher than what?

    Answer: Only severity codes higher than 18 are considered fatal errors.

91. Name some of the uses for the monitoring tool sp_sysmon.

    Answer: sp_sysmon is a system stored procedure that can be used to monitor the server's performance. It is used to take a snapshot of the server activity for a specific period of time. It should be used to monitor the server when performance is sluggish, as well as a benchmarking tool for before and after tuning activities take place.

92. Name the three basic types of locks that might be acquired on a row, page, or table.

    Answer:
    Shared lock – acquired during a select
    Exclusive lock – acquired during an insert and during some updates and deletes
    Update lock – acquired during some updates and deletes

93. Assume userA has an exclusive lock on pageA, but cannot complete the transaction until he can acquire a shared lock on pageB. userB, however, has an active transaction with an exclusive lock on pageB and he cannot complete until a shared lock is acquired on pageA. What is this situation called?

    Answer: Deadlock. In this case the server will choose one of the transactions as the deadlock victim and it will be terminated. The application will receive an error 1205.

94. Name the three different types of locking schemes that are present in ASE 11.9.2+, and indicate which one of these is the installation default.

Answer:
(APL) All Pages Locking – default
(DPL) Datapages Locking
(DRL) Datarows Locking

95. What type of locks are taken on index pages for DOL (Data Only Locking) scheme tables?

    Answer: No transaction locks are taken on the index pages of DOL tables. A short-duration structure known as a Nested Top-Level Action (or a latch) is taken on these pages.

96. What system tables were added in 11.9.2 to manage database statistics?

    Answer: sysstatistics and systabstats

97. What is a latch?

    Answer: A latch is a mechanism used by ASE on index pages of DOL table (datapage or datarow locking schemes) which guarantees consistency by allowing only a single process access to an index page at any point in time. However, unlike locks, which are held until the end of the transaction, a latch is removed immediately after the modification is complete.

98. What system stored procedure can be used to change the default locking scheme for a server?

    Answer: sp_configure "lock scheme", 0, [allpages | datapages | datarows]

99. Explain the difference between a row being deleted from an APL (allpages) locking scheme table and a DOL (data only) locking scheme table.

    Answer: When a row is deleted from an APL table, the remaining rows are moved up and free space is kept in a contiguous block at the end of the page. When a row is deleted from a DOL table, the row is marked as logically deleted and the space becomes "garbage." The free space on the page becomes fragmented.

100. What command can be used to manually collect garbage (unused space) and improve performance?

     Answer: The reorg command.

101. What type of reorg would allow you to reclaim unused space, un-forward any previously forwarded rows, and improve clustering of the placement index structure?

     Answer: reorg rebuild

102. When utilizing a DOL table (data-only locking schemes), which utility should be run periodically to determine if reorg needs to be run?

     Answer: The optdiag utility can be run to look for low cluster ratios in clustered index structures, and large numbers of forwarded or deleted rows in a table.

103. What option can be used on the create index command of a clustered index to avoid free space fragmentation on index pages?

     Answer: You may create the clustered index with the "with fillfactor = percent" parameter.

104. Resource limits can be set to restrict any valid login to the server from monopolizing resources, based on what three criteria?

Answer:
io_cost
row_count
elapsed_time

105. What utility allows you to copy out the structure definitions of objects in the database to an operating system file?

    Answer: defncopy

106. What is the purpose of the –b option on the bcp utility?

    Answer: It is used with a number of rows to specify batch size. This is good to use when bulk copying extremely large tables to avoid the server running out of locks.

107. What utility can be used to balance skewed partitions in a partitioned table?

    Answer: The bcp utility can be used to balance partitions by specifying first and last rows in a bulk copy file, and the partition number in which to copy them into.

Appendix C

Tips

A special thanks to all those who sent in tips:
John Bidwell
Todd Boss
Philip Brantley
Wayne O. Estep
Robert Fenstermacher
Simon Fixter
Tony Prusa *
Ravinder Singh
Malathy Sundaram
Peter Toivonen
Angel Tyrone
* Sent in over half of the material for this appendix!

Backing Up UNIX Systems

1. Automate running dumps and dbcc utilities with daily crons and e-mail the results to yourself. This gives the DBA assurance that the dbcc output shows no errors and the dumps completed successfully.
2. When making dumps use a date variable to add to the name of the dump, and when all the dumps are complete, use the tar command to combine them into one file and then compress that file. This saves about 50% of the space needed to store dumps.
3. Use a cron to search your dump directory and remove old dump files depending on the number of days you want to store. This method assures the DBA the HD slice will not fill up and dumps will proceed normally.

Deadlocking

The deadlock checking period configuration option should be used very wisely, because deadlock checking is a time consuming process. It also puts an overhead for applications that experiences no or very minimal deadlock. In the sp_sysmon report, if deadlock searches has a low value and searches skipped wasn't significant enough, then slightly increase the deadlock checking period in the configuration parameter. If searches skipped had a very low or no value, and the deadlock searches find very few, then increase the deadlock checking period by a large value. This is only to avoid unnecessary deadlock checks to the application if that is not required.

Default Database

Make the default database of all logins (except SAs) tempdb. All servers have a tempdb database. It avoids users accidentally "doing things" in the master database. This makes migrating logins between servers easier since all servers have a tempdb.

Loading Production Databases

When loading production databases into a development environment (for example, where the development users are different from those in production), I always use "select into" on sysusers and sysalternates to create tables in tempdb prior to beginning the load. Then I truncate sysusers and sysalternates and insert the rows back from tempdb post-load.

Performance Tuning

Performance tuning is a constant and recurring activity, even more so with today's ever-changing development life cycle. Changes that used to take months or even years to get rolled out to production now take weeks or sometimes days.

Standards

Don't let your developers freely develop or implement SQL standards on the fly. Know the optimizer and development coding standards that will allow you and the optimizer to pick the most effective plan. Stick to those standards; developers are going to resist, but when you have 2,000 stored procedures to review and maintain, you do not want to have to re-edit each one just to review it.

Review

Implement a development and review process for your developers. You will get minimal argument from management for augmenting the development process to include a step for quality assurance that will be used in your production environment.

Process

Have a roll-out process: development, staging, production. Changes to the queries, as well as changes to the server configuration, should go through the same process. One of the things I considered a year ago was parallelism. We configured and tested in our development environment, and then in our staging environment. We did see some gains and all looked good, so we rolled it out to production over a weekend during some scheduled downtime. Come Monday morning all heck broke loose. The one thing that our development and staging environment could not emulate was the concurrent activity of 700 online users. The parallelism had a negative impact on the application and on the system.

Tune

ASE has come a long way in 10+ years. There are things we can configure to allow the server to perform optimally. Memory is always key: the more the better. Larger buffer pools can have a positive impact. At a minimum, set up the 4 K pool for the logs. The key thing here is to do your homework. Read the *Performance and Tuning Guide*, and anything else you can get your hands on regarding performance tuning (watch for e-mails on the Sybase list server from Eric Miner, Jim Egan, Jeff Garbus, and others…). The Sybase list constantly has discussion threads regarding the performance issues and tweaking that can be done. Know what you are going to tweak, what it's going to impact, why it is going to add value to your system and your applications, and what the users expect to see from the change.

Free DB

The ASE can be tuned and tweaked, and all the users' code can be reviewed and tuned optimally, but if you cannot get any CPU time, then all of it is for naught. Be sure to work with your hardware administrator to make sure that your box is tuned optimally and that you are getting as many CPU cycles as you can. If you have web access to your dataserver, make sure you have a separate box for your web server or your dataserver hardware is appropriately sized to handle the load of both the dataserver and the web server.

Analysis

Always perform recurring performance and tuning analysis. Take the time periodically to go back and look at your system. If you have multiple systems (as most of us do), go through round-robin and peek at your systems to see how they are doing. In my case, I use a significant amount of stored procedures for data access. I utilize the stored procedure monitor within Monitor Server and I take a look at the top 50 by logical I/Os. I have found over time (and observation) a number that I use to measure what is normal and what is offensive. If I find a stored procedure that appears to be doing more I/O than I expect, we go through and do performance and tuning on the procedure to see why the I/O or performance model has changed. Sometimes it leads nowhere, but more often we have found that the data volume has changed, or the actual implementation of a code set has skewed to make the index useless.

Historical Server

- Historical Server can add value. I recently went through an exercise creating execution classes for each of my application user groups. I was able to do this dynamically and programmatically for 95% of my users. Each of these execution classes gets the same access to engines and priority as if they logged in without it (or the equivalent of EC2 on your default server, any engine, medium priority). I took the time and defined other execution classes and bindings for the other 5% so that now I have all the programs/users defined to an execution class.

  Now with a very simple view in Historical Server I can track and measure the usage of my applications, the groups within the application, and do some measure of capacity planning.

  ```
  hs_create_view appl_sum
  ,"Application Name"                ,"Value for Sample"
  ,"Application Execution Class"     ,"Value for Sample"
  ,"CPU Time"                        ,"Value for Sample"
  ```

  This has also been beneficial in identifying those applications/users that have been very offensive. Which brings me back to the recurring performance and tuning check. What was running good a year ago may not be running as well now that the volume of data has increased 2000%. I had to configure the ASE to support the Monitor Server and this Historical Server view. I configured number of event buffers per engine to 150,000 (significantly higher than default) and I configured the Historical to two times its default settings in the configure file (there are only four items in the file).
- Each server we install is different. The applications that are going to run on that server are most likely going to be different then the last one we installed and configured, and how the users use that application will be different.
- Knowledge is power when it comes to performance and tuning. Know what can be tweaked at the server level, and how it will impact both the system and the application. Know the application, how it accesses and manipulates the data, and what the volume of users (if applicable) will do to the application and contention. Know your users and how they will use/abuse the application.
- Read the manuals *System Administration*, *Performance and Tuning*, and *Troubleshooting*. Know your server!

Tuning

- When running sp_sysmon for performance monitoring there is one thing we need to remember: Since both sp_sysmon and SQL Monitor rely on dbcc monitor, avoid running both at the same time because when running Historical Server, the monitoring routines can interfere with each other. Therefore sp_sysmon can be run to do the "spot checking" of the machine and Historical Server SQL Monitor can be used to check the "trend in the CPU utilization."
- One of the things that makes my job easier is dbschema.pl (a tool developed by Michael Peppler and David Owen — see http://www.isug.com/Sybase FAQ/ASE/section9.html.) dbschema.pl is a DDL reverse engineering tool for ASE. It runs under UNIX/Linux or NT. I run it in two different modes to back up all of the tables, triggers, procs, and views (everything that is DDL) on all of my servers.

  Create a DDL directory, and under that create a subdirectory for each server, as follows:

  ```
  \opt\sybase\DDL\PROD
  \opt\sybase\DDL\DEV
  ```

  Then run dbschema.pl nightly in two modes for each server.

  ```
  dbschema.pl -A -m -O1 -Usa -SSERVER -Ppassword
  ```

  and

  ```
  dbschema.pl -A -m -O2 -Usa -SSERVER -Ppassword
  ```

  Parameters:

  -A
  : Selects all databases to be extracted.

  -m
  : Creates the server disk inits and create database statements.

  -O1
  : Puts all of the SQL into one file per object type (tables, procs, triggers).

  -O2
  : Puts the SQL in one file per object and puts each object type into a subdirectory.

So, we wind up with a directory for each server that contains the DDL to do disk inits/create databases, and then a subdirectory for each database that contains DDL for procs, tables, views, users, etc.

This comes in really handy when a developer comes to you and says that they blew away a stored proc or something that they were working on. This also comes in handy for reapplying users/groups/aliases when dumping and loading databases across servers where the logins do not match (such as development versus production).

The scripts also help in speeding disaster recovery or if you need to rebuild a server because most of the scripts that you would need are created for you.

Just create the server, run the disk inits, bcp in the syslogins, run the create database scripts (for load), load your dumps and reapply the users, groups, and aliases.

However, dbschema.pl can't help you if you don't have backups.

Monitoring

- Simple monitoring stored procedure

```
use sybsystemprocs
go
if object_id("sp_upsall") is not null
begin
drop proc sp_upsall
end
go
create procedure sp_upsall as
declare @length int, @usedb smallint, @usename varchar(30),
@lockcount int, @user_dbname varchar(30)
declare db_cur cursor for
select name
from master..sysdatabases
where dbid not in (1, 3)
order by dbid
for read only
set nocount on
open db_cur
fetch db_cur into @user_dbname
while @@sqlstatus = 0
begin
/*
**
** Get the id of the current database.
**
*/
select @usedb = db_id(@user_dbname)
select @usename = rtrim(@user_dbname)
select @lockcount = count(dbid)
from master.dbo.syslocks
where master.dbo.syslocks.dbid = @usedb
if ( @lockcount != 0 )
begin
/*
**
** show all the process info for the default database.
**
*/
print
"----------------------------------------------------------------------------"
print "                        Processes in the %1! database",@usename
print"---------------------------------------------------------------------------"
select spid =
convert(char(4), master.dbo.sysprocesses.spid),
fid = convert(char(4),
```

```
master.dbo.sysprocesses.fid),
table_name = convert(char(16),
object_name(master.dbo.syslocks.id,@usedb)),
page = convert(char(10),page),
program=convert(char(8),program_name),
trans= convert(char(12),tran_name),
blk=convert(char(3),blocked),
blk_time = convert(char(6),
master.dbo.sysprocesses.time_blocked),
line = convert(char(5),
master.dbo.sysprocesses.linenum)
from    master.dbo.syslocks, master.dbo.spt_values,
master.dbo.syslogins, master.dbo.sysprocesses
where master.dbo.syslocks.type =
master.dbo.spt_values.number
and     master.dbo.sysprocesses.suid =
master.dbo.syslogins.suid
and     master.dbo.spt_values.type = "L"
and     master.dbo.syslocks.spid =
master.dbo.sysprocesses.spid
--      and master.dbo.sysprocesses.spid =
--      master.dbo.sysprocesses.fid
and     master.dbo.syslocks.dbid = @usedb
union
select spid=convert(char(4),spid),
fid=convert(char(4),fid),
table_name="--Locked--" ,
page="--Locked--",
program=convert(char(8), program_name),
trans=convert(char(12), tran_name),
blk=convert(char(3), blocked),
blktime=convert(char(6), time_blocked),
line = convert(char(5), linenum)
from master.dbo.sysprocesses
where blocked>0
order by spid, table_name, program, page
end
fetch db_cur into
@user_dbname
end
close db_cur
deallocate cursor db_cur
go
```

- If you are not real-time monitoring your system with Monitor Server, start! When performance starts going downhill, no matter the reason, the first place most people go is to the DBA and state that database performance is less than optimal. If you cannot, at a minimum, visibly observe the performance of your system, you have no grounds with which to state otherwise. Capture those statistics and trend your usage — management loves reports. Okay, that's a bit extreme, but the message is, "Be able to state and document your performance."

Monday is report day in my shop, and Tuesday is high user day, which means CPU utilization at 10 a.m. is approximately 80%.

- Use sp_sysmon; it is a great tool. I pull this one out of the toolbox only when I have detailed issues I want to address. Sybase has taken the time to document this better over the years as well.
- sp_objectstats is another great tool. Contention on objects is perceived as negative performance by the end user. The process may only take a second but if it takes 45 seconds to obtain a lock because of a blocked object then the user perceives almost a minute of wait time.

Unique Users by Database

Problem Description

We don't know who is using our databases. Which databases are routinely used vs. periodically used? What data is being heavily served off of our data server? Who should be paying and how much for this database service we're offering? What are the trends in the past, of database usage? How many of these users are actual users and how many are developers?

Requirements Derived

- Maintain a log of users and developers for each database.
- Build a report suitable for management.
- Make it versatile, so that trends by date or database can be done.
- Make it run frequently during the day and a few times at night.
- Keep track of the user counts, but not the individual names.

Behind the Scenes

Developers should have the text ", developer" in the fullname field of the syslogins table. An example of this would be "Tony Prusa, developer". The program uses this text to differentiate between garden-variety users and developers. Developers in one realm are considered to be developers everywhere.

The program is run as part of a sybase-user cron at 21 minutes after the hour between 5:21 and 18:21. Other than that, it's also run at 2:21, 20:21, and 22:21.

Only unique DB+user name combinations are counted. If user "prusa" has five connections to the same database, he's only counted once. This was specifically requested to prevent counting users with a connection for each instance of the application running. Hence, this is not a good tool to determine total user connections.

Running the Script

```
cd $SYBASE/sysadm/cronscripts
./users_by_db.csh [user name] [password] [VERBOSE (optional)]
```

Log File

Sybase logs directory. This file is added to whenever the program is run via interactive use or cron execution.

```
$SYBASE/log/Users_by_db.log
```

Shell script: users_by_db.csh

```
#!/bin/csh
#
##########################################################################
#
# FILENAME:
#   users_by_db.csh
#
# PURPOSE:
#   Shell script to count users by database
#
# STANDARDS VIOLATIONS: None
#
# PARAMETERS:
#      $1 = SERVER (optional, no entry means $DSQUERY)
#      $2 = PASSWORD (optional, no entry means look in pw file)
#      $3 = VERBOSE  ("ON" turns this on)
#
# DEPENDENCIES:
#      Requires $SYBASE to be defined,
#      If $1 is not supplied, $DSQUERY env var must be.
#      If $2 is not supplied, file /sybase/sysadm/.pw.(servername) is
#         assumed to exist
#      Uses stuff only available in Sybase SQL Server System 10 and 11
#
# SCCS VERSION: @(#)users_by_db.csh     1.2 01/28/00
#
# REVISION HISTORY:
# DATE:        AUTHOR:     CHANGE ID:         DESCRIPTION:
# 06/04/98     Tony Prusa  1.1                New
# 01/28/00     Tony Prusa  1.2                isql password visible.
#                                             added spacing to make it
#                                             invisible to 'ps' command.
#
##########################################################################
#
# Get server
#  - if user inputs nothing, give it $DSQUERY
#  - if user types HELP, give them a usage message
#  - if they give us a $1 parm, use it as the server name
#
if ( "$1" == "" ) then
   set server=$DSQUERY
else if ( "$1" == "?" || "$1" == "help" || "$1" == "HELP" ) then
   echo Usage\: $0 \[server\] \[sa password\] \[Verbose\]
   echo \ \ \ \ \ \ \(defaults\: $DSQUERY\, Password File\, OFF\)
   exit 0
```

```
else
   set server=$1
endif
#
# Get password:

#  - if user supplies $2, use it as the password
#  - if not, get the password from the password file for that server
#      ( assumes read permission on that file )
#
if ( "$2" == "" ) then
   if ( -f /sybase/sysadm/.pw.$server ) then
      set passwd="'cat /sybase/sysadm/.pw.$server'"
   else
      set passwd="'cat /opt/sybase/sysadm/.pw.$server'"
   endif
else
   set passwd=$2
endif

#
# Get verbose:
#  - if not supplied, OFF
#  - if = "ON", "on", "Verbose", "VERBOSE", "verbose", "V", or "v"
#
if ( "$3" == "" ) then
   set vbose="off"
else
   if ( "$3" == "ON" || "$3" == "on" || "$3" == "Verbose" || \
        "$3" == "VERBOSE" || "$3" == "verbose" || "$3" == "V" || \
        "$3" == "v" ) then
      set vbose="on"
      echo "verbose on"
   else
      set vbose="off"
   endif
endif

#
# script-wide variables
#
set out_file="/opt/sybase/log/users_by_db.out"
set this_out="/tmp/users_by_db.out"
set working_dir="/opt/sybase/sysadm/cronscripts"
if ( ! -f $this_out ) then
   touch $out_file
endif
if ( -f $this_out ) then
   /bin/rm -f $this_out
endif
$SYBASE/bin/isql -Usa -S $DSQUERY \
   -w 0000000000000000000000000000000000000000000000000000000999 \
   -P$passwd -i $working_dir/users_by_db.isql -o $this_out
```

```
if ( -f $this_out ) then
   cat $this_out >> $out_file
endif
if ( "$vbose" == "on" ) then
   cat $this_out
endif
```

ISQL Script: users_by_db.isql

```
/*++ users_by_db.isql
 ***********************************************************************
 *
 *  ENTERPRISE DATABASE:  DBA
 *
 *  SUBJECT AREA:  DBA
 *
 *  PURPOSE:
 *    This script creates a report showing who is logged in to the
 *    various databases. Broken down by developer / non-developer
 *
 *  STANDARDS VIOLATIONS:  none
 *
 *  DEPENDENCIES:
 *    Tested only for System 11.
 *
 *  SCCS VERSION:  @(#)users_by_db.isql     1.3 07/06/98
 *
 *  REVISION HISTORY:
 *    DATE:     AUTHOR:         CHANGE ID:      DESCRIPTION:
 *    --------- --------------- --------------- -----------------------
 *    6/4/98    Tony Prusa      New             New program
 *    6/7/98    Tony Prusa      1.2             Totals line checks for
 *                                              null and reports zero.
 *    7/6/98    Tony Prusa      1.3             added date to every
 *                                              detail line
 *
 ***********************************************************************
 --*/
set nocount on
go
/* create table in tempdb, so we don't leave trash everywhere */
use tempdb
go
/* get rid of table if it already exists */
if exists (select "X" from sysobjects where type = "U" and name =
"dbusers")
begin
   drop table tempdb..dbusers
end
go
/* now, create it again */
create table tempdb..dbusers (dbid int NULL, total int null,
   developers int null)
go
```

```
/* need an unique index so that the cursor can walk through this table */
/* later on */
create unique index db_ndx1 on tempdb..dbusers  (dbid)
go
/* let's get dbs with users and databases in use */
/* Note that this thing doesn't count usage of "supporting */
/* databases, like common, or report, as users never really */
/* change their focus from their "working" database. */
insert tempdb..dbusers (dbid,total)
select p.dbid,count(distinct p.suid)
from master..sysprocesses p
where p.suid != 0 and
      p.dbid not in (select dbid from master..sysdatabases
                           where name in
                           ("master", "model", "pubs2", "tempdb",
                            "sybsecurity", "sybsyntax")
                     )
group by p.dbid
go
/* let's get a cursor to fill in the number of developers using these */
/* databases */
declare update_developers cursor for
select dbid from tempdb..dbusers
for update of developers
go
open update_developers
go
declare @current_dbid int, @counted_num int
fetch update_developers into @current_dbid
/* count the number of developers for each database in dbusers table */
while (@@sqlstatus = 0 and @@error = 0)
begin
   /* kind of complicated, but this is the number of users           */
   /* We don't care about the usual databases                        */
   /* The list of developers is determined by the word ", Developer" */
   /* in their syslogins entry, as part of their fullname field      */

   select @counted_num = count(distinct p.suid)
     from master..sysprocesses p
    where p.suid != 0 and
         p.dbid not in (select dbid
                        from master..sysdatabases
                        where name in
                                    ("master", "model", "pubs2",
                                     "tempdb", "sybsecurity",
                                     "sybsyntax")
                         ) and
         p.suid in (select suid
                    from master..syslogins
                    where upper(fullname) like "%, DEVELOPER%"
                   ) and
         p.dbid = @current_dbid
   /* update the number of developers for this db */
```

```
   update tempdb..dbusers
      set developers = @counted_num
    where current of update_developers
   /* go on to the next database */
   fetch update_developers into @current_dbid
end
go
close update_developers
go
deallocate cursor update_developers
go
/* Done getting info, report out results */
select convert (varchar(20), getdate(), 0) + "   Counts of Users by
Database"
print ''
select name       = substring(d.name,1,18),
       date       = convert (varchar(20), getdate(), 0),
       total      = u.total,
       developers= u.developers,
       users      = u.total-u.developers
  from master..sysdatabases d,
       tempdb..dbusers u
 where d.dbid = u.dbid
go
select " ** TOTALS **       "+
       convert(char(20), getdate(), 100 ),
       isnull(sum(u.total),0), isnull(sum(u.developers),0),
       isnull(sum(u.total-u.developers),0)
  from master..sysdatabases d, tempdb..dbusers u
 where d.dbid = u.dbid
go
drop table tempdb..dbusers
go
```

Sample Output

```
--------------------------------------------------
Jan  28 2000 09:21AM   Counts of Users by Database
name            date                      total    developers     users
----            ----                      -----    ----------     -----
procurement     Jan 28 2000  9:21AM         26          4           22
templar         Jan 28 2000  9:21AM          1          0            1
webgroup        Jan 28 2000  9:21AM         12         10            2
edie            Jan 28 2000  9:21AM          2          0            2
iso9001         Jan 28 2000  9:21AM          8          2            6
nren            Jan 28 2000  9:21AM          6          0            6
bizRules        Jan 28 2000  9:21AM          2          0            2
odin            Jan 28 2000  9:21AM         36          2           34
serva           Jan 28 2000  9:21AM          2          0            2
serve           Jan 28 2000  9:21AM          2          0            2
useraccts       Jan 28 2000  9:21AM         13          6            7
assetload       Jan 28 2000  9:21AM          2          0            2
webpb           Jan 28 2000  9:21AM          2          0            2
oldserve        Jan 28 2000  9:21AM         14          1           13
```

```
arrts           Jan 28 2000  9:21AM      40          7          33
olduseraccts    Jan 28 2000  9:21AM       2          0           2
oldservm        Jan 28 2000  9:21AM      14          0          14
oldservu        Jan 28 2000  9:21AM       8          0           8
                                       -----    ----------    -----
  ** TOTALS **                          192         32         160
```

Killing User Connections to Database

Problem Description

There seems to be occasional problems with a specific database. In some situations, it appears that more and more user connections are mounting, even after the user logs off an application. Sometimes, we need to quickly kill off all user connections to the database to perform maintenance, repair problems, or perform ad hoc reporting.

Requirements Derived

- Given a Sybase server name and database name, pick out all of the server process IDs and issue a Sybase ISQL "kill" command against those processes.
- Don't waste any time reporting who we're killing, what they were doing, or what objects they were working with — we're looking for speed in cleaning out user connections, not elegant reports.

Behind the Scenes

Walk through some of the code from sp_who, and generate an ISQL script that will perform the kill command for each SPID with a connection against the named database. Run the ISQL script.

Script: kill_all_4_db.csh

```
#!/bin/csh
#
########################################################################
#
#   Filename:       kill_all_4_db.csh
#
#   Purpose:        Script to find users from a named database
#                   and kill the sybase process for them. There
#                   is an application out there that leaves user
#                   connections hanging after the user is finished.
#
#   Standards Violations:   None
#
#   Parameters:     $1   SERVER          [ default: DSQUERY ]
#                   $2   PASSWORD        [ default: sa password file ]
#                   $3   DATABASE        [ required ]
#
#   Dependencies:
#
#
#   SCCS Version:   @(#)kill_all_4_db.csh   1.2 01/28/00
```

```
#
#  Revision History:
#  Date     Author  SCCS ID Description
#  ======== ======= ======= =========================================
#
#  9/28/99  EMM/TAP 1.1     New program
#  1/28/00  TAP     1.2     Removed sql file after it was run.
#
######################################################################
#
# setup
#
#
# give us a good input file. If it's not writable give an error
# and exit
#
  if (-f /tmp/kill_all_4_db.sql) then
     /bin/rm -f /tmp/kill_all_4_db.sql
  endif
  if (-f /tmp/kill_all_4_db.sql) then
     echo "ERROR: Can't kill sql file permissions"
     exit
  endif
#
#  Get Server
#   - if user inputs nothing, give it to $DSQUERY
#  / - if user types Help, give them a message
#   - if they give us a $1 part, use it as the server name
#
  if ("$1" == "") then
     set server=$DSQUERY
  else if ("$1" == "?" || "$1" == "help" || "$1" == "HELP") then
     echo "Usage: ${0}[server] [sa password] (default: ${DSQUERY}) \
     [database name]"
     exit 0
  else
     set server=$1
  endif
echo $0\: running for $server
#
#  Get Password
#   - if user supplies $2, use it as the password
#   - if no, get the password from the password file for that server
#              (assumes read permission on that file)
#
  if ("$2" == "") then
     if ( -f /sybase/sysadm/.pw.$server ) then
        set passwd="`cat /opt/sybase/sysadm/.pw.$server`"
     else
        set passwd="`cat /opt/sybase/sysadm/.pw.$server`"
     endif
  else
     set passwd=$2
```

```
  endif
  if ("$3" == "") then
     echo "ERROR: Must specify a database name."
     exit 0
  else
     set dbname = "$3"
   endif
endif
#
# Find users for selected database and setup file to be used to
# kill logins found
#
isql -Usa -S $server \
   -w 0000000000000000000000000000000000000000000000000000000000000000999 \
   -P $passwd << EOF >! /tmp/kill_all_4_db.sql
select "kill "+convert(varchar(6),p.spid) +char(10)+ "go"
  from master..sysprocesses p, master..syslogins l
 where p.suid = l.suid
   and l.dbname = "$dbname"
   and l.dbname not in ("master", "model", "tempdb", "sybsystemprocs",
                        "sybsecurity")
go
EOF
set numkills = `cat /tmp/kill_all_4_db.sql | grep "kill " | wc -l`
echo "Killing $numkills proccesses accessing the $dbname database(s)"
#
# Use this information to kill logins found
#
isql -Usa -S $server -w
00000000000000000000000000000000000000000000000000000000999 -P $passwd
-i/tmp/kill_all_4_db.sql
#
# After we run it, get rid of the old SQL file
#
if (-f /tmp/kill_all_4_db.sql) then
   /bin/rm -f /tmp/kill_all_4_db.sql
endif
if (-f /tmp/kill_all_4_db.sql) then
   echo "ERROR: Can't kill sql file permissions"
   exit
endif
echo "done"
```

Database Device Utilization Report

Problem Description

The databases are constantly in use. Which databases are filling up? How fast? What is the status of each of the databases on a particular server? What is full? Which segments?

Requirements Derived

- Build a general purpose script to give the percentage full of all of the databases on a named server.
- Give the total amount of space available too.

Shell script: segment_check.csh

```
#!/bin/csh
##########################################################################
#
# FILE NAME: segment_check.csh
#
# PURPOSE:   To check databases to see if segments are getting full.
#
# STARDARDS VIOLATIONS: none
#
# PARAMETERS:
#           $1 = Server Name
#           $2 = Password
#
# DEPENDENCIES:
#              If $1 not supplied, $DSQUERY env var must be used.
#              If $2 not supplied, file
[/opt]/sybase/sysadm/.pw.(servername)
#              is assumed to exist.
#
# SCCS VERSION: @(#)segment_check.csh   1.4 02/25/99
#
# REVISION HISTORY:
# DATE:       AUTHOR:         CHANGED ID:      DESCRIPTION:
# 04/14/1998  E.Mulleda       1.1              New
# 05/14/1998  TonyPrusa       1.2              Peer review, minor
#                                              changes
# 01/26/1999  TonyPrusa       1.3              Y2K changes to date
#                                              formatting
# 02/25/1999  TonyPrusa       1.4              Output results of script
#                                              to screen after run is
#                                              done
#
##########################################################################
#
#
# Get server
#  - if user inputs nothing, give it $DSQUERY
#  - if user types HELP, give them a usage message
```

```
#  - if they give us a $1 parm, use it as the server name
#
if ( "$1" == "" ) then
   set server=$DSQUERY
else if ( "$1" == "?" || "$1" == "help" || "$1" == "HELP" ) then
   echo Usage\: $0 \[server\] \(default\: $DSQUERY\) \[sa password\]
   exit 0
else
   set server=$1
endif
echo $0\: running for $server
#
# Get password:
#  - if user supplies $2, use it as the password
#  - if not, get the password from the password file for that server
#      ( assumes read permission on that file )
#
if ( "$2" == "" ) then
   if ( -f /sybase/sysadm/.pw.$server ) then
      set passwd="'cat /sybase/sysadm/.pw.$server'"
   else
      if ( -f /opt/sybase/sysadm/.pw.$server ) then
         set passwd="`cat /opt/sybase/sysadm/.pw.$server'"
      else
         echo "password file not available, error."
         exit 0
      endif
   endif
else
   set passwd=$2
endif
#
# script-wide variables
#
echo Starting at\: 'date'
set out_file="/tmp/segments.txt"
pwd
#
# Set list of ALL database names for segment check
#
isql -Usa -S$server \
-w 00000000000000000000000000000000000000000000000000000000000999 \
-P$passwd <<EOF | tail +3 >! $out_file
set nocount on
go
use master
go
select name from sysdatabases where name not in ("model", "master",
                "sybsystemprocs", "tempdb", "sybsecurity", "pubs2")
go
EOF
set DB_LIST = 'cat $out_file'
/bin/rm $out_file
```

```
if ( "" == "$DB_LIST" ) then
   echo Error\, DB_LIST not populated\. Exiting \. \. \.
   exit 0
endif
#
# Got the DB_LIST, now check the segments on each DB.
#
set dump_file="/tmp/segments.$server"
/bin/rm -f $dump_file
touch $dump_file
foreach db ( $DB_LIST )
   echo "Running check for: $db"
   echo "- - - - - - - - - - - - - - - - - - - - - - - - - - - - - - - -" >>
$dump_file
   echo "" >> $dump_file
   echo "Database Device Fragment Utilization Report 'date +%m\/%d\/%Y'" \
      >> $dump_file
   echo "Server: $server          Database: $db" >> $dump_file
   echo "" >> $dump_file
# run SQL
  $SYBASE/bin/isql -Usa -S$server \
   -w 00000000000000000000000000000000000000000000000000999 \
   -P$passwd << EOF | grep -v "affected)"
>> $dump_file
use $db
go
declare @numpgsmb       float        /* Number of Pages per Megabyte */
select @numpgsmb = (1048576. / v.low)
  from master.dbo.spt_values v
 where v.number = 1
   and v.type = "E"
declare @curdbid smallint              /* the one we're currently */
select @curdbid=db_id()
declare @pagekb          int
select @pagekb = (low / 1024)          /* kbytes per page */
                from master.dbo.spt_values
                where number = 1
                  and type = 'E'

declare @dbname          varchar(30)
select @dbname=db_name()
declare @sptlang         int
select @sptlang = @@langid
select device_fragments = substring(v.name,1,15),
             total_size = str(size / @numpgsmb, 8, 1) + " MB",
                  usage = substring(m.description,1,15),
                free_mb = str((curunreservedpgs(@curdbid, u.lstart,
                             u.unreservedpgs) * @pagekb / 1024.0),8,1)+"MB",

               free_pct = str((((curunreservedpgs(@curdbid, u.lstart,
                             u.unreservedpgs) * @pagekb / 1024.0) /
                             (size / @numpgsmb) )* 100), 8, 1),
               full_pct = str(100-(((curunreservedpgs(@curdbid, u.lstart,
```

```
                              u.unreservedpgs) * @pagekb / 1024.0) /
                              (size / @numpgsmb) )* 100), 8, 1)
  from master.dbo.sysdatabases d,
       master.dbo.sysusages u,
       master.dbo.sysdevices v,
       master.dbo.spt_values a,
       master.dbo.spt_values b,
       master.dbo.sysmessages m
 where d.dbid = u.dbid
   and v.low <= u.size + vstart
   and v.high >= u.size + vstart - 1
   and v.status & 2 = 2
   and d.name = @dbname
   and a.type = "E"
   and a.number = 1
   and b.type = "S"
   and u.segmap & 7 = b.number
   and b.msgnum = m.error
   and isnull(m.langid, 0) = @sptlang
 order by 1
go
EOF
end
   if (-f $dump_file) then
      echo "All segment checks completed."
   else
      echo "All segment checks were unsuccessful."
   endif
echo "Segment check of Test databases is finished."
echo "Output files should be reviewed. Output file is $dump_file"
echo Finished at\: 'date'
echo "=============================================================="
echo ""
cat $dump_file
```

Sample Output

```
Database Device Fragment Utilization Report
01/28/2000
Server: IAS                                                Database:
arrts
 device_fragments  total_size  usage      free_mb   free_pct  full_pct
 ----------------  ----------  ---------  -------   --------  --------
 syb07             10.0 MB     log only   10.0 MB   99.7      0.3
 syb19             20.0 MB     data only  10.8 MB   54.0      46.0
 syb20             17.0 MB     data only  17.0 MB   100.0     0.0
 syb20             53.0 MB     data only  53.0 MB   100.0     0.0
- - - - - - - - - - - - - - - - - - - - - - - - - - - - - - - - - - - - -
```

Active vs. Inactive Connections

Problem Description

There are a lot of longstanding connections to the database server. When is something going on with these connections? What objects are they locking? We don't want to set up full accounting, we just want a snapshot occasionally of the idle and busy processes on the system.

Requirements Derived

- Make a handy tool for DBAs, not managers.
- For an inactive system, provide only one detail line.
- For active processes, tell us as much as you can about the locks.
- Make it run as a cron occasionally.

Behind the Scenes

Much of the code required for this is located in the Sybase stored procedures sp_who and sp_lock. Liberal use and customization of this code was done to gather together the SQL to build this script.

As a result of this, the program locks roughly the same data as the sp_who and sp_lock programs. If the database server is messed up, this program probably will not help. This is meant as an historical diagnostic tool, not a troubleshooting tool.

Running the Script

```
cd $SYBASE/sysadm/cronscripts
./sp_who.csh [user name] [password]
```

Log File

Output goes to stdio. The cron for this will need to output text to the $SYBASE/log dir.

Shell script: sp_who.csh

```
#!/bin/csh
#
########################################################################
#
#   Filename:        sp_who.csh
#
#   Purpose:         Summarize user connections to database server as
#                    "running", "lock sleep", "nothing", "something".
#                    For those that are not "nothing", give us a list of
#                    lock type and pages for whatever objects are in use.
#
#   Standards Violations:   None
#
#   Parameters:  $1 SERVER [default: DSQUERY]
#                $2 PASSWD [default: pw file for this DSQUERY/user]
#
#   Dependencies:#
#
#   SCCS Version:    @(#)sp_who.csh   1.4 01/13/00
#
```

```
#   Revision History:
#   Date     Author  SCCS ID Description
#   ======== ======= ======= ============================================
#
#   4/13/99  TAP     1.1     New program
#   4/21/99  TAP     1.2     Whoops. Not reporting "something"
#                            correctly
#   4/24/99  EMM     1.3     Doc. Final review, peer review
#   1/09/00  TAP     1.4     Add code to run as user or sybase=sa
#
########################################################################
#
# setup
#
if ( "$1" == "" ) then
   set svr = $DSQUERY
else
   set svr = "$1"
endif
if ( "$2" == "" ) then

   if ( -f  ~/sysadm/.pw.$svr ) then
      set pw = 'cat ~/sysadm/.pw.$svr'
   else
      echo 'PW not set, error'
      exit 0
   endif
else
   set pw = $2
endif
#
# Need two temp files to hold SQL output
#  1 is the sp_who output
#  2 is the sp_lock output
set temp_file = "/tmp/ms$$"
set temp_file2 = "/tmp/m2$$"
#
# Run as user unless user is sybase, then be sybase "sa" user.
#
if ( "$LOGNAME" == "sybase" ) then
   set user="sa"
else
   set user=$LOGNAME
endif
#
# special use of -H parameter. This shows up as HOST in sp_who output.
# We can use this to program in the "ignore" my own connection checking
# status.
#
#
# sql code almost snipped word for word from sybase stored proc sp_who
#
isql -U $user -S $svr -H SPWHOCHK \
```

```
   -w 00000000000000000000000000000000000000000000000000000000000999 \
   -P $pw << EOF | grep -v "NETWORK HANDLE" | grep -v "DEADLOCK TUNE" | \
   grep -v "MIRROR HANDLER" | grep -v HOUSEKEEPER | \
   grep -v "CHECKPOINT SLE" | grep -v "AUDIT PROCESS" | \
   grep -v "SPWHOCHK" >! $temp_file
select spid         = convert(varchar(4),sp.spid),
       status       = convert(varchar(10),sp.status),
       loginame     = substring(sl.name,1,10),
       hostname     = convert(varchar(8),sp.hostname),
       blk          = convert(varchar(4), sp.blocked),
       dbname       = convert(varchar(9),sd.name),
       cmd          = substring(sp.cmd,1,14),
       program_name = convert(varchar(12),sp.program_name)
from master..sysprocesses sp,
     master..syslogins sl,
     master..sysdatabases sd
where sp.uid = sl.suid
  and sp.dbid = sd.dbid
go
EOF
#
# Now that we have sp_who, let's also steal the sybase stored proc sp_lock
# to get the lock info for the processes
#
isql -U $user -S $svr \
   -w 00000000000000000000000000000000000000000000000000000000000999 \
   -P $pw << EOF | grep -v "NETWORK HANDLE" | grep -v "DEADLOCK TUNE" \
   | grep -v "MIRROR HANDLER" | grep -v HOUSEKEEPER | \
   grep -v "CHECKPOINT SLE" | grep -v "AUDIT PROCESS" >! $temp_file2
select "NOPE", spid,
       locktype = name,
       table_id = id,
       page,
       dbname = db_name(dbid),
       class
  from master..syslocks l,
       master..spt_values v
 where l.type = v.number
   and v.type = "L"
go
EOF
#
#
# One lousy lock? Forget about it!
set howmanylocks='cat $temp_file2 | grep '(1 row affected)' | wc -l'
if ( "$howmanylocks" == "1" ) then
   /bin/rm $temp_file2
endif
#
# "nothing"   is defined as AWAITING COMMAND roughly
# "something" is defined as not "AWAITING COMMAND"
# "lock"      is defined as any line with the keyword "lock" in it
# "running"   is defined as any line with the keyword "running" in it.
```

```
#
if ( -f $temp_file ) then
   echo -n "$svr"
   echo -n " 'date +%m\/%d\/%Y\ %H\:%M\:%S'"
   set nothing = 'cat $temp_file | grep 'recv sleep' | grep 'AWAITING COM'
        | wc -l'
   set something = 'cat $temp_file | grep -v 'AWAITING COM' | grep -v NULL
        | \
                     grep -v 'affected)' | grep ' ' | grep -v 'spid
                           status' | \
                     grep -v '\-\-\-\-\-\-\-\-' | wc -l'
   set lock = 'cat $temp_file | grep -v NULL | grep -i lock | wc -l'
   set running = 'cat $temp_file | grep running | wc -l'
   echo -n "  Running: $running"
   echo -n "  Lock sleep: $lock"
   echo -n "  Something: $something"
   echo "  Nothing: $nothing"
   cat $temp_file | grep -v 'AWAITING COM' | grep -v NULL | grep -v
        'affected)'
endif
#
# If the "locks" file still exists, output it. Otherwise, skip it
#
if ( -f $temp_file2 ) then
   echo ""
   echo "Details of locks"
   set detailock='cat $temp_file2 | grep NOPE | awk '{print $2}' | sort
        | uniq'
   foreach onelock ( $detailock )
      echo "For process: $onelock"
      cat $temp_file2 | grep " $onelock " | \
               awk '{print "object: "$4" type: "$3" DB: "$6}'
      echo ""
   end
endif
#
# clean up
#
/bin/rm -f $temp_file $temp_file2
# Done
```

Sample Output

```
SERVER1 04/17/2000 01:31:01  Running: 0  Lock sleep: 0  Something: 0  Nothing: 3
 spid status    loginame   hostname blk  dbname      cmd           program_name
 ---- --------- ---------- -------- ---- ----------- ------------- ------------

SERVER1 04/17/2000 03:01:09  Running: 0  Lock sleep: 0  Something: 0  Nothing: 3
 spid status    loginame   hostname blk  dbname      cmd           program_name
 ---- --------- ---------- -------- ---- ----------- ------------- ------------

SERVER1 04/17/2000 03:31:04  Running: 0  Lock sleep: 0  Something: 1  Nothing: 3
 spid status    loginame   hostname blk  dbname      cmd           program_name
 ---- --------- ---------- -------- ---- ----------- ------------- ------------
 7    sleeping  sa         unixsys1 0    procurement COND          ctisql
```

```
Details of locks
For process: 7
object: 757577737 type: Sh_intent DB: procurement
object: 757577737 type: Sh_page DB: procurement
For process: 8
object: 448004627 type: Sh_intent DB: master

SERVER1 04/17/2000 05:01:10  Running: 0  Lock sleep: 0  Something: 2  Nothing: 3
 spid status     loginame   hostname blk  dbname      cmd           program_name
 ---- ---------- ---------- -------- ---- ---------   ------------  ------------
 7    send sleep sa         unixsys1 0    procurement SELECT        loadSewp2Cat
 8    runnable   sa         unixsys1 0    procurement SELECT        loadSewp2Cat

Details of locks
For process: 11
object: 448004627 type: Sh_intent DB: master
For process: 7
object: 757577737 type: Sh_intent DB: procurement
object: 757577737 type: Sh_page DB: procurement

SERVER1 04/17/2000 05:31:06  Running: 0  Lock sleep: 0  Something: 0  Nothing: 3
 spid status     loginame   hostname blk  dbname    cmd           program_name
 ---- ---------- ---------- -------- ---- --------- ------------- ------------

SERVER1 04/17/2000 07:01:01  Running: 0  Lock sleep: 0  Something: 0  Nothing: 3
 spid status     loginame   hostname blk  dbname    cmd           program_name
 ---- ---------- ---------- -------- ---- --------- ------------- ------------

SERVER1 04/17/2000 07:31:06  Running: 0  Lock sleep: 0  Something: 1  Nothing: 3
 spid status     loginame   hostname blk  dbname    cmd           program_name
 ---- ---------- ---------- -------- ---- --------- ------------- ------------
 7    runnable   sa         unixsys1 0    useraccts    UPDATE        ctisql

Details of locks
For process: 7
object: 937770398 type: Ex_intent DB: useraccts
object: 937770398 type: Update_page DB: useraccts
object: 937770398 type: Ex_page DB: useraccts
object: 937770398 type: Update_page DB: useraccts
For process: 8
object: 448004627 type: Sh_intent DB: master

SERVER1 04/17/2000 09:01:02  Running: 0  Lock sleep: 0  Something: 0  Nothing: 3
 spid status     loginame   hostname blk  dbname    cmd           program_name
 ---- ---------- ---------- -------- ---- --------- ------------- ------------

SERVER1 04/17/2000 09:31:01  Running: 0  Lock sleep: 0  Something: 0  Nothing: 3
 spid status     loginame   hostname blk  dbname    cmd           program_name
 ---- ---------- ---------- -------- ---- --------- ------------- ------------

SERVER1 04/17/2000 11:01:02  Running: 0  Lock sleep: 0  Something: 0  Nothing: 3
 spid status     loginame   hostname blk  dbname    cmd           program_name
 ---- ---------- ---------- -------- ---- --------- ------------- ------------
```

Database Creation Checklist

When you create a database, you should document what resources you are using, and what the database's use will be and by whom. Here's a sample form to contain some of the information your potential successor will need to know, and which you may forget if you are away from the system for a while.

DBName:		Date:	/ /
Owner:		Password:	
Project:		Contact:	
Summary:			

Server: ❑ IAS ❑ TEST ❑ DEVELOP ❑ SYBASE ❑ CCBS

❑ SERVER1 ❑ ________ ❑ ________ ❑ ________ ❑ ________

Devices:

Device Name	Segment	Size	Device Name	Segment	Size
	Default				
	Default				
	ncindexes				
	logsegment				

Users: ❑ Task 41 ❑ Others: ________________________________

____

Groups, Membership, and Permissions:

Use	Group Name	Members	INS	UPD	DEL	EXE
❑			❑	❑	❑	❑
❑			❑	❑	❑	❑
❑			❑	❑	❑	❑
❑			❑	❑	❑	❑
❑			❑	❑	❑	❑

(Permissions: INS, UPD, DEL, EXE)

To Do:

enough "open dbs?" ________	users ________	drop constraints ________
Create database ________	permissions in other dbs ________	add constraints again ________
Add DBO ________	aliases ________	add procedures again ________
DBO aliased in other dbs ________	defaults ________	check available space ________
Initial DB dump ________	rules ________	ncindexes: ________
Set sp_dboption ________	types ________	default: ________
Object Creation #1 ________	binding defaults ________	Check errorlogs ________
Extract DDLs: ________	tables ________	Compare old vs. this ________
Source: ________	foreign keys ________	Object Creation Done ________
Modify DDLs ________	binding defaults again ________	DB Backup / Baseline ________
Load DDLs: ________	views ________	DBCC everything ________
Destination: ________	unresolved references ________	Source files dir stru ________
Object Creation #2 ________	foreign db references ________	SCCS dirs ________
segments ________	procedures ________	copy to prod scripts ________

ncindexes	unresolved references	backupdbs script
___________	___________	___________
threshold	foreign db references	Update statistics script
___________	___________	___________
last chance pages:	BCP DATA	log dump times:
___________	___________	___________
# of pages	Source:	check backups
___________	___________	___________
doc: (LOG)	triggers	
___________	___________	___________
doc: (default)	indexes	
___________	___________	___________
groups	add constraints	
___________	___________	___________

Simple Data Mining

Problem Description

When attempting to understand a new system, database, or customer site, it's often difficult to get a detailed understanding of databases and tables. The manual effort of examining each table to see what is inside it is often a manual process that is time prohibitive. Locating the nonexistent database documentation is more frequently a waste of time. Frequently, the push for results requires a relatively quick ramp up on the database with little to no supporting documentation to be found. What is this database? What data is in it? What is the distribution of the data in the rows? Is there an obvious primary key in this table?

Requirements Derived

- For a given server, database, and table give exhaustive information on table contents.
- Provide a detailed report showing table structure, type definitions, indexes, and defined keys.
- Don't go overboard. Give the top 20 data elements in a table, but not every last single solitary data item in the entire table.
- Give useful statistics about the table too.
- This program is not intended for runs on production.
- Don't make it fast, make it thorough.

Behind the Scenes

This program is very useful for finding out about all of the tables in all of the databases on a server. If run against a development server, it's an extremely useful thing to start on Friday afternoon so that it can work through the weekend and give you results.

Uses code from sp_help and sp_helpdb stored procedures.

This program can be exceedingly slow and extraordinarily resource hungry. It makes liberal use of select distinct, group by, order by, and having. It is not for use on any production system.

Running the Script

```
cd $SYBASE/sysadm/
./reporter.sh [table (required)] [database (required)] [server (optional)]
[user (optional)] [password (optional)]
```

Example:

```
reporter.sh solicitations procurement SERVER1 sa SECRET1
```

Output File

None. Output reflected to standard output. Redirect to a file to save output.

Shell script: reporter.sh

```
#!bin/sh
########################################################################
#
# FILE NAME: reporter.sh
#
# PURPOSE:   Given a DB and table, get me the following information:
#            - table info (sp_help (table) info basically)
#            - data info (for each column)
#            - how many null / non-null rows
#            - distinct values in column vs total rows in table
#            - min, max values in column
#
# STARDARDS VIOLATIONS: none
#
# PARAMETERS:
#            $1 = Table name      required
#            $2 = Database        required
#            $3 = Server Name     optional
#            $4 = User Name       optional
#            $5 = password        optional
#
# EXAMPLE RUN:
#               sh reporter.sh containers pms KIVA_DEV dbown password
#
# ASSUMPTIONS:
#               1. (for now) Assume I have SYBASE permission to
#                  read table, and columns in table. unsafe assumption
#                  will be fixed in rev 2.
#               2. Don't know yet which column types NOT to pick.
#               3. Assumes DBO
#
# DEPENDENCIES:
#               If $3 not supplied, $DSQUERY env var will be used.
#               If $4 not supplied, $LOGNAME env var will be used.
#               If $5 not supplied, automatically look for file
```

```
#                            $HOME/.pw.(servername).(username)
#
# SCCS VERSION: %W% %G%
#
# REVISION HISTORY:
# DATE:       AUTHOR:         SCCS ID: DESCRIPTION:
# =========== =============== ======== ================================
# 08/10/2000  TonyPrusa       1.1      New
#
########################################################################
#
#
# process parameters
#
#
# $1 is TABLE NAME required. If they ask for help, give it to them.
#
table=""
if [ "$1" = "" ] ; then
   echo "ERROR: table name must be supplied"
   exit 0
else
   if [ "$1" = "USAGE" -o "$1" = "usage" -o "$1" = "Usage" -o "$1" = "Help"
        -o "$1" = "HELP" -o "$1" = "help" ] ; then
      echo "Usage: reporter.sh (Table name) (Database) [Server Name] [User
           Name] [Password] "
      exit 0
   else
      table="$1"
   fi
fi
#
# $2 is DATABASE required.
#
database=""
if [ "$2" = "" ] ; then
   echo "ERROR: DATABASE name must be supplied."
   exit 0
else
   database="$2"
fi
#
# $3 is SERVER optional
#
# if not supplied, use env var $DSQUERY
#
server="$DSQUERY"
if [ "$3" != "" ] ; then
   server="$3"
fi
#
# $4 is USER optional
#
```

```
# if not supplied, use env var $LOGNAME.
# If value of user variable is SYBASE, change it to "sa"
#
user="$LOGNAME"
if [ "$4" != "" ] ; then
   user="$4"
fi
if [ "$user" = "sybase" ] ; then
   user="sa"
fi
#
# $5 is password
# if not supplied, try to find the right password in user's
# home directory
#
passwd=""
if [ "$5" != "" ] ; then
   passwd="$5"
else
   if [ -f "$HOME/.pw.${server}.${user}" ] ; then
      passwd='cat $HOME/.pw.${server}.${user}'
   else
      if [ -f "$HOME/.pw.${server}." ] ; then
         passwd='cat $HOME/.pw.${server}'
      else
         echo "ERROR: Password not Available"
         exit 0
      fi
   fi
fi
#
# defined script-wide variables
#
# $table, $database, $server, $user, $passwd
#
# check whether $user can log in to $server with $password
#
# define output file
outfile="/tmp/reporter.1$$"
# test isql login and database use with data provided by inputs to program
isql -U $user -S $server -o $outfile -w
000000000000000000000000000000000000000000000000000000000000000000000000000
0000000000000000000000999 -P $passwd << EOF
use $database
go
set nocount on
go
select "WORKS"
go
EOF
# if the word "Msg error or failed" comes up, it's a message to Sybase that
there was some kind of error
```

```
answer='cat $outfile | grep -v "WORKS" | grep -v " -----" | egrep -i
"msg|error|fail" | wc -l | sed 's/ //g''
if [ "$answer" != "0" ] ; then
   echo "ERROR"
   cat $outfile | grep -v "WORKS" | grep -v " -----" | grep -v "Line " |
        grep -v "CT-LIBRARY" | grep -v "ct_connect" | grep -v "server name
        not"
   cat $outfile | grep "Requested server name not found"
   /bin/rm -f $outfile
   exit 0
else
   echo "Login attempt successful"
   echo "======================="
fi
/bin/rm -f $outfile
#
# now, I know that $user/$passwd combination on this $server for this
$database is valid
#
#
----------------------------------------------------------------------------
# assumption
# modification needed to make this work 100%. As I'm checking columns,
# first make sure that I have sybase permissions to allow me to look at
# this table and column
#
----------------------------------------------------------------------------
#
# get all column names for this table.
#
isql -U $user -S $server -o $outfile -w \

00000000000000000000000000000000000000000000000000000000000000000000000999 \
   -P $passwd << EOF
use $database
go
declare @tabname varchar(15)
select @tabname="$table"
select "FIELD: "+ sc.name
  from sysobjects so
     , syscolumns sc
     , systypes st
 where so.id       = sc.id
   and sc.usertype = st.usertype
   and so.name     = @tabname
   and so.type     = "U"
 order by sc.colid
go
EOF
col_list='cat $outfile | grep 'FIELD: ' | sed 's/FIELD: //g' | sed 's/
//g''
/bin/rm -f $outfile
echo $col_list
```

```
#
# first, count the number of rows in the table and remember it
#
isql -U $user -S $server -o $outfile -w \

0000000000000000000000000000000000000000000000000000000000000000000000999 \
   -P $passwd << EOF
use $database
go
select "COUNT: ", count("X")
from $table
go
EOF
table_rows='cat $outfile | grep "COUNT:" | sed 's/COUNT://g' | sed 's/
//g''
/bin/rm -f $outfile
#
# give entire table info first
#
isql -U $user -S $server -o $outfile -w \

0000000000000000000000000000000000000000000000000000000000000000000000999 \
   -P $passwd << EOF
use $database
go
sp_help $table
go
sp_helprotect $table
go
sp_helpconstraint $table
go
EOF
echo ""
cat $outfile
echo ""
echo ""
echo "Rows in table: $table_rows"
for column in $col_list
do
   #
   # message to user first
   #
   echo ""
   echo ""
   echo ""
   echo "Working on SERVER: $server, DATABASE: $database, TABLE: $table,
        COLUMN: $column"
   echo
"========================================================================="
   #
   # count number of distinct values for this column
   #
```

```
   isql -U $user -S $server -o $outfile -w \000000000000000000000000000000
        00000000000000000000000000000000000999 \
      -P $passwd << EOF
use $database
go
select "COUNT: ", count(distinct $column) from $table
go
EOF
   distinct_rows='cat $outfile | grep "COUNT:" | sed 's/COUNT://g' | sed
        's/ //g''
   echo "Distinct rows: $distinct_rows"
   /bin/rm -f $outfile
   if [ "$table_rows" = "$distinct_rows" ] ; then
      echo "Column is unique"
      unique="true"
   else
      echo "Column is not unique"
      unique="false"
   fi

   if [ "$unique" = "false" ] ; then
      #
      # Provide the top twenty lines in this file to user
      #
      isql -U $user -S $server -o $outfile -w \

000000000000000000000000000000000000000000000000000000000000000000000999 \
         -P $passwd << EOF
set nocount on
go
use $database
go
select "value"   = $column
     , "matches" = count("X")
     , "percent" =
convert(numeric(7,2),round(((count("Y")+0.0)/($table_rows+0.0))*100,2))
  from $table
 group by $column
 order by 3 desc
go
EOF
       echo ""
       head -23 $outfile
       echo ""
       /bin/rm $outfile
   fi
   #
   # Give MIN, MAX and number of times this value appeared
   #
   isql -U $user -S $server -o $outfile -w \

000000000000000000000000000000000000000000000000000000000000000000000999 \
      -P $passwd << EOF
set nocount on
```

```
go
use $database
go
select "Minimum Value"=min($column), "Maximum Value"=max($column) from
$table
go
EOF
   echo ""
   cat $outfile
   echo ""
   /bin/rm -f $outfile

done
exit 0
```

Sample Output

```
 Name           Owner          Type
 -------------- -------------- ----------------------
 solicitations  dbo            user table

 Data_located_on_segment        When_created
 ------------------------------ --------------------------
 default                        Mar 22 1999  2:00PM

 Column_name    Type             Len Prec Scale Null Default      Rule Ident
 -------------- ---------------- --- ---- ----- ---- ------------ ---- -----
 sol_no         artificial_type    4 NULL NULL     0 zero_dflt     NULL    0
 buyer_id       opl_type           4 NULL NULL     1 zero_dflt     NULL    0
 sol_date       datetime           8 NULL NULL     0 NULL          NULL    0
 return_pricing datetime           8 NULL NULL     1 NULL          NULL    0
 comments       description_type 255 NULL NULL     1 NULL          NULL    0
 title          varchar           50 NULL NULL     0 NULL          NULL    0
 created        created_type       8 NULL NULL     0 clock_dflt    NULL    0
 creator        creator_type      30 NULL NULL     0 operator_dflt NULL    0
 updated        updated_type       8 NULL NULL     1 NULL          NULL    0
 updater        updater_type      30 NULL NULL     1 NULL          NULL    0
 deleted        deleted_type       8 NULL NULL     1 NULL          NULL    0
 deleter        deleter_type      30 NULL NULL     1 NULL          NULL    0

 index_name  index_description                         index_keys
 ----------- ----------------------------------------- ------------------
 sol_pk_ndx1 nonclustered, unique located on ncindexes solicit_no
 sol_ndx2    nonclustered located on ncindexes         solicit_no, buyer_id

 keytype object         related_object object_keys related_keys
 ------- -------------- -------------- ----------- --------------
 foreign solicit_dealer solicitations  sol_no      sol_no
 foreign solicit_item   solicitations  sol_no      sol_no
 primary solicitations  -- none --     solicit_no

 Object is not partitioned.

 grantor grantee type  action     object        column grantable
 ------- ------- ----- ---------- ------------- ------ ----------
 dbo     public  Grant Delete     solicitations All    FALSE
```

```
dbo     public  Grant Insert     solicitations All    FALSE
dbo     public  Grant References solicitations All    FALSE
dbo     public  Grant Select     solicitations All    FALSE
dbo     public  Grant Update     solicitations All    FALSE

name            definition
--------------- ------------------------------------------------------------
clock_dflt      create default clock_dflt as getdate()
operator_dflt   create default operator_dflt as suser_name()
zero_dflt       create default zero_dflt as 0

Rows in table: 1127

Working on SERVER: SERVER1, DATABASE: procurement, TABLE: solicitations,
COLUMN: sol_no
=======================================================================
Distinct rows: 1127
Column is unique

Minimum Value Maximum Value
------------- -------------
            1          1127

Working on SERVER: SERVER1, DATABASE: procurement, TABLE: solicitations,
COLUMN: buyer_id
=======================================================================
Distinct rows: 7
Column is not unique

value       matches     percent
----------- ----------- ----------
      35455         503      44.63
      14255         270      23.96
      11371         164      14.55
      16764          75       6.65
      34095          55       4.88
      16457          38       3.37
     219497          22       1.95

Minimum Value Maximum Value
------------- -------------
          155        219563

Working on SERVER: SERVER1, DATABASE: procurement, TABLE: solicitations,
COLUMN: solicit_date
=======================================================================
Distinct rows: 832
Column is not unique

value                      matches     percent
-------------------------- ----------- ----------
       Aug 28 1999  5:13PM          37       3.28
       Apr 15 2000 12:54PM          34       3.02
       Jan 10 2001 11:45AM          28       2.48
       Feb  8 2000 12:15AM          16       1.42
       Nov 29 1995  9:44AM          12       1.06
       Dec 20 1995 12:56PM          12       1.06
```

```
       Mar 27 2000  5:31PM          10        0.89
       Nov 27 1995 12:13PM           8        0.71
       May 17 1999  3:00PM           8        0.71
       Apr 29 1999 12:54PM           7        0.62
       Mar 21 2000 12:21PM           6        0.53
       Mar 28 1996  4:43PM           6        0.53
       Dec 21 1995 12:56PM           5        0.44
       Feb 21 1995 12:31PM           5        0.44
       Feb 23 1995  9:43AM           5        0.44
       Feb 29 2000 12:54PM           5        0.44
       Apr  4 1996 12:50PM           5        0.44
       Apr 22 1996 12:04PM           5        0.44
       Nov 28 2000 11:41AM           4        0.35
       Jan  6 1996 10:32AM           4        0.35
       Feb  3 1996 06:30PM           4        0.35

Minimum Value              Maximum Value
-------------------------- --------------------------
       Nov 21 1995 12:00AM        May  3 2001  9:21PM

Working on SERVER: SERVER1, DATABASE: procurement, TABLE: solicitations,
COLUMN: return_pricing
=======================================================================
Distinct rows: 666
Column is not unique

value                      matches     percent
-------------------------- ----------- ----------
       Apr 29 1998  5:06PM          35        3.11
       Apr 16 2000  9:00AM          32        2.84
       Aug  5 1996 11:46AM          30        2.66
       Jan 11 1996  4:38PM          28        2.48
       May 16 1998 12:18PM          28        2.48
       Feb  9 1998  3:42PM          22        1.95
       Jun 10 2000 12:04PM          15        1.33
       Jun 14 1996  5:14PM          15        1.33
       May 20 1999 12:42PM          14        1.24
       May 31 1996  3:43PM          14        1.24
       Aug  9 1998  4:00PM          12        1.06
       Nov 30 2000  4:42PM          11        0.98
       Dec 21 1995 12:35PM          11        0.98
       Sep  6 1996  2:13PM          11        0.98
       Mar 28 1998  9:42AM           9        0.80
       Aug 26 1996  4:43PM           9        0.80
       Sep  4 2000  8:53AM           9        0.80
       Nov 28 1998  5:55PM           8        0.71
       May 20 1996  3:41PM           8        0.71
       Apr 30 1999  5:34PM           7        0.62
       Jul 11 1996  3:21PM           6        0.53

Minimum Value              Maximum Value
-------------------------- --------------------------
       Nov 24 1995  5:00AM        May  3 2001  9:00AM
```

```
Working on SERVER: SERVER1, DATABASE: procurement, TABLE: solicitations,
COLUMN: comments
========================================================================
Distinct rows: 51
 Column is not unique

value                                               matches     percent
-------------------------------------------------   -------     -------
NULL                                                 1068        94.76
(See Attached Quote)                                    3         0.27
List of Parts attached                                  3         0.27
Quote Attach                                            3         0.27
(See attached Quote)                                    2         0.18
Computer Spec Per NSA-430503 Single Source              2         0.18
(See attahced Quote)                                    1         0.09
(See attached Quote)                                    1         0.09
3/18/99 - working too                                   1         0.09
Garth, don't mess with this one.                        1         0.09
JE-543                                                  1         0.09
List attached                                           1         0.09
Listed parts not attainable, select alternatives        1         0.09
Necessary per requestor                                 1         0.09
Needs 3 poly coats on cases                             1         0.09
Need ASAP - QUOTE NOW                                   1         0.09
No customer order for this one yet.                     1         0.09
PRIORITY ITEMS - QUOTE EXACTLY AS LISTED                1         0.09
Quote att                                               1         0.09
STS-93 backup system                                    1         0.09
Two requests                                            1         0.09

Minimum Value  Maximum Value
----------------------------------  ----------------------------------
(See Attached Coupon)  just in time delivery

Working on SERVER: SERVER1, DATABASE: procurement, TABLE: solicitations,
COLUMN: title
========================================================================
Distinct rows: 1022
Column is not unique

value                 matches        percent
-----------------     -------        -------
                         6             0.53
AZA-509                  4             0.35
SIX-064                  4             0.35
IAR-063-0                3             0.27
IYS-559                  3             0.27
APL-514-4a               3             0.27
AOO-406                  3             0.27
TEA-445-5T               3             0.27
FOT-506                  3             0.27
OXT-017-1                3             0.27
OXT-138                  3             0.27
SGT-341                  3             0.27
```

```
SST-006-2                  3            0.27
SST-1437                   3            0.27
GS-008                     2            0.18
O-020-1                    2            0.18
TIA-104                    2            0.18
TIA-064-1                  2            0.18
TIA-108                    2            0.18
IXC-441                    2            0.18
ICX-093-2                  2            0.18

Minimum Value               Maximum Value
--------------------------- ---------------------------
                            XTS-405-2

Working on SERVER: SERVER1, DATABASE: procurement, TABLE: solicitations,
COLUMN: created
======================================================================
Distinct rows: 1127
Column is unique

Minimum Value              Maximum Value
-------------------------- --------------------------
Oct 24 1995  2:19PM        May  3 2001  9:04AM

Working on SERVER: SERVER1, DATABASE: procurement, TABLE: solicitations,
COLUMN: creator
======================================================================
Distinct rows: 8
Column is not unique

value                  matches            percent
--------------         -------            ----------
vargas                   500                  44.37
hubert                   262                  23.25
tracey                   152                  13.49
martington                71                   6.30
prasad                    59                   5.24
tran                      37                   3.28
alvarez                   35                   3.11
vo                        11                   0.98

Minimum Value                  Maximum Value
------------------------------ ------------------------------
adams                          vo

Working on SERVER: SERVER1, DATABASE: procurement, TABLE: solicitations,
COLUMN: updated
======================================================================
Distinct rows: 62
Column is not unique
```

```
value                         matches       percent
--------------------          -------       ----------
                NULL           1065             94.50
 Nov 27 1996 12:00PM              1              0.09
 Nov 27 2000 12:36PM              1              0.09
 Nov 29 1997 11:40AM              1              0.09
 Dec  4 1996  1:24PM              1              0.09
 Dec 11 1998 12:32PM              1              0.09
 Jan 23 1997  1:37PM              1              0.09
 Jan 23 1997  1:41PM              1              0.09
 Jan 23 1998  1:47PM              1              0.09
 Jan 23 2000  2:31PM              1              0.09
 Jan 23 1996  2:34PM              1              0.09
 Feb  1 1998  3:15PM              1              0.09
 Feb  3 1998  1:43PM              1              0.09
 Feb  3 1998  1:51PM              1              0.09
 Feb  3 1997  1:55PM              1              0.09
 Feb  5 1998  4:01PM              1              0.09
 Feb  8 2001  9:08AM              1              0.09
 Feb  8 1997 10:36AM              1              0.09
 Feb  8 2000 10:42AM              1              0.09
 Feb  8 1996 11:00AM              1              0.09
 Feb  8 1996 12:20PM              1              0.09

Minimum Value                Maximum Value
-------------------------- --------------------------
Nov 27 1995 12:00PM          Apr 29 2001 10:37AM

Working on SERVER: SERVER1, DATABASE: procurement, TABLE: solicitations,
COLUMN: updater
======================================================================
Distinct rows: 9
Column is not unique

value            matches         percent
----------       -------         -------
NULL             1065            94.50
hubert           24              2.13
tracey           14              1.24
vargas           7               0.62
martington       6               0.53
belliard         4               0.35
adams            4               0.35
prasad           1               0.09
franks           1               0.09
tran             1               0.09

Minimum Value                    Maximum Value
------------------------------ ------------------------------
adams                            vo
```

```
Working on SERVER: SERVER1, DATABASE: procurement, TABLE: solicitations,
COLUMN: deleted
==========================================================================
Distinct rows: 10
Column is not unique

value                          matches          percent
--------------------           -------          -------
                NULL             1111             99.12
 May  6 1999  3:57PM                1              0.09
 May  7 1995  8:33AM                1              0.09
 Jul 11 1997  1:37PM                1              0.09
 Jul 24 1999  1:26PM                1              0.09
 Jul 31 1999 10:08AM                1              0.09
 Jul 31 1997 10:14AM                1              0.09
 Feb  4 2001  2:03PM                1              0.09
 Sep  4 1998  1:14PM                1              0.09
 Nov 27 1999 12:49PM                1              0.09
 Dec  4 1996  2:03PM                1              0.09

Minimum Value                Maximum Value
-------------------------- --------------------------
May  7 1995  8:33AM          Feb  4 2001  2:03PM
Working on SERVER: SERVER1, DATABASE: procurement, TABLE: solicitations,
COLUMN: deleter
==========================================================================
Distinct rows: 5
Column is not unique
value                          matches          percent
--------------------           -------          -------
                NULL             1111             98.58
               adams                7              0.62
              vargas                4              0.35
                tran                2              0.18
               perez                2              0.18
                ross                1              0.09

Minimum Value                  Maximum Value
------------------------------ ------------------------------
adams                          vargas
```

Space Requirements

When defining space requirements for a segment that will hold data, make sure that you plan for free space to be at least 125% larger than the largest table (clustered index) in that segment.

I have found that defragmenting tables by rebuilding their clustered indexes has been the simplest and most rewarding performance maintenance task (after optimizing queries and building the appropriate indexes).

I would recommend rebuilding all of the indexes (clustered and nonclustered) either once a week or once a month, depending on the volatility of your data and the availability of system resources.

Index Maintenance

If the page shrink count in the index management section keeps increasing after repeated checks using sp_sysmon, consider dropping and re-creating the NC index. Because page shrink count indicates that there have been significant deletes or updates, there may be fragmentation in the index pages or index pages that have few entries remaining.

Contention

The use of datapages and datarows locking can be your best friend when it comes to contention. Our implementation has approximately 400 active objects, of which less then 10% of those objects have real contention. By implementing a mix of allpages, datapages, and datarows locking, we were able to significantly reduce the contention and change the users' perception of performance. The SQL did not change, but the transaction time changed dramatically. This also brings up another tweak that may be required. As we have learned, the default lock escalation number is 200; if I have 200 shared page locks, then I am going to escalate to a shared table lock. When I was doing page level locking, if I had 5 rows per page, I was not escalating until I hit approximately 1,000 rows. If/when I implement datarows locking on that same object, I will escalate when I have accessed 200 rows or what was the equivalent of 40 pages. My point is that the lock promotion scheme will have to change for those objects that are tweaked.

Solaris, Total Physical Memory

There are two methods of accurately determining the total physical memory in a Sun Solaris 2.4+ system.

Reboot the system. Examine /var/adm/messages for the reboot log.

```
May 30 20:20:49 dev1 unix: cpu0: SUNW,UltraSPARC-II (upaid 1 impl 0x11 ver
0xa0 clock 400 MHz)
May 30 20:20:49 dev1 unix: cpu1: SUNW,UltraSPARC-II (upaid 2 impl 0x11 ver
0xa0 clock 400 MHz)
May 30 20:20:49 dev1 unix: SunOS Release 5.6 Version Generic_105181-05
[UNIX(R) System V Release 4.0]
May 30 20:20:49 dev1 unix: Copyright (c) 1983-1997, Sun Microsystems, Inc.
May 30 20:20:49 dev1 unix: mem = 2097152K (0x80000000)
May 30 20:20:49 dev1 unix: avail mem = 2086912000
May 30 20:20:49 dev1 unix: Ethernet address = 8:0:20:b1:4f:b5
May 30 20:20:49 dev1 unix: root nexus = Sun Enterprise 450 (2 X
UltraSPARC-II 400MHz)
May 30 20:20:49 dev1 unix: pci108e,80000 at root: UPA 0x1f 0x4000
May 30 20:20:49 dev1 unix: pci108e,80000 is /pci@1f,4000
May 30 20:20:49 dev1 unix: glm0:        Rev. 3 Symbios 53c875 found.
May 30 20:20:49 dev1 unix: PCI-device: scsi@3, glm #0
May 30 20:20:49 dev1 unix: pci1000,f0 is /pci@1f,4000/scsi@3
May 30 20:20:49 dev1 unix: glm1:        Rev. 3 Symbios 53c875 found.
May 30 20:20:49 dev1 unix: PCI-device: scsi@2, glm #1
```

This example indicates that the system has 2 GB internal physical memory. More information can be obtained by using the UNIX manual (man) command on prtconf.

```
System Configuration: Sun Microsystems sun4d
Memory size: 256 Megabytes
System Peripherals (Software Nodes):
. . . . . . . . .
```

Passwords

One of my favorite tips is to grant sa_role to a regular login so that the DBA has a "backdoor" or a safeguard against losing the SA password.

IDs

ASE DBAs face problems of login IDS and database user IDS getting mismatched quite often, when database dumps from one server or environment are loaded into another server or environment. The recommended approach is to either re-create login IDS in the same order as created in the original server, or drop and re-create all the user IDS in the database.

I prefer to run a single SQL command to match login and user IDS in the database. The SQL commands are as follows:

```
sp_configure 'allow updates',1
go
use <database_name>
go
begin tran
update sysusers
set suid=suser_id(user_name(uid))
from sysusers
where uid between 2 and 16000
and suser_id(user_name(uid)) is not null
go
sp_helpuser
go
/* if no mismatch, commit, else rollback */
commit tran
go
use master
go
sp_configure 'allow updates',0
go
```

The above query ensures that all user IDS except for dbo user, all groups and all role names are matched in accordance to the login IDS. Any user ID for which no login exists remains matched to NULL.

Problem

```
------------
%UNIX% isql -Usa -P NOTASECRET      ←      BAD BAD BAD!
```

The UNIX system process table holds an 80-character buffer of the commands typed to it. The example above allows anybody on the system (and I do mean anybody) to view the sa password by listing the process status. This is such a huge security risk that it's best to build something to make this password invisible. But typing the password 200 times a day is no fun either. Try out this alias for a single day and you'll be hooked.

Solution

```
------------
Create PW file for all possible DSQUERY values:
 1. touch file /sybase/sysadm/.pw.SERVER1
 2. chmod 600 /sybase/sysadm/.pw.SERVER1
 3. echo "SECRET                     " > /sybase/sysadm/.pw.SERVER1
```

```
Create alias:
alias is 'echo "User: sa Server: $DSQUERY";isql -Usa -S $DSQUERY -H
SYBASE-DBA -w
00000000000000000000000000000000000000000000000000000999 -P'cat
/sybase/sysadm/.pw.$DSQUERY''

Type "is"
%UNIX% is
User: sa Server: SERVER1
1> quit
%UNIX% setenv DSQUERY SECOND
%UNIX% is
User: sa Server: SECOND
1> _
```

The Danger

This approach only works where the DBA team is careful to absolutely know where they are and what they're doing at any given time. Don't laugh. A heck of a lot of people dive into systems without any concept of making sure they're able to recover if they break something. Do not use this alias approach when there are trainee-level DBAs. The absolute last thing you ever want to hear from someone who is cavalier about their access is, "I thought I was in development."

DBA Reference Sheet

Title	Description	Commands
DB Name	Name of the database	select db_name()
Date	Date form was filled in	select getdate()
Owner	Database owner	use <db>;sp_helpuser dbo
Password	Password of database owner	sp_password to change
Project	Project Title	
Contact	Civil servant contact for user surveys	
Summary	Short description of Database / Project Purpose	
Server	Server(s) where database exists	
Devices	History of initial creation and alterations	part of sp_helpdb <db> output
Device Name	Sybase logical device name	"device_fragments" section of sp_helpdb

Title	Description	Commands
Segment	Segment name mapped to this device	"segment" section of sp_helpdb
Size	Amount of space allocated	"size" section of sp_helpdb
Users	Specific user names added to database	use <db>;sp_helpuser
Task 41	Checked if all developers for Task 41 are added	
Others	Names of other users	sp_adduser <login name>, <alias name>, <group name>
Groups...	Groups defined in the database	sp_helpgroup (ignore system-defined groups: navigator_role, oper_role, replication_role, sa_role, sso_role, sybase_ts_role)
Use	Checked if group has members	
Group Name	Name of group	individual group names
Members	User names that are members of the group	sp_helpgroup <group name>
Permissions	General permissions that group holds	sp_helprotect <group name>
To Do	Checked as each task is completed	
enough open dbs	Configuration parameters set high enough	sp_configure "open databases"
create database	create database command issued	create database <name> on <device> =<size>, .., log on <device>=<size>
Add DBO	Add dbo login and change database owner	sp_changedbowner <login name>
DBO aliased in other dbs	Does this dbo own other databases too?	
Initial DB dump	Save copy of database completely empty	dump database <name> to "<file>"
Set sp_dboption	Check and changed database-specific options	sp_dboption (set "trunc log on checkpoint", and "abort tran on log full" during object creation)
Object Creation #1	First, easiest method of object creation	
Extract DDLs	Get database definitions from existing database	SQL Server Manager: (Server -> Generate DDL) or UNIX (execute dbschema.pl)

Title	Description	Commands
Source	Server and Database name of source of DDLs	
Modify DDLs	Check DDLs carefully and modify where needed	
Load DDLs	Load DDLs into new database	isql ....
Destination	Server and Database name of destination	
Object Creation #2	Second, harder method of object creation. Usually hand-run from source files of DB	
segments	Special segment names added	sp_addsegment ...
ncindexes	Size of ncindexes segment	sp_helpsegment ncindexes
threshold	Thresholds added to database	sp_helpthreshold
last chance pages	(required), number of pages in last chance	sp_helpthreshold (where "last chance?" column = 1)
# of pages	(optional, recommended) earlier threshold	sp_helpthreshold (where "last chance?" column = 0 and threshold procedure is called sp_thresholdaction)
doc: (LOG)	(optional) errorlog doc of nearly full log	sp_helpthreshold (where segment name is logsegment and procedure name is sp__thresholdmsg)
doc: (default)	(optional) errorlog doc of nearly full DB	sp_helpthreshold (where segment name is default and procedure name is sp__thresholdmsg)
groups	Groups added to database	sp_addgroup script
users	Users added to this database	sp_adduser script
permissions in other dbs	Users given permissions in other databases	usually in sp_adduser script, permissions problems may arise if this step is missed.
aliases	Aliases for users, aliased DBOs assigned	sp_addalias script, usually not used
defaults	Created all defaults	create default ... script
rules	Added rules	
types	Added type definitions	sp_addtype ....
binding defaults	Bindings of defaults to types	sp_bindefault ....
tables	Tables created	create table .... scripts

Title	Description	Commands
foreign keys	Foreign key definitions defined.	sp_foreignkey scripts, sp_primarykey scripts if they exist.
binding defaults again	Binding column names and types to defaults.	Rerun these scripts to bind columns in tables directly.
views	Created all views.	create view … scripts
unresolved references	Resolved errors in views due to references.	Watch for errors and fix permssions, nonexistent object names, or failed references.
foreign db references	No errors arose due to foreign database refs.	Watch for errors due to developers' assumption of user access to other databases.
procedures	Added stored procedures to database.	create procedure …. scripts
unresolved references	No errors in sp's: variable errors, table ref error	Watch for undefined variables, or nonexistent table name errors.
foreign db references	Foreign and remote references are okay.	Watch for potential user permission errors related to access to foreign and remote databases.
BCP DATA	If data comes from existing DB, copy data now.	Use bcp… scripts on ENDOR in /sybase/sysadm/bcp*. Watch bcp out / in carefully. Record tables with problems and retry copies by hand.
Source	Record source (Server / Database) of data.	
triggers	Create triggers on tables.	create trigger …. scripts
indexes	Added clustered / nonclustered indexes.	create .. index …. scripts
add constraints	Add constraints to tables.	alter table add constraint …. scripts, if they exist.
drop constraints	Remove constraints and check that all are gone.	Make sure there is an alter table DROP constraint for every add.
add constraints again	Add them again.	This will make sure you can restore the constraints as they originally existed.
add procedures again	If errors occurred in proc creation, try again.	If no problems occurred in the original create procedure … scripts, skip this step.
check available space	Record space after objects, data added.	sp_helpdb <db> will show how much space is left now that we're done

Title	Description	Commands
ncindexes	Record space in ncindexes segment.	Add up individual lines for available space in the ncindexes segment device fragment.
default	Record space left in default data space.	Use the same procedure to get the available space in the default segment.
Check errorlogs	Check server errorlogs for errors during creation.	(UNIX) more $SYBASE/install/errorlog. <SERVER>
Compare old vs. this	Compare source database objects with this one.	Make sure all database objects are present in new database.
Object Creation Done	Done with object creation.	
Database Backup	Make another copy of the database. Store it separately with a name of "<db>.full.baseline".	Select development system and create the directory structure for server-side files.
DBCC everything	Run the DBCC commands against this database. Make sure all output is clean.	dbcc checkdb (<db>) dbcc checkalloc (<db>), dbcc checkcatalog (<db>)
Source files dir stru	Record system/full path name of source files.	Select a development system and create the development directory structure for server-side files.
SCCS dirs	SCCS directories added to source tree.	Make sure there is an SCCS directory where necessary.
copy to prod scripts	Copy to production scripts tested.	Make sure there is a MOVE_TO_GEORGE directory where necessary.
backupdbs script	Database added to nightly backups.	backupdbs script in /sybase/sysadm/cronscripts
Update statistics script	Database added to weekly update statistics.	update_statistics script in same place
log dump times: _______	Logs to be dumped automatically at what times.	If logs are to be dumped at specific times, make sure there is a script to perform this task.
check backups	Results of nightly backups checked, working!	The next day, unzip and load database from backup file. Make sure that database is restored completely.

Appendix D

Other Resources

OK, you've read the book, and you've got other questions. Perhaps they are platform specific; perhaps they pertain to subjects that simply didn't exist when the book was written. Where do you look?

- Online Documentation Set

  You can go to http://www.sybase.com/support/manuals/ for online manuals of all supported Sybase products. This is a great place to start.

- *ASE Troubleshooting and Error Messages Guide*

  Of the books online, this is the one that will contain some of the internal information that you want.

- Sybase-sponsored news groups

  You can go to www.sybase.com/support/newsgroups, and register for newsgroups on a variety of subjects, from administration to performance and tuning to programming.

- Non-Sybase-sponsored list server

  Subscribe/unsubscribe at listserv@listserv.ucsb.edu (by sending an e-mail with that keyword in the message title).

  Send postings to SYBASE-L@LISTSERV.UCSB.EDU.

- International Sybase Users Group (ISUG)

  ISUG membership benefits include savings on Sybase education classes, discounts on affiliated conferences, and a subscription to the *ISUG Technical Journal*. Information available at www.isug.com, including lists of local user groups, sharable code, and white papers.

Appendix E

Tuning Sybase ASE Using Solid State Accelerators

A technical white paper by Imperial Technology, Inc. This document can be found online at www.imperialtechnology.com/technology_whitepapers_sybase.htm.

Abstract

Sybase Adaptive Server Enterprise has a history of success in very transaction intensive environments, especially Financial Services, Telecommunications and Government. The architecture has long supported large numbers of users and fast response times. But even the latest version of Adaptive Server Enterprise[1], like most relational database systems, has vulnerable areas that are performance limited by the laws of physics. This paper explores solid state disk technology as a quick and cost-effective way to solve those problems and supercharge your Sybase application.

Introduction

Solid state disk devices are not a new technology. They have been around for over 20 years, but were historically limited to mainframes because of their bulk and expense. But tremendous strides have been made in the last ten years with regard to both parameters. Solid state devices are now available in configurations from a 3-1/2" format that will fit in a PC, to rack mount units that will fit in a modern data center. The cost, while still much higher than rotational hard drives, can be easily justified when performance, maintenance and investment protection are taken into consideration.

1 The current version of Sybase ASE is 12.5 at the time of this article.

Since the early 1990's when Sybase took Wall Street by storm, the database has been known for a very efficient architecture that gets top performance from less hardware. So why should you consider a hardware solution for gaining a major performance improvement in your Sybase application? In a phrase — "no moving parts." CPUs get faster by the month, components get smaller, and network bandwidth is blazing new paths with high speed Ethernet and Fibre Channel. However, the hard disk arena has improved primarily in the direction of creating greater capacity and a lower cost per megabyte. Progress has not been very great in improving the speed of data access from the disk drive. Speed of access in a drive is still limited by the rotating speed of the disk or the linear speed of the access arm — the moving parts. This is illustrated in **Figure 1**.

Figure 1: Mechanical latency in a rotational device

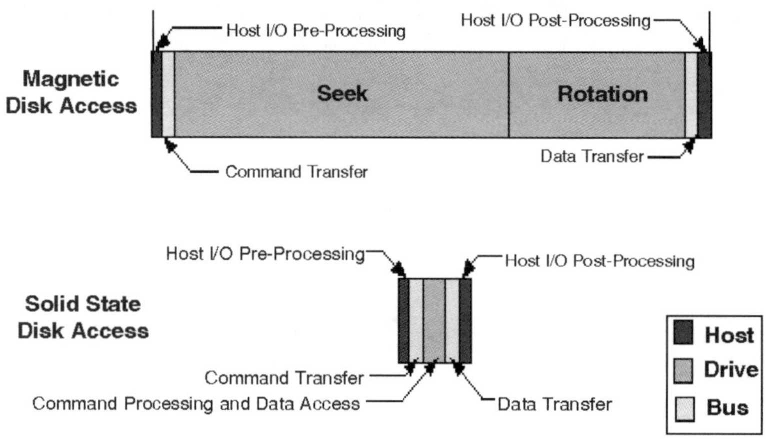

Solid state access times are typically hundreds of times faster than mechanical drives, and there are no moving parts to wear out.

But data residing in memory is volatile and will disappear as soon as the power is turned off. How can you trust your production Sybase data to a volatile device? Solid state disk manufacturers have effectively resolved this situation by adding built-in UPS functionality and packaging regular hard disk drives with the solid state drive as one all-inclusive and compact device. In the event of power interruption, circuits inside the solid state accelerator sense the loss and automatically switch to power from the internal battery-backed UPS. All data from the solid state drive is then written to the internal disk drive. Once data is safely saved to the internal disk, the device will switch off and wait for the power to return as the data is now protected. When stable power is re-established, data is copied from the internal disk drive back to the solid state accelerator (memory area) and the files are made available again to be accessed at memory speeds. There is virtually no risk of losing data with these safe guards in place. A file created on a device like this is equally if not more safe than a file created on a regular disk drive.

Solving the Right Problem

There are performance problems, and then there are performance problems. Solid state technology is not a solution for all of them. Sybase documentation currently has three volumes on Performance and Tuning tips alone. There are many tunable parameters within the Sybase architecture that allow a knowledgeable DBA to improve the performance of the database — everything from lock management to number of engines to procedure cache. Then there is application tuning — how to write the best queries, how to build indices, how to use stored procedures. And all of these factors should be considered to have a well running production application.

But many of the Performance and Tuning tips also point to system problems, and even the best DBA will be left banging his or her head (and wasting time) trying to solve a hardware problem with software. System performance problems usually fall into three main categories — CPU resource bottlenecks, memory bottlenecks, and I/O bottlenecks. It is fairly easy to identify when CPU resources are exhausted and more processing power is necessary. But do not waste your money on additional CPUs if the ones you have are waiting on other system resources. Adding system memory is traditionally a good rule of thumb for improving performance in a Sybase server. More memory can be used for Joins, Sorts, Temp Tables, Procedure Cache, etc. The drawbacks are that this memory is volatile, it can take quite a bit of effort to balance properly, and any memory assigned to the database is taking away valuable resources from the overall system. The diagram in **Figure 2**, from Volume 1 of the Sybase Performance and Tuning Guide, shows the default memory configuration. If the problem is actually an I/O problem, i.e. getting data to and from the disk, then you might try to make the data cache extremely large. You can even split this area into named caches and bind a specific table to a named cache. But memory assigned to data cache is memory that is not available for other operations. Data cache also does not guarantee a cache hit because more data coming in can flush it.

Figure 2: How Adaptive Server uses memory

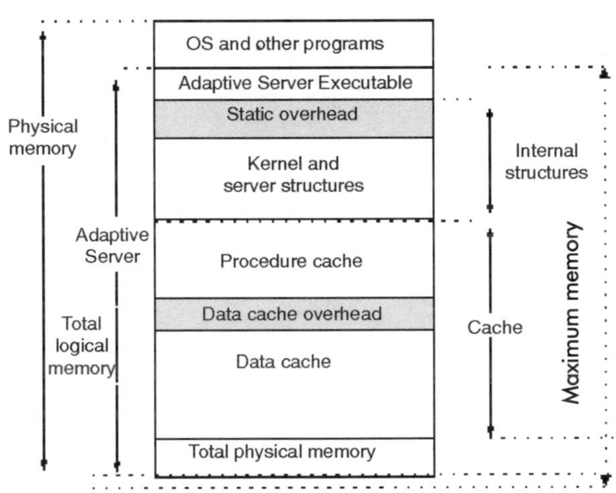

An I/O bottleneck, then is the ideal target for solid state technology. We have seen 200% to 1000% performance improvement in just a couple of hours by moving hot files onto a Solid State Accelerator. Let's now consider the tools used to identify these hot spots and look at specific Sybase files.

Identifying Problem Areas

The first thing you can do is use one of the monitoring procedures available to you within Sybase itself. **sp_sysmon** is a system procedure that produces Adaptive Server performance data. First, take a look at the "Requested disk I/Os" and "Completed disk I/Os" figure. If the data indicates a large number of requested disk I/Os and a smaller number of completed disk I/Os, there could be a bottleneck that is causing delays. The "Device Semaphore Granted" and "Device Semaphore Waited" categories report the number of times that a request for a device semaphore was granted immediately and the number of times the semaphore was busy and the task had to wait for the semaphore to be released. When Adaptive Server needs to perform a disk I/O, it gives the task the semaphore for that device. A large percentage of I/O requests that waited could indicate contention for a particular device.

The following sample shows **sp_sysmon** output for the "Disk I/O Management" section.

```
Disk I/O Management
-------------------

  Max Outstanding I/Os        per sec   per xact    count  % of total
  ------------------------- --------- --------- -------  ----------
    Engine 0                      n/a       n/a     1354         n/a
    Engine 1                      n/a       n/a     1421         n/a
    Engine 2                      n/a       n/a     1221         n/a
    Engine 3                      n/a       n/a     1554         n/a ............
  Total Requested Disk I/Os       n/a       n/a     5550         n/a

  Completed Disk I/O's
    Engine 0                     25.0       0.2     1512      28.3 %
    Engine 1                     21.1       0.2     1274      23.9 %
    Engine 2                     18.4       0.2     1112      20.8 %
    Engine 3                     23.8       0.2     1440      27.0 %
  ------------------------- --------- --------- -------  ----------
  Total Completed I/Os           88.3       0.8     5338     100.0 %
............
  Device Semaphore Granted       52.6       1.0     3218      89.1 %
  Device Semaphore Waited         4.1       0.1      394      10.9 %
```

There are also utilities available to you within most operating systems for measuring system I/O. In an NT system you can use Performance Monitor. In a UNIX environment you can use **iostat** and **sar**. "**iostat –D –c 1**" will give you reads and writes for each disk, and the user, system, wait and idle times for the CPU, at one second intervals. (check your OS for the exact parameters) "**sar –u –d 1 10**" will give you a similar set of information plus disk queue figures. The numbers in the following figure typify the condition of a system with a heavily utilized disk. The CPU is waiting for I/O to be completed, indicating a bottleneck. Another problem is the 90% disk utilization.

Figure 3: Sample iostat data

	sd2			cpu		
rps	**wps**	**util**	**us**	**sy**	**wt**	**id**
0	**90**	**90**	**20**	**40**	**40**	**0**

Finally, there are various performance analysis tools available on the Internet free of charge. Imperial Technology provides one called MiniMon. MiniMon runs on your system as a background task and does not interfere with any normal system operations. The program simply collects raw data from the system over a period of 72 hours using a series of performance "snapshots." Raw data is then uploaded to the portal for detailed analysis. Within 48 hours, a performance report is prepared and available for review. The report averages 12-14 pages and focuses on three main areas: CPU, memory utilization, and physical disk performance. You may see more detail at the Imperial website: imperialtech.com/products_minimon.htm.

Sybase Adaptive Server Hot Spots

The *Transaction Log* and *tempdb* are the two most obvious areas that a solid state accelerator can provide a quick and significant performance improvement. The Sybase documentation recommends placing both of these on separate devices from the data to avoid contention. The *transaction log* is the most contentious area for I/O performance in any OLTP system. All modifications (inserts, updates, deletes) to a database, as they are committed, are passed through the database's transaction log. The implication of this is that the transaction log becomes a fundamental bottleneck to database performance. The speed at which transactions can be written to the transaction log is the speed that data can be processed. Adding memory to the database cache has no effect on the performance of a database's *transaction log*. This is because the performance of transaction logging is directly related to the performance of the device upon which the transaction log has been placed.

The other hot spot is *tempdb*. Anyone can create objects in *tempdb*, and many processes use it silently. It is a server-wide resource that is used primarily for internal sort processing, creating worktables, reformatting, and storing temporary tables and indexes created by users. Many applications use stored procedures that create tables in *tempdb* to expedite complex joins or to perform other complex data analysis that is not easily performed in a single step. Again quoting from the Sybase Performance and Tuning Guide, "Keep *tempdb* on separate physical disks from your critical application databases. Use the fastest disks available. If your platform supports solid state devices and your *tempdb* use is a bottleneck for your applications, use those devices."

Heavily hit tables and indices are also good candidates for solid state. If you are concerned about security and make heavy use of audit records, the *sysaudits* table could be placed on one of these devices. With access times that are hundreds of times faster than a hard disk, you do not need to make a trade-off between security and performance.

Finally, if you are constantly dropping and rebuilding your key indices for peak performance, you can minimize down time and increase the speed of your system by applying solid state to that process. We know one major web auction company that greatly improved performance because they were able to go from rebuilding their search engine indices once a day to four times a day.

Benefits of Solid State Disk

While the cost per megabyte for Solid State Disk is significantly more than that of magnetic disks, there are several benefits of solid state that one must consider as well. First, SSD is not intended to replace entire disk farms, but only to store a small number of files that are causing your I/O bottleneck. This is typically about 3% of your files.

Figure 4

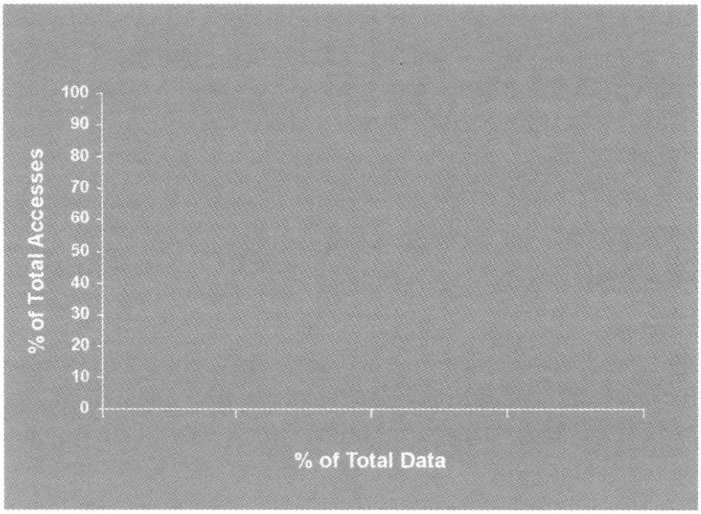

Second, SSD prices are comparable to system memory that one would add for database cache. But considering the earlier discussion, SSD does not have the negative impact on the overall system that giving memory to the database can have. And opposed to system memory, which is usually hardware vendor specific, SSD just looks like a standard SCSI device and can be moved from system to system or shared between systems.

Third, SSD can provide a very quick and proven performance fix. Consider the cost of DBA time involved in the hit-and-miss tweaking of system parameters, or the cost of a multi-month consulting effort to re-write an application. We have seen cases where SSD achieved better performance improvement in half a day than a consultant had been able to achieve in six months.

Fourth, SSD has a lower maintenance cost and higher reliability than magnetic devices. Because there are no moving parts to wear out, you are less likely to be faced with down time or the loss of critical data.

Finally, remember that your original goal is better performance. SSD applied to an I/O bottleneck promises not just incremental performance, but performance gains of 2x, 3x and more. What would your company pay to quickly and easily cut the response time of a critical application in half or support twice as many users without buying new servers?

Conclusion

Whether you are building a new Sybase application or maintaining one already in production, you are looking to get the highest performance and support the most users for the least cost. There are many options to tune your application and all options should be considered and applied in the appropriate situation. Solid State Disk/Accelerators solve the specific problem of I/O bottlenecks quickly, completely and cost-effectively. With warp speed performance, easy installation, investment protection and low maintenance, it is a solution you should consider for your high-performance Sybase application.

Appendix F

Fragmentation and Database Performance

A technical white paper by White Sands Technology, Inc. (http://www.whitesands.com/).

> **WARNING:** Page numbers in this section refer to the online documents which can be found at www.whitesands.com.

About the Authors

White Sands Technology produces the ProActive DBA family of products and is a leader in the development of performance tuning, maintenance, diagnostics and disaster recovery solutions for Sybase ASE and Microsoft SQL Server databases. Their home page on the Web is located at .

Also assisting with this white paper was John McVicker. John achieved nearlegendary status in the Sybase community as a performance-tuning guru. He is currently a Systems Architect and Performance Manager within the Enterprise Systems Management division of Inventa, and was a Principal Consultant for over five years with Sybase Professional Services, the consulting division of Sybase, Inc. He can be reached via e-mail at jmcvicker@yahoo.com or jmcvicker@inventa.com.

Preface

This white paper is intended for DBAs and managers who must be concerned with keeping production Sybase database systems running at peak performance levels. It assumes a good degree of familiarity with Sybase database servers.

Microsoft SQL Server versions 6.5 and earlier share a common data structure with pre-11.9.2 versions of Sybase; thus, much of the information in this white paper applies to those versions of Microsoft SQL Server as well.

Introduction

One of the last things client/server developers often think about is the long-term storage considerations of their database objects, namely tables.

The production-support DBA is going to support the application in its day-today usage, so it is up to the DBA to watch over active database objects such as disk devices, segments, table sizes, and index usage.

The developers work from a blueprint of the application as it will be used and create specific logical designs to match. However, the next step is to create a good physical design to support the application's logical design work.

The physical design steps should include making sure that the correct data types are selected for tables, ensuring that the proper normalization is done, and planning for the long-term growth and maintenance of the Sybase server and its databases.

Why Be Concerned with Fragmentation?

During normal operations, the Sybase DBA must maintain a high performance RDBMS environment. This includes keeping service levels and performance ratings of the system, which include average response times of OLTP applications and batch jobs, as well as maintaining a high amount of availability of the system for the users.

While Sybase ASE and SQL Server are high-performance RDBMS engines, the database engine can perform only as well as the applications that are written for it allow.

Standardized benchmarks such as TPC-C aside, well-written applications perform very well only if all pre-production application development is done with an eye towards long-term performance requirements of the business as well as the RDBMS engine that the application is written for.

The topics of defragmentation and performance-related aspects of table design have not been as mainstream with Sybase ASE and SQL Server as with other RDBMS products. Defragmentation of Sybase database tables is not considered a requirement by Sybase or by many Sybase DBAs, since tables do not have pre-set size parameters such as extent size and growth size factors found in other vendors RDBMS engines.

However, tables in Sybase databases can become fragmented in various ways. And, as many DBAs have discovered in recent years, the proper design of database tables and indexes, as well as the use of ongoing defragmentation steps, will allow the Sybase DBA to maintain higher performance and retain the value of the hardware investment, rather than having to move to a new, higher level of hardware in order to maintain performance levels of an initially deployed production system.

Currently, most if not all RDBMS engines from various vendors do not automatically maintain compactness in their data structures, since the overhead of dynamic maintenance of data can be a burden on a busy production server.

Sybase has always provided a high-performance RDBMS server and continues to do so with its latest release—ASE version 12.5.

However, Sybase has also made advances in dynamic maintenance of the environment, starting with the Housekeeper task added in Sybase SQL Server System 11. This task helps keep database checkpoint times much lower than they were in older versions of SQL Server, and, starting with ASE version 11.9.2, the housekeeper task performs automatic, background cleanup of certain aspects of DOL (data-only locked) tables.

Let's hope this is only the first step in a more proactive approach to the DBA's maintenance chores, such as automated data defragmentation housekeepers and index statistics gatherers.

This white paper illustrates how important table defragmentation is to achieving high performance in Sybase database servers. This importance is magnified in Sybase 11.0 and later versions, due to the availability of large I/O, and in Sybase ASE 11.9.2 and later which include the ability to perform OAM-based table scans on DOL tables using extent I/O. However, earlier versions also show increased performance following proper table defragmentation.

What is Fragmentation?

At this point, we assume the reader knows the basics of Sybase data storage internals. Also, most readers of this paper (DBAs, rather than developers) will be interested in production Sybase database support issues.

However, developers may also be interested in the capacity planning and fragmentation-causing topics here.

For more detailed information on Sybase database structure, you can refer to the resources listed below:

- White Sands Technology, Inc.'s *ProActive DBA User's Manual*, Chapter 2 (Overview of SQL Server Data Storage)
- *Sybase Adaptive Server Enterprise Performance & Tuning Guide*, Chapter 3 (Data Storage) and Chapter 4 (How Indexes Work)
- *Sybase Internals* (Kirkwood, John; International Thomson Computer Press, 1996), Chapter 8 (Storage)

Definition of Terms

The following section lists basic data structures and other terms that will be mentioned in this white paper.

Page

Sometimes known as a block, a page is 2KB in size (or larger, up to 16K, in Sybase ASE 12.5 and later versions). A data or index page holds one or more rows of data, and rows cannot span pages—that is, a row must exist on a single page.

Extent

A group of 8 contiguous pages (or 7 pages if the first page number of the extent is a multiple of 256, where the first page in the extent is reserved for the allocation map page).

Extent Reclaim

Occurs when all data pages on an extent become unused; the database extent is removed from use by its owning table and placed back into the free list of extents in the database.

Reserved Page

A page within an extent which has been assigned to a specific table, but does not necessarily contain data yet.

Data Page

A page within an extent which actually has rows on it and is not empty.

Unused Page

A page which does not have rows on it but is a reserved page.

Overflow Page

A type of data page maintained for nonunique clustered indexes, overflow pages hold duplicate index rows.

Cache Buffer

A database page which is resident in the database server's cache.

Segment

One or more logical chunks of a database typically used for table placement on specific disk drive(s).

Seek Time

Time it takes a disk drive head to move to and start reading a requested piece of data.

Fragmentation Defined

Fragmentation is defined as any condition which causes more than the optimal amount of disk I/O to be performed in accessing a table, or causes the disk I/Os that are performed to take longer than they optimally would.

Optimal performance of SELECT queries occurs when data pages are as contiguous as possible within the database, and the data pages are packed as fully as possible.

Note that achieving optimal SELECT performance can be at odds with maximizing performance of INSERT, UPDATE and DELETE statements, which will be discussed later in this paper (see page 6).

Defragmentation can be defined as the set of operations that a DBA performs to an RDBMS to remove any wasted space and make the storage space contiguous and well-ordered within individual database rows, pages, extents, segments, databases, and cache memory, all of which leads to better system resource usage and performance.

Types of Fragmentation

Fragmentation can manifest itself in different ways in the database. The different types of fragmentation are described in the following sections.

Messy Page Chains

This condition occurs when the pages within the page chain of a table or index are not contiguous and in sequential order within the database. Messy page chains cause excessive disk seeking during full table or index scans and range queries (partial scans).

The drawing below illustrates discontiguous pages within a page chain:

Figure 1: Fragmented page chain

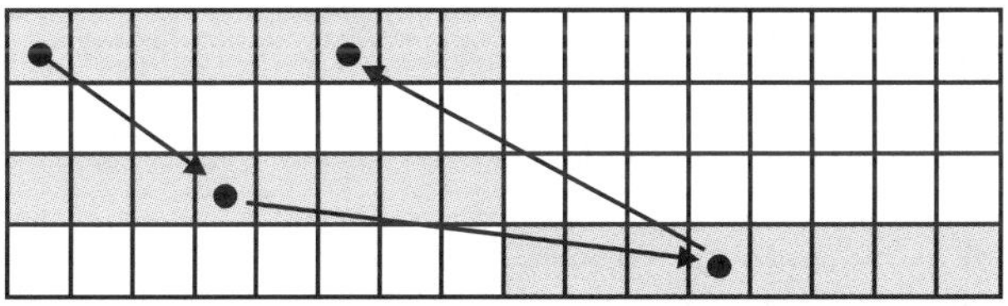

As you can see, the pages within the page chain are not physically contiguous (next to each other); thus, to read the pages in the page chain involves seeking the disk heads to each new page in the chain—a very time-consuming operation.

The page chain shown below, on the other hand, is in optimal order with no disk seeking required to move from page to page within the page chain—the I/Os can be performed sequentially, with no disk seeking:

Figure 2: Properly organized page chain

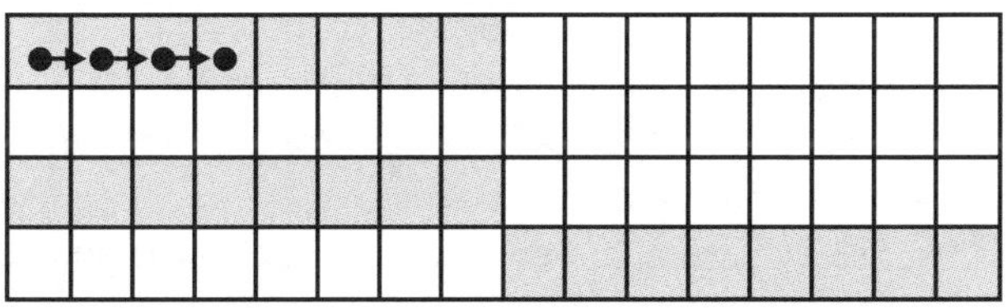

A random I/O (defined as an I/O involving a disk seek) typically takes 10-20 times longer than a sequential I/O of the same size; thus, messy page chains can harm performance to a much greater degree than other types of fragmentation in objects on which full or partial scans (i.e., table scans or range queries) are performed.

Messy page chains can be caused by any of the following:

- Page splits due to inserts to a clustered index which is set up to spread randomly across the table;
- Page splits due to row growth (i.e. a row being updated to a larger row size);
- Pages being removed from the page chain due to heavy deletes, which leaves the page chain discontiguous between the pages surrounding the deleted page.

Data-only locked (DOL) tables in Sybase ASE 11.9.2 and greater do not utilize page chains in the data layer (heap) of tables. However, indexes (both DOL pseudo-clustered and nonclustered) utilize page chains, and messy page chains can harm performance for full or partial scans of these indexes, such as in covered queries which use the index.

As new database pages are allocated to satisfy new storage required by a table (e.g. due to inserts or page splits caused by rows which grow in size), the new pages are allocated first from a list of unused pages within the table, and then from new free extents within the database segment.

However, the grabbing of random unused pages creates non-contiguous database pages spread out over the segment of the database, as you can see in the diagram below:

Figure 3: Page splitting causes messy page chains

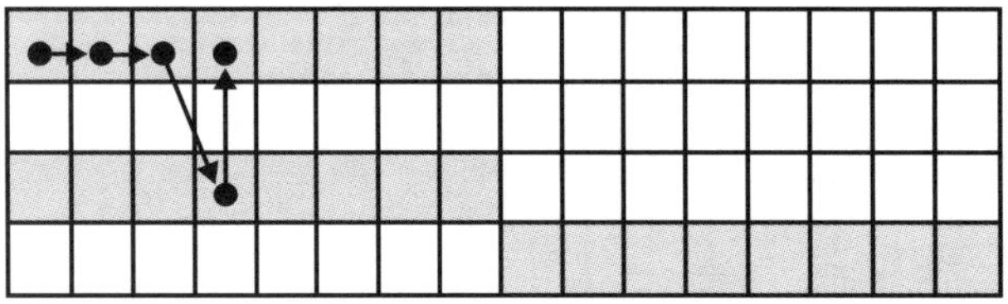

The third and fourth pages used to be contiguous within the page chain, but after the page was split, there is now a break in the contiguity of the page chain.

The randomness of data pages causes larger seek times when following a page chain during operations such as a table scan, index scan, and range queries. Larger seek times translate to slower response times for both long-running queries as well as OLTP operations.

In order to help you understand random page ordering, you can refer to ProActive DBA's Page Chain Order report, which shows you the effects of poor page ordering and its effects on performance at various I/O sizes (2KB to 16KB). ProActive DBA also includes higher-level reports which summarize your tables' and databases' overall fragmentation levels.

As an alternative, the DBCC pglinkage command can be used to traverse the data pages of the table, so you can get an idea of how well or poorly the page chain is ordered.

Microsoft SQL Server 6.0 and greater offers the DBCC showcontig command, which provides a report of certain types of fragmentation on a table or index.

To run this command, you must use an administrator's account such as sa and also have the sybase_ts_role granted to you. Typically, the DBA of the database server should be the one using the command.

First, use the query below to obtain the starting page number of the table's data page chain:

```
/* show print output */
dbcc traceon(3604)
go
/* find the starting page # of the table's heap or CI */
SELECT name, first
FROM sysindexes
WHERE indid in (0,1)
AND id = object_id(your_tablename)
go
name first
---- -----
Customer 14092
```

Next, issue the DBCC pglinkage command as shown below to walk the page chain of the table:

```
/*
* dbcc pglinkage (dbid, start_pg#, number_pgs,
* print_option, search_for, search_order)
*
* dbid - the database id of the database being reviewed
* start_pg# - first page in the heap or CI (see above)
* number_pgs - how many pages to read (0=all)
* print_option - 0 = show count of pages read
* 1 = show last 16 pages read
* 2 = show all pages read
* search_for - page # to stop at (0=end of table)
* search_order - 0 = follow previous page pointer,
* 1 = follow next page pointer
*/
go
/* Example - show all page numbers, starting from first,
continue to end of table */
dbcc pglinkage (5, 14092, 0, 2, 0, 1)
go
```

This command will be time-consuming for large tables; look to use a limiting number_pgs value, such as 5000.

You will see the page numbers for all pages within the page chain, and you can determine how random the page linkage is and plan for table defragmentation accordingly.

For a perfectly linked table, the pages in each extent should be linked together so that the page numbers increase by 1 within each extent. Every extent has a starting page number which is evenly divisible by 8.

Ideally, the extents will be contiguous as well, so that the page numbers will all be sequential (with the exception of breaks for allocation map pages, which occur every 256 pages).

Poor Page Utilization

When pages are less than fully used, the part of each page that is unused constitutes a form of fragmentation, since the table's or index's rows are no longer packed together as tightly as they could be. The drawing below illustrates poor page utilization:

Figure 4

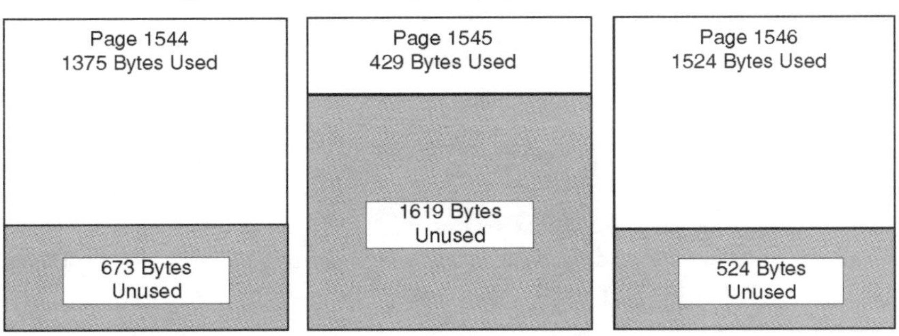

The effect of poor page utilization is that more disk I/Os are required in order to read a table of a given size, due to the wasted space on each page, whereas fewer disk I/Os would be required if the pages were packed more fully with data.

Poor page utilization is caused by the following conditions:

- Random delete operations, which leave individual pages in use but not completely full of rows;
- Page splits due to inserts or updates, which leave each page approximately half-full;
- Row shrinkage of rows that contain nullable or variable-length columns;
- Placement of duplicate clustered index rows onto overflow pages, which are likely not to be fully utilized;
- Using a fillfactor of less than 100 when rebuilding an index on a readonly table or very large, lightly modified table; this will leave gaps within database pages which are unlikely to become filled in;
- Using very large row sizes, which prevent rows from being able to occupy all the space on a page; for example, if rows are 800 bytes each, then only two rows can fit on a 2K page, leaving approximately 400 bytes unused on every page.

When you build a clustered index on an APL table using a low fillfactor setting, it results in fewer rows on the data pages than could otherwise fit.

This can have both advantages and disadvantages, and it is up to the DBA to weigh the benefits and drawbacks to determine the optimal fillfactor setting.

The main reason to use a fillfactor lower than 100% is so that, when performing randomized inserts across the entire table, rows that are inserted will not cause page splits immediately—in other words, each page will, on average, have room for a certain number of new rows to be inserted before a page split must occur.

Over time, of course, page splits will inevitably occur as individual pages fill up with newly-inserted rows, but using a fillfactor when you create or rebuild a clustered index can delay the onset of page splitting, in effect buying you some time before it becomes cost-effective to rebuild the index again.

On the other hand, setting the table's fillfactor too low results in excessive wasted space on pages, which negatively impacts the performance of SELECT queries against the table due to the extra disk I/Os that are required to read the selected rows.

These tradeoffs can be summarized as follows:

Fillfactor Setting	Pro	Con
Higher Fillfactor	Best utilization of page space.	Random inserts more likely to result in page splits, harming performance of inserts and updates, and causing excessive disk seeking.
Lower Fillfactor	Page space is less effectively utilized, meaning more disk I/O is required for large SELECT queries.	Inserts spread across the table are less likely to cause page splitting.

In general, page splitting harms performance to a greater degree than having a certain amount of unused space within rows and pages, because the extra disk I/O and disk seeking incurred by page splits outweighs the slight additional cost of performing extra disk I/Os (if those I/Os are sequential) due to lower page space utilization. Thus, use of a fillfactor lower than 100% should be strongly considered for those tables that will receive a moderate to high degree of random inserts across the range of the clustered index.

If the table's clustered index is not designed so as to spread out inserts across the table's data pages, then the wasted space which exists due the low fillfactor setting only results in fewer rows being locked while page locks are in effect, but will confer no benefits in terms of reducing page splitting. In such cases, a fillfactor of 100% is recommended unless you need to use a lower setting in order to reduce contention due to page locking.

The DBA must also understand that using a low fillfactor can also result in more rows being considered by the query optimizer during query optimization, and may even lead to indexes not being chosen on tables due to the larger amount of data pages within the table.

In general, we recommend that a fillfactor of either 100 or at least 90 percent be used unless carefully planned. However, this formula may not apply to smaller, highly-accessed tables, because points of contention (blocking) should be addressed with a fillfactor or the use of the dirty-read feature within Sybase.

Applications built around the use of low fillfactors should probably be redesigned based on the newer features of SQL Server 11.0 and later, or use of row-level locking features available starting with ASE 11.9.2 should be considered.

ProActive DBA's Object Information Report lets you view a table's page utilization level in detail, so you can keep an eye on page splitting and other causes of poor page utilization.

Extent Fragmentation

Similar to page fragmentation, extent fragmentation occurs when the extents of a table or index are not contiguous with the database. This can occur due to:

- Random deletes throughout a table, which leave some of the pages in an extent unused while the extent itself is still reserved as part of the table's space allocation.
- Deletes on ranges of contiguous rows within the table, causing one or more entire extents to become deallocated, thus leaving a gap between the surrounding extents of the table or index;
- Interspersion of a table's data extents with its own indexes' extents or with the extents of other tables, resulting in excessive disk seeking.

The diagram below illustrates extent fragmentation:

Figure 5

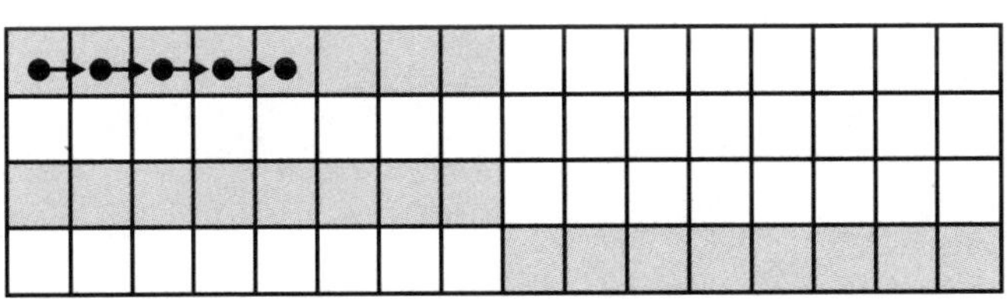

The areas highlighted in gray represent the extents allocated to a particular table in the database. As you can see, the table's extents are not contiguous within the database, but rather are intermingled with the extents of other objects and with empty extents.

Extent fragmentation is very common in Sybase. It occurs, for example, when two or more tables are built in parallel, thus causing new extent allocations to alternate between the two tables; or, when a table which has indexes is loaded with data, new extent allocations alternate between the table's data layer and its indexes, causing the extents for each object to become interleaved with the other(s).

You can reduce the amount of extent interleaving on tables by allocating selected tables to their own segments in the database, so that when the tables grow, new extent allocations will not be interleaved with the allocations of other tables.

Row Fragmentation

This type of fragmentation occurs when columns in a tables are wider than needed to store application data. For instance, if a customer table has a column of CUST_NAME with a datatype of CHAR(30) NOT NULL, then any right-padding spaces in this column would be considered as fragmentation since they take up space but do not apply to the application specifically.

Changing this column to a VARCHAR(30) NOT NULL datatype would cause only the usable data to be stored, but not the trailing spaces. This is more space efficient, and the developer could even plan more proactively for larger names and use VARCHAR(255) NOT NULL as the datatype since only the name is stored and not the spaces.

The tradeoff in making this change is that if the customer name changes to a longer string, page splitting can occur, which results in lower page utilization as well as page chain fragmentation.

In general, page splitting harms performance to a greater degree than a certain amount of unused space within rows and pages, so for columns that are likely to grow in size, it is often better to use a fixed-length datatype which will not grow, rather than a variable-length datatype whose data can grow and cause a page split. In this case, the extra space used by the fixed-length column harms performance less than the extra I/Os and inevitable disk seeking caused by page splits.

But, it may make more sense to use variable-length datatypes for columns that will not grow or change in size once the rows have been inserted. This will realize the space-saving benefits of variable-length columns, yet will not allow row growth or shrinkage which can increase the fragmentation level in the table.

Dealing with Fragmentation

Now that we understand the different types of fragmentation that can occur, let us turn to what can be done to reduce the occurrence of fragmentation in your databases, and how to cope with fragmentation if and when it does occur.

With the proper planning during the application development and table design phase, and by planning appropriate maintenance schedules for ongoing database maintenance, DBAs can achieve the proper levels of space efficiency and reduced fragmentation that will result in optimal performance of the database as a whole.

The following sections list techniques you can use as part of your strategy for keeping fragmentation-related performance degradation at a minimum.

Analyzing Effects of Deletes

The design of tables in Sybase should include the analysis of whether random deletes to the table will occur. Since Sybase databases only reclaim space at the extent level, not the page level, the DBA and developer should understand the condition of page fragmentation.

When a row is deleted, its space is not utilized by new inserts unless the same, or a very similar, clustered index value is used. For tables without clustered indexes (i.e. heap tables), new inserts are only applied to the last data page of the table. Unused deleted row space within data pages on tables without clustered indexes is never reclaimed.

The effect of this is to reduce overall page utilization in the table, which means more disk I/Os are required in order to scan a given number of rows in the table, than would otherwise be required if the pages were as full as possible.

Analyzing Effects of Inserts

As discussed earlier (see page 7), inserts to APL tables with clustered indexes can cause page splitting, which is a serious degrader of performance. Analysis should be done to determine what level of inserts will occur against the larger and/or more heavily used tables in the database, and where those inserts will occur.

If the inserts will occur primarily at the end of the table, it is usually best to use a higher fillfactor setting (or even 100%), and use the dbcc tune(ascinserts) setting to prevent 50-50 page splitting (see below).

Tables with random insert points mixed with random delete points will experience the most fragmentation if a clustered index is used to cause the random inserts. This is because page splits occur on data pages when no more room is found on the page but the clustered index value falls between two existing values.

When this occurs, the Sybase server creates two half-full pages out of the original page, and the new row being inserted is placed on one of the two split pages.

Subsequently, the data that used to occupy 2048 bytes (on a single page) now consumes 4096 bytes in two pages with about 50 percent full data pages. Over time, if the table is inserted into and deleted from either heavily or lightly, the table becomes heavily fragmented at the database page level.

When using database tables with clustered indexes that allow for all inserts to go to the last database page, the DBA can allow for the use of the DBCC TUNE feature with the "ascending inserts" option, to allow the page split to occur at the end of the data page, rather than the middle of the data page. The following table is one that could benefit from using DBCC TUNE:

```
CREATE TABLE Customers
(Customer_Number NUMERIC(10,0) IDENTITY
NOT NULL, Customer_data...)
CREATE INDEX cidx ON Customers (Customer_Number)
```

As new records are added to this table, application developers will expect the rows to be added in numerically increasing order based on the identity attribute of the Customer_Number column.

Using the following command in Sybase versions 11 and higher, the DBA can force page splits to occur at the offset where the row would be inserted:

```
DBCC TUNE(ascinserts, 1, Customer_Number)
```

To turn off ascending inserts, the following command would be issued:

```
DBCC TUNE(ascinserts, 0, Customer_Number)
```

It is best to use this command when the data in the table is inserted in sequential order based on the clustered index, or if the clustered index of the table is a composite index and the last column increases monotonically.

In the latter case, even though not all inserting is done at the end of the table, if enough of the inserts will be in sequence at a small number of insert points in the table, it can be beneficial to force page splits to occur at the end of the page. Some fragmentation will result, but overall, less fragmentation will occur than if pages were split using the normal "50-50" method.

NOTE: This command is a runtime-only command and must be re-issued upon dataserver startup. The DBA may want to create a startup batch which is run following dataserver startup to set certain tables up for ascending inserts. In addition, this command can be used prior to a large BCP operation.

Sybase 11.0 as well as prior versions all benefit from defragmenting to remove database page fragmentation. More data on a database page means the possibility of fewer logical and physical I/Os during database disk usage, as well as lower requirements of data cache size. Data cache can keep more rows of data in memory with fewer cache buffers (data pages in memory) if the pages are more fully packed with rows.

Analyzing Effects of Updates

Like random inserts, updates which cause rows to grow in size can cause page splitting on APL tables. On DOL tables, these updates can cause another problem known as row forwarding, where Sybase relocates the grown row on a new database, but leaves a marker at the row's old location which indicates the new location of the row.

Both of these conditions harm performance by causing extra disk I/O and disk seeking, and thus developers and DBAs should work together to avoid these conditions as much as possible.

You can prevent rows from growing in size by using only fixed-length, nonnullable column datatypes. Obviously, this is not feasible in all situations, but DBAs and developers alike should be aware of the tradeoffs in using variablelength and nullable datatypes.

Variable-length types can save storage space if used wisely; yet, they do incur additional overhead, which can end up wasting space if they are used indiscriminately.

But perhaps the worst problem of all is that, when a variable-length column grows in size, it can cause a page split, which itself not only takes much longer to execute, but also causes fragmentation, leading to poorer performance for subsequent queries that have to scan that part of the table.

Thus, special care should be taken to ensure that variable-length columns are used only where the following conditions are met:

- There is a significant spread between the average and maximum column length; and,
- The maximum column length is reasonably large (e.g. 5-10 characters or more), so the variable-length column overhead does not outweigh the potential space savings.

Preventing Extent Fragmentation

When a table undergoes a variety of operations, data pages may become empty within an extent of the table. The extent continues to store data on some of its pages, while other pages are marked as unused (these pages show up in the output of sp_spaceused under the unused column).

Since these unused pages are never reclaimed by Sybase unless new inserts are done which cause a new page requirement, they contribute to the overall unused space of the table. These pages add up over time, and use disk space which otherwise would be available for other tables.

Extents are deallocated from a table when all data pages of the extent become unused. As the last row of a data page is removed, the extent is reviewed to see if that page is the last one in the extent with data on it, and if so, the whole extent is removed from the table's allocation map and returned to the free list of extents within the database.

Larger amounts of unused pages for a table should be reclaimed by the database in order to provide the pages to other tables on the database segment. The operations of defragmentation will reclaim this space. With the large-block I/O offered starting in SQL Server 11.0, extent fragmentation becomes much more significant a performance problem, because entire extents with unused pages are read into cache but only those pages with data on them will be utilized by the server during the query that fetched the extent into cache.

Capacity Planning for Defragmentation

When planning a Sybase database environment, most DBAs and development teams plan for expected data sizes as well as affording space for fault tolerance in the form of mirroring or RAID configurations.

However, space considerations for table defragmentation are often overlooked. Typically, capacity planning should include allocating database segments to defragmentation areas to allow tables to move from one database segment to another when defragmentation occurs.

For instance, the following tables show you how to allow for space planning for a large table.

Database Name	Size
Customer_History	5GB

Segment Name	Size	Usage
history_seg_01	1GB	Customer_History data only
history_seg_02	1GB	Customer_History data only
ncidx_seg_01	1GB	Nonclustered indexes only
ncidx_seg_02	1GB	Nonclustered indexes only
default	500MB	
system, log	500MB	

Table	Typical Size	Initially Assigned to Segment
Customer_History	800MB	history_seg_01

The steps to defragment this table would be as follows:

- Drop Customer_History non-clustered indexes
- Drop Customer_History clustered index
- Rebuild Customer_History clustered index on history_seg_02 (if on 01 today)
- Use fillfactor of 100% (plan accordingly, depending on usage)
- Rebuild Customer_History non-clustered indexes on ncidx_seg_02 (if on 01 today)
- For nonclustered indexes, use a fillfactor of 90% (plan accordingly, depending on usage)
- Optionally execute DBCC Tune(ascinserts, 1, tablename)
- Execute sp_recompile "Customer_History"

The effects of properly allocating space for defragmentation are:

- The nonclustered indexes are kept separate from the data layer of the table (heap or clustered index), thereby reducing fragmentation at the data layer;
- The data layer and the nonclustered indexes can be rebuilt onto a clean segment (either _01 or _02, whichever it is not currently using), so the page allocations will be perfectly contiguous with no extent interleaving fragmentation.

When rebuilding a clustered index, consider the space requirements within the segments being used for the new clustered index. You will need space to accept new data pages which will hold the rows being moved from the older clustered index.

Typically, the space requirements will be equal to or less than the current size of the table (for example, as shown in the data column of sp_spaceused for the table).

The reason the space requirement may be less is that unused page space may exist in the table—for example, if a table's clustered index currently uses 500MB, it may only require 400MB after defragmentation.

A good estimate is based on the first clustered index rebuild done on the table. Compute the row count and divide by the number of pages shown in the data column of sp_spaceused after the clustered index is created. Use that to judge the average number of rows per page and continue to use that average number for further space estimates when rebuilding clustered indexes. The steps would be:

- Defragment the table to pack the pages as fully as possible
- Run sp_spaceused tablename
- Compute rowtotal / data / 2
- Catalog the result as the table's average rows-per-page value

When defragmenting a non-clustered index, you simply need to drop and recreate it. Many times, it will be smaller than its original size, as reported by:

```
sp_spaceused table_name, 1
```

Use Fixed-Length Row Sizes

If you try to avoid as much as possible variable-length datatypes and datatypes which allow NULL values which later change to non-NULL values, you will prevent row size growth, which can cause page splitting on updates or row forwarding on DOL tables—i.e. fragmentation.

Row size growth can also lead to overflow page usage. If a duplicate row cannot fit back onto the page it was updated on, a new page will be created for the page split, causing data page fragmentation.

For smaller VARCHAR NOT NULL datatypes, consider CHAR NOT NULL. A rule of thumb could be to use CHAR for 10-byte and smaller character columns, and VARCHAR for ones larger than 10 bytes, where column size is not deterministic.

ProActive DBA's Row Information Report lets you examine a table's average row size versus its defined minimum and maximum row size. If the average size is close to the maximum, consider replacing variable-length columns with fixedlength equivalents.

Use Monotonically-Increasing Clustered Index Keys

Create tables with clustered indexes which increase in value over time—such as identity-based clustered index columns or a date/time value based on the current date and time. This will help reduce fragmentation due to page splitting because new rows will always be added to the end of the table.

Some DBAs do not like to do this because they consider the last page of the table a point of contention which will cause blocking. This is only a problem if users have multi-step transactions which take excessive amounts of time to insert onto the last page of a table.

Applications may be able to have such transactions broken out into multiple transactions if the unit of work is not critically dependent on such bundling of transaction activity.

If many users are updating the last page of the table, the typical point of contention is the speed of transaction log writes during the commit phase of the transaction. Such contentions can be alleviated with faster transaction log disks or even Solid State Devices for log segments.

Also, in version 11.5 and greater, proper sizing of the PLC (also called ULC, or user log cache) can improve transaction commit throughput, thus alleviating last-page contention on clustered indexes with monotonically-increasing index key values.

Use Unique Clustered Index Keys

Where possible, you should only use unique-valued clustered indexes to keep overflow page usage down.

When a significant number of duplicate key values exist in a clustered index, Sybase creates overflow pages to hold the duplicate rows. This lowers space efficiency and index performance for two reasons:

- The duplicate rows are not part of the B-tree index structure and thus require extra disk I/O for the server to locate these rows within the index;
- The overflow pages are often not packed very fully, and may contain only one or several rows; this reduces overall page utilization and cache efficiency, and increases fragmentation.

The best way to eliminate overflow pages in a clustered index is to create the clustered index on a unique column or columns in the table. As an alternative, you can often reduce the level of overflow pages in a clustered index by adding one or more columns to the index to increase the level of uniqueness of the index.

Large I/O Considerations

Starting with Sybase SQL Server version 11.0, multiple pages can be read at one time into I/O pools configured in the default cache and any DBA-defined data caches.

Because the ability to effectively use large I/O depends on the data page chain being contiguous, the DBA should pay attention to the output of sp_sysmon in SQL Server 11.0.1 and greater.

Running sp_sysmon at 10 minute intervals while large I/O operations are being done will give the DBA an idea of how efficient the page chains are. The numbers to review are the comparison between the large I/Os that are done and number of pages used.

If the percentage of pages used is below 60 percent, consider examining the table's fragmentation level—for example, via ProActive DBA's Fragmentation Summary Report, or by using the DBCC pglinkage function to determine the number of contiguous pages in the table; then, plan a table defragmentation for those tables and indexes being scanned with larger I/Os that could benefit from defragmentation.

ProActive DBA's Fragmentation/Performance Report shows the effects of fragmentation in terms of disk seeking and increased disk I/O levels when using regular 2K disk I/O versus the larger 16K I/O size. This can help you identify tables that could benefit from the larger I/O size, as well as tables that could effectively utilize larger I/O if defragmented.

The Big Picture

With the proper amount of table defragmentation, the Sybase DBA can proactively keep a database server environment operating in top condition.

Sybase continues to review operating procedures of ASE and may offer built-in table defragmentation operations in future version of ASE.

However, in today's customer environments, the database can only offer those features which are available today.

In our experience, it is not uncommon for defragmentation to reclaim database space of 30-40% or more. For example, one customer saw savings in the 6-7 GB range following defragmentation of 14GB of tables which had not had their indexes rebuilt in over a year.

Subsequently, overall user performance was enhanced on their Sybase 11.0 system, especially for table scans using 16KB I/Os.

Other customers have reported performance increases of between 5-50% or more in batch and on-line processes running against Sybase databases after defragmenting critical tables in heavily-used databases.

With the data pages in a contiguous format, all eight pages of each extent could be used following a 16KB I/O, and disk seeking was reduced during table scans due to the extents now being contiguous.

Many of the latest disk drive arrays and controllers contain read-ahead caches. Such caches may perform more physical I/O than requested if they "predict" that additional data will be required—for example, for a 2KB I/O request, a readahead cache may read 16KB or 32KB from disk.

This means that a properly defragmented table will allow for a much higher throughput for such caching environments since many of the reads done following an initial 2KB read will be satisfied by the disk controller's RAM cache, instead of wasting (discarding) the pre-read blocks of data.

It can allow random read rates which might typically occur at 100KB to 200KB per second to be increased to over 1MB and sometimes 2MB per second, even when performing 2 KB I/Os during a table scan on Sybase 11.0.x and older versions.

Sybase versions 11.0 and greater can also utilize the cache better if the cache does pre-reads of data blocks of 16KB or larger.

Finally, Database Consistency Checker (DBCC) execution times are dramatically improved by defragmentation of tables.

Checking a table with DBCC incurs reads of all data pages within a table, similar to a table scan.

Speeding up of DBCCs allows for more end-user availability to the tables as the shared locks placed on the tables being checked do not occur for as long a period. Checking of non-clustered indexes is also sped up by defragmenting them along with the data portion of the table, though some sites can skip running DBCCs against non-clustered indexes and, in the event of a problem within the nonclustered index, the index can be rebuilt.

Conclusion

Hopefully you now have a better understanding of what causes fragmentation in Sybase, and the various options you have at your disposal for dealing with it when it occurs.

As we have seen, with the right tools and the right information, you are no longer at the mercy of fragmentation.

For further information on the White Sands Technology, Inc. products mentioned in this white paper, including ProActive DBA, contact us at:

Voice: 1-818-349-8900
Fax: 1-818-349-8988
Web: www.whitesands.com
Email: info@whitesands.com

Finally, we at White Sands would like to thank you for reading this white paper, and we hope you find it beneficial in tuning and maintaining your Sybase databases.

If you have any feedback regarding this white paper, feel free to contact us using any of the above methods.

Appendix G

Disaster Recovery: A Practical Handbook

A technical white paper by White Sands Technology, Inc. (http://www.whitesands.com/).

WARNING: Page numbers in this section refer to the online documents which can be found at www.whitesands.com.

Preface

This white paper is intended for DBAs and managers who must be concerned with keeping production database systems running and error-free. It assumes some familiarity with database servers (particularly Sybase Adaptive Server Enterprise).

While the focus of many of the details in this document is on Sybase database servers, the general principles apply to all major RDBMSs.

Introduction

It's late Friday afternoon. Most businesses on the U.S. West Coast are wrapping up their week's work, and the rest of the country has already started heading out for happy hour.

At 3:30pm PST, a support technician at White Sands Technology, Inc. receives a call from a frantic Jeff, the senior DBA at a major Wall Street financial services company[1]. Their Sybase online trading database server is logging cryptic errors that report an incorrect object ID on a page in one of their mission-critical webaccess account tables, and certain users are getting knocked out of the system.

1 All names and some identifying details of this story have been changed to protect the anonymity of the client.

Since the database server is replicated to a warm standby server, Jeff naturally checked the standby server and found that it too had data corruption, but in different places from the production server. So there is no possibility of restoring from the standby server.

Jeff has also tried loading last month's backups onto their smaller test server, to see if the corruption occurred recently. To his dismay, he determined that the index corruption has existed for at least 30 days, undetected until now.

They cannot simply reload a backup older than 30 days and reapply the changes made since then, because the time required to do that would bring their whole trading system down for the better part of a day, thus costing the company millions of dollars in lost orders.

They cannot simply run a DBCC command to fix the table, because DBCC will truncate the table at the point where the page chain corruption exists, thus dropping thousands of rows from the table.

It seems to Jeff that this is a no-win situation.

However, the White Sands technician has a much different take on it.

She presents Jeff with the following options, all of which are made possible by White Sands's Disaster Recovery Toolset:

- Use the Disaster Recovery Toolset to scan the database, identify **all** the pages belonging to the corrupt table—even pages inaccessible to Sybase—and export the rows on all the pages to an ISQL script in a flat file, so the data can be reloaded later.
- Use the Disaster Recovery Toolset's Database Page Editor to repair the corruption on-line.

Since downtime is Jeff's paramount concern, the second option, while more labor-intensive, works much better for him.

Over the next couple of hours the White Sands technician works with Jeff to dig deeper into the problem. Using the Disaster Recovery Toolset from White Sands, we determine that the table's page chain is corrupt in one area of the table—specifically, the data page chain is broken. The Disaster Recovery Toolset quickly identifies the page where the page chain break existed, and also identifies the most likely page to which the corrupt page should have been joined.

Further checking identifies a nonclustered index row that points to the invalid page. This and the broken page chain appear to be the entire extent of the damage.

How did everything turn out? Well, fortunately the story has a happy ending and, of course, a moral. Using the Disaster Recovery Toolset, the technician was able to repair the damaged pages while keeping the database online. The fix was made first on their standby server, so they could verify that the repairs would work correctly. After testing the fix on the standby server, a similar fix was done on the production server. No data was lost, and no downtime was incurred.

The moral is that while backups and replicated systems are an important part of your data integrity assurance plan, these methods alone are not enough to ensure zero downtime and zero loss of data.

So how was this seeming miracle worked? Let us take a closer look.

Understanding Data Corruption

Before we can discuss how to fix data corruption in your databases, we must first explain exactly what data corruption is and how it occurs.

What is Data Corruption?

In a nutshell, data corruption (which we also refer to as *database* corruption in this white paper) is any error in the data storage structure used by your database.

Sybase databases have a well-defined storage structure, which consists of *database pages* at the lowest level of granularity, and has higher-level structures based on blocks of pages within the database. Each database page is 2K in size (or larger in newer server versions).[2]

Within each database page, data is stored in a well-defined format which depends on the type of page (data, index or other page types).

Data corruption occurs when the formatting of one or more pages becomes damaged, often rendering information on that page (and/or other pages) inaccessible to the database server.

Database corruption may be *transient*, meaning the corruption only exists in the cached copy of data which is resident in the server's RAM memory; or, it may be *persistent*, meaning the corrupted data has been permanently written to the server's hard disk(s).

As a result of corruption, the database server (and thus your users) may encounter errors any time it tries to access a corrupt table at all, or it may get errors only when accessing certain rows or pages in the table, or only when accessing the table through a certain index.

Whatever the case, when data corruption occurs, it can prevent access to large amounts of your organization's data by your users and applications, and thus can obviously have a significant impact on your operations!

How Does Corruption Occur?

There are several hardware and software elements which comprise your database server:

- The server's CPU, RAM and associated hardware (including power source)
- The disk controllers and drives, which are also hardware but warrant special consideration due to their central role in the database server.
- The operating system (Windows or Unix "flavor")
- The Sybase database server software

If any of these elements fail, data corruption can result. Let us take a closer look at how each of these elements can fail, and how these failures can cause data corruption.

2 For a detailed description of the exact data structure of Sybase databases, see the references on page 21.

Failures in Computer Hardware

Today's enterprise-class server machines are extremely reliable, to a degree that might have been unfathomable ten or twenty years ago.

But, as reliable as computer hardware is today, it still does fail occasionally. Fortunately, when a failure occurs, it is usually in an obvious way, so that errors do not go undetected.

This is fortunate, because when a hardware error or failure occurs, you will want to know about it as soon as possible, and with the least possibility of incorrect information getting stored into the computer permanently.

To see why undetected failures are so rare in computers today, let us examine the different components in the computer which can fail.

Disk Drives

Far and away the most common component to fail in a computer is the hard disk drive, since it has the most moving parts (and also the fastest-moving parts). Since disk drives are a uniquely integral part of a database server, very special measures are taken to deal with their failures, which we will discuss in detail in the section starting on page 4.

Other Failures: CPU, RAM, Network

Aside from disk drives, most of the components in a computer are solid-state (meaning they are entirely electronic and have no moving parts).

If operated within the proper ranges of temperature, humidity and shock (physical vibration), these components will typically run for decades without any failures, and will require little or no maintenance.

For the rare occasions when electronic circuitry does fail, built-in error detection mechanisms are used so that the hardware and/or the computer's operating system can detect the failure and deal with it accordingly.

The result is that systems today generally handle these situations appropriately so that the computer can proceed to a known state whenever a critical hardware failure occurs.

Power Failures

System power failures are a type of hardware failure that is common enough to be planned for by system hardware designers.

Uninterruptible power supplies (UPSs) are typically used in high-availability environments to ensure that short power outages will not affect the servicing of end-users.

Two other database system facilities also help ensure that data integrity will be maintained in the event of a power failure:

- UPSs typically provide a "low battery" signal to the computer system, so that if the UPSs battery will soon run out, the operating system, database server and other applications running on the machine can begin an orderly shutdown so that all transactions in progress will either be rolled back or will get saved to disk correctly.

- The database's transaction log (described more fully in the next section) helps ensure data integrity, even if power is removed from the computer suddenly while transactions are in progress.

Disk Drive Failures

Disk failures are given special consideration by typical enterprise-scale operating systems and database servers. This is done for two reasons:

- First, because disk failures are probably at least an order of magnitude more common than failures in any other critical component of a computer system;
- Second, because undetected errors or inconsistencies in the information stored on a computer's disk drives can compromise the integrity of a company's critical business data, thus potentially jeopardizing the company's entire business as well as the businesses of its customers.

Let's discuss these two points in more detail.

Hard disk drives today have a *mean time between failure* (MTBF) ranging from 300,000 to over one million hours, and a *service life* of 5 years or more. Since the MTBF is so much greater than the service life, this means that, on average, a high percentage of disk drives will run for a period of time at least as long as the service life without an *unrecoverable* failure.[3]

An unrecoverable failure means an error or failure in writing or reading data to or from the disk, such that the error remained after all available *error correction* methods were tried.

In actuality, disk failures can start to occur much sooner than the MTBF, as we will discuss below; also, keep in mind that the MTBF is an average, meaning that some disk drives will fail much sooner than the manufacturer's specified MTBF. (True, some drives will also last much longer than the MTBF, but you should be a lot more concerned about the ones that fail sooner!)

Before you (or a disk drive) can try to correct any errors that might occur, you first need to know that an error has in fact occurred. To do this, disk drives employ various *error detection* techniques, such as checksums, cyclic redundancy checks (CRCs) and other algorithms. Methods used today can detect at least 99.99% of all unintended modifications to data on the disk.

Once a disk error has been detected, there are a number of strategies typically employed to try to correct the error.

Error correction methods include retrying the read or write operation 5 or 10 times; they might also include application of *redundant error correction data* to the erroneous data to see if the correct data can be restored.

---

3 See http://www.storage.ibm.com/storage/oem/tech/mtbf.htm for more information on understanding MTBF.

The upshot of all this is that, depending on the effectiveness of these errorcorrecting measures, a disk might start to experience failures long before the average failure time of 2 to 10 years, but these failures go undetected (and in fact are not significant—yet) because they were automatically corrected by the disk drive's hardware, circuitry and/or embedded firmware.

It is when these errors can no longer be corrected by the disk drive itself that they start to have a real impact. Depending on what type of failure occurred in the disk drive, you might see different symptoms:

- You might see errors reported by your database server or operating system very infrequently, and the errors slowly and gradually become more and more prevalent;
- You might see errors only in certain locations of the disk (i.e. when accessing certain files, tables, etc.)
- In the worst case, an entire disk might "die" suddenly, taking all of its data with it to that "big databank in the sky."

Today's enterprise-scale database server systems (and the people who design, install and configure them) employ various methods to prevent loss of your organization's data in the event of any of the above types of disk failures.

Database Logging

As any experienced DBA knows, database servers such as Sybase use a logging mechanism (the *transaction log* in Sybase), one of the major benefits of which is *recoverability* of the data stored in the database—if one or more of the database's data or log disks should fail, the data can be reconstructed to a consistent state from the last backup combined with the transaction log data since the last backup.

Maintaining a disk-based transaction log, and using it to correctly update the data in a database, is an enormously complex task. Why, then, do database servers go to all this trouble? Why not just keep a record of transactions in RAM, and finish updating data on the disks when transactions are completed (committed)?

The answer is simple: because sooner or later, disks are all but guaranteed to fail. And when they do, the database server does its best to prevent any loss of data, or loss of integrity in the data stored in the database. The transaction log provides a form of *disk redundancy*, in that if either the data device or log device (but not both) in a given database should fail, the server can recover the database to a known, transactionally consistent state automatically.

Incidentally, this is a good argument for **not** enabling the Sybase "truncate log on checkpoint" option on any production databases. If you use this option, in the event that corruption occurs, you will be unable to recover the database from backups to a point in time close to when the corruption occurred. The same argument holds in the event of a disk failure.

By performing regular database dumps to tape, and performing frequent transaction log dumps to tape in between the database dumps, you ensure that you can recover the database up to that point in time when the failure occurred.

The point is that, unless you can stand to lose the changes made to the database since the database dump occurred, database dumps alone are not enough—you need the transaction log backups also.

Disk Redundancy

Today's operating systems, enterprise-class database servers and disk storage subsystems all can provide various options for providing redundant disk storage. This means that every block of data (on a disk, a database or an entire system) is stored two or more times, on different disks (and possibly accessed through different controllers or entirely different subsystems). Thus, should a single hardware failure occur in any of the disks, its redundant backup disk will take over, and in theory no data loss should occur.

Replication

Many database servers including Sybase offer the option to *replicate*, or maintain a copy of, databases on a completely separate system. As data is added, changed or deleted on the main, or *primary*, server, these changes are sent to the replicated server and mirrored there, so that an exact logical copy (typically within a lag time of a few minutes or less) is maintained on the replicated system.

This has the advantage of full redundancy—every component of the database system (CPU, disks, network cards, etc.) is backed up by the replicated system.

There are other potential benefits to using replication, depending on the situation—you can split users between the two systems for load-balancing; or, you can keep one server offline to users as a "warm standby" and perform maintenance on it while users use the primary system, for example. After performing the maintenance on the standby system, you would then switch the standby into production, and switch the former production server into standby mode.

Failures in the Operating System

Although a computer's operating system is no more than a specialized type of software program, it is unique in that all application software running on the computer depends on the operating system for various classes of services such as allocating system resources, disk I/O, communications, etc.

Because the OS supports all the other software running on the computer, it tends to "disappear into the background" in the eyes of users (and even system administrators) and become part of the machine itself.

Also because of this, the OS is usually the most stable, reliable piece of software on the computer—almost as reliable as the computer hardware itself.

These two factors conspire to make the OS seem "above reproach"—when a failure occurs, it often does not occur to anyone to investigate the operating system itself.

However, experienced DBAs and system administrators know that this is not true at all—the OS, like any other highly evolved and complex piece of software, is not perfect and does contain bugs which can surface from time to time.

Depending on the seriousness of bugs which may occur in the OS, database corruption can in rare cases occur, and database integrity can be compromised as a result.

Failures in the Database Server Software

Sybase Adaptive Server Enterprise (and older versions known as SQL Server) is a software application which, owing to its general-purpose nature, tends to become used by many different applications in an organization; because of its ubiquity, it tends to "blend into the background" much like a computer's operating system, until it is hardly thought about in terms of reliability, stability and bugs.

However, like any other software application (including the operating system itself), the database server can have bugs, and these bugs can have varying degrees of severity.

The bugs might simply be minor annoyances, such as a typographical error in a message displayed by the database server.

The bugs might be fairly serious, such as an inability to process a SQL statement of a certain type in a specific situation.

Or, the bugs might be critical, such as causing data corruption or a server crash when certain SQL commands are run in a certain sequence.

All of these types of bugs do exist, both in database servers and in operating systems, and they must be planned for by the vigilant DBA and system administrator, so that appropriate steps can be taken should they occur in a production environment.

!@#&% (Corruption) Happens, So You Need a Recovery Plan!

It might seem, with all these protective measures system designers and administrators take to ensure data integrity, that data corruption would be all but unheard of today.

Unfortunately, this is not true—despite all these measures, in certain cases, failures in the hardware, software or a combination of both *do* occur, and data corruption results. If and when it does, you will want to make sure you have a good contingency plan in place.

Merely using backups, or even replication, is not good enough to ensure that data corruption will have a minimal or no impact on your production servers. This is true for two reasons:

1. Because when corruption occurs, the corruption might not be detected when backups are performed, and thus the corruption will be silently propagated to the backup systems so you no longer have a completely good copy of your data anywhere; and
2. Because even if you have a good copy of the data (e.g., in a replicated database), getting it back on-line and into production may require more downtime than your operation can afford.

As we will see later, further measures must be taken to deal with corruption if and when it occurs, so that minimal downtime and loss of data occur.

We talk to many people who say, "If corruption occurs, why not just let DBCC fix it?" The short answer is that using DBCC to repair corruption is analogous to "fixing" an infected finger by amputating it! When using DBCC's "fix" options on a corrupt table, the way it often fixes the corruption is to truncate the table at the point of corruption, and/or to deallocate the corrupt pages it finds.

This can add up to thousands or millions of lost rows of data! This may be acceptable in certain cases, but in the majority of instances, your business cannot sustain that kind of data loss. This was one of the major reasons White Sands developed its Disaster Recovery Toolset: we knew customers were unwilling to live with the limitations of DBCC for fixing data corruption.

Detecting Database Corruption

Now that we have discussed what database corruption is and how it occurs, how do you find out whether corruption exists in your databases?

First Defense: Run Regular DBCCs!

As most DBAs know, the primary method for detecting database corruption is running DBCCs (database consistency checks) against each production database on a regular, frequent basis.

NOTE: While DBCC commands are very useful as part of a plan for detecting corruption, in general we do not recommend any of the DBCC "fix" options to repair corruption; see page 14 for more information.

Running regular DBCC checks is so important that we view it as virtually a requirement, yet we encounter many production environments where this essential step is not being performed.

In many situations, especially 24x7 environments that require very limited database downtime, special steps must be taken in order to perform DBCC checking against production databases. Generally, DBAs will make a dump of the production database, load it onto a backup server and run the DBCCs there, this has two benefits:

- The DBCCs (which are disk I/O-intensive) do not impact the performance of the production server;
- The DBCCs execute reliably and without generating spurious or transient error or warning messages, since no users are making data modifications to the backup server while the DBCCs run (in fact, ideally each of the backup server's databases should be placed into single-user mode as the DBCCs run against it)

In replicated environments where a warm standby server is used, the DBA can take the standby system offline to run DBCCs while users use the primary system; then, after the DBCCs complete, the warm standby can be brought back on-line and caught up with the primary.

Because of the extra work that must be done to perform DBCCs in a highavailability environment (and the extra hardware that may be required), many DBAs forego them entirely.

This is unfortunate, because data corruption often works its way into your databases in such a way that it does not immediately become noticeable or affect users.

If you do not perform DBCCs at least on a daily or weekly basis, your database backups may become worthless because they will contain corrupted data. Then, when the corruption surfaces, your backups may be useless since the backups for the last few weeks or more may all contain the corruption as well.

Another important point to mention is that you should run DBCC checks against your production *and* backup systems, since corruption can arise in one or the other independently. This is also true in replicated environments—corruption can occur in the replicated system that does not exist in the primary system, and vice-versa.

Improving on DBCC: Third-Party Solutions

A few third-party software vendors, including White Sands Technology, Inc., offer database verification products that complement the use of DBCCs and help the DBA identify database corruption.

Keep in mind that these solutions should be used *in conjunction with* DBCCs, and not instead of them! The more checks you run against your databases, the more likely you are to detect corruption as soon as it occurs. Furthermore, most third-party tools do not provide as thorough checking of your database as DBCC does.

So we strongly recommend that you investigate third-party solutions, but only as an addition to your existing suite of regular DBCC checks!

Some third-party products we are aware of include:

- ProActive DBA and the Disaster Recovery Toolset, from White Sands Technology (of course!)
- SQL-BackTrack and Database Verifier for Sybase, from BMC Software

Finding Data Corruption the Hard Way (From Users)

Running regular DBCCs is your first and best line of defense against database corruption. Unfortunately, however, even if you run regular DBCCs, all too often you will find out about database corruption from irate users who start getting application error messages because of the corruption.

In other cases, the corruption might be such that your entire server may be brought down. Obviously, the server is designed to prevent this from happening, but as software is never perfect and cannot account for every possible case, this too can and does happen from time to time in the real world.

It is in these sorts of situations that you most need a disaster recovery plan, since a simpler solution utilizing backup/restore or replication may not be feasible, either because it will require taking the database offline for too much time, and/or because it will not be able to preserve the latest changes made to the database since the last backup.

When !@#&% (Corruption) Happens

Let's say you, being a conscientious DBA, have set up a daily DBCC script to run against each of your production databases. Let's also say you have set up mirrored disk arrays, replication and backups so you are making regular copies of your data at the physical disk, logical database and transaction levels.

So why is your phone ringing off the hook with dozens of angry users complaining about page and buffer errors? Because, my friend, !@#&% (corruption) happens!

We hope this situation never happens to you. But if it does, we want you to have a good plan for dealing with it. In this section, we submit a set of recommended steps for determining the cause of the corruption, and isolating the exact extent of corruption in your server.

Investigating the Cause of the Corruption

Before even thinking about how to fix corruption, it is essential to find out exactly what caused it. This seemingly obvious step may at times be overlooked in an effort to quickly bring the corrupted database or table back on-line; however, since of course you don't want the corruption to keep occurring, it is best to isolate and fix the cause before proceeding with a fix for the symptom.

In the section starting on page 2, we discussed the various causes of corruption. In general, you will want to follow these steps:

1. Check for disk hardware failures, such as an entire disk or array having failed, or a power failure that was not recovered from properly. If you have a mirrored disk subsystem with automatic failover, failure of an entire disk may not even be a critical failure, and you may be able to bring a replacement disk or disks online without users even noticing. On the other hand, if something went wrong during the failover or restoral process, corruption may have worked its way into the primary disk(s), which will now need to be repaired.
2. Check for other hardware failures; methods for doing this might include:
   - Checking operating system error logs for any failure notifications;[4]
   - Checking other running applications on the database server's host system for failures;
   - Running hardware diagnostics to ensure the rest of the system is operating properly.
3. Check for any operating system failures:
   - Checking operating system error logs for any failure notifications;
   - Checking other running applications on the database server's host system for failures;
4. Finally, check the Sybase dataserver's error log for a full description of the failure(s) which it encountered. We provide explanations of some of the more common error messages starting on page 21.

4 Steps for viewing the OS error logs are described in the topic "Checking the Operating System Error Log" in Sybase's ASE Troubleshooting and Error Messages Guide.

The point is to check the underlying hardware and software which supports the Sybase server first, in case any problems turn out to be what originally caused the corruption to surface.

In some cases, more than one factor may have contributed to a corruption problem. As we mentioned earlier, the software involved here (namely Sybase itself, and the operating system) is very complex, and very rare bugs can manifest themselves only when certain circumstances occur in both the operating system and the Sybase software, making it difficult to attribute the problem to one or the other alone.

Additionally, failures can occur in the hardware or in the operating system which go undetected, so you may not be able to find any evidence that this has occurred. In this case, you may have no alternative but to proceed with fixing the corruption and then waiting to see if it happens again.

Determining the Extent of the Corruption

Once you (hopefully) have a handle on what caused your corruption, the next step is to find out just how bad it is. This is best done in three general steps:

- First, determine which database(s) are affected by the corruption;
- Next, identify which table(s) in each database are affected;
- Finally, determine which and how many pages are affected within the corrupt table(s).

By starting at a high level and working down, you can determine whether the corruption is so bad that you will save the most time by just reloading the entire server or an entire database, or if the system can "limp along" while you make smaller repairs to affected areas of the database or individual tables.

To find out the full extent of the corruption, you will want to check each database as thoroughly as possible to determine where corruption exists. To do this, use the same methods as described starting on page 8:

- Run full DBCCs against the affected database and, if possible, against all the other databases;
- Use DBCC PAGE and third-party tools such as White Sands Technology's Disaster Recovery Toolset to provide additional verification and crosschecking of your DBCC results.

Initially, to save time or reduce downtime, you may want to run the DBCC checks against a replicated server or against a copy of the database(s) restored from backups. This is often done as a first step in order not to have to bring the production system or databases down to run the checks.

This is a useful way to obtain some information about the corruption. BUT—never assume that whatever you find (whether it's corruption or a lack thereof) on a restored backup or on a replicated database will be exactly the same as what exists on your production database.

When corruption occurs, it may or may not have made its way into your backups. Also, the corruption may have occurred after the most recent backup was made, in which case the corruption will not exist in the backup.

Since a replicated database is a logical copy of the primary (but not necessarily an exact physical copy), running DBCCs against a replicated database will not catch corruption that occurred only in the primary database. Because the replicated database is a complete, separate database system from the primary, it can experience its own corruption that does not exist in the primary database.

Thus, the best strategy, when corruption occurs, to run DBCCs against the database in question, as well as its replicated database, if any.

Standard Disaster Recovery Strategies: Benefits, Drawbacks and Limitations

There are several standard disaster recovery strategies known to the DBA community, which can be researched using various resources such as DBA reference manuals, Sybase Technical Support or consultants.

Much of this can be found in the Sybase ASE Troubleshooting and Error Messages Guide, Chapter 2, in a section titled "Avoiding Disaster Through Good DBA Practices."

As we shall see in the following sections, while these practices are a good start and form the backbone of a good disaster recovery plan, they are not always a complete solution and may not cover you completely.

Copy Out and Reload the Data

A standard solution recommended by Sybase when corruption is discovered is to copy the data out to another database using SELECT INTO, or to make a copy of the data using BCP; then, drop the table and reload it from the copy that was made.

The problem with doing this is that the corruption may prevent SELECT or BCP from being able to access all the rows in the table—leaving you with a copy of only part of the data.

At best, the SELECT or BCP will return an error, or (if a circular loop exists in an object's page chain) it may simply run forever without completing (or at least run until there is no more disk space on the output device and then return an error).

At worst, however, the SELECT or BCP may *appear* to have completed successfully while still not having copied all the rows; this can happen if an object's page chain is incorrectly terminated, causing SELECT or BCP to believe it has read all the pages in the table, when there are really other (stray) pages in the table's page chain that SELECT or BCP cannot see.

So, when corruption exists in your database, it can be very risky to rely on SELECT or BCP to retrieve your data from the corrupt database. If you can verify that the row count is correct in the copy of the table you made, then it is probably a good copy. But, if you are not sure how many rows should be in the table, you are better off not relying on these methods to recover your data.

White Sands's Disaster Recovery Toolset includes powerful export tools that can recover *all* of the pages in a corrupt table, not just the ones accessible to Sybase. This gives you more options when faced with corruption—you don't have to live with being able to recover only part of a corrupt table; instead, you can save out all the rows that can be physically accessed, and then reload the corrupt table, load the data into another table for comparison, etc.

Rebuild the Corrupt Object

If the corruption exists only on an index, you can often simply drop and recreate the affected index to solve the problem.

This may not work, however, if there is incorrect (corrupt) data in allocation maps, OAM or GAM pages, since new page allocations may fail or may cause corruption in other tables when you rebuild the index.

This solution also requires locking the table or making it otherwise unavailable for the duration of the index rebuild, so this may cause significant user delays if the affected table is very large. If you cannot afford the downtime to rebuild the object, you may have to look at other options.

Rebuilding a clustered index on an APL (allpages-locked) table presents another challenge: if you want to use the SORTED_DATA option to rebuild the index (which saves significant time because it only rebuilds the index layers of the table, without copying and resorting the data layer), you must ensure that the index key values do not change while the index is being rebuilt. This may require keeping users out of the database or putting the database in single-user mode, neither of which option may be very attractive in today's high-availability environments.

Switch In Your Mirrored Disk

On systems with mirrored disks, the mirror provides 100% redundancy against failure of the main disk. This should provide complete protection against erroneous (corrupt) data which may get written to one of the disks—you can move the mirrored disk into the primary position, and then at your leisure (relatively speaking) you can install a new mirrored disk to replace the original.

However, when the corruption occurs at a software level (in Sybase or in the operating system), the corrupt data will get written to both the primary and the mirrored disks, rendering them equally useless to your production operation. In this case, you must look for another solution.

Restore from a Backup

Restoring your database from a backup made before the corruption existed is generally the least labor-intensive and most reliable method of removing corruption from a database. However, it has several potential (and likely) drawbacks:

- Current releases of Sybase ASE (through Version 12.5) only support backup and restoral of an entire database, not of specific objects within a database, so the downtime and/or disk space required to do this may be prohibitive in your situation;
- You may not be able to recover any of the changes made since the last backup without reintroducing the corruption into the system;
- The corruption may have existed and gone undetected for some time, meaning that the last backup made which did not contain the corruption may be too old to be useful.

In short, because of the downtime requirements and because the corruption may have worked its way into the backup stream at some unknown time in the past, restoring from backups often becomes a last resort in dealing with corruption.

Restore from a Replicated Database

Restoring the affected table(s) from a replicated database offers the benefit of being able to restore a much more up-to-date copy of the tables than the most recent backup is likely to contain.

Additionally, you can restore only the affected tables from the replicated server, without having to bring the entire database down to do the procedure. This may be a significant benefit over restoring from a database backup.

If you will be replacing an entire corrupt table with a good copy from a replicated database, you will need sufficient free space to load the new copy of the table into the database (that is, if you want to keep the table on-line while you load the copy in); depending on the size of the table, this might be prohibitive.

Use DBCC to Repair the Corruption

Various DBCC commands have options to let you repair corrupted areas of a table or database when it discovers these problems. Using DBCC has the advantages that it is relatively simple to execute, and it will often return the database and all its tables to a known good state.

However, using DBCC has several substantial drawbacks:

- DBCC may drop (delete) a large amount of data from any tables that are affected by corruption, and you will not know beforehand that it is going to do so;
- DBCC may not be able to fix the corruption, and if so, will not do anything to correct it;
- Certain DBCC commands require that you put the database in single-user mode to repair corruption.

For example, when DBCC encounters a broken page chain, its solution may be to sever the page chain at that point. If it encounters any further pages that should be part of the object's page chain, it typically deallocates all of the pages, thus potentially dropping thousands of rows from the table under the guise of "repairing" the corruption.

If you do decide to use DBCC to fix the corruption, make sure you do the following things:

- Before using DBCC to fix the corruption, do a full dump of the database so you can restore it to its current state if the DBCC repairs do not work (or make things worse)
- Before using DBCC, obtain row counts on all the affected tables using as many indexes as possible (because you may get different row counts using different indexes—the largest row count is generally the correct one), so that after DBCC repairs the table(s), you can see whether any rows were dropped

Advanced Disaster Recovery Techniques

When standard disaster recovery methods fail or have limitations which make them unusable in your situation, you must turn to more advanced techniques.

Currently, the only way we know of to go beyond the standard Sybase recovery facilities is by using White Sands Technology's **Disaster Recovery Toolset**, which provides advanced data recovery and data repair tools for on-line disaster recovery of databases.

The benefits of using the Disaster Recovery Toolset's advanced recovery and repair features are:

- You can recover all of the most up-to-date data in a table, even from areas that lie beyond the corruption and are inaccessible to Sybase;
- You can target specific areas of the database to repair, without having to reload entire tables or the whole database;
- Repairs can be made to your data while the database and all tables remain completely on-line;
- You can fix *any* type of corruption (except an actual hardware failure), not just the few types correctable by DBCC.

The only real drawback to using these techniques is that you have to be very knowledgeable in Sybase's data structure[5] to make on-line repairs to a production database—otherwise, you are putting your data at even more risk.

Fortunately, White Sands Technology's Technical Support staff is a valuable resource with great experience in disaster recovery. With our help, you will be able to evaluate the state of your database and weigh the risks, if any, in performing the recovery, before you proceed.

General Corruption Repair Strategies

The general approach to use when attempting to repair a corrupt Sybase table is:

- Repair any affected data-layer pages; in APL (allpages-locked) tables, these exist in a doubly-linked page chain, so the page chain pointers may need to be repaired in addition to any other corrupt information on the affected pages;
- Repair any allocation map, OAM or GAM page inconsistencies, so that the pages belonging to the corrupt object(s) can be "seen" properly by Sybase;
- Rebuild or repair any indexes affected either by the original corruption or by the repairs made to the data layer of the table.

These steps are discussed in more detail in the following sections.

5 See the references starting on page 21 for more information on learning about Sybase database storage structure.

Repair the Data-Layer Pages

The first step in repairing a corrupt table is to repair the data layer of the table; once this has been done, then as a last resort you will at least be able to perform a table-scan query to retrieve all the rows from the table for later reloading into a good (non-corrupt) database.

The method for repairing the table's data layer depends on which type of table it is: allpages-locked (APL) or data-only locked (DOL), also known as RLL (for rowlevel locked). The locking strategy used by a table greatly affects the data structure of the table, and has a number of implications for how the table must be repaired.

Repairing APL Tables

For allpages-locked (APL) tables (which are the only kind of tables supported on pre-11.9 versions of Sybase), repairing the data layer entails repairing any breaks in the page chain of the data layer. Allocation map and OAM page inconsistencies generally do not affect the ability of the server to walk a table's page chain, so you can deal with any allocation errors afterward.

White Sands's Disaster Recovery Toolset makes this process much easier. Its Page Chain Consistency Checker produces a simple report that shows you where the breaks in a table's page chain are, and what pages should be linked in where the breaks exist. You can use this information to repair the affected pages, thus rejoining the pages into a single intact chain.

The Database Page Editor, also part of the Disaster Recovery Toolset, provides an easy-to-use graphical interface which lets you change the next-page and previous-page pointers in corrupt pages so as to repair the page chain. Keep in mind that you will need to repair both the next-page and the previous-page pointers on any affected pages. Again, the Page Chain Consistency Checker's report will identify exactly where you will need to make repairs.

Dropping a Page from the Page Chain

If one or more pages are so corrupt that there is no possibility of recovering data on them (or if, due to a hardware error, the pages cannot be recovered or repaired), you may want to drop the pages completely out of the table's page chain.

This can be done as shown in the diagram below:

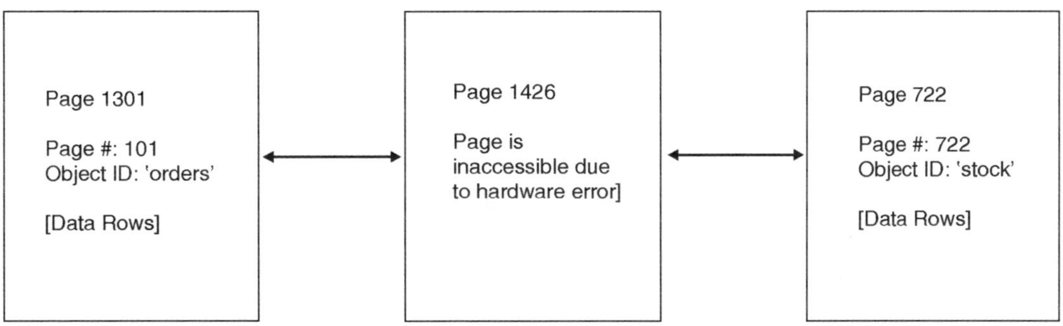

For each corrupt page (such as page 1426 in the above example), you will need to make repairs in two places:

- Change the *next-page* pointer of the page in the page chain before the damaged page, so it points to the page in the chain after the damaged page;
- Change the *previous-page* pointer of the page in the page chain after the damaged page, so it points to the page in the chain before the damaged page.

In the above example, the repairs would be made as follows:

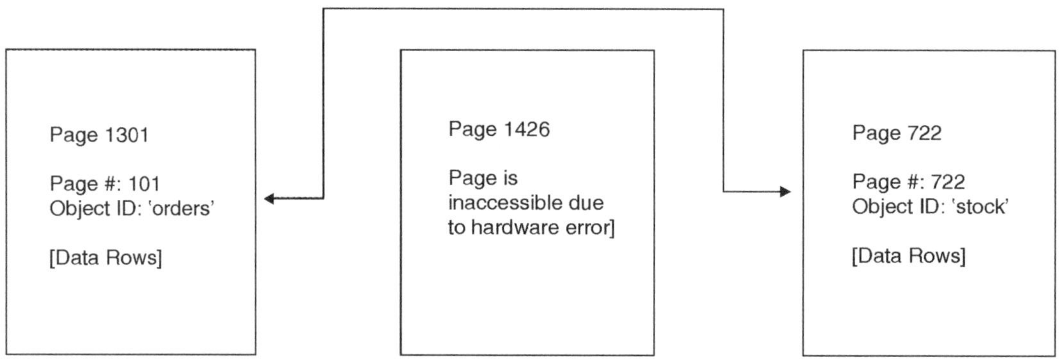

Then, after making the repairs to the page chain, the page that was dropped out of the page chain (page 1426 in this example) would be deallocated by marking it unused in the allocation map page.

Of course, after doing this, you will need to repair or rebuild any affected indexes also.

Before performing the above steps to repair the table, you will want to try to save the row data from the affected page(s).

White Sands's Disaster Recovery Toolset provides a useful facility for doing this: its Page Detail Window lets you build an ISQL script of INSERT statements from any single page or a page chain fragment. Additionally, the Disaster Recovery Toolset can scan the entire database to locate any pages or page chain fragments that are not linked to the table, so you can recover the rows from those pages as well (even if Sybase cannot access the data on those pages).

Repairing DOL Tables

Repair of the data layer of a data-only locked (DOL) table is quite different from repairing an APL table.

For DOL tables, allocation maps and OAM pages are critical to being able to scan a table; these tables are essentially heaps and have no page chain at the data level (that is, the page chain pointer values may or may not be valid and in any case are not used by the server).

The access method used by the server to scan a DOL table is called an *OAM scan*, and proceeds like this:

- Look up the table's first OAM page number by retrieving the *doampg* value from the *sysindexes* table for the heap (which is the row where *indid=0*)
- For each allocation unit referenced by the OAM page:
- Read the allocation map page for that allocation unit;
- For all data pages belonging to the desired table and marked as being in use, read and process those data pages.
- After processing all allocation units referenced by the OAM page, check the OAM page's next-page pointer to go to the next OAM page, if any, in the OAM chain.

Thus, when corruption occurs on a page, you need only repair that page, or drop it completely from the table; there are no page chain pointers to be concerned with.

To drop a page from the data layer of a DOL table, you need only deallocate the page from its allocation map and update the OAM page to reflect the deallocated page; these steps are described in the next section.

Repairing Allocation Errors

The *allocation map* page in Sybase keeps track of the allocated pages in a 256-page block. Allocation map pages exist every 256 pages in every database—at page 0, page 256, etc. The allocation map has a 48-byte page header, followed by 32 structures of 16 bytes each—one structure for every 8-page extent contained within the allocation unit (32 extents x 8 pages per extent = 256 pages in the allocation unit).

Here is a section from a page dump of an allocation page, as presented by the Disaster Recovery Toolset's Page Detail window:

```
Page 39680 - Page Type: Allocation Page
Page not found in Cache.
--------------Page Header Information--------------
Page Number: 39680 Next Page: 3 Prev Page: 24510464
Object ID: 99 Index ID: 0 Level: 0
Timestamp: 0x000000000000
Free Offset: 0 Next Row Number: 11 Min Row Len.: 0
Status Bits: [None]
Extents mapped by this allocation page:
Extent 39,688: APL Table 'dbo.customer' (8 of 8 pages used) NextX=1,
PrevX=0
Extent 39,696: APL Table 'dbo.customer' (8 of 8 pages used) NextX=1,
PrevX=0
Extent 39,704: APL Table 'dbo.customer' (8 of 8 pages used) NextX=1,
PrevX=0
Extent 39,712: APL Table 'dbo.customer' (8 of 8 pages used) NextX=1,
PrevX=0
Extent 39,720: APL Table 'dbo.customer' (8 of 8 pages used) NextX=1,
PrevX=0
```

Here is the corresponding section of the hex dump from the page:

```
0: 00 00 9B 00 00 00 00 03 01 76 00 00 00 00 00 63 .........v.....c
10: 00 00 00 00 00 0B 00 00 00 00 00 00 00 00 00 00 ................
20: 00 00 00 00 00 00 00 00 00 00 00 00 00 00 00 00 ................
30: 00 00 00 00 00 00 00 00 00 00 00 00 01 00 00 00 ................
40: 00 00 00 01 00 00 00 00 04 C4 C0 F4 FF 00 00 00 ................
50: 00 00 00 01 00 00 00 00 04 C4 C0 F4 FF 00 00 00 ................
60: 00 00 00 01 00 00 00 00 04 C4 C0 F4 FF 00 00 00 ................
70: 00 00 00 01 00 00 00 00 04 C4 C0 F4 FF 00 00 00 ................
```

The first three 16-byte rows comprise the allocation page header; then, subsequent rows describe the usage of each extent within the allocation unit.

The third extent, for example, at offset 50 on the allocation page, is owned by object 04C4C0F4 hex, or 80003316 decimal, and the FF hex byte in the fourth position from the end of the row is the *page-usage byte*, which in this case indicates that all 8 pages in that extent are in use by the object.

The page-usage byte contains one bit for each page in the extent. The low bit (with a value of 1) corresponds to the first page in the extent, and the high bit (with a value of 128, or 80 hex) represents the last page in the extent.

By modifying the page-usage bits, you can allocate or deallocate pages in an extent.

Keep in mind that if you manually add or remove pages to a table in this manner, you will also need to update the OAM page for the affected table or index. DBCC can usually accomplish this, so that you do not have to manually update the OAM page values.

Repairing a Corrupt Index

When faced with repairing an index, you should take into account the following:

- What is the extent of the corruption on the index?
- How long would it take to simply drop and recreate the index? (For a clustered index on an APL table, you can use the SORTED_DATA option to save time, as long as the key-value order of the rows will not change while you are rebuilding the index)
- How will users be affected during the index rebuild (since the table will be locked while it is in progress)?

Examining these issues lets you decide whether it is better to rebuild or reload the entire affected object, or perform repairs on a more narrowly-targeted basis.

The following sections give more detailed information on repairing specific error conditions that can occur in Sybase.

Recovering Damaged Data

Before attempting to repair a corrupt database, it is prudent to make a backup of at least the affected pages, and preferably the entire affected table(s), if time permits. This ensures that you have some kind of recourse should the attempts at repairing the database fail.

The best way we know of to recover all the data in a corrupt table is to use White Sands Technology's Disaster Recovery Toolset. It will build an ISQL script from the rows contained on all the pages belonging to a corrupt object. To do this, it performs the following steps:

- First it scans the page chain of the affected object and generates ISQL INSERT statements for all the rows on the pages in the page chain;
- Then, it scans the entire database for any stray, unlinked pages or page chain fragments that may exist due to breaks in the main page chain.

In this manner, the Disaster Recovery Toolset can quickly and reliably recover all the rows that are present in the data layer of a table, regardless of page chain breaks or other errors it may encounter in the process. You can then reload all or part of the table as necessary.

An alternate, but potentially much slower, option is to work around the corruption by not using the data-layer page chain. This means issuing SELECT statements to access the table by a nonclustered index; for example:

```
SELECT * INTO new_table FROM corrupt_table (INDEX nc_good_table)
```

This requires that you have a nonclustered index on the table which was not affected by the corruption. If you have such an index, then this method may be able to access all, or almost all, of the rows in the table.

Another, similar option is to use WHERE clauses to work around the corruption:

```
SELECT * FROM table
WHERE key_val >= 0 AND key_val <= 10000
SELECT * FROM table
WHERE key_val >= 10000 AND key_val <= 20000
etc.
```

Use an ORDER BY or forced-index clause to require the optimizer to use the nonclustered index, if necessary.

Yet another method we have heard of is using the DBCC PGLINKAGE[6]command to locate the ends of the page chain fragments in an object having a broken page chain, then hand-modifying the *sysindexes* system table's *first* column so as to make the broken parts of the page chain (temporarily) accessible to Sybase via a clustered index scan.

The downside to using this method is that it requires that you know at least one page number in each fragment of the broken page chain. If you know one page number in a particular page chain

6 The syntax of DBCC PGLINKAGE is "semi-undocumented"; for more information, refer to http://my.sybase.com/detail?id=20405.

fragment, you can use DBCC PGLINKAGE to trace the page chain forward and backward from that page until it finds the break in the page chain.

Unfortunately, if you don't know where the page chain fragments are, it can be difficult to locate them. The Disaster Recovery Toolset makes this job much easier by automatically locating all page chain fragments in a corrupt table for you.

Understanding Sybase Error Messages

Most of the error messages you will see in your Sybase server's error log which pertain to data corruption are intimately related to the data storage structure used by Sybase. So, to best understand and diagnose corruption in your database, you will need a thorough knowledge of how Sybase stores data internally.

Some good descriptions of Sybase's data storage structure, available in print or on the Web, are listed below:

- *ProActive DBA User's Manual*, Chapter 2 (Overview of SQL Server Data Storage)
- *Sybase Adaptive Server Enterprise Performance & Tuning Guide*, Chapter 3 (Data Storage) and Chapter 4 (How Indexes Work)
- *Sybase Internals* (Kirkwood, John; International Thomson Computer Press, 1996), Chapter 8 (Storage)

About Sybase Error Logs

Often, when a user receives a corruption-related error, detailed information about the error will be written to the Sybase server's error log file. Here you may see information about the user process that received the error, along with all or part of the SQL that was being executed. Be aware that the SQL statement(s) shown here may or may not be the exact ones that triggered the error. The SQL shown in the error log (often as part of a stack trace) comes from the process's *network receive buffer*, which may only contain the last network packet received and not the entire SQL batch that was being executed.

In short, do not necessarily count on the SQL text shown in the error log as being the exact SQL command that triggered the error, although it may be a good place to start looking.

Often, corruption-related error messages report database and object ID numbers instead of names. However, you can easily convert the IDs to the names by using the *db_name()* and *object_name()* system functions. Refer to your Sybase Reference Manuals for more information.

Also note that object ID 99 is sometimes seen in error messages; the object_name() function reports its name as 'ALLOCATION'. This is an internal ID (not appearing in *sysobjects*) used for allocation map pages, which exist at every 256th page in every database. Any error messages in Sybase which mention object ID 99 are related to accessing allocation map pages in a database.

The following sections describe some of the more common corruption-related errors reported by Sybase database servers.

Error 605

An attempt was made to fetch logical page '722' in database 'Sales' from cache 'default data cache'. Page belongs to object with id '112003431', not to object 'orders'.

This is one of the more common corruption-related errors, but the true cause of it can be difficult to discern from the information that is reported in the error log.

The 605 error, categorized under Access Methods Errors, indicates that the server was trying to access a table ('orders' in the above example), but the page that was read had the object ID of a different object in its page header, as shown in the example below:

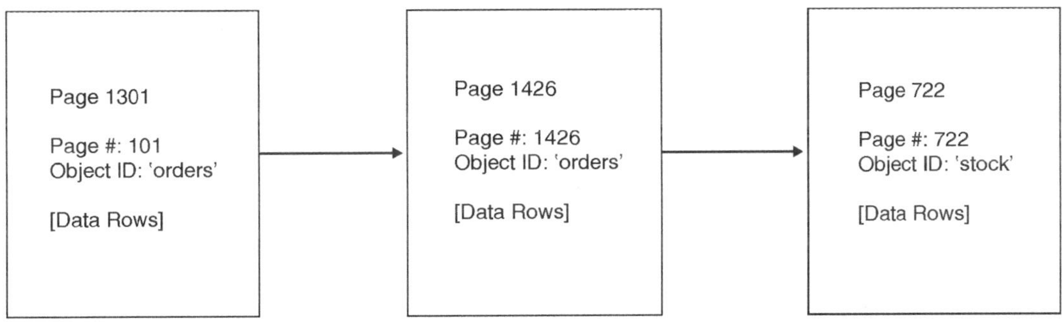

By using the *object_name()* system function, you can find the name of the table whose object ID is given in the error message (112003431 in this example).

In essence, this message means that the page that was read contained the wrong object ID value in its page header. This can have a number of causes:

- The page chain of table 'orders' or one of its indexes is corrupt and points to a page belonging to another object (in other words, page 722 is a valid page for some other table—in this case, the table having object ID 112003431);
- The page being read (page 722 in this example) used to belong to table 'orders', and in fact is still allocated to that object and is part of its page chain, but the page was erroneously overwritten with data from the other object (object ID 112003431);
- The data on the desired page was corrupted in some other fashion (and may still contain some or all of the original data); this is most likely the case if the object ID shown (here, 112003431) is not a valid object in this database.

Diagnosing 605 Errors

To properly diagnose and correct this error without loss of data, the following questions must be answered accurately:

- Does page 722 contain data for table 'orders' or for the other table (the table with object ID 112003431)? To answer this, you will want to do the following:

  - First, look at the page header, to see what other pages, if any, page 722 is linked to. If it is linked to pages from the other table, chances are it does not belong to table 'orders'. If it is linked to pages which also belong to table 'orders', it probably belongs with that table.
  - Next, look at the other fields in page 722's page header, such as the minimum row length and index ID, to see if they match the page chain for table 'orders'—if they do not, the page probably contains data for the other object.
- Do the page chains for any other tables or indexes, or any *sysindexes* rows, point to the affected page (here, page 722)? If so, page 722 may have been allocated to table 'orders' incorrectly (i.e. when that page was already in use by another object). The other object will need to be identified and repaired as well as the 'orders' table.

To answer these questions, you will first want to run DBCC commands CHECKTABLE and TABLEALLOC against the affected table(s) to verify the integrity of the indexes and other structures of those tables. It is basically a good "first shot" at identifying which tables have corruption.

The Page Detail Window in White Sands's Disaster Recovery Toolset can make answering these questions much easier—it provides a formatted dump of the rows on a given database page. From this, you can identify whether the row data looks valid or not (as determined by the column definition of the table which the page is supposed to belong to—the 'orders' table in this example).

In addition, the Disaster Recovery Toolset lets you quickly and easily identify which page(s) of which table(s) point to the affected page, so you can narrow down the scope of the corruption. It will also produce a report showing you where any breaks in the object's page chain are, so you can repair the affected areas or work around them in recovering the data from the table.

Finally, the Disaster Recovery Toolset contains tools which let you safely and accurately extract **all** the rows from the affected table, even near the location of the corruption, in case you need to truncate and reload the table.

Repairing 605 Errors

Once you know the extent of the corruption relating to a 605 error, the steps involved in fixing it can be fairly simple—that is, if the damage is localized to one part of the affected table.

Typically, you will need to repair the page that pointed to the page number reported in the 605 error, so that its "next-page" pointer points to a valid page. You will also need to fix up the "previous-page" pointer of the true next page, so the page-chain linkage is intact in both directions.

Then, if any indexes pointed to the corrupt page, these indexes will have to be rebuilt, or the index pages will have to be modified (by having rows deleted or modified) so they are no longer pointing to the corrupt page.

Finally, if any rows were dropped as a result of fixing the corruption, they will need to be reinserted into the table so that all the original data remains present in the affected table(s).

Error 692

Uninitialized logical page '722' was read while accessing object '112003430' in database '11'. Please contact Sybase Technical Support.

This error is relatively rare, which is fortunate because it is one of the more serious corruption-related errors (as evidenced by the request to contact Technical Support at the end of the message).

It occurs when a page is read from disk, and the page number and object ID values found in its page header are both zero (thus implying that the rest of the page probably contains zero bytes as well). The following diagram illustrates this condition:

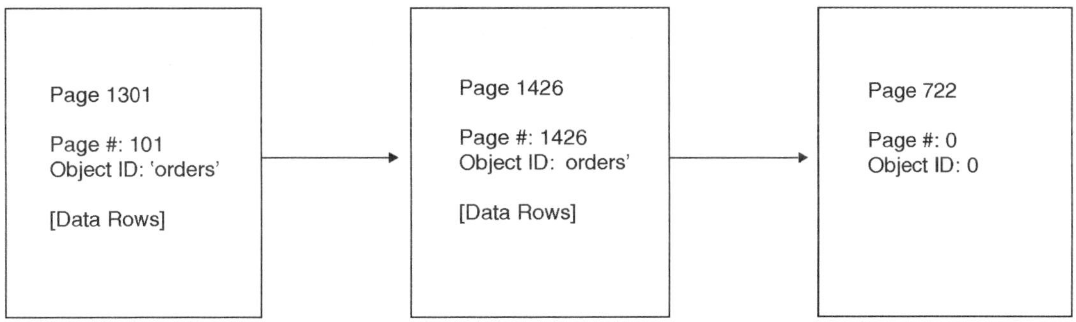

Possible causes of this error include:

- The page in question (and possibly others) was overwritten with zero bytes by the operating system's disk-formatting command or another utility such as 'dd';
- An error was made in the configuration of the disks or disk partitions used by Sybase, causing the data in one or more partitions to inadvertently get formatted or overwritten (systems not utilizing a Logical Volume Manager, or LVM, are particularly prone to this);
- Due to a bug or configuration error, the operating system read some uninitialized (zero) data from the wrong location on the disk, or from the wrong disk altogether.
- Due to a hardware failure, the disk controller or drive returned incorrect (zero-byte) data but failed to signal the failure to the operating system.

Diagnosing 692 Errors

With 692 errors, depending on what actually caused the error, it is likely that a whole section of a disk (or at worst, an entire disk) is affected, rather than the problem being localized to a single page or several pages.

The first thing you should do is run full DBCCs against the database, and against any other databases which share any of the same disks with the affected database.

The Disaster Recovery Toolset's Database Page Map is also helpful in getting a "bird's-eye" view of the database so you can see what areas are affected by the corruption.

If you discover that entire databases or large areas of databases have been zeroed out or are inaccessible, your only recourse may be to reload the entire database(s) from backups—i.e., "surgical" repair of individual pages of the database may not be possible.

On the other hand, if a small number of pages were corrupted, it is usually possible to recover most of the data, although you may have to go to a backup tape in order to recover the rows on the page(s) that were zeroed out.

Repairing 692 Errors

Usually when a 692 error occurs, the entire corrupt page's contents are no longer accessible. This may be due to a hardware failure (such as a bad spot on a disk) which should be investigated immediately!

In any case, to repair the error, the corrupt page must be dropped out of its page chain (if any) and deallocated. Then, if possible, the rows that were on that page should be reloaded from some other source, such as a database backup loaded onto another machine.

If the corrupt page was a nonclustered index leaf or intermediate page, the page cannot be simply dropped, because the index structure will no longer be consistent. Furthermore, it can be very difficult to reconstruct the index page unless you can load a fairly recent backup copy of the database onto another server—this is because there is usually no other way to know which rows (i.e. which nonclustered index key values) were stored on the page before it became corrupted. For these reasons, rebuilding the nonclustered index is usually your only option when a 692 error has occurred on a nonclustered index page.

If the corrupt page was a clustered index leaf (data) page, it may be easier to determine which rows were on the page, but you may still need to refer to a recent backup copy of the database to obtain the exact contents of the rows.

Error 695

An attempt was made to read logical page '722' for object '112003430' in database '11' from disk. Wrong logical page '66258' was brought into cache 'default data cache'.

This message indicates that the server was trying to access a database page (page number 722 in this example), and because the page was not found in cache, it attempted to read the page from disk. The actual page that was read, however, had the wrong page number (here, 66258) in its page header, as shown in the following diagram:

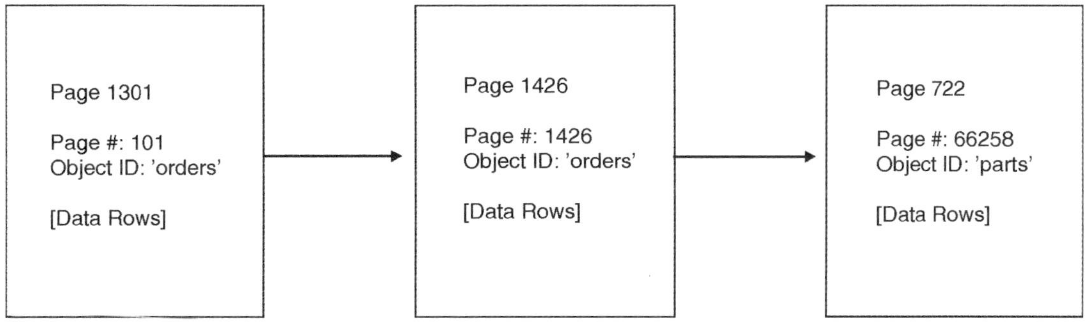

The database and object IDs for the object the server was trying to access are shown in the error message; using the *db_id()* and *object_id()* T-SQL system functions, you can find the names of the database and table in question.

The cause of this error is usually one or more of the following:

- The page data for a particular database page (page 66258 in this example) was written to the wrong location in the database (here, it was written to the location of page 722) due to an error or bug in Sybase;
- The page data for a database page was written to the wrong location on the device, or to the wrong device altogether, by the operating system;
- The page data on the disk is actually correct, but the server, in attempting to read data from database page 722, read the data from the wrong location and thus received the data for page 66258;
- The data on the disk is correct, but the operating system read the requested page from the wrong location or the wrong device;
- The data on page 722 was corrupted somehow, and may still contain some or all of the original data.

Diagnosing 695 Errors

This error can be a little more difficult than others to track down and correct, because it may involve failures in the LVM (logical volume manager), in the operating system or in the hardware. If the Sybase database server cannot reliably read or write to the correct location on the disk, any attempts at repairing the corruption at that location may not work either.

If, however, it is just a case of the wrong data having been written to that page, the error can probably be repaired. You must gather information pertaining to two pages in the database:

- The page whose number is given by the location at which the page was read (page 722 in the above example), which we refer to as the "*target page*";
- The page whose number was found in the page header (page 66258 in this example); we'll call this the "*source page*."

The data read by the server for the target page may belong to one or the other of these pages, and to one or other of the objects which own each of these pages. To find out, you must gather the following information:

- Using, for example, DBCC PAGE or the Disaster Recovery Toolset's PageDetail Window, examine the page to determine whether the data on the page really belongs to the source page or the target page. This can be determined by looking at the "minimum row length," "index ID" and other fields in the page header, and also by examining the contents of the rows on the page.
- Also examine the contents of the real source page (page 66258 in the above example) to determine whether it can be read correctly by the server and whether the table that owns it is also corrupt.
- Finally, if the source and target pages are owned by two different tables, perform full DBCCs and use the Disaster Recovery Toolset's Page Chain Consistency Checker to identify any other breaks in the objects' page chains or any other corruption in either of the two tables.

The above steps should tell you the extent of the corruption and what object the damaged page really belongs to.

Repairing 695 Errors

Usually with 695 errors, one page (the target page) has been overwritten with the contents of another page (the source page). This has two implications:

- The original contents of the target page may have been overwritten and are lost (except as may exist in any backups that did not contain the corruption);
- If the current contents of the source and target pages differ, you will need to decide which contains the most current version of the data that you will wish to keep.

Once you know what to do with the data on the corrupt page, the steps to take will include one or more of the following:

- If the corrupt page is a duplicate (i.e., you don't need to preserve the rows on it), deallocate the page by removing it from its allocation page and possibly the OAM and GAM pages;
- If you will be keeping the corrupt page, repair it by changing the page number in its page header;
- Remove the corrupt page from one or both affected objects' page chains, or repair the page chains as necessary so the corrupt page is included in only the correct object's page chain;
- If you can identify which rows were on the lost page, and if you have a recent enough database backup, you can reload the lost rows by loading the backup onto a test server, for example, selecting the rows in question, and reinserting the rows back into the production database;
- Repair or rebuild any affected indexes.

Error 697

An attempt was made to fetch logical page '722' for object '112003430' in database '11' from cache 'default data cache'. Wrong logical page '66258' was found in cache.

This message is very similar to error 695—it indicates that the server tried to access a database page, and received the wrong page number.

The difference here is that the page was already found in cache, but had the wrong page number in its page header. If a 694, 695 or other error occurred previously on the same page, then further attempts to access the page will result in 697 errors, so the 697 error is really just a "reminder" of the corruption that was found on the disk.

The rest of this write-up assumes the 697 error occurred on a page without previous 695 or other errors; in this case, it indicates the corruption probably occurred in memory alone, which is indicative of either a hardware (RAM) problem that went undetected when it first occurred, or a serious Sybase bug.

Diagnosing 697 Errors

Recycling (rebooting) the Sybase server is probably your best first strategy for correcting 697 errors. Due to their nature, 697 errors should not persist across a server reboot. If after rebooting the problem does not recur, you can probably continue using the server for some time—with the following caveats:

- You will want to run full hardware diagnostics on the server machine, to make sure there have been no RAM or other component failures;
- Make sure you are using the correct (usually most recent) releases of the Sybase and operating system software, since a problem like this will usually not go for very long without being uncovered and corrected by the software manufacturer;
- You may want to formulate a plan to migrate production work off of that server, if necessary, until you can determine what was causing the problem, because other corruption could occur at any time, and could go undetected for some time as well.

Repairing 697 Errors

Because 697 errors arise from in-memory corruption rather than corruption on the disk, recycling the server is usually your only remedy. If the 697 errors persist through a reboot, there may be some other problem (bug) in the reporting of this error or related errors.

In this situation, the remedies available for correcting 695 errors (see the previous section) could possibly apply here also, but your best bet would be to check with Sybase Technical Support to be sure.

Error 806

Could not find virtual page for logical page 16843724 in database 'Sales'.

This cryptic little error implies a page could not be found in the server. But what is it really saying?

In actuality, what happened was that somehow the server ended up looking for an out-of-range page number within a database.

The error message is in effect saying that Sybase, for some reason, had a logical page number within a database that it was trying to read, and in doing so it found that there was no corresponding device-relative page number for that logical page; specifically, the logical page number could not be found within the range of any of the device/database fragments listed in the *master..sysusages* system table.

This can have several possible causes:

- The page chain of a particular page in the database was linked to an incorrect, and out-of-range, page number;
- A clustered or nonclustered index row had a pointer to an incorrect, outof-range page number;
- An incorrect value in *sysindexes* pointed to a root, first or distribution page number that was out of range;
- A more rare case is that one or more *sysusages* entries for the database became corrupt, and while the page number shown in the 806 error message is actually correct, the server thinks it is an out-of-range page number.

Diagnosing 806 Errors

With an 806 error, the first thing to check is whether the page number shown in the error message is actually a valid page number within the database. The lowest valid logical page number in any database is Page 0 (i.e., no negative page numbers are allowed). The highest valid page number can be found using the following formula:

```
Highest Page # = (Database Size in MB * 512) - 1
```

For example, a 500MB database would have a maximum page number of (500 * 512) – 1, or 255999; valid page numbers would be anything from 0 to 255999 (but any page numbers 256000 or higher are invalid).

Note that, with 806 errors, you should **not** rely on querying *sysusages* to determine the database size. If you do not know it already, try to verify the database size from another source besides *sysusages*, since in rare cases it may be corrupt and the size reported by querying it can be misleading.

If the page number in the error message is valid, then your *master..sysusages* table is probably corrupt and will need to be hand-modified using an ISQL tool or other means to make it correct again. Or, if other databases' entries in *sysusages* are affected as well, you may have to reload your *master* database.

If the page number in the 806 error message is not valid, then the problem is probably more localized (but may exist in more than one place). In this case, since the page number in the error is not valid, it is not the true source of the corruption, and you will need to do a little digging to find out exactly where the corruption is.

Repairing 806 Errors

Unfortunately, the 806 error message itself does not show which table the server was accessing which led to the invalid page number. The server error log may show part or all of the SQL which accessed the invalid page, however, so this may be a starting point. (Note, however, that as mentioned on page 21, the SQL shown in the error message comes from the network receive buffer, and may not reflect the actual SQL command that caused the error.)

Otherwise, you can use DBCC and/or White Sands's Page Chain Consistency Checker to identify which table(s) are corrupt, and which page pointed to the outof-range page number. The pointer to the invalid page number will probably come from one of two places:

- A break in the page chain of at least one object in the database;
- An entry in *sysindexes* points to the out-of-range page as a first, root or (on pre-11.5 servers) an index distribution page for some object.

Once you know where the bad page pointer(s) are, you can correct them by:

- Hand-modifying the *sysindexes* entries using an ISQL tool; and/or
- Repairing the damaged page chain(s) as described in the section on 605 errors starting on page 21.

Error 1133

Page 115298 was expected to be an OAM page for 112003430 and it is not.

This error occurs when the Sybase server has read what is supposed to be an OAM page for a table or index (specifically, for the table whose object ID is given in the error message), but the page that was read is not actually an OAM page.

The server locates OAM pages in one of two ways:

- The page number of the first OAM page for an object is given by the *ioampg* field (for indexes) or the *doampg* field (for a table's data layer, or heap) in the *sysindexes* system table;
- Subsequent OAM pages are linked from the first OAM page in a circular page chain.

The diagram below gives an example of this:

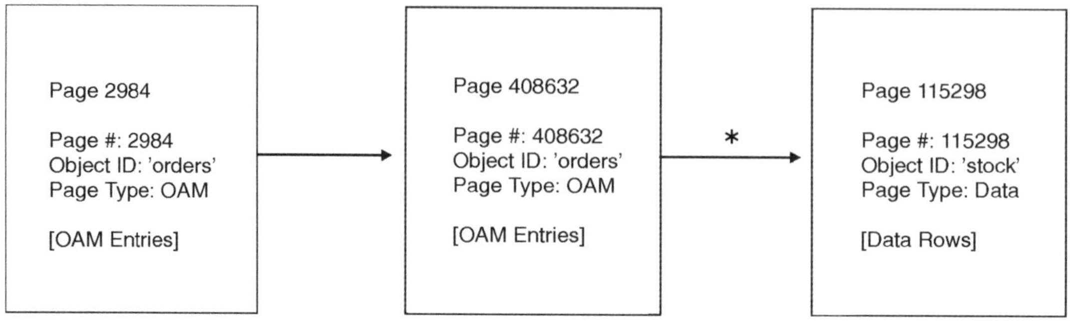

*Corrupt page chain link

When the server locates and reads an OAM page using one of the above methods, it then checks the page header of the page that was read in; the "status" field of the page header must contain a certain setting (called PG_OAMPG), which indicates that the page is in fact an OAM page. If the page does not contain this setting, then an 1133 error is raised.

Diagnosing 1133 Errors

These errors arise due to one of the following causes:

- An incorrect page pointer exists in *sysindexes* or in the next-page pointer of another OAM page;
- The OAM page used to be at the location that was read, but was overwritten with the contents of another page or with corrupt page data.

To find out which of these is the case, you will need to use DBCC PAGE or White Sands's Page Detail Window to look at the contents of the page in question (page 115298 in the above example).

The page is likely to belong to some other object, and is also likely not to be an OAM page. Or, the page may be empty. If the page belongs to another object, you will want to run full DBCCs against that object, as it may contain corruption.

You will also need to determine whether the corrupt object listed in the 1133 error message (object ID 112003430 in this example) has a valid first OAM page and (optionally) other OAM pages in a valid page chain. Here again, using DBCC PAGE or White Sands's Page Detail Window, you can follow the OAM page chain until you reach the first OAM page, and in doing so you can verify the integrity of the next- and previous-page pointers on each OAM page.

Note that if the object only has one OAM page (which it typically does if it is less than about 130MB in size), that OAM page will be linked forward and backward to itself.

Repairing 1133 Errors

Depending on whether the object's OAM page chain is intact, you may need to add or remove OAM pages to/from the OAM page chain, and then run DBCC to fix up the allocation errors in the OAM page(s).

Conclusion

Hopefully you now have a better understanding of what causes database corruption in Sybase and other database servers, and the various options you have at your disposal for dealing with it if and when it occurs.

As we have seen, with the right tools and the right information, you are no longer at the mercy of data corruption.

For further information on the White Sands Technology, Inc. products mentioned in this white paper, including ProActive DBA and the Disaster Recovery Toolset, contact us at:

Voice: 1-818-349-8900
Fax: 1-818-349-8988
Web: www.whitesands.com
E-mail: infor@whitesands.com

Finally, we at White Sands would like to thank you for reading this white paper, and we hope you find it beneficial in dealing with data corruption.

If you have any feedback regarding this white paper, feel free to contact us using any of the above methods.

Index

C

D

ASE 12.5 NT Evaluation Installation

Notice to User: By installing this software you accept all the terms and conditions of the license agreement on the following page. Please read it carefully. If you do not accept the terms, then DO NOT install, or use the software.

System Requirements: Pentium 133 MHz or higher; Windows NT, Release Level 4.0 (Service Pack #6a, or higher); 128 MB RAM; 406 MB available disk space (Typical Install)

Installation Instructions: Before starting the installation you should access and read the Installation Guide at: http://www.sybase.com/support/manuals. This installation guide provides general installation and configuration instructions. You should follow these instructions during the product installation.

License keys for this evaluation are available at: http://www.sybase.com/ase12_5eval.

Below are additional installation instructions specific to this Evaluation Software:

1. To ensure compatibility with all utilities, do not use spaces or exceed eight characters in the name of the installation directory or its subdirectories.
2. During the Install you may encounter an error message about a missing dll clusapi.dll. You can ignore this unless you intend to run the High Availability (HA) functions. If you do intend to run HA, then you will need to install on an NT Server Cluster configuration, which should already include the clusapi.dll.
3. Follow the instructions in the Installation Guide except for entering the license key. A specific License Authorization Key has been generated for your timed evaluation usage and will be sent to you via e-mail. This is different from the procedure described in the installation guide. The expiration date, software version, and authorization code, (license key), should be entered into the three fields upon request of the Sybase Installer.

   Then click "Continue Install" and proceed with configuring Adaptive Server Enterprise, as described in the Installation Guide.

Technical Product Information:

You can access Sybase Technical Library Product Manuals at: http://www.sybase.com/support/manuals.

Additional Technical Information:

Technical documentation at the Sybase web site is updated frequently. Please consult http://www.sybase.com/support/techdocs.

Support Contact Information:

If you are not a registered Sybase SupportPlus user you can still access the publicly available areas of http://www.sybase.com/support, and you can also use the relevant public newsgroup forums at sybase.public.sqlserver.nt, and sybase.public.sqlserver.general.

ASE 12.5 Eval Linux Version: http://www.sybase.com/ase12_5eval

WARNING: By opening the CD package, you accept the terms and conditions of the CD/Source Code Usage License Agreement.

Additionally, opening the CD package makes this book non-returnable.

SYBASE, INC. ADAPTIVE SERVER ENTERPRISE 12.5 for NT 60-DAY SOFTWARE EVALUATION LICENSE AGREEMENT

IMPORTANT - READ CAREFULLY BEFORE USING THE ACCOMPANYING SOFTWARE

NOTICE TO USER: BY INSTALLING OR USING THIS SOFTWARE YOU ACCEPT ALL THE TERMS AND CONDITIONS OF THIS AGREEMENT. PLEASE READ IT CAREFULLY.

THE FOLLOWING TERMS AND CONDITIONS ("AGREEMENT") SHALL GOVERN YOUR INSTALLATION AND USE OF THE ACCOMPANYING ADAPTIVE SERVER ENTERPRISE SOFTWARE PROGRAMS AND RELATED EXPLANATORY MATERIALS (THE "PROGRAMS"). IF YOU DO NOT ACCEPT OR AGREE WITH THESE TERMS, YOU MAY NOT INSTALL OR USE THE PROGRAMS AND YOU SHOULD IMMEDIATELY RETURN THE UNOPENED PROGRAM MEDIA TO SYBASE.

UPON YOUR ACCEPTANCE OF THIS AGREEMENT, SYBASE GRANTS YOU A LIMITED, NON-EXCLUSIVE LICENSE TO USE THE PROGRAMS AS FOLLOWS:

1. USE OF PROGRAMS. You may install and use the Programs (and accompanying documentation) internally in your organization solely for evaluation and testing purposes on a single computer system. You may not use the Programs for any development, commercial or production purpose. The Programs may not be transferred, sold, assigned, sublicensed or otherwise conveyed (whether by operation of law or otherwise) to another party without Sybase's prior written consent.

2. COPY RESTRICTIONS AND OTHER RESTRICTIONS. You may not copy the Programs except that you may either install the Programs on your hard disk or make one copy for inactive back-up and archival purposes for your own use. Except as expressly permitted in the Documentation, you may not modify or adapt the Programs in whole or in part (including but not limited to translating or creating derivative works) or reverse engineer, decompile or disassemble the Programs (except to the extent applicable laws specifically prohibit such restriction). You may not use the Programs for timesharing, rental or service bureau purposes. You shall not remove any copyright notices or other proprietary notices from the Programs or Documentation and you must reproduce such notices on all copies or extracts of the Programs and Documentation. Results of benchmark or other performance tests run on the Programs may not be disclosed to any third party without Sybase's prior written consent.

3. COPYRIGHT AND OWNERSHIP. The Programs are owned by Sybase, its subsidiaries or their suppliers and are protected by copyright laws and international treaty provisions. You acquire only the non-exclusive right to use the Programs as permitted herein and do not acquire any rights of ownership in the Programs or any other implied rights or licenses under any intellectual property rights of Sybase.

4. SUPPORT. These Programs are provided on an "as is" basis and are unsupported. This Agreement does not entitle you to any maintenance or other services or any updates or new versions of the Programs.

5. U.S. GOVERNMENT RESTRICTED RIGHTS. The Programs are Commercial Computer Software. Use, duplication and disclosure of the Programs and Documentation by the U.S. Government is subject to restrictions set forth in this license or in a written agreement specifying the Government's right to use the Programs. Sybase reserves all unpublished rights under U.S. copyright laws.

6. TERMINATION. Your license to use the Programs will automatically terminate as of the date sixty (60) days after your receipt of the Programs. YOU ACKNOWLEDGE AND UNDERSTAND THAT THE PROGRAMS MAY CONTAIN A DEVICE WHICH SHALL CAUSE THEM NOT TO OPERATE AFTER SUCH SIXTY (60) DAY PERIOD. In addition, Sybase may immediately terminate this Agreement on notice to you. Upon termination, you shall cease using the Programs and shall destroy all copies of the Programs (and associated Documentation) in any form. All disclaimers of warranties and limitations of liability shall survive any termination of this Agreement.

7. WARRANTY DISCLAIMER. The Programs are provided AS IS, without any warranty whatsoever. SYBASE DISCLAIMS ALL WARRANTIES AND CONDITIONS, EXPRESS OR IMPLIED, INCLUDING WITHOUT LIMITATION THE IMPLIED WARRANTIES OR CONDITIONS OF MERCHANTABLE QUALITY, NONINFRINGEMENT, AND FITNESS FOR A PARTICULAR PURPOSE.

8. LIMITATION ON LIABILITY. NEITHER SYBASE, ITS SUBSIDIARIES NOR ANY OF ITS LICENSORS SHALL BE LIABLE FOR ANY LOSS OR DAMAGE HEREUNDER, INCLUDING, WITHOUT LIMITATION, ANY INACCURACY OF DATA, LOSS OF PROFITS OR INDIRECT, DIRECT, SPECIAL, INCIDENTAL OR CONSEQUENTIAL DAMAGES, EVEN IF SUCH PARTY HAS BEEN ADVISED OF THE POSSIBILITY OF SUCH DAMAGES.

9. EXPORT. You agree to fully comply with all laws and regulations of the United States and other countries ("Export Laws") to assure that neither the Programs or any direct products thereof are (1) exported, directly or indirectly, in violation of Export Laws, or (2) are used for any purpose prohibited by Export Laws, including, without limitation, nuclear, chemical or biological weapons production.

10. GOVERNING LAW; COMPLETE AGREEMENT. This Agreement constitutes the complete agreement between the parties with respect to the Programs and is governed by the laws of the State of California (other than its conflict of law provisions).

WARNING: By opening the CD package, you accept the terms and conditions of the CD/Source Code Usage License Agreement.

Additionally, opening the CD package makes this book non-returnable.